the definitive guide to
managing the numbers

Prentice Hall
FINANCIAL TIMES

In an increasingly competitive world, we believe it's quality of thinking that will give you the edge – an idea that opens new doors, a technique that solves a problem, or an insight that simply makes sense of it all. The more you know, the smarter and faster you can go.

That's why we work with the best minds in business and finance to bring cutting-edge thinking and best learning practice to a global market.

Under a range of leading imprints, including *Financial Times Prentice Hall*, we create world-class print publications and electronic products bringing our readers knowledge, skills and understanding which can be applied whether studying or at work.

To find out more about Pearson Education publications, or tell us about the books you'd like to find, you can visit us at
www.pearsoned.co.uk

PEARSON
Education

the definitive guide to
managing the numbers

the executive's fast-track to mastering
spreadsheets, budgets, forecasts,
investment metrics...

Richard Stutely

Prentice Hall
FINANCIAL TIMES

An imprint of **Pearson Education**
Harlow, England • London • New York • Boston • San Francisco • Toronto • Sydney • Singapore • Hong Kong
Tokyo • Seoul • Taipei • New Delhi • Cape Town • Madrid • Mexico City • Amsterdam • Munich • Paris • Milan

PEARSON EDUCATION LIMITED

Head Office:
Edinburgh Gate
Harlow CM20 2JE
Tel: +44 (0)1279 623623
Fax: +44 (0)1279 431059
Website: www.pearsoned.co.uk

First published in Great Britain in 2003

© Pearson Education Limited 2003

The right of Richard Stutely to be identified as Author of this Work
has been asserted by him in accordance with the Copyright, Designs and
Patents Act 1988.

ISBN 0 273 66103 5

British Library Cataloguing in Publication Data
A CIP catalogue record for this book can be obtained from the British Library

10 9 8 7 6 5 4 3 2 1

Typeset by Pantek Arts Ltd, Maidstone, Kent
Printed and bound in Great Britain by Bell & Bain Ltd, Glasgow

The Publishers' policy is to use paper manufactured from sustainable forests.

about the author

RICHARD STUTELY

Richard has been *managing the numbers* throughout his career, which has spanned banking and finance, government, and business in Europe, North America, the Middle East and Asia-Pacific.

As a manager at all levels and a director, he has produced, managed and analysed hundreds of project plans, departmental and enterprise budgets, cash flow statements, income accounts and balance sheets.

Richard received a solid grounding in finance and accounting with NatWest, one of the largest banks in the world. He went on to become an investment analyst and senior economist with top investment banks – acquired by Shearson Lehman, American Express and Chase Manhattan – and a member of the London International Stock Exchange. Richard also worked at HM Treasury, the British finance ministry, where he dealt with public expenditure planning and cash controls on a national scale.

Subsequently, as chief economist of an international bank, the results of his forecasting and financial modelling were in regular demand with various government agencies and with journals such as *Institutional Investor*. Richard was also secretary to the bank's assets and liabilities committee, analysing the numbers with the objective of improving performance.

As executive vice president of a multinational software company, Richard developed and directly managed financial reporting and analysis for subsidiaries in several countries, as well as handling aggregation of group accounts.

In addition, Richard developed one of the world's first PC spreadsheet applications. He has also designed and developed many other well-known computer programs for financial decision-making, risk assessment and reporting, and is Microsoft Certified.

Richard has written extensively for such journals as *Accountancy*, *The Economist* and *The Banker*, and his books include the international bestsellers *The Definitive Business Plan*, *The Economist Guide to Economic Indicators* and *The Economist Numbers Guide*.

When Richard is not writing books or managing a multinational software company, he runs seminars and lectures to MBA students and corporate audiences.

acknowledgements

It is my pleasure to acknowledge and thank the countless individuals and organizations that contributed to the development of this book. I cannot list them all, but special mention should be made of the International Accounting Standards Board, the Financial Accounting Standards Board in the US, and the Accounting Standards Board in the UK (the IASB, FASB and ASB – you will meet these and other acronyms in Chapter 2 and beyond) and their counterparts in many other countries.

I must also thank Microsoft Corporation (www.microsoft.com) and the Cyber-dynamics Group (www.cyber-dynamics.com) for their assistance with the spreadsheet issues and for developing various financial tools which are available for download from this book's website, **www.ManagingTheNumbers.com**.

Of course, sincere thanks are due to my family, friends and colleagues for their input and especially for putting up with my quirks and idiosyncrasies while I was writing this book. My son Alex made a sterling contribution. He is definitely not a beanie, but there is a likeness of him in Chapter 3.

contents

Contents

how to use this book

As you can see from the foregoing contents pages, this book is somewhat wide ranging. It starts from the assumption that you want to try to run the numbers yourself using spreadsheets. However, this is not essential and you can skim or skip the chapters on this topic if you find them heavy going. Much the same applies to the arithmetic of finance. At the end of the day, you can always fake it by using the calculators on this book's website (**www.ManagingTheNumbers.com**). If you are wearing a particular hat today, you may find the following fast track guides useful. The list is not exhaustive. Many other fast tracks will be self-evident from the list of contents.

▶ Where do you want to go today?

I want to focus on using spreadsheets to analyse numbers. The most important chapter for you is number 4 *The financial wizard's toolbox*. This is followed closely by 5 *Explaining and reporting*, 9 *Tracking trends* and 10 *How to forecast anything*. You will find useful tricks in 8 *Managing money* and 23 *Making better decisions*. You should also check the spreadsheet sections in Chapters 11 to 18 covering financial statements, 21 *Appraising projects* and 22 *Brilliant budgets*.

I want to know about forecasting. Chapters 9 *Tracking trends*, 10 *How to forecast anything* and 12 *Controlling costs* are most relevant; you may also find useful material scattered through most other chapters.

I want to understand financial statements. Take a look at Chapter 7 *Keeping score*, then read Chapters 9 to 17 which cover various aspects of the financials. Parts of Chapters 18 to 20 will also be helpful.

I want to analyse financial statements. Follow the route for understanding financial statements, but pay particular attention to Chapter 18 *Figuring financials*.

I am responsible for appraising a project. You probably need to follow the routes for forecasting, some of the fast track for analysing financial statements (Chapters 11 to 13 especially), Chapter 23 *Making better decisions* and, of course, Chapter 21 *Appraising projects*.

I am responsible for managing a project. Follow the fast track for appraising a project, then read Chapter 22 *Brilliant budgets*.

My budget is due to be presented/reviewed tomorrow. Go straight to Chapter 22 *Brilliant budgets*, then read any of the prerequisites listed in that chapter's survival toolkit as necessary.

I want to manage better. Read Chapter 2 *Where managers and numbers meet*. Then read the rest of the book. Sorry.

I want to be better at personal investment. Chapter 6 *How money grows* is a good starting point. Then follow the route for analysing financial statements, paying particular attention to Chapter 19 *Financing and investing*.

introduction

If you are an entrepreneur, manager or other executive, you simply can't do your job if you can't manage the numbers. It is essential to have a firm grasp on metrics. This applies equally whether you work in a small business, a corporation or a not-for-profit organization. At the very least you need to be able to plan, set targets, measure and interpret progress, and analyse the results. In the words of management guru Peter Drucker; 'if you can't measure it, you can't manage it'.

However, the need for numeracy drives much deeper than this. No one would argue against the suggestion that you make better decisions when you quantify the factors at play. If you have your fingers on the figures, you can delegate better and, perhaps more important, be one step ahead of what you are being told. In addition, nearly all managers have to draw up budgets or at least operate within them during their careers. Almost as many have to undertake some form of project appraisal or management, even if under a different name. Moreover, techniques for managing money make us all more capable both in the office and in personal investment and finance. Everyone has to deal with finances and financial experts.

This book is not written for financial experts or statistical specialists. It is written for executives in all walks of life. It aims to provide the basic tools for managing the numbers – reviewing, analysing, interpreting, estimating, forecasting, projecting, and so on. It covers a wide range of techniques, but, since you can get away with a little less of the statistical stuff, it puts a little more emphasis on the financials. It debunks some of the myths about accounting. It highlights the scope for creativity, obscuration and outright cheating – and shows you how to catch and counter this. It discusses current international issues in finance which could affect you as a manager. In short, it gives you the inside track. This will assist you not only in building your own financials, but, significantly, in interpreting those prepared by others. It will also help to you hold your own when dealing with the finance director and other bean counters and propeller heads.

One final point. Supplemental material is available on this book's website. Even if you don't have time to master underlying mathematical concepts or accounting techniques, you will be able to produce results using the wizards and calculators which are available for download. Whatever your needs, and however you approach *managing the numbers*, I hope that this book helps you in your mission.

Richard Stutely
June 2003

the journey starts here

'If you can't measure it, you can't manage it.'

Peter Drucker

Chapter survival toolkit

▶ Overview

Each chapter in this book contains a survival kit similar to this one. This idea is to provide an outline of what to expect, what you need to bring to the chapter and what you might take away with you. I hope that you will revisit the survival kit when you have finished the chapter, and make sure that I was successful in conveying the message intended.

This chapter provides a quick overview of what you can expect from the book and where to find it. Note that there is additional supporting material on this book's website **ManagingTheNumbers.com**.

▶ Prerequisites

The general objective is to make this book stand-alone. All you need to bring to it is general business common sense and/or business competence. Where one chapter relies on material from earlier pages, this is outlined in the *prerequisites* section of the survival kit.

This chapter, of course, requires no prior knowledge other than an ability to read and a desire to achieve mastery over managing the numbers or, more realistically, to achieve competence with a numbers-related task that you have to find out how to solve before a deadline.

▶ Mastering this book

The aim of the *Mastering this book* section is to provide a ten-point checklist of questions that you should be able to answer after reading the chapter. If you can answer the questions, you can speak with confidence and walk with financial giants. Well, that's the plan. It seems that I have failed at the first hurdle. I can explain away this failure by saying that since this chapter is just an introduction, I have let you off with just five questions (answers in the text):

1 Are you a muppet?
2 Do you want to be a brilliant with numbers (or, at least, just get by)?
3 What is a bean counter? What is a dough kneader?
4 What is in this book?
5 Where can you find supplemental information?*

* Hint: what is **www.ManagingTheNumbers.com**?

> 'I am always doing that which I can not do, in order that I may learn how to do it.'
>
> **Pablo Picasso**

▶ Jargon watch

Finally, each survival toolkit contains a list of new buzz words in the chapter and, where appropriate, a reminder of jargon encountered in previous pages which is critical to the current chapter. I try not to insult your intelligence by labouring the definitions of new terminology, but if I have been too brief, try the glossary at the back of the book (or this book's website). There is not really any new gobbledygook in this chapter, but here are a couple of new-in-this-chapter terms by way of illustration:

muppet
bean counter
dough kneader

> 'A journey of a thousand miles must begin with a single step.'
>
> Lao-tzu

▶ Start here

We are about to embark on a journey through the realm where managers and numbers meet or, perhaps, collide. It depends how you feel about figures. This book is intended primarily for non-financial managers and entrepreneurs. It is a meld of finance and investment; financial, management and cost accounting; economics; forecasting; statistics; quantitative analysis and other numerical techniques. But do not let that put you off. No prior specialist knowledge is required. Yet, by the time you reach the end of the book you should be able to produce solid forecasts and financials, present and defend them even in hostile environments, and do some pretty snappy analysis of numbers provided by your colleagues and competitors. Indeed, the book should help you to hold your own when dealing with any professional number crunchers, including accountants, bankers and your chief financial officer. Never again risk intimidation or being snowed under by the numbers, and win some tough arguments.

▶ Is the book for you?

This book is for you if you want a little help with (or a complete guide to) doing the numbers. If you are a bit hazy about them and you answer yes to any of the following, you should definitely read on:

◆ Daunted by financials?
◆ Have to develop a budget? Present it? Defend it? Report on progress?
◆ Want to forecast sales?
◆ Need to prepare a sales and marketing plan or business plan?

◆ Wondering how to account for product development costs?

◆ Preparing for a project or planning meeting?

◆ Need to make a forecast in a hurry?

◆ Have to decide between two projects with differing costs and rewards?

◆ Have to draw up financial statements?

◆ Want to work out net income or produce a balance sheet?

◆ Want to read someone else's balance sheet?

◆ Worried about cash flow?

◆ Need to look for funding or estimate the amount required?

◆ Have to revise the numbers to cope with lower than expected sales, economic recession, or some other unexpected event?

◆ Presenting to your chief financial officer, bankers or shareholders?

◆ Going to meet the auditors or accountants?

◆ Have to make a decision based on the numbers?

◆ Going to stake your reputation on a recommendation based on financial analysis?

◆ Being judged by how you perform in relation to some financial target?

In fact, the list goes on and on. Take a look at the *Places to meet numbers* section on p. 16 and you will see many more reasons why this book could help you.

> This book is able to answer so many questions because of the fascinating interrelationship of financials. I will show you how to unlock these relationships and use them to your advantage.

▶ Who are you travelling with?

Most people who read this book are non-financial managers – or soon-to-be mangers – in corporations and non-profit organizations. Some readers are entrepreneurs running their own businesses. Students of business studies and finance use it as an introductory text. We might even have some bean counters turning the pages.

> Accountants are frequently known as bean counters, or beanies, perhaps because beans are sometimes used as a simile for money. Indeed, cocoa beans were used as cash in pre-Columbian Mexico, and some early metallic coins were bean shaped. However, the origin of the term bean counter probably relates to being tight-fisted and counting the last bean in a grocery store (see Chapter 3). Given the way that accountants can manipulate numbers, it seems that 'dough kneaders' might also be a good tag for them.

▶ Batteries (more or less) included

Let me reiterate that no special knowledge is required to read this book. I am going to assume that you are a bit of a muppet (one up from a dummy) when it comes to numbers, finance and computers. This is not meant to be an insult. You must be competent at what you do, or you would not be reading a Financial Times Prentice Hall book. I will just start from scratch with these numbers things and try to explain it all as we go along. You can skip over the material that you already know or use it as a refresher for things that you have forgotten.

You do not necessarily have to have a personal computer (PC), but they make doing the numbers so easy that you ought at least to arrange access to one. You will soon see how great they are as management tools. If you need convincing, go to an Internet café in a town where no one knows you and have a play with Microsoft Word and Excel – after you have taken a look at Chapter 4.

Incidentally, I fibbed a little when I said that I would start from scratch. I have to assume that you can at least turn on a PC, although not necessarily do much more. It will be ideal if you know how to use MS Word to write and print memos or letters. There is not room in this book to digress into the great mysteries of computing, so we will job through the essentials at a rapid pace. Chief executives and other real computer beginners are welcome to download the supplementary introductory material from the website accompanying this book (see p. 7).

Other than being able to power on a PC, if you can add up and subtract (with or without a calculator), and if you have a rough idea what a bank is, you'll be fine.

▶ How simple is simplified?

We (you and I together) have already established that you are not stupid. Accordingly, I am not going to insult your intelligence by giving you a superficial overview which will leave you vulnerable. We are going to discuss the financials in some detail so that you are ready to do battle with financial professionals. Accordingly, this book has a simple approach but it is not over-simplified. We will tackle some heavyweight topics, but I will try not to bog you down with unnecessary details. We are going to be highly focused on getting results – doing the numbers and making the right decisions based on the numbers.

No royal we's

Incidentally, as I write I have a picture of you in my mind. If I say that we are going to do something, I mean you and I together. There are no royal we's in this book.

▶ I'm on your side

I want you to know before we start that I am completely on your side. I am not a bean counter. I am a manager just like you and I talk your language. I had to start somewhere – close to the bottom actually – and I remember the pain of learning this stuff from dull textbooks and kindly bean counters. But I did learn it. I also picked up many useful wrinkles along the way and I retain some healthy scepticism about much of this. I hope that my sense of humour has not been beaten out of me completely, and will try to pass on some of my knowledge while making it fun for you at the same time. No, really, there is no reason why doing the numbers cannot be entertaining and interesting.

▶ Financial law and lore from the sharp end

Where did I pick up all this beanie stuff? In the early days of my career I was an analyst with investment banks – crawling over financials, looking for value and for danger signs – and a professionally qualified member of the London Stock Exchange. Later, I was secretary to a bank's assets and liabilities committee, chief economist, adviser to a bank's chairman, and a general manger of an international commercial bank. Along the way, I also worked at HM Treasury (the British finance ministry) where I was involved with world economic reporting, monetary policy and exchange rates, national public spending, cash controls, and corporate taxation. You come to see and do quite a lot of numbers in those positions. A good chunk of the work was forecasting, analysing, interpreting and troubleshooting.

Moreover, even if banking and finance is one step removed from the oily reality of the real world, I had to prepare my own budgets and business plans just the same as any other manager. I was also governor and treasurer of a preparatory school for which I prepared financial plans to reverse a decade of losses. And for the past 10 years I have been running and directing multinational businesses, preparing feasibility studies, business plans, budgets and financials – and dealing with officials, auditors and accountants in a score of different jurisdictions around the world. Many of these businesses are in the new high-tech economy where doing the numbers is similar to doing them in the old economy, except that they plunge faster.

Also, back in about 1980, I designed and programmed one of the world's first PC-based spreadsheets. I have been a heavyweight user of number-crunching software ever since then. My interests include running a technology company and, for what it is worth, I am Microsoft certified. I provide corporate training in finance and technology related issues.

One more thing. Working in sometimes very large corporations I have been well-exposed to the pleasures of corporate backstabbing and politics. Regrettably, I have seen executives fiddling the books, and entrepreneurs who ran off with the petty cash. Well, one of them emptied the bank account actually. As a result, I think I understand the environment in which you work. But enough of this. We need to consider our action plan.

The website

There is a website at **ManagingTheNumbers.com** which contains additional material relating to this book. You can download spreadsheets containing the examples from each chapter. Also you will find useful definitions, various financial calculators and links to many other sites of relevance to managers. I will try to keep the site up to date and I welcome suggestions and feedback.

Divided by a common language

This is intended to be a truly international book. Two times two is four anywhere in the world (with one exception), and a profit, by any other name, would smell as sweet. True, government regulations and accounting rules vary, but the information that managers need does not. Moreover, accounting standards are slowly coming into line internationally – and this book looks at how these developments might affect you.

The largest problem is nomenclature. One person's *profit and loss account* is another's *income statement*. Such variations are explained when first encountered in the text, and summarized in the glossary. But it would be tiresome to keep referring to the alternatives. Accordingly, I have opted to standardize on the least ambiguous term in each case. For example, the British *cheque* could only be one thing, so I use this word in preference to the American *check*. For similar reasons I favour the American word *inventory* over the British *stock*. I hope you find this helpful.

I have also opted to use the dollar (but not necessarily the US dollar) for the monetary values in the examples. My perception is that this is universally familiar, while many national units of currency and even the euro are perhaps less memorable.

By the way, the exception to the rule that two times two is four is explained on p. 65.

Here are some examples of variations on a name; numerous others are mentioned throughout this book. Terms are defined when first encountered and in the glossary, *The finance director's language*, at the back of the book.

British	American
annual general meeting (AGM)	annual stockholders' meeting
authorized share capital	authorized capital stock
base rate	prime rate
bonus or capitalization issue	stock dividend or stock split
building society	savings and loan association
cheque	check
company	corporation
current account	checking account
gearing	leverage
gilt-edged stock (gilts)	Treasury bonds (Treasuries)
memorandum and articles of association	bylaws

British	American
merchant bank	investment bank
ordinary share	common stock
profit and loss account	income statement
land, property	real estate
quoted company	listed company
share	stock
shareholder	stockholder
sources and uses of funds statement	cash flow statement
Stock, stock-in-trade	inventory
trade creditors, creditors	accounts payable
trade debtors, debtors	accounts receivable
turnover	sales
unit trusts	mutual funds

▶ The plan of the book

You have already browsed the table of contents, so you have a good idea of what is covered in this book. There is overlap between the various themes woven into this book, but let me explain the broad logic by listing and describing the chapters:

▶ Executives, entrepreneurs and numbers

First, I will help you suit up with the weapons and armour needed to do battle.

◆ Chapter 2: **Where managers and numbers meet** reviews this magical kingdom and starts to show you how to use the numbers to your advantage.

◆ Chapter 3: **How the finance director thinks** looks at mindset of the professionals with whom you will be dealing.

▶ Attaining mastery over numbers

Next, I want to introduce spreadsheets and remind you about some numerical basics.

◆ Chapter 4: **The financial wizard's toolbox** investigates the tools you use to hammer the numbers – primarily spreadsheets.

◆ Chapter 5: **Explaining and reporting** provides a refresher about some numerical techniques.

◆ Chapter 6: **How money grows** describes the basic arithmetic of investment and finance.

▶ Managing money

Forearmed, we can move on to income and expenditure. I will start to show you how you dominate every penny that comes into and flows out of your coffers.

◆ Chapter 7: **Keeping score** introduces the rudiments of bookkeeping.

◆ Chapter 8: **Managing money** reviews the roll-up-your sleeves business of managing petty cash, bank balances, cash flow, expenses claims, debtors and so on.

▶ Look both ways

Now we take a short digression into analysing what has happened and forecasting the future.

◆ Chapter 9: **Tracking trends** introduces ways of looking at the way that numbers change over time – and how this highlights what is happening to the business.

◆ Chapter 10: **How to forecast anything** explains how to form a realistic view about potential future trends – with particular attention on forecasting sales.

◆ Chapter 11: **Counting capital** considers the special factors surrounding capital spending on fixed assets (often huge outlays where there is longer-term benefit and perhaps short-term pain).

◆ Chapter 12: **Controlling costs** looks at assessing other spending – the cash that seems to go up in smoke instantly when you pay telephone bills, rent, and so on.

◆ Chapter 13: **Getting to gross profit** pulls together sales and production costs. This is the link between this section and the next.

▶ Feeling the financials

With all the foregoing out of the way, you are ready to pull together the numbers to produce, interpret, analyse and review the financial scorecards.

◆ Chapter 14: **Producing a profit** investigates income statements, known in the UK and elsewhere as profit and loss accounts. These are just budgets or project plans restated.

◆ Chapter 15: **Building balance sheets** looks at balance sheets – misunderstood (to say the least) medical reports about of the health of any business.

◆ Chapter 16: **Watching cash flow** considers sources and uses of funds – highlighting ways of recasting the figures already dealt with to give you better management control over cash – and projecting your own cash needs.

◆ Chapter 17: **Reviewing reports** looks at published financial statements, introducing a couple more financial reports and discussing the blurb that surrounds them all.

◆ Chapter 18: **Figuring financials** at last gets down to analysing financial statements. The analysis is continued in Chapter 19.

▶ Serious management issues

The next few chapters review financial control of the enterprise – although the topics are every bit as applicable and important at the departmental level.

◆ Chapter 19: **Financing and investing** looks at the interesting topic of financing a business, debt, equity, mergers and acquisitions, joint ventures and the cost of capital.

◆ Chapter 20: **Business across borders** reviews the increasingly important topic of international commerce, with particular attention on managing exchange rate risks.

◆ Chapter 21: **Appraising projects** describes how you assess, select and manage projects for financial success.

◆ Chapter 22: **Brilliant budget**s covers the budgeting process – addressing the control of finances throughout the business.

◆ Chapter 23: **Making better decisions** provides some tools to help you make decisions where numbers are involved.

◆ Chapter 24: **The finance director did it** pulls together the themes running through the book.

▶ I want to manage better

Managing better is the crux of this book. Without further ado, let's really get down to it and look at that mysterious realm where managers and numbers meet.

2
where managers and numbers meet

> 'If you're a CEO and you think you can fudge the books in order to make yourselves look better, we're going to find you, we're going to arrest you and we're going to hold you to account.'
>
> **President Bush, July 2002**

▶ Chapter survival toolkit

▶ Overview

This chapter is very straightforward. It explains why managers need to be proficient with numbers. It outlines the concepts of numerical and financial methods. It lists what you should look out for as a manager. It explains that directors, and therefore managers, have responsibilities to report financials accurately. It examines accounting principles, requirements and reporting around the world and looks at current trends. And it throws acronyms around as if they were going out of fashion. Of course, they are not. They are very much in vogue, and being familiar with a handful will stand you in good stead for meetings with bean counters.

▶ Prerequisites

None, given that this is the first chapter in this book to really get down to business. Or, perhaps, the prerequisite is a desire to manage better.

▶ Mastering money management issues

After reading this chapter, you will be able to answer the following questions:

1 Why do managers need to be proficient with numbers?

2 How can managing numbers help you to manage better?

3 Are you familiar with the analytical approaches (in concepts at least) listed in the *Jargon watch* section opposite?

4 What should you keep in mind while reading this book?

5 What is financial reporting? How can it ruin your marriage?

6 Why are there national differences in the approach to accounting?

7 How did financial reporting spread around the globe, and why is it coming back together again?

8 Are you familiar with accounting acronyms FASB, ASB and IAS?

9 How do differing accounting principles allow flexibility in reporting?

10 What will happen in 2005, and are you ready for it?

> 'It has been said that figures rule the world.
> Maybe. But I am sure that figures show us whether
> it is being ruled well or badly.'
>
> **J.P. Eckermann**

▶ **Jargon watch**

Essential accounting acronyms		Analytical approaches
GAAP	Generally accepted accounting principles	Numerical methods
IAS/IASB	International Accounting Standards/Board	Quantitative analysis
SEC	Securities and Exchange Commission (US and other countries)	Financial analysis
FASB	Financial Accounting Standards Board (US)	
SFAS	Statement of Financial Accounting Standards (US)	
ASB	Accounting Standards Board (UK)	
FRS	Financial Reporting Standard (UK)	

▶ Figuring better ways to manage

There is no escaping it. Managers have to deal with numbers. The little digits come at you from all angles. They bubble up from below – your subordinates continuously bombard you with data. They are fired in sideways. You will receive all manner of potentially exciting or troubling figures from marketing and sales, production, research and development and, especially, accounting and finance. They drop in from above, often uninvited, in missives and instructions. You will receive them from customers, suppliers, business partners, bankers, brokers and other well-meaning outsiders. You will find them in every newspaper, magazine and journal. You will even hear them on broadcast media – in

Managers have been dealing with numbers since time immemorial. The earliest known writing is a 5,500-year-old inscription on pottery vessels found in the Indus Valley – the script was probably a bookkeeping entry.

Almost concurrently, in the overall scheme of things, the Mesopotamians were keeping written accounting records and running banks. And recently, archaeologists have concluded that the majority of Egyptian hieroglyphs on clay tablets from the same era are tax records. Now there's a thought.

programming apparently intended for six-year-olds which fills the short gaps between endless, mindless adverts, themselves full of useful facts, such as nine out of ten cats love whiskers.

There is no getting away from the fact that there is no getting away from numbers. Moreover, once you have them in your possession, you have to do something useful with them. You have to turn chaos into order, data into information. You will analyse, interpret, review and criticize (this last one is fun). And then you will make a decision, prepare a report, present to your colleagues or a committee, argue a case, delegate, or take some other action based on the numbers.

This is not something to take lightly. It can make or break your career. It can even ruin your marriage. Directors who intentionally or accidentally mislead can be personally liable. Pop a number in the wrong place in the balance sheet and you could end up in jail, as demonstrated in numerous corporate scandals in 2002 – more on this fascinating matter later.

The central theme in this book, as you may have guessed from its lengthy title, is *managing the numbers*. Together, you and I will see how to make short work of all these sources and uses of numbers. Or, to put it another way, how to manage better using the numbers. We will set the ball rolling in this chapter.

▶ Safety in numbers

Many people are frightened of figures. There is no need to be. If you have ever argued over whether a given colour was green or blue, or if a rice allowance should be replaced with a cash payment (we are talking Asia-Pacific here), you will know that some issues have no easy answer. Yet numbers adhere obligingly to the laws of logic. One apple plus one apple is unquestionably two apples.

Moreover, you do not have to have a mathematics chip implanted in your brain in order to deal with numbers. You can always use a calculator, as demonstrated amply in fast-food establishments every time you do tricky stuff such as using a $10 note to pay for a $4.99 Big Burger with fries.

> Ancient shoppers and traders tried using various objects as money, including cattle, stones, shells, miniature metal tools, copper rings and iron bars. Most endearingly, perhaps, cocoa beans were used as money in pre-Columbian Mexico.
>
> Incidentally, the first true coins seem to have been in use in Asia Minor and China about 2,700 years ago.

> Accounting and finance are inextricably linked. The former being perhaps more concerned with record keeping and the latter with money matters in general. To save a few words here and there, references to accounting in this book usually mean accounting and finance unless otherwise indicated.

Indeed, in order to have an adequate mastery over the numbers, you need nothing more than a modicum of common sense, the ability to coexist with everyday office equipment, and a willingness to master a few straightforward and logical methods and procedures. It is well worth the effort. It will elevate you to the status of one of the Big Five in the UN Security Council. You will not necessarily be able to make things happen, but you will certainly have the power of veto in management meetings. Who will be able to argue with you if you can demonstrate with a few undisputable figures that Kim's project is not financially viable?

Of course, the power of numbers goes much further than this. With a reasonable command of the figures, you will be able to manage more effectively and efficiently, make better decisions, produce stunning reports, be a better communicator and at least hold your own in difficult meetings. There is, indeed, safety in numbers.

By the way, I found that replacing the rice allowance with cash in hand was a bad idea. At first it was well received and easy to administer. It meant more spending power for the staff and no more humping sacks of food around. Yet, within months, the employees were complaining that it was unfair that they did not have a rice allowance while their friends did. The rationality underpinning numerical analysis is not found everywhere. That is where your other management skills are needed.

▶ Just enough and no more

You will meet numbers cloaked in various guises:

1 Frequently they will be raw and unadorned, as in: 'my best programmer writes 20 lines of code a day' (the industry average is between eight and 20 lines, honestly) or 'output rose by 101 units'.

2 Sometimes the figures have been squeezed through an analytical process: 'there is a one in eight chance that the next spangle out of the box will be red' or 'a 10% increase in advertising spending will boost sales by 1.2%'.

3 More often than not, the data will be dressed up with a dollar or other currency sign in financial amounts such as 'sales exceeded $23 million in March'.

Generalizing a touch, these examples of digit dress-sense are known grandly as numerical methods, quantitative analysis and financial analysis (respectively). Do not let that worry you. Each one is straightforward enough in its own way.

The financial figures are the most pervasive because, after all, businesses and probably your performance are usually measured in beans: net profit, cash flow, assets, share price, etc. Consequently, we will touch on all three of these numerical techniques, but with a special focus on finance. Frankly, you have to be competent with the beans, but you can get by with a little less of the statistical skills.

With just a few hundred pages in this slim book, it is going to be necessary to concentrate on the things which, to borrow a phrase, give the biggest bang for the buck. I will try to focus on practical issues, without meandering down academic side routes. We might have to go quite fast to complete our journey, but you can pull off into a lay-by and take a break whenever you wish.

Fig. 2.1 What they worry about

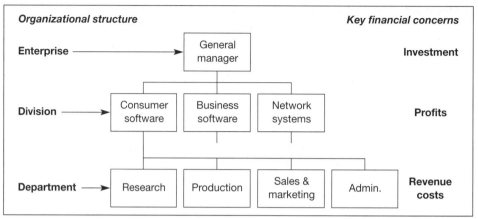

▶ Places to meet numbers

This is an easy bit. I want to tell you what is not in this chapter. It seems to me that it is useful to outline some of the places where you will meet numbers, so you know what to look out for as we travel together. A handful of examples follow. These are useful things to think about as you read the rest of this book.

Dealing with beanies. How do you deal with your chief financial officer, finance director, financial controller, financial managers, external accountants, internal and external auditors, commercial bankers, investment bankers, etc? Are they different from other professionals?

Meetings about numbers. How do you prepare for and handle such meetings? They include: kick off, review and approval meetings for the annual budget exercise, sales forecasts, financial planning, etc.; monthly, quarterly and annual reviews of budget/sales/financial performance (actual against forecast); financial post-mortems; getting approval for new projects and business units; funding, borrowing, raising equity, initial pubic offerings (IPOs), annual shareholders meetings, pre-audit planning, post-audit reviews, investment reviews, and, well, I could go on but I guess you get the point.

When you are in the spotlight and on the defensive. What questions will you be asked, and how do you answer? Where will they pick holes in your analysis and shoot you down? How do you get buy-in? How can you defend your assumptions, projections and forecasts? How can you allocate responsibility and pass the buck legitimately?

When you are in the spotlight and on the attack. What questions should you ask and what answers could you expect? Where do you look for holes and flaws in the numbers shown to you? How should you question forecasts? How do you find fixes – where other managers have used bookkeeping trickery (capitalizing costs, fiddling depreciation and amortization, provisions, cheating with timing, off-balance sheet items) or real-world trickery (skimping on maintenance, using sub-contractors, leases, etc.)?

Re-jigging the numbers. What do you do when the numbers are off-target before you start or during the year? How can you revise your forecasts, cut costs, boost revenues, and get to a better bottom line?

Financial reporting. What do you want from your managers? What do you have to send upwards? How can you set up reporting procedures, make them work, get value from financial reports, and generally manage better?

Better decision-making. How profitable is your business? Which product lines are most profitable? Which business units are most vulnerable? What indicators of operating efficiency, liquidity, debt, and investment should you track? How do you value and choose between projects, estimate net present value and the internal rate of return, use activity-based costing, calculate return on investment, manage inventory, receivables and payables, and so on?

▶ Reporting responsibilities

There is one important issue which I do want to touch on now – what might be called public financial reporting. All businesses have to file various financial returns with government regulators; public corporations publish glossy annual reports; and most if not all companies will at some time give financial information to trade partners, creditors, bankers, investors, shareholders and other nosey people. It hardly needs to be said that the law imposes certain obligations on such reporting. As already mentioned, directors can be held personally liable for misreporting. It is, therefore, rather important for managers to understand the basics of these obligations. Let me introduce the concepts here, but deal with the specifics a bit later in the appropriate chapters.

In the UK, the Companies Act 1985 includes provisions relating to:

- maintaining accounting records;
- the form and content of annual accounts;
- generally acceptable accounting practices;
- the publication to shareholders and the public filing of annual accounts;
- the requirements for annual accounts to be audited;
- the enforced correction of unsatisfactory annual accounts.

A new companies Bill went onto the drawing board in 1998 and was due to be finalized in 2003. (Check for updates on this book's website.) The stated aim was to develop **a simple, modern, efficient and cost effective framework for business activity in Britain for the twenty-first century**. Among other things, this means codifying directors' responsibilities.

▶ What is financial reporting?

A company's financial reports summarize its historical financial performance. A full set includes a profit and loss account (showing totals for sales and net profit in specified periods – usually each covering three months or a year), a balance sheet (showing debts, assets and other indicators of financial standing at a given date) and usually a cash flow statement. There will also be other figures and written notes to aid interpretation. We will discuss all this in detail later.

▶ National differences

As we will see, there are often many ways of dealing with the same numbers. Various countries have adopted differing accounting conventions. As a result, for example (picking a company at random), the Royal Bank of Scotland's net profit in the first half of 2002 was well over US $500 million higher under the US generally accepted accounting principles (GAAP – note the jargon) than under the UK's GAAP. Who would have though that by crossing the Atlantic you could magic up half a billion in six months? Of course, there is no sorcery. It is all down to bookkeeping entries.

> The origin of modern accounting can perhaps be traced to double entry accounting used by Venetian merchants in the 1200s. Luca Pacioli, a Franciscan monk, took the trouble to document the system thoroughly in a paper dated 1494; and Gutenberg's printing press helped ensure that the concept spread rapidly through Europe to Britain – and thence to the world at large.

In just about every country, regulators impose rules or guidelines governing the way that financial reports are produced. Mostly, the watchdogs also require these reports to be published. It is interesting to examine the way that accounting has evolved, and why. Some examples of the motivating factors, and the results, will make this clear.

The stage of economic development

◆ Countries such as the US, Japan and many in western Europe (which have large and multifaceted corporations with widespread public ownership) have developed complex accounting structures with detailed requirements for the disclosure of information.

◆ Less-developed economies such as many in the Middle East and Asia-Pacific, particularly where company ownership is more closed, have less complex accounting rules with more relaxed disclosure requirements.

The type of economic system

◆ Laissez-faire, common law countries, such as the UK, allowed the private sector to develop accounting principles to suit the needs of joint-stock companies and their financiers.

◆ Where laws are codified, as in western Europe, governments have attempted to document standard accounting rules which apply uniformly across all types of business. These rules may be tax based (France, Spain), legalistic (Germany) or socialistic (Sweden).

◆ Communist states such as those in the former Soviet bloc were concerned with measuring production quotas rather than profit, and with state ownership rather than the interests of shareholders.

The rate of inflation

◆ High-inflation countries in Latin America have adopted current cost rather than historic cost accounting (discussed in Chapter 18, p. 275).

Spheres of influence

◆ The British carried their accounting system throughout their former Empire, which at its peak covered more than 25% of the world's land area and people – and has included North America, Australia, New Zealand, India, parts of the Middle East, Atlantic and Pacific Islands, the south-east Asian power houses of Singapore and Hong Kong, and countless other places too numerous to list here. British investments in North American railways also helped to cement British accounting in the US in its postcolonial period.

◆ Other colonial trends had similar effects: Dutch accounting was exported to South Africa and Indonesia, and Spain's to Latin America.

◆ Accounting in Japan was influenced by the country's close ties with Germany early in the last century, then by the US after the Second World War.

◆ The US influenced neighbouring Canada and Mexico, and its former colony, the Philippines.

◆ In the last few decades, the economic dominance of the US carried its accounting practices to most corners of the map.

Internationalization

And there, in a nutshell, you have a rough and ready overview of how accounting spread around the globe. Except that it is still evolving. The growth of multinational corporations, the internationalization of capital markets and the general trend to globalization has led to pressures for unification of international accounting standards. You can see the logic. If everyone plays by the same rules, it will be easier to operate, invest and raise capital in world markets. It does not take too much thought to see that global convergence would be tricky, but the lesser goal of harmonization is easier to achieve.

The International Accounting Standards Committee (IASC) was founded in 1973 and reconstituted in 2001 as the International Accounting Standards Board. It is a private-sector body largely sponsored by the accounting profession, with representatives from around 100 countries. Its goal is to promote worldwide *convergence on a single set of high-quality, understandable and enforceable global accounting standards*. It is doing pretty well so far. In 1998, new laws in Belgium, France, Germany and Italy allowed large companies to use International Accounting Standards (IASs) domestically. More recent European Union (EU) regulations *require* all EU listed companies to produce consolidated financial statements under IAS by 2005. Many other countries already accept, or soon will accept, IASs, and even mighty Uncle Sam seems to be bowing to pressure. Whether companies will have their IAS accounts ready in time is another question.

▶ OOA – an overload of acronyms

When it comes to accounting standards, your Finance Director will rattle off all manner of AMAEs (acronyms meaningless to anyone else). To give you a fighting chance of understanding this beanie-speak, Fig. 2.2 outlines standards-setting in the US, UK and internationally. It is, after all, odds on that you are working in a country with beanie rules influenced by one of these two English-speaking nations. I will not labour the point, but note the rule-making roles of FASB (pronounced fas-bee) in the US and the FRC/ASB in the UK. These bodies, and others similar to them around the world, will coexist with the International Accounting Standards Board for the foreseeable future.

Specific rules are called Statements of Financial Accounting Standards (SFAS) in the US. In the UK, they are referred to as Financial Reporting Standards (FRS), although you will occasionally hear the term Statements of Standard Accounting Practice (SSAP) which dates back to pre-1990. As already mentioned, the International Accounting Standards Board uses the term IAS (even if you have not been paying attention, I am sure you can work out what it means).

Fig. 2.2 Acronyms in US, UK and international standards

US standards
Overview: Since 1973, standards in the US have been set by the FASB, with minimal input from the AIPCA, nominally under the authority of the SEC (which has power to establish GAAPs but does not do so).

The bodies	
SEC	Securities and Exchange Commission – sets basic reporting requirements, allows FASB to define standards.
AICPA	American Institute of Certified Public Accountants – 1938–73; professional organization which set standards
CAP	Committee on Accounting Procedures – 1938–59; standard-setting arm of the AICPA; issued 51 ARBs
APB	Accounting Principles Board – 1959–73; standard-setting arm of the AICPA ; issued 31 APB Opinions
FASB	Financial Accounting Standards Board – current standard-setting organization; established 1973; has issued over 140 SFASs

Fig. 2.2 continued

Their pronouncements	
ARB	Accounting Research Bulletin
SFAS	Statement of Financial Accounting Standards

UK standards

Overview: Since 1990, standards in the UK have been set by the ASB and policed by the FRRP, both subsidiaries of the FRC.

The bodies

ICAEW	Institute of Chartered Accountants in England and Wales – set standards 1942–69
CCAB	Consultative Committee of Accountancy Bodies – 1970 to date; established by ICAEW, expanded to include six UK professional bodies for accountants
ASSC	Accounting Standards Steering Committee – 1970–76; standards-setting arm of CCAB
ASC	Accounting Standards Committee – 1976–90; standards-setting arm of CCAB; with its predecessor the ASSC, it set 25 SSAPs
FRC	Financial Reporting Council – Current standards-setting organization; independent not-for-profit, dating from 1988 Dearing Committee Report; adopted 22 SSAPs; four have since been replaced and at the time or writing five more are being withdrawn; has issued 17 FRSs
ASB	Accounting Standards Board – established 1990; subsidiary of FRC
FRRP	Financial Reporting Review Panel – subsidiary of FRC; polices accounting requirements
UITF	Urgent Issues Task Force – assists ASB when unsatisfactory or conflicting interpretations of accounting requirements emerge

Their pronouncements

SSAP	Statements of Standard Accounting Practice
FRS	Financial Reporting Standard – successor to SSAP; equivalent to US SFAS
SORP	Statement of Recommended Practice – developed by ASC and other bodies; now reviewed by ASB
FRED	Financial Reporting Exposure Draft – ASB paper issued after Discussion Paper and before an FRS
FRSSE	Financial Reporting Standard for Smaller Entities – optional cut-down standard for small companies (i.e. essentially those with annual sales turnover under £2.8 million)

International standards

The bodies

IASC	International Accounting Standards Committee – 1973–2001; the predecessor of the IASB
IASB	International Accounting Standards Board – established 2001; with its predecessor the IASC has set over 40 standards

Their pronouncements

IAS	International Accounting Standards
IFRS	International Financial Reporting Standards

Room for manoeuvre

The interesting thing is that the US has a greater number of specific rules than any other country. To save you counting (acronyms explained in Fig. 2.2), it has 31 APB Opinions, over 140 FASB Statements, dozens of Interpretations, Statements of Position and Accounting Guides issued by the ACIPA, and goodness knows what else.

With all these rules, you would expect US beanies to be the best behaved in the world. As it is, this lawyer-dominated society has found ways to follow the rules while pulling the wool over our eyes. Some very devious ways that the books were cooked came to light in 2002. They are discussed in various places in this book. These discoveries led to the hastily introduced Corporate Responsibility Act in mid-2002, which established stronger penalties for corporate malfeasance, an SEC-controlled oversight board for the accounting industry and new rules for corporate executives and directors.

In on the Act

In the US, the Securities Act of 1933 and the Securities Exchange Act of 1934 require the filing of certain financial statements with the Securities and Exchange Commission (SEC) – such as Forms 10-Q (quarterly) and 10-K (annually – I expect there is a reason for designating it K). There is a full list of these forms on this book's website.

In contrast to the US, there are only about 30 standards in the UK, and there are more relaxed rules for private limited companies. The overriding principle, enshrined in the 1985 Companies Act, is that accounts should give a *true and fair view* of a corporation's financial position. It is much harder to cheat if you have to comply with this sort of moral code (although, to be fair to all concerned, I have to say that the UK has had its own share of corporate accounting scandals).

Consequently, the International Accounting Standards Board has stated categorically that it does not intend to follow the over-regulated US model. We all held our breath for a while, but in October 2002 the US *seemed* to agree to implement IAS by 2005. Time will tell.

Multinationals (corporations operating or raising finance in more than one country) often have to prepare several sets of accounts – one for each country's GAAP. For example, software giant Infosys reports its financial statements under the accounting principles of (alphabetically) Australia, Canada, France, Germany, India, Japan, the UK, and the US. As International Accounting Standards become accepted, the job of producing and interpreting financial reports is becoming greatly simplified. I have to say, though, that it does seem something of a miracle that everybody is working together so well. If only politics were as friendly as accounting.

Ten hard questions to ask or be asked

1 Why are we interested in managing *these* numbers? What is it that we want to do with them or find out from them?

2 By what duties, ethics and laws am I personally bound when managing and reporting the numbers?

3 Do our internal and published financial reports give a true and fair view of the business?

4 Under which country's set of generally accepted accounting principles (GAAP) do we operate? Do we report under more than one GAAP? Why? What is the cost?

5 How do international accounting standards (IAS) affect the operations of our company?

6 What do our national accounting and regulatory bodies have to say about IAS? Is there any clash between our national and the international accounting standards?

7 Are our implementation plans effective and on target? What will be the costs and benefits?

8 How will the move to IAS affect our reporting and disclosure?

9 How will our customers and competitors react?

10 Are we ahead of the market in adopting and understanding IAS?

The website for this book has some excellent sources of information on national accounting principles in various countries, the national and international regulatory bodies, and the standards themselves.

Checklist

The choice here was for me to do some work or for you to do some work. Guess who won? I am going to ask you to turn back to the *Mastering money management* questions at the start of this chapter and look over the *Ten hard questions*. They provide a useful summary of what you might take away from this chapter. Actually, I was not being lazy. I just did not want to be repetitive. Perhaps we can strike a deal. I will not repeat the obvious, if, in return, when you reach to end of each chapter you will look back to the *Survival toolkit* to ensure that you hit upon the key points that I wanted to make. Let me know if I failed anywhere and I will amend the next edition.

▶ Conclusion

Back to the topic in hand. There are a few lessons to learn from all of the above.

◆ The first and most obvious is that you have some statutory reporting requirements to consider. You need to know the basics even if you let your beanies worry about crossing the t's and dotting the i's – and at the end of the day it is you, not they, who could be prosecuted for non-compliance.

◆ The second is that there is some flexibility in accounting and financial reporting. You need to know about this when you are creating and interpreting accounts.

◆ The third observation is that if you operate in more than one country, you may have to prepare your financials differently in each.

◆ The fourth is that it is all changing. National GAAP may be supplemented with or replaced by International Accounting Standards, depending on where you are operating.

Read on to find out more.

3

how the finance director thinks

'Our experts describe you as an appallingly dull fellow, unimaginative, timid, lacking in initiative, spineless, easily dominated, no sense of humour, tedious company and irrepressibly drab and awful. And whereas in most professions these would be considered drawbacks, in … accountancy they are a positive boon.'

John Cleese, Graham Chapman, Terry Jones, Michael Palin and Eric Idle
(*Now for Something Completely Different*, 1971)

▶ Chapter survival toolkit

▶ Overview

This chapter takes a rather cynical look at the accounting profession. Do not take it too seriously. It describes the rigorous training which imbues beanies with a meticulous, conservative approach to business. It looks at their qualifications and job titles and touches on the underlying principles which shape their view of the corporation. It discusses briefly the role of auditors – and how their work affects you directly. And it provides a gentle warning about following financial procedures.

▶ Prerequisites

None, other than a pinch of salt.

▶ Mastering the beanie mind set

After reading this chapter, you should be able to answer the following questions:

1 What are the on-the-job training requirements for would-be accountants?

2 Why does their training emphasize logic, attention to detail and risk aversion?

3 What is the role of the chief financial officer?

4 What is the distinction between the treasurer, financial controller and various other accountancy roles?

5 What is the difference between financial, cost, management and environmental accounting?

6 What is the distinction between accountants and auditors? Should the internal auditor report to the finance director?

7 What are the roles of the internal and external auditors?

8 Why is shareholder protection important?

9 What is the significance for you of the finance manual and internal audits?

10 Can you describe the bean counter's belief system?

> 'The nice part about being a pessimist is that you are constantly being either proved right or pleasantly surprised.'
>
> **George F. Will**

The second oldest profession?

No doubt you have seen pictures of those ancient cave paintings where a bunch of woolly savages are chasing a woolly mammoth off a cliff. You probably noticed that the stick figure at the back was an accountant.

As soon as there were things to count, there were beanies. They went by other names back then, given that the first in their trade were probably preoccupied with divvying up woolly mammoth steaks, or counting bushels of grain going into storage for leaner days. All that tallying and remembering was tricky and prone to later argument, so it is quite possible that accountants had a significant hand in the invention of the written word. Indeed, with such a long history they have had plenty of time to develop a rich jargon which has developed almost into a separate language – one that is up there with Egyptian hieroglyphics, Ancient Greek and Gibberish.

In addition to beanie-speak, accountants have built an impressive system of qualifications and a range of job titles that would make anyone proud. Most remarkable, perhaps, is their unique level of optimism. Apparently they do not have any. Presumably this comes from handling other people's money all the time.

> The first written use of the term bean counter was in a 1975 Forbes magazine article which referred to "a smart, tight-fisted and austere 'bean counter' accountant from rural Kentucky".

> When you see letters after a beanie's name, a C usually stands for certified or chartered, a P for public, and A, well, take a wild guess. You sometimes see M for management.
>
> - In the US and many countries in Asia the most common beanie designation is CPA – certified public accountant.
>
> - British beanies are usually CAs (chartered) or CCAs (chartered and certified).

▶ Pessimism can be learned

When you chat with your finance director, you'll probably get the impression that he is a born pessimist. This may not be the case. The pessimism could well have been learned during accountancy training. Finance directors and the people they surround themselves with are, not surprisingly, mostly accountants by training – birds of a feather, so to speak. Anthropologists must find this an interesting group of people.

▶ How accountants are made

Almost every country regulates bean counters, either through government bodies or professional institutes. Generally, anyone can call himself or herself an accountant, but only beanies who have completed specific professional training can put the appropriate letters, such as CPA, after their name and call themselves certified or chartered accountants.

Accountants increasingly complete a formal education to at least degree level before beginning their professional qualification (the US is generally pretty fussy in requiring an undergraduate degree, although the UK and many other countries are more flexible). Given their bent, many wannabe beanies will have studied finance or business, although this is not normally a prerequisite. They usually begin their formal professional training only after they start work as powder monkeys.

> The P in CPA indicates that the accountant can sell services to the public. It is tempting to make a quip about selling their souls or prostituting their services, but I will refrain.

Generally, the bodies that award accountancy qualifications insist that candidates are engaged in approved on-the-job training while they study. Money-minded people who are not in finance-related work are usually barred from taking accountancy examinations. Even financial geniuses cannot walk into suitable employment and sit the examinations right away. There are strict timescales laid down to ensure that would-be accountants have been stacking and polishing beans for long enough to be able to do so blindfolded. (Most states in the US require two years' experience; many other countries require three years on-the-job training. Would-be beanies in Thailand have to put in at least 3,000 hours before qualifying.)

Anyway, after several years, and several sets of rigorous examinations, those dedicated enough to complete the training become qualified accountants. Three interesting points about this training are worthy of mention.

> 'It doesn't hurt to be optimistic. You can always cry later.'
>
> **Lucimar Santos de Lima**

1. Machiavelli apply here

Would-be accountants have to find employment where they are provided with on-the-job training. Very small companies do not employ their own accountants. Slightly larger companies do, but they cannot justify or support the cost of having trainees cluttering up the place and eating into the finance chief's time. The consequence is that wannabe bean counters have to start their careers in bigger ponds.

Big ponds have a unique culture and political structure which imprints itself on financial fledglings at the very time when they are most impressionable – when they are waddling around behind mother duck carrying the printouts and carefully learning how best to advance their own careers.

The culture and politics of big business is a fascinating topic. Large organizations are usually highly structured with a clearly defined hierarchy. Important and not-so-important proposals are analysed in excruciating detail before decisions are taken, often by committees. There are also less clearly defined but probably more important pecking orders based on influence and power. By understanding how this works, ambitious executives can flutter over their apparently pre-ordained stopping points and follow an accelerated route into senior management and the board.

Indeed, or perhaps because, white-collar life can be so deadly dull at times, playing this promotion game can become a major preoccupation. Is it possible that executives sometimes make decisions based first on 'what this means for my career' and second for the good of the company? Can it become second nature to surreptitiously and ever so nicely peck away at other people's proposals and performance? Of

> Certified or chartered? It makes little difference to you and me. It's basically down to snobbish rivalry between what are usually well-established and respectable accounting institutes.

course, there is one instance when Machiavellians praise others: when something risky needs to be done. If you suddenly find a corporate adversary enthusiastically supporting you, you might want to carefully re-examine your figures. But I digress. The message is that accountancy training by design gives accountants a solid grounding in big-pond decision-making. You must decide for yourself whether this is a good thing or not.

2. No turtles

My second point relates to the nature of accountancy study courses and examinations. All the topics are somewhat structured and mechanical. They include a smattering of mathematics and statistics, some law relating to corporations, taxation, and so on, and a whole bundle of stuff about bookkeeping, accounting and finance. There is no time for the metaphysical. It is logic and mechanics all the way down. To start accountancy training requires a certain way of thinking. To complete the course requires a lot more of the same.

By the time that accountants order name-plates with CPA or whatever after their name, they will have totally forgotten how to make decisions on instinct – if they ever did know. Accountants are, quite properly for their profession, indoctrinated with the need for meticulous precision and attention to detail. Everything will be decided by careful analysis of the possible outcomes. And, as already hinted, there will be considerable emphasis on avoiding risk. Whether this is good or bad I will leave for you to decide. I am merely drawing your attention to how the training pushes their thought processes in a particular way.

> The International Federation of Accountants (IFAC), working to harmonize standards in the profession, has 156 member bodies in 114 countries, representing 2 million bean counters

3. No free spirits

Many brilliant and successful business people are accountants by training, but their approach is necessarily different from that of entrepreneurial risk takers. Accountants are not university dropouts who have built empires as did Bill Gates with Microsoft or Michael Dell with Dell Computers. Those accountants who do create and run big corporations usually do so by following a more conventional approach. If you are a seat-of-the-pants entrepreneur, then before you sit down for coffee with the finance director, think back to the most rigorous subject you studied – preferably from the areas of maths or science. The discussion will not be 'I have a hunch we'd sell more widgets if we painted them green'. It will be 'based on empirical evidence from market research by McKindred, with sampling as detailed in this handout, which indicates that we can be 99.5% confident that 3.91% of consumers prefer the colour approximated by Pantone Process 281–1, we could…'.

> The US Bureau of Labor projects that between 2000 and 2010 the number of accountants in the US will increase by one-third – making the profession one of the top 20 fastest-growing sources of employment in the nation.

What's in a name?

- ◆ **Financial accountants** are preoccupied with financial reporting (as you can see, this box is not going to be too taxing conceptually).
- ◆ **Cost accountants** concentrate on working out how much you spend producing a unit of something or other.
- ◆ **Management accountants** try to make sense of it all from a decision-makers' perspective, and spot inefficiencies in your operations.
- ◆ **Environmental accountants** have nothing to do with this book and got into the act because they thought the word accountant gave them extra credibility.

Fig. 3.1 The evolutionary process

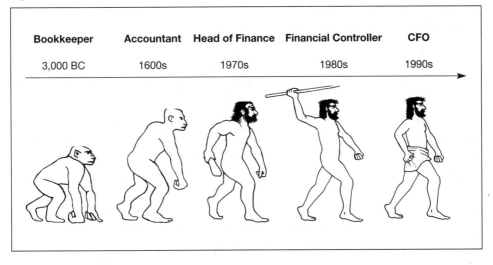

Bookkeeper	Accountant	Head of Finance	Financial Controller	CFO
3,000 BC	1600s	1970s	1980s	1990s

▶ What do all these people do?

Beanie titles are evolving rapidly (see Fig. 3.1). For ambitious accountants, the goal these days is to become the chief financial officer (CFO) – the mother duck of all accountants. This title first saw the light of day in the US. Across the Atlantic, the beanie at the top of the pecking order is also known with typical British understatement as the finance director. In smaller companies, or those lagging in the evolutionary process, the position is often termed financial controller (when treasury responsibilities might fall to a different person).

> The CFO, or equivalent, reports to the chief executive officer, keeps the board informed, directs financial plans and policies, and oversees audits, accounting, budgeting, tax, treasury, and anything else that involves beans.

Reporting to the CFO, there could be a bewildering array of titles (see Fig. 3.2). Most of the titles are fairly self-explanatory. A few that might need elucidation are as follows:

- The **treasurer** manages the corporation's cash position, ensuring that there is just enough folding stuff to meet daily obligations, and that any excess is not idle but is earning interest somewhere.

> Accountants wield extreme power, because they have power of veto. By demonstrating that an idea is not financially viable, they can stop it dead in the water. A good game you can play is to try to prove them wrong.

- **Accounts receivables** and **collections** people work to ensure that the cash from customers rolls in promptly.

- **Accounts payable** bods basically pay the bills on time so that the lights do not go out.

◆ Anyone with **Information** in his or her job title is concerned with some aspect of your computer systems.

◆ **Bookkeepers** maintain the basic financial records.

◆ **Auditors** try to ensure that everyone is being honest and truthful. Too often, they report direct to the CFO but, for reasons which will become clear in a moment, they should be independent of the finance director and should report directly to the chief executive or the board.

The way things are going, the list of job titles here probably went out of date while this book was being printed. New designations are being invented almost daily. I have recently come across a **forensic accountant** (tracking fraud) and a **software accountant** (valuing software and web applications). Let me know what creative designations you have in your company.

> 'An accountant is a man hired to explain that you didn't make the money you did.'
>
> Anon.

Fig. 3.2 The names they call themselves

Choose a title	OR	Pic-and-mix: select one from column A (optional), one from column B and one from column C		
		A	B	C
Accountant				
Actuary		Assistant	Accounting	Clerk
Auditor		Senior	Accounts Payable	Analyst
Bookkeeper		Chief	Accounts Receivable	Supervisor
Controller			Audit	Manager
Financial Analyst			Billing	Officer
Financial Controller			Bookkeeping	
Information Systems Auditor			Budget	
Internal Auditor			Cash	
Management Accountant			Collections	
Tax Accountant			Cost Accountant	
Treasurer			Credit	
			Credit & Collections	
			Collections	
			Financial	
			Financial Analysis	
			Information Systems Audit	
			Internal Audit	
			Investment/Portfolio	
			Payroll	
			Taxation	
			Treasury	

Variations on a theme

Use of the designations finance and financial varies. *Finance director* is slightly more common than *financial director*, but *chief financial officer* is far more popular than *chief finance officer*. The term *comptroller* is also used sometimes – it is a variation on *controller*, derived from compute.

Other numbers people

Other people who deal with numbers include actuaries, mathematicians, statisticians and economists. You may have such propeller heads in your company. They inhabit their own world again, also with its own jargon. We will demystify some of it in this book. The most important thing to remember at this stage is that they are mostly every bit as meticulous and precise as accountants. By the way, an actuary is a statistician who calculates insurance risks and premiums – someone who, as the old joke goes, found accounting too exciting.

Fig. 3.3 Accountants in the boardroom

If you meet 100 directors who are (or were) accountants, these will be their roles.
Note: this is highly subjective, i.e. an educated guess.

Role	No. of accountants
Chairman	6
CEO/MD	7
Company Secretary	12
CFO/Finance Director	40
Chief Accountant	5
Treasurer	3
Other executive	5
Non-executive	22

▶ Watch out for the auditors

It has to be said that auditors can be scary people. Their job is basically to ensure that good finance and accounting procedures are being followed and that no one is quietly dipping their fingers in the till. Auditors do not usually check every last transaction and voucher, but instead they will check a sample of your financial records. Be aware that fraudsters will know this and will often attempt to have the 'right' sample reviewed. By the way, just in case *sample* sounds too lax, bean counters call this a *test of the accounts*.

Internal auditors

Internal auditors are employed by the company and are, shall I say, generally pretty pernickety. They do not earn beanie brownie points by reporting that there is nothing to report. They make their name according to the number of things that they identify as being wrong. The more nitpicking they do, the faster they will be recognized as *Good Chaps* and get promoted out of a dull job. They will swoop on you uninvited and unannounced in the hope that the element of surprise will catch out some laxity of ticking boxes and duplicating dockets.

> Most stock exchanges require listed companies to conduct internal audits, and there is usually a statutory requirement for an independent external audit.

Watch out. You will be penalized if you or your people are doing something that the auditors think is incorrect, even if no one told you that the company prefers if it is done some other way. For example, a friend once had his knuckles rapped because he signed and countersigned the bank reconciliation report and initialled the corresponding bank statement, instead of signing both. This is a reasonable requirement. But considering that head office gave absolutely no guidance in advance, I think it was a bit unfair that he had to spend a day in the stocks.

When you take over a business unit with accounting or finance responsibilities, insist on either of the following – or preferably both:

♦ Ask your beanies for a finance manual relating to the job, and document in writing that you cannot be held responsible for non-compliance with amended or additional policies that have not been notified to you in writing.
♦ Request an internal audit so that you have a benchmark of what is required. The beanies will say that they are too busy. Make it clear that you will follow pre-existing policies for which you are not responsible until they have completed the audit and give you a copy of the report, together with details of any new or amended procedures.

External auditors

External auditors work for those big public firms that are always in the news and seemingly always changing their names. They are essentially consultants. Remember that consultants earn their money by telling you what you want to hear and, usually, what you already know. Their success is not measured by a scorecard in your internal audit department, but by a fat fee paid to them for doing what they are told to do.

External auditors are concerned more with good practice and compliance with regulations, rather than with the minutiae of internal financial policies. At the broadest level, these financial police are concerned with protecting the interests of shareholders and, essentially, providing an independent opinion on the financial report – which until about now was often pre- pared by someone else in the auditors' own firm. All this is changing. Regulators are demanding a greater degree of separation between account- ing and auditing, and auditors are treading very carefully.

When an external audit is required, it will be requested by you or your beanies. You will know about it beforehand, and you should ask for a meeting with the auditors before they start. This gives you the chance to find out what they need from you, and to tell them about any areas where you want them to check carefully what is being done by your staff, your accounting and finance department, and your external accoun- tants. Their report will not absolve you from blame, but it will provide a handy third-party check on internal financial and accounting pro- cedures and processes.

> **And then there were four**
>
> In 2002, following accounting scandals that wiped Andersen off the map, the Big 4 accounting firms were Deloitte Touche Tohmatsu, Ernst & Young, KPMG and PricewaterhouseCoopers.
>
> This was down from eight in 1960: Arthur Andersen, Ernst & Ernst, Haskins & Sells, Lybrand, Ross Bros & Montgomery, Peat Marwick, Price Waterhouse, Touche Ross, and Arthur Young.
>
> Second-tier accounting practices are known as Group B.

Bankers

Bankers are not usually accountants, although there will be some bean counters lurking amongst their midst. However, bankers are steeped in financial matters and their training will have included analysing and interpreting financial statements. Moreover, investment bankers have rafts of analysts who spend their day tracking the financial performance of corporations. Expect them to behave very similarly to beanies.

▶ What is there to be cheerful about?

We have already noted that accountants are not long on optimism. They have been taught to see the financial downside in everything and, in general, ignore the upside. For example, if they become aware of some pressing need to spend money in the future, they will usually insist on showing this in your financial accounts right away. But try getting them to recognise income in advance. That would rank somewhere between getting blood from a stone and walking on water. Indeed, the system of accruals accounting (see Chapter 8) is so-named because it requires accounts to show any commitments to spend money (accrued expenses). Never mind that these same accounts also have to include pre-paid expenses. The system could have been called prepayments accounting, but I am sure you agree that would sound too cheerful. Figure 3.4 outlines the bean counter's belief system.

Fig. 3.4 Five of your bean counter's top beliefs

1 **Beans are everything.** Accountants insist that everything can be measured with money. Accounts do not take account of competitive forces, goodwill, quality, location, etc.

2 **Business is an ongoing concern.** Beanies work on the basis that the business will keep going for ever. Financial statements do *not* purport to show what you would be left with if you closed the business tomorrow.

3 **The value of something is what you paid for it.** Accountants base all their records on purchase prices. The current value of anything will be shown in the accounts as its cost less some arbitrary allowance for wear and tear. Things that appreciate are rarely revalued upwards. In most cases, it will be an accident if the recorded value of a factory or machine coincides with the current market value or replacement value.

4 **Always play it safe.** Bean counters steadfastly refuse to anticipate revenue. They include it in the accounts only when a sale is made. However, they insist on making provision for every expected expense or loss just as soon as someone thinks about it.

5 **Policies are set in stone.** Accountants try to prevent you from changing accounting policies and want the basis on which your accounts are prepared to remain consistent from month to month and from year to year.

▶ A unique jargon

In common with every other discipline, accounting has a mystifying jargon of its own. Your finance people will pepper their sentences with mystifying terms such as contingent liabilities, contra accounts, accruals, net present value, hurdle rate, discount rates and so on. Moreover, there is a surfeit of financial acronyms, some of which we bumped into in Chapter 2. I will attempt to demystify as much of this as possible as we move forward.

To make matters worse, some of the terms have completely the opposite meanings to those which we recognize from every day life. For example, if you have money in your bank account, your bank statement will have a credit balance. Well, do not be alarmed if your finance director's notes indicate that the company bank account has a huge debit balance. From a bean counter's perspective, a debit balance is often good news. This is discussed on p. 102.

> 'In a 2003 survey of CFOs, 38% of respondents identified "a positive attitude" as the most important interpersonal skill for accountants. Least important, with just 1% of the vote, was reckoned to be "a sense of humour".'
>
> **Anon.**

Hard questions to ask about your finance department

How does your finance department score? More than one or two no's are cause for concern.

1 Are monthly figures available within a day or two of month end?

2 Are quarterly figures available within about 10 days of the end of the quarter?

3 Are your financials stable (i.e., rarely revised or restated)?

4 Do you get clear answers quickly when you query any figures?

5 Can you find out easily if a payment has been made or received?

6 Is inventory trim?

7 Are receivables collected quickly?

8 Are bad debts small?

9 Do you receive clear internal notification when payments are received?

10 Can you say that your company never paid a bill twice?

11 Are refunds processed smoothly?

12 Are finance duties properly split (e.g., are cheques written and signed by different people)?

13 Does your internal auditor report to the CEO or someone other than the finance chief?

14 Is your cash flow well managed without unexpected or excessive surpluses or deficits?

Conclusion

Having had a reasonable shot at assassinating the personality of beanies, I should perhaps reiterate that my cynicism should be taken with a large pinch of salt. Accountants and financiers are essential to the functioning of every business. Their cool logic and analytical approach provides a valuable balance for risk-taking managers and entrepreneurs. Moreover, there are some things, such as understanding tax regulations and filings, that no one else can be expected to do. Love them or hate them, you just can't live without them.

By the way, I should give you a little warning. I am going to switch tack for a few pages, and review spreadsheets and some ways of handling numbers. These topics are very interesting in their own right, but they also lay the groundwork for managerial success with the numbers – as discussed in the final chapters of this book.

the financial wizard's toolbox

'Should I refuse a good dinner simply because I do not understand the process of digestion?'

Oliver Heaviside
(when criticized for using numerical techniques without understanding how they worked)

▶ Chapter survival toolkit

▶ Overview

This chapter is about spreadsheets. It is intended mainly as an introduction for novices. Nevertheless, if you can do the things in this chapter, you will be able to do everything in this book, and possibly everything that you ever need to do with these electronic helpers. Probably, 90% of us use 10% of their features, and frankly this is usually more than enough.

Spreadsheets have a gazillion amazing features, many of them of interest to only the most dedicated propeller heads. Moreover, there are many ways of achieving the same results and you can use what you do know to get the answers you need, even if you are neglecting some advanced techniques for doing the same thing. However, if there is one important message to take away from this chapter, it is probably *use the online Help*.

▶ Prerequisites

None, other than a basic familiarity with common computer tasks such as using Word or email.

▶ Mastering spreadsheet basics

After reading this chapter, you should be able to answer the following questions:

1 What is the concept of a spreadsheet?
2 How do you save and print spreadsheets?
3 How do you create well-formatted tables?
4 How do you produce first-class reports by copying spreadsheet tables into Word documents?
5 How do you dynamically-link spreadsheet tables and charts to Word documents?
6 How do you create intelligent spreadsheets
7 How do you use arithmetic and built-in formulas in a spreadsheet?
8 How do you use brackets to control the order in which spreadsheets perform calculations?
9 How can you use a spreadsheet to help you manage lists?
10 How do you sort and find data?

'Logic is the art of going wrong with confidence.'

Morris Kline

> ▶ **Jargon watch**

PC (personal computer) basics	Computer actions	Spreadsheets stuff
Desktop	Click	Spreadsheet/workbook
Operating system	Point-and-click	Table
Application	Double-click	Cell
Document	Right-click	Cell reference
File	Select	Formula
	Drag-and-drop	Dynamic linking
	Cut, copy and paste	
	Clipboard	
	Keyboard shortcuts	
	Menu bar	
	Toolbars, buttons and icons	
	Dialog box	

▶ Power on your PC

I want to apologize in advance. In the previous three chapters you and I chatted happily about things finance-related. In this chapter I am going to ask you to actually do something. I will start gently, but in the second half of the chapter I want you to experiment with spreadsheets. I will try to explain each task in plain English before degenerating into the *press this and click that* of books for computer dummies. I think that if you have made it thus far, you will probably find this all very easy. Moreover, if you are already slick in the spreadsheets, you can skip over much of this. Incidentally, though, there are some secret spreadsheet shortcuts revealed here which are great timesavers.

▶ The power of PCs

With the previous thoughts out of the way, let me get back to the story. My first job was in a bank, operating monstrous adding machines (I also made the tea and fed the canary). I totalled, in the constructive sense, anything that did not move, and some things that did: cheques, share certificates, piles of money.

I learned two lessons. First, do everything in two different ways. If the totals disagree, you have made a mistake. Second, if the error is divisible by nine, it is odds on that you have reversed two digits. For example, if you enter 54 instead of 45, the total will be out by 9 exactly. Try swapping two digits in any number and checking by how much it increases or decreases. The difference is always a multiple of nine. For me, this discovery was the beginning of a life-long fascination with numbers.

But I digress. The point I really wanted to make was about adding machines or *comptometers*. These were noisy mechanical monsters with arrays of over 100 buttons. Originally, driven by obstinate crank handles, they were later powered by whirring motors in much the same way as old electric typewriters. They were too heavy to move around easily. Indeed, accountants would send their adding up to a room full of nimble-fingered machine operators and wait anxiously for the results. The alternatives were mental arithmetic, slide rules and books of look-up tables. A lucky few in the latter days before PCs could send a box of punch cards to the electronic data processing (EDP) department, as information technology (IT) was then known, and wait even longer for results – which were invariably useless because the cards were punched wrongly or somebody had dropped them and mixed up the order.

Electronic calculators that rendered all this obsolete hit the market in 1972. True, at first, their capabilities were limited, but their impact cannot be underestimated. They were, however, overshadowed within a mere decade by innovations with even greater significance: desktop computers and spreadsheet programs.

Imagine how difficult it was to prepare forecasts in the days before personal computers. By and large, financials had to be fairly rudimentary. Today, common office software has matured to the extent that a non-financial manager can do tricks with numbers that were previously undreamed of even by mathematical specialists. We will discuss some of this wizardry in this chapter and develop the ideas as we work through the book together.

▶ What's in the electronic toolbox?

If you sneak into the office of a financial whiz, you will find only one real tool – a PC with spreadsheet software such as Microsoft Excel. PCs used by real beanies will also contain an electronic accounting package, which we will discuss in Chapter 7. If you look really hard, you will find some other software to help with obscure calculations. Beyond this, everything else is obsolete or obsolescent. Calculators, adding machines and look-up tables are still used sometimes, but the humble spreadsheet fulfils their roles and does much more. Even reference books containing hard-to-remember formulas are unnecessary, because spreadsheet software generously provides the formulas in built-in crib sheets.

However, if you think that spreadsheets are the exclusive preserve of propeller heads and beanies, think again. Spreadsheets can help every manager manage better. Even if you are coming in cold, I guarantee that within an hour of working through this chapter you will have thought of a way to use a spreadsheet to improve at least one of your tasks (connect to this book's website and tell me what it was). You can probably see where we are heading. It is time to get under the covers with a spreadsheet.

> 'I cannot do it without comp[u]ters.'
>
> **William Shakespeare**

PCs vs Macs

Some 90% of desktops are dominated by the PC – a box of incomprehensible bits and bobs based on the design of IBM's first popular microcomputer released in 1981. This has become the undisputed tool for business use. You will also come across the Mac, which evolved from Apple's machine of the same era as the IBM PC. The Mac has become the tool of choice for some creative types, while left-brain financial wizards use PCs almost without exception. Most software mentioned in this book runs on PCs and Macs, so I will use the term PC as synonymous with Mac. Apologies to staunch aficionados of either who object to this.

So what is this spreadsheet thing?

A spreadsheet is to numbers what Word is to text or Outlook is to email. Essentially, spreadsheets just provide a framework or grid to help with the layout of their content, and a range of formatting and calculating options. The grid carves up the electronic page into boxes – or cells – which fall into neat rows and columns.

What is the content of spreadsheets? It is simply words and figures that you want to lay out neatly in rows and columns (for an example, flick ahead to Fig. 4.3). The real magic starts as soon as you want to do any summarizing (e.g. adding numbers in a column) or analysing (such as calculating ratios). Once you have told the spreadsheet what you want, you have the framework for ever more. You can change one number and the calculations will update automatically.

Two other features are of huge significance. First, you can produce a chart (see Fig. 5.1) faster than a rat descending a greased drainpipe. Second, you can insert such pictures, or for that matter any other extract from a spreadsheet, into a Word document. Reports will never be the same again.

Spreadsheets we have known

In the brief history of the PC, there have been only two or three dominant spreadsheet applications. Worthy of mention is the first-ever spreadsheet, VisiCalc, released on the Apple II (Mac) in the early 1980s. It was quickly swallowed up by the revolutionary Lotus 1-2-3 (now known as 123) which first hit the market in 1983. For most of the 1980s, 123 battled it out with upstart rivals such as SuperCalc and Quattro Pro. Microsoft introduced Excel in 1985; but, remarkably, for the Mac only. By the late 1980s Excel had been ported to the business-minded PC, and within a few years Excel was the undisputed winner. It remains so a decade later.

Despite this supremacy from Seattle, there is something of a choice today. The Lotus (office) SmartSuite in which 123 lives on, and Sun Microsystems' Star Office are both significantly cheaper than Microsoft Office (which includes Excel). Both these rival products include spreadsheets which their makers claim are fully compatible with the Microsoft package.

The spreadsheet examples in this book are based on Excel because it is on more than three-quarters of all corporate desktops. You can do all the tricks demonstrated here using its rivals. Moreover, given that this book is about managing numbers, I should exhort you to consider using one of the lower-cost competitors. You could be a hero for cutting your company's software licensing costs significantly. (And, by the way, Microsoft did not bother to reply when I asked for permission to use Excel screenshots in this book; the Corporation's standard terms for doing so are legalistically unhelpful.)

▶ What you need to bring to the party

If you can do very simple arithmetical sums, with or without a calculator, and find your way around a computer, you can do everything in this chapter – and indeed in this book. If you can power on a computer, open, say, MS Word and write a short note or memo, and then save and print your work, you are well placed. Why? Because all the common office applications – Word and Excel included – have the same look and feel. If you can use Word, you can use Excel. If you are not wholly familiar with tech-speak, please browse Figs 4.1 and 4.2. There is not room in this book to digress into great mysteries of computing, so we will job through the essentials at a rapid pace. You are welcome to download supplementary material from this book's website.

▶ Why bother?

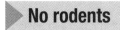

> Using a standard PC with the software that probably came with it gives you at least five basic advantages over pen and paper:
>
> 1 You call tell the PC to do all the arithmetic for you, and even build in cross-checks to ensure it has done it right.
>
> 2 You can make changes effortlessly and see how they ripple through to the bottom line.
>
> 3 You can update the figures over the coming months to monitor results and compare actual events with your budgets or forecasts.
>
> 4 You can link and copy tables into your written reports and/or produce wonderfully neat results on paper.
>
> 5 Once you have set up the template, you can use it over and over again, for years to come.

There is at least one more benefit to doing the numbers yourself with a PC. The act of keying figures, assumptions and relationships helps them sink in more effectively than when you just read them. It is almost therapeutic. No, really. It is.

▶ No rodents

A blank spreadsheet is potentially enormous. The bit of it you are using is a table. (I'm not sure my spreadsheet manual defines it this way, but it makes sense to me.)

It helps to try to make to your tables fit neatly into one or more printed pages. With small print you can get 12 months' budget figures, together with captions and totals in the width of A4 or letter paper.

I want to give you a little warning. The remainder of this chapter outlines the basics of spreadsheets. The easiest way to understand these incredible tools is to use one. Accordingly, I am going to assume that you have this book in one hand and a mouse in the other. If you are wondering why you need to hold a small, furry rodent you should skip the next few pages. If you know what I mean by mouse, but you do not have one to hand, you can skim the remainder of this chapter and return to it, say, during your lunch break at the office.

How to excel at numbers

Think of a spreadsheet as being a page in a note pad. Each page is ruled off into a large number of rows and columns. This creates a grid of little boxes, each of which is called a cell. You type descriptive text (e.g. budget categories, names), numbers or instructions into the cells. The layout of cells gives order to your text and numbers, but the real power of spreadsheets is that they can understand and act on your instructions. You can tell the spreadsheet to perform useful tasks such as 'add up the numbers in the five rows above this cell and show me the result' or 'if the number in this cell is negative display it in red'. Generally, when you look at a spreadsheet, you see the results rather than the underlying instructions. A couple of keystrokes will reveal the instructions if you need to review them.

To save your spreadsheet for future use, choose **Save** or **Save As** from the **File** menu, and in the dialog box that appears type a name for the file.

By default, Excel files have the ending '.xls'. such as 'salary .xls'. You can probably work out what xls indicates. Actually, they should perhaps be designated xlw files, because they contain workbooks, each of which can contain one or many spreadsheets.

Note that the xls **extension** might be hidden from view, depending how your version of Windows is set up.

If this sounds too good to be true, there is a rub. To get round the problem that people might issue their commands differently, the instructions are standardized in a kind of shorthand. Its not much of a rub, though. The shorthand is mainly self-evident. Moreover, the instructions that you will use 90% of the time are so easy to remember that you will not have to refer often to the helpful built-in guides.

Getting started

When your spreadsheet application springs into life you will be greeted with a screen such as that shown in Fig. 4.1.

Note how the columns are labelled with letters and the rows are indicated with numbers. A spreadsheet can have over 250 columns and more than 65,000 rows – enough for most expenses claims. In case you wondered, when you get to column Z, the lettering continues at AA, AB, and so on. Each cell can be uniquely identified by the appropriate column and row designators.

To gain some familiarity with a spreadsheet application, open it and drop down (i.e. click on) each menu in turn to see what is on it. Much of it won't make sense if it is completely new to you, but you will spot some things which are self-evident. On most Microsoft products you will have to click on the double arrow at the bottom of a menu (or double-click at the top) in order to see all the options. I guess that the Seattle Giant thinks that an abbreviated menu is more user-friendly. It makes me incredibly irritated.

Also, right-click on the work area and on some surrounding elements and up will pop more menus with more options – such as the one at the bottom of Fig. 4.1 which can be used to add and rename spreadsheets.

A virtual desktop

Figure 4.1 shows a computer desktop with Excel in use. Note that cells A4 to A15 are selected.

Fast shortcut: The months were entered as follows: Cell A4 was selected by clicking it with the mouse. The word *Jan* was keyed into the cell, and the fill handle was then dragged down another 11 rows with the mouse. The spreadsheet automatically generated the months Feb–Dec. The same trick works with numbers, and you can create your own lists – choose *Tools/Options* and in the dialog box that appears, click the tab marked *Custom Lists*.

For the experienced: Right-click on the very edge of a selection box, drag to a new location, and release the mouse button. A popup menu will offer you various handy options. I frequently use the one listed as Copy here as values to freeze the results of formulas and prevent recalculation.

Table 4.1 A virtual desktop

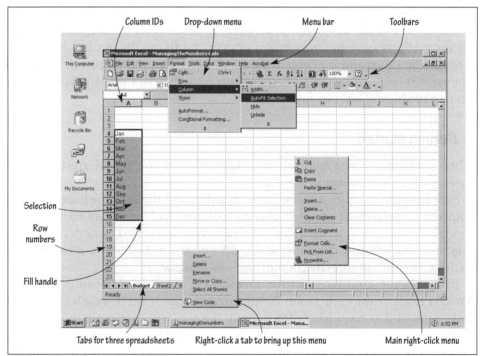

A handy trick is to select *What's This?* from the *Help* menu (or press Shift-F1 – hold down the shift key and press the F1 key at the same time, then release both keys). The cursor will acquire a question mark. If you now click on anything on the Excel screen, a little pop-up description will appear. Go ahead and click on things to see what they do.

Documents and files

◆ **Operating system:** Probably Windows 98, ME, 2000 or XP – software that acts as an interface between you and your machine. Essentially, it creates the *desktop*, gives you access to *files*, and helps *applications* do their job.

◆ **Application:** Software which helps you do something useful (e.g. Word or Excel).

◆ **Document:** A Word text file, an Excel spreadsheet, or a similar electronic equivalent of the printed page.

◆ **File:** A document or software which is stored on a CD or disk.

Mouse and keyboard jargon

◆ **Point-and-click:** issue a command using the mouse. Move the mouse and a pointer on the screen echoes the movement; position the screen pointer over something (e.g. a menu item) and click the mouse buttons briefly to make things happen. The standard **click** is a quick press on the left button. A **double-click** is two rapid clicks on the left button. A **right-click** (right mouse button) often does useful stuff.

◆ **Mac right-click:** Apple Computers decided that the creative types who use Macs would not be able to cope with more than one mouse button – and stubbornly refuse to admit that they are wrong. To *right-click* on a Mac, hold down the *Shift* key on the keyboard and press the single mouse button. That's easier?

◆ **Select/highlight:** choose something (e.g. text) with which you want to work. *Left-click* and hold the button down, move the mouse, release the button – and whatever was under the mouse movement will be highlighted (assuming it was selectable).

◆ **Drag-and-drop:** move something (e.g. text) using the mouse. First *select* the item, then point at it again, *right-click* and hold, move the mouse to the required location, and release the button.

◆ **Cut, copy and paste:** a useful method of duplicating or moving things. For example, if you select some text and *copy* it to the *clipboard*, the text will be available to *paste* (insert) elsewhere in the same or a different document. If instead of using *copy* you *cut* the text, it is deleted from the original location. You can issue the commands using various menus and icons and, usually, a right-click. Handy *keyboard shortcuts* are *Shift-Del* to cut and *Shift-Ins* to paste. *Ctrl-Ins* performs a copy (i.e. without a cut). A right-click on selected text often brings up a menu with copy, cut and paste options.

◆ **Clipboard:** a temporary and usually invisible storage area inside the computer.

◆ **Keyboard shortcuts:** quick ways of doing things using the keyboard instead of the mouse. The shortcuts usually involve pressing two or more keys at the same time. For example, *Shift-Del* (see *cut*, *copy* and *paste*) is done by holding down the shift key, pressing *Del* and then releasing both keys.

▶▶

Personalizing

When I use a new software application, the first thing I do is look to see how I can change the way the application behaves. This is not as perverse as it might sound. For example, with Excel, user-choices are set by pointing at the *Tools* menu and selecting *Options*. (abbreviated to *Tools/Options* from now on.) One of the options you might want to specify is what happens when you press *Enter* (e.g. nothing – my preference – or move the selection to the cell below or to the right).

▶ Your first day at the office

▶ Making it look good

Plain English: this section focuses on the basics of entering and formatting text and numbers.

Entering text. To input text, you simply click on a cell and start typing. Hit the *Enter* key when you have finished, or end the typing by pressing an arrow key. For example, if you are typing a list into a column, pressing the down arrow after entering each value will speed things up.

> To format a cell super-fast, select a cell (or range of cells) with your mouse and then press **Ctrl–1** (hold the **Ctrl** key down, press the number **one** and let go of them both).

Text display. Text that is too long to fit in a cell will not be lost. If the cell to the right is completely empty, the text will be displayed in its entirety. Any character in the cell to the right – even a space – will chop off the display. To see all the text, you can reduce the font size, make the column wider or wrap the text (using *Format/Cells/Alignment*).

Formatting text. Figure 4.2 shows the main formatting options and is, I hope, self-explanatory. Simply select one or more cells and click a toolbar button to apply a style. You can achieve more extensive control over formatting by selecting *Format/Cells*. Note that some *number formats* display positive numbers in black and negative numbers (e.g. losses) in red. This is handy for highlighting, say, underperformance.

Changing column widths and row heights. Double-click on the boundary between two column headers, and the column width will adjust automatically so that the longest entry displays fully. Drag the boundary to manually change the column width. Similar options apply to rows.

Fig. 4.2 The format toolbar

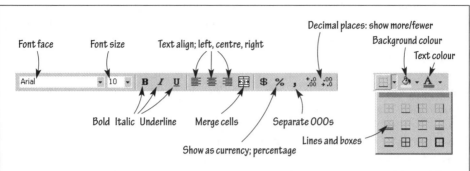

If this toolbar is not visible, *right-click* on a blank grey area at the top of the spreadsheet window, near to another menu or toolbar. A menu will appear. Check the *Formatting* option. Incidentally, some of the other toolbars on the menu are not normally visible, but can be usefully displayed if you have enough screen real estate.

Establishing a dialog

When you make a selection from the drop-down menus, a dialog box usually opens (*usually*, because sometimes the menu item acts like a switch as with *Help/What's This*). Dialog boxes are where you give instructions to the application. Sometimes these look similar to tabbed notebooks. If so, by clicking a tab you get to view a different page of the dialog. Any one page of a dialog will offer options you can select and/or input boxes you can fill in.

▶ Creating a table

Plain English: the previous page gave you enough information to create a table. This section explains how you get it onto paper.

If you are with me up to here, you know enough to produce a very professional-looking table. Of course, it will be a dumb table. In a moment, we will add some intelligence. Figure 4.3 on page 52 (ignore the annotation for the moment) shows a simple table produced with the techniques mentioned above. More complex examples are scattered through this book. Printing a table is straightforward enough. Save your work, then follow the next few steps.

Selecting the print area. Start by selecting *File/Page Setup*. The dialog box that appears allows you to choose which part of the spreadsheet you want to print. By default the whole *active area* will print (i.e. from cell A1 to the cell with content which is furthest away towards the bottom right). To specify that only part of the spreadsheet will print, click on the *Sheet* tab, click inside the *Print Area* input box, and then use your mouse to select the area of the spreadsheet to print.

Page features. While in the *Page Setup* dialog, you can also enter headers and footers for the printed page, specify if you want certain rows to appear at the top of each printed page and certain columns to appear to the left, and so on.

Make sure it stays on its paper. Now – still in the *Page Setup* dialog – click on the *Print Preview* button. This allows you to see if the table will fit neatly onto paper. To adjust the amount of paper that is covered, you can click *Margins* and drag the guides that appear. If you click *Preview Page Breaks*, the view will change and you will be able to amend the page breaks, font size and column widths. You can also insert extra page breaks by clicking anywhere in the row where you want the break, and choosing *Insert/Page Break*. You need to select *View/Normal* after using the *page breaks preview mode*.

Note that the *Print Preview* button is available on the *File* menu and in the *Page Setup* and *Print* dialog boxes. The *Page Breaks Preview* option can be accessed from the *Print Preview* mode or the *Insert* menu.

▶ Converting a table into a report

> **Plain English**: this section explains how to insert a spreadsheet table into a word document. You can do a once-only *copy-and-paste*. Or you can insert a *dynamic link* so that when you change the spreadsheet, the word document is automatically updated.

Almost every report requires a cover and some explanatory text. You could do this in a workbook, using the first and last tab sheets as the cover and endnotes, and so on. However, you will soon discover that the relationship between a spreadsheet and a printed page is rather vague, and it is easier to write text in Word because that is what it is designed for.

Copy-and-paste. The easiest way to produce good-looking reports is to format your tables in Excel, and then insert them into your Word document. To copy data from a spreadsheet to a word document, which must both be open on your computer screen:

◆ Select all the cells containing your table, *right-click* and choose *copy*; and then switch to the word document (*alt-tab*), *right-click* in the required location, and choose *Paste*.

Dynamic linking. *Copy-and-paste* could not be any easier. However, on many occasions you will want to use a sort of smart paste called *dynamic linking*. After you have created a dynamic link between two documents, any changes you make to the source will automatically be fed through to the target. For example, if you change a figure in the spreadsheet, next time you look at your Word document, it will have been mysteriously and automatically updated. This is a very powerful feature. To create a dynamic link requires only one more click:

◆ In Excel, select all the cells containing your table, right-click and choose *copy*; and then switch to the Word document (*alt-tab*), choose *Edit/Paste Special*, and in the dialog box that appears choose *Paste link* and *Microsoft Excel Worksheet Object*, then click *OK*.

Now switch back to the spreadsheet (*alt-tab* again), change some figures in the table, flick back to the Word document, and the report will already contain the changes. If this appears to have potential, wait until you make your spreadsheet intelligent.

> By and large, it is easiest to keep closely related sheets in the same workbook, while trying not to make one workbook too large. For example, you might put balance sheet, income statement and cash flow in one book, with separate books for each year, and keep your asset register and depreciation schedules in different workbooks.

▶ Making dumb tables smart

> **Plain English:** this section introduces formulas. These automated calculations take all the agony out of *doing the numbers*.

At last it is time to try a little trick which turns a dumb table into a very powerful thingamabob. Let me use a bit of simple arithmetic to demonstrate. Suppose you want to know the total of a column of numbers – such as those in Fig. 4.3. With a mouse click and a key press you can have the spreadsheet do the sum for you. This is how:

◆ Click on the empty cell under the column of numbers (cell A14 in the example), and then click on the Σ tool button. A busy dotted line will appear around the numbers to indicate which *range* will be summed. Hit the *Enter* key and the total will magically appear in the selected cell. You probably noticed that the spreadsheet guessed which cells you wanted to add up. You can override this electronic guessing game and use the mouse to select a different range of cells (i.e. move the dotted selection rectangle) before pressing enter.

All calculations in spreadsheets are called formulas. Once you have planted one, it will quietly watch the numbers it is guarding. If you change so much as one digit in its ambit, the table will update automatically. Try it. Download the sample spreadsheet for this chapter from this book's website and press F9 a few times.

By the way, Σ is the Greek S, which mathematician geeks use as shorthand notations for 'take the sum of' – sorry if this makes a simple operation seem unnecessarily alien.

> 'Part of the inhumanity of the computer is that, once it is competently programmed and working smoothly, it is completely honest.'
>
> **Isaac Asimov**

Fig. 4.3 A simple table

	A	B
1		**Amount**
2	Jan	76
3	Feb	1
4	Mar	11
5	Apr	23
6	May	32
7	Jun	54
8	Jul	92
9	Aug	81
10	Sep	69
11	Oct	26
12	Nov	10
13	Dec	42
14	**Total**	**517**
15		
16	**Average**	**43.08**

Cell A14 contains the formula '=SUM(A2:A13)

Cell A16 contains the formula '=AVERAGE(A2:A13)

To display the formulas instead of values, key *Ctrl-`* (*Ctrl* and the *apostrophe*, which on most keyboards is at the top-left corner). Repeat these keystrokes to switch back to displaying values.

Formulas decoded

When you were entering the summation formula and the hectic rectangle of little dots appeared around the selected range, you might have noticed that the target cell contained the code =SUM(A2:A13). I am sure you can decode it:

1 The equals sign indicates that the content of the cell is a formula.

2 SUM( ) means, well, take the sum of everything in the brackets.

3 The characters A2:A13 indicate the *range* of cells to which the formula is applied.

You can use the mouse to change the selected cells immediately before pressing *Enter*, when the range will be updated automatically. You can also edit the range using the keyboard, or enter a new formula by typing it directly into the cell.

▶ Common calculations

> **Plain English:** this section discusses ways to enter formulas. I urge you to read it even if you are not beside a PC.

You are probably ahead of me, and realize that spreadsheets do more than Greek addition. They have several hundred other built-in functions. Yes, several hundred. However, unless you want to do something out of this world, such as plan a NASA expedition to Mars or program a video recorder, you will never use more than a mere handful.

The surprising thing is that even though there are all these built in functions, the ones you use the most are the ones you create yourself. And to create them, all you need to know is a couple more things. I will demonstrate them with another example.

> The 123 spreadsheet uses an @ instead of an equals sign to indicate that a formula follows.
>
> If you want to type in plain text that starts with an = sign or another reserved character, prefix it with a single quote (as in : ' = my salary).

◆ Suppose that you want to multiply the value in the top left-hand cell by the one immediately below it. In a third cell of your choosing, type =A1*A2 and press *Enter*. That is all there is to it.

Why the little star? Because there is no multiplication sign on a standard computer keyboard. Similarly, since there is no division key you indicate this operation with a forward slash: /. Addition and subtraction work as normal: + and –.

My logic is different

Spreadsheets calculate the answer to a formula by working through the instructions in their own unique way, doing multiplication and division before addition and subtraction, and so on. This can get fairly confusing. However, spreadsheets also do things in brackets first. If there is more than one set of parentheses, the calculation works from the *inside* outwards. Some examples will help make this clear. If cell A1 contains the value 100:

> When you have keyed in some coded calculation, the cell contains a **formula**, but displays the result as a **value**. In fact, all the characters and numbers you usually see when you view a spreadsheet are values. Click on a cell to see the underlying formula, if there is one. Click and then press F2 to **audit** the formula – i.e. to highlight the cells on which it operates.

=A1 * 5 + 10 produces the result 510, but

=A1 * (5 + 10) gives the answer 1500.

Likewise:

=A1 * 5 + 10 / 2 generates 505, but

=A1 * (5 + 10) / 2 means that you get 750, and

=A1 * (5 + 10 / 2) results in 1000.

Note that you can mix reference to cells (such as A1) *and* constant values (such 5) *and* built-in functions, such as in the following:

=SUM(A1:A10) + A15 + 500 or

=SUM(A1:A10,A15,500)

Or you can omit cell references completely, as in:

= 10 * 5 + 24.

When I give my electronic friend more-complicated calculations, I tend to ignore its built-in sequence order of arithmetic and **always use brackets** to indicate the required sequence. I find it easier to read and check later what the code was intended to do.

I also switch between the mouse and keyboard depending on the complexity of working out which cell I am referring to. For example, as well as keying the above formulas straight into the cell, you can key = click on cell A1 and then type *5+10. In other words, after an equals sign or an arithmetic operator (+ - * /) the spreadsheet expects a cell reference and it will accept it via a mouse selection or a couple of key strokes.

> For more information, see the Excel Help topic *Creating Formulas and Auditing Workbooks*. *Examples of commonly used formulas* is particularly useful.

▶ Built-in functions

> **Plain English:** the next few paragraphs describe how you can access and understand the hundreds of built-in spreadsheet formulas. Again, you do not need to have a spreadsheet active to read about this topic.

So, you ask, if there are hundreds of built-in functions where are they on the tool-bars? Good question. They are all accessed by the f_x button or *Insert/Function*. Click a cell and then click the button (or use the menu option) and the *Paste Function* dialog box will pop up and probably scare you silly. However, look again and it will not seem so bad.

The functions are grouped by category in the list box on the left. Click on one of these, and the right-hand list will change to show the available functions in that group. For example, if you click on *Math and Trig*, and then scroll down the right-hand list box, you will find our Greek friend SUM. Click on this word, and a little description obligingly appears below the list boxes. When you have found the function you are looking for, double-click it, or click OK. This current dialog box will close and another one will open. This new dialog guides you through entering the required information.

There is no point in me listing all the functions available. It would bore both of us silly and neither of us will ever use more than a small fraction of them. What I will do, is describe the useful ones as we work though this book. For example, averages are listed in Fig. 5.4 on page 68. If you have a quiet moment and you want to know more, open your spreadsheet, press F1 to bring up the Help file, and read *Creating Formulas and Auditing Workbooks* – or browse the *Paste Function* dialog box:

```
Paste Function                                    ? X
Function category:          Function name:
All                    ▲   SUBTOTAL               ▲
Financial                  SUM
Date & Time                SUMIF
Math & Trig                SUMPRODUCT
Statistical                SUMSQ
Lookup & Reference         SUMX2MY2
Database                   SUMX2PY2
Text                       SUMXMY2
Logical                    TAN
Information            ▼   TANH
User Defined           ▼   TRUNC                  ▼

SUM(number1,number2,...)
Adds all the numbers in a range of cells.

 ?                              OK         Cancel
```

► Lists

> **Plain English:** this short section outlines the way that spreadsheets can be used to store data. At first glance, this might appear to have little to do with managing numbers. However, it is a useful facility, and you will see that there are numerical applications.

The grid pattern of a spreadsheet makes it very useful for managing lists. You might use it to store a list of employees (together with their contact and salary details), a record of your inventory (the items you stock, cost and retail prices, names of suppliers, and so on), invoices issued, etc.

> Always make a copy of a workbook before you make major changes to it. It can take hours to rebuild after one inadvertent booboo. Creating and subsequently re-opening a clean copy takes seconds.

It is conventional to use one row per item (employees, widgets, etc.), and enter details for that item across the page. The very first row can be used for *field names* – e.g. name, address, salary. This layout is what the spreadsheet expects when you use the tools provided for managing lists. Let me show you one such tool.

To sort a table into alphabetical and/or numerical order

Select the whole table and then choose *Data/Sort*. The *Sort* dialog box allows you to choose which column or columns to sort on and whether to sort in ascending or descending order. It is self-explanatory when you look at it – and quite handy. You can sort individual rows or columns, but take care because you can totally muddle up a previously useful table. (This is one of the occasions when the Undo button ↰ can be very useful.)

Further reading

If you are interested in lists, I recommend the spreadsheet *Help* topic titled, believe it or not, *Managing Lists*. The use of data filters (see sub-topic *Finding Rows That Meet Specific Conditions*) is worth looking at.

Error trapping

It is all too easy to mis-key a number or formula when using a calculator or spreadsheet. As a check on the accuracy of your work, always do a similar but easier sum in your head, on a scratch pad, or even in another area of the spreadsheet – and compare the results. For example, when multiplying 138.51 by 0.1135, you can temporarily simplify this to 140×0.1. The answer to this latter sum is 14. If your electronic helper produces a result that is significantly from 14 you know you have made a mistake. Other cross checks are covered elsewhere in this book.

Ten hard questions to ask or be asked

1 Have formulas, such as the sum of a column, been entered correctly?*

2 Has the correct order of complex calculations been preserved with brackets?

3 Does the word 'Circular' appear in the status bar, indicating that a formula erroneously references itself?

4 Is any part of a text entry erroneously truncated by the value in the next cell?

5 Has any row or column been omitted or truncated during printing because it did not fit in the printable area of the paper?

6 Have all relevant columns been correctly included when sorting a list? (For example, it is possible to sort names while leaving corresponding addresses unsorted.)

7 Was a table in a Word document correctly copied from a spreadsheet, or have any subsequent changes been made to the spreadsheet?

8 Are currency units, row and column labels, and so on correctly identified? A common mistake is to assume that the reader will guess that amounts are in millions or dollars, or whatever.

9 Is the copy saved to disk the most recent version?

10 Do you have unexpected characters in a formula (which might not display on in the cells) such as an apostrophe ('), caret (^), quotation mark("), at sign (@) and so on? These can result from importing a spreadsheet created in, say, 123 into Excel.

*Believe it or not, I know of one quantity surveyor's office where all the totals were being found with a calculator and then keyed into the spreadsheet by hand.

Conclusion

I hope that this whirlwind introduction to spreadsheets has got you started. As already mentioned, the online *Help* is well worth spending some time reading. Having laid the groundwork here, I will introduce many practical and useful tricks as we work through this book – starting in the next chapter.

5

explaining and reporting

'I've come loaded with statistics, for I've noticed that a man can't prove anything without statistics.'

Mark Twain

Chapter survival toolkit

▶ Overview

This chapter builds on the spreadsheet techniques discussed in the previous few pages and provides the foundations for explaining and reporting numbers. We will look at charts, numerical accuracy, summarizing, reviewing and comparing figures. These ideas are very relevant for managing numbers and we will develop them in subsequent chapters.

▶ Prerequisites

If you want to be able to perform the calculations introduced in this chapter, you really need to be on top of the spreadsheet basics and associated jargon outlined in the previous chapter.

▶ Mastering explaining and reporting

After reading this chapter, you should be able to answer the following questions:

1 Charts – how do they aid and mislead?

2 How do you create charts in spreadsheets and insert them in reports?

3 What is meant by significant figures, decimal places, effective figures, rounding and accuracy, and the 4/5 rule?

4 Where do you use the following averages: mean, median, mode, weighted averages?

5 What is spread (range, standard deviation, z-scores)?

6 What is skew?

7 What is the normal distribution? Why is is useful?

8 How do you compare numbers using relationships and changes?

9 What are index numbers? Why are they useful?

10 What are relative and absolute cell addresses in spreadsheets?

'Going to work for a large company is like getting on a train. Are you going sixty miles an hour or is the train going sixty miles an hour and you're sitting still?'

J. Paul Getty

▶ Jargon watch

Summarizing

Rounding: significant figures, decimal places, effective figures

Averages: mean, median, mode, weighted averages

Spread: range, standard deviation, z-score, tails

Distributions: skew, normal

Illustrating

Charts: including line, area, column, bar, pie, high-low.

Miscellaneous

Index numbers: index number, base

Spreadsheet stuff: relative and absolute cell addressing

▶ Understand better, report better

This chapter runs through some basics related to analysing and reporting numbers. The aim is to help you enhance your understanding and explanation of what the figures show, which will lead automatically to better reporting. Most people gain an improved picture of the numbers when they see a chart. I will kick off with delightfully simple techniques for creating charts and inserting them in written reports. Then we will look at some ways to summarize and compare figures. All this lays a good foundation on which we will build as we move through this book together.

▶ A picture tells a thousand words

If numbers can talk, charts positively sing. Creating charts with spreadsheets is even easier than creating formulas. To insert a simple chart:

◆ Select a range of values in your spreadsheet (such as sales figures for 12 months), click the little chart icon 📊 (or choose *Insert/Chart*) and in the Chart Wizard dialog box which appears immediately click *Finish*.

> A super-fast way to generate a chart is to select a range of values and hit **F11** or **Alt–F1**. A chart will magically appear in the workbook as a new tab sheet (**right-click** on the tab and choose **Delete** if you want to get rid of it).

As soon as you click *Finish*, the Wizard will close and a chart will appear in the spreadsheet. You can move and resize this image by clicking on the borders.

If you double-click and right-click on various parts of the chart, dialog boxes open allowing you to change the content and appearance of the chart. I will leave you to experiment with this (see also the *Working with Charts* topic in the spreadsheet *Help* file). The *Chart Wizard* in Fig. 5.1 hints at the range of options available. In the instructions given a moment ago, I ignored the Wizard. When you first insert a chart you are, of course, free to step through the Wizard immediately, before clicking *Finish*.

There are examples of charts in this chapter, in the book as a whole, and in the sample spreadsheets available for download from the website.

▶ Keep it simple

When you have created a spreadsheet chart style which suits you, you can save it for future use. Right-click the chart, choose **Chart Type/Custom Type** and click the **Add** button. To make the chart the default, in the same dialog box, click **Set as default chart**.

The inset provides suggestions on choosing chart types. I suggest keeping charts simple. A mass of lines on a graph, too many components in a bar or pie chart, and dominant colours can be overwhelming. You rarely even need gridlines (horizontal lines which spreadsheets tend to include by default), because you cannot accurately read figures off of a chart. If you expect users to want the detailed figures include them in a table, perhaps in an annex. Note that if the chart is still in a spreadsheet, you can click on the plot and the underlying value will be displayed.

By the way, some purists complain that 3D charts are a waste of time because they also obscure detail. Maybe. I happen to think that they can look good when used sensibly.

Inserting pictures in reports

Including charts in written reports helps readers interpret and understand the figures. To insert a chart in a report as an image:

◆ Click on the outer border of the chart in your spreadsheet, right-click and choose *Copy*, switch to your Word document (alt-tab), right-click at the location where you want the chart, and choose *Paste*.

To insert a chart as a *dynamic link* (as discussed in Chapter 4):

◆ Click on the outer border of the chart in your spreadsheet, right-click and choose *Copy*, switch to your Word document (alt-tab), from the menu bar choose *Edit/Paste Special* and then click the *Paste Link* option.

With this dynamic link, the chart in your report will update automatically if you change the numbers in the spreadsheet. This can be useful when you are developing budgets and plans, or using standard reports over and over again.

'Summaries can be very useful, but they are not the details.'

J.W. Tukey

Charts: choosing and using

Common name	Spreadsheet jargon	Use
Line	Line	Ideal for continuous data, frequently used for trends over time and to highlight relationships between points. See Fig. 9.5.
Area	Area	Adds emphasis to simple lines, highlights trends and breakdowns. Usually the shaded area represents relative values – as in Fig. 16.4.
Bar or column chart	Column	Good for categories (sales by region) or discrete data (e.g. monthly totals). Helps highlight differences between adjacent columns. Good for comparing, say, budgeted and actual spending – see Fig. 22.4.
Horizontal bar	Bar	Variation on bar/column chart – also good for categories, especially for showing which one is ahead. An example is in Fig. 3.8, where I thought this presentation was more effective than a more conventional pie chart.
Stacked bar	Stacked column	Shows totals and breakdowns – see diagram on p. 240. It can be difficult to compare elements from bar to bar – it's a good place to bury one poor result among otherwise good figures. (When inserting in a spreadsheet, note that each element in a vertical bar is one series.)
Pie	Pie	Good for illustrating breakdowns (shares of the pie). Two pies side by side can also show relative changes, but it is hard to judge how much the pie has grown – when twice the width means increases the area four-fold – and too many slices add clutter. See Fig. 18.1.
Scatter	XY (scatter)	Plots points but does not join them. Good when looking for relationships between two series (such as household income and spending on widgets, or time and sales – see Fig 9.6).
Cobweb or radar	Radar	A cross between a scatter diagram and a line graph. Sometimes useful for comparing three series, especially when one is time – such as average household spending and average sales, where each point represents the plot for a given year.
Bubble	Bubble	As previous chart, but the size of the bubble (the plotted point) represents the third series – which must be a value (i.e. not a year).
Hi–lo, high–low	Stock	Usually used for stock prices or exchange rates – each plot shows the low, high and close or average for one period.

Fig. 5.1 The Chart Wizard

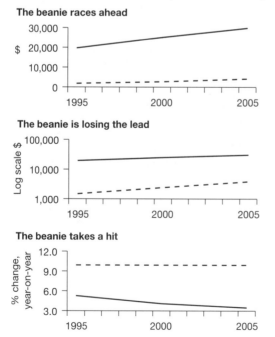

How to cheat with charts

There is an old story about an accountant who, when asked *how do the figures look?* whispered confidentially 'how do you want them to look?' Here are a few examples of how charts can be used and abused. They are based on the monthly salaries of an office cleaner (the dotted lines) and an accountant (the solid lines).

The beanie races ahead

The cleaner has read this book in your office in the evenings and produces this plot of actual pay to support a claim for a pay rise.

The beanie is losing the lead

Your wily accountant starts with a logarithmic scale. This is actually the most valid way of comparing growth, and it appears to suggest that the gap is narrowing.

The beanie takes a hit

Next, the beanie plots year-on-year percentage increases which show, validly, that the growth *rate* of his pay is declining (but note that the rates are positive and both salaries *are* growing).

The beanie is caught

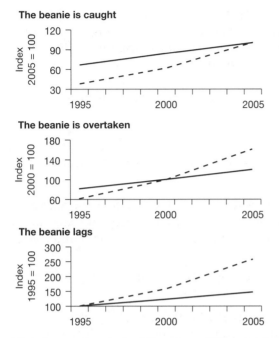

Then the beanie converts the salaries into index form (as discussed below) and with 2005 = 100 suggests – inaccurately – that the cleaner's pay is catching up. Indices show nothing more than *relative trends* – as the next chart reveals – and they always converge at their base where they equal 100.

The beanie is overtaken

Spurred by this success, the beanie rebases the indices to 2000 = 100 and, again misleadingly, claims that the cleaner's pay has overtaken his.

The beanie lags

Finally, for the moment, the accountant rebases the indices again, this time to 1995 = 100 to show falsely that the cleaner's pay is above the beanie's.

This is not the end of the story. Other tricks include compressing or expanding the vertical scale to hide or exaggerate changes, inverting the vertical scale so that declines appear to be increases, and plotting averages, totals or end-month figures which hide the detailed figures. There are other examples of interpreting charts in this book (see especially Chapter 10 and Fig. 22.4).

Significant accuracy

Making figures significant

A certain company's net profit was a few cents over $18,208,371 last year. When the CEO reported the results, he described the profit as 'just over $18.2 million'. This was more sensible than reading out the amount to the last dollar, because the audience would have been struggling to make sense of a number read to eight *significant figures*. The precise figure was there in an annex for anyone with particular interest to read.

Detailed figures should be calculated to an appropriately high degree of accuracy, but numbers summarized in the body of reports or given in presentations are usually better rounded. Normally, you can make the number easier to comprehend, especially for large amounts, as follows:

◆ Round them to two or three *significant figures* (the first number above has *eight* and the second number *three significant figures*), and

◆ include at most two *decimal places* (i.e. two digits after the point).

The combination is known as the number of *effective figures*. A good rule of thumb it to use as few effective figures as possible, while ensuring that relevant differences are apparent (for example, if you were describing production tolerances to one-thousandth of an inch, it would not make sense to round to the nearest half-inch). With sensible rounding, your audience can focus their attention on what you are saying, rather than on decoding complex numbers.

▶ Maintaining accuraccy

As surprising as this might sound, you can have problems with spreadsheet accuracy. Let me give you an example.

1 Suppose you divide 100 by 7. A spreadsheet will tell you that the answer is 14.2857142857143000... If this figure is, say, your retail price for some cog or sprocket, you will probably round up to $14.29. If you sell 1,000 units, your revenue will be $14,290.00.

2 If you do the entire sum using a spreadsheet *without* rounding, the total *when rounded* is $14,285.71.

> ### The 4/5 rule
>
> Calculators and spreadsheets generally round using the 4/5 rule. That is, values ending in four are rounded down, while those ending in five are rounded up. For example, 1.4 is rounded down to 1, while 1.5 is rounded up to 2. You will, perhaps, be in good company if you adopt this convention: for example, the European Central Bank follows it for exchange rate calculations.

The spreadsheet's answer is a few dollars lower than the rounding-at-each-stage example. Repeat such discrepancies over thousands of items, and the amounts involved could be huge. Even one penny out of balance is too much for the grey suits – and when you project your financials using spreadsheets you often find that your figures are out by just this amount. This is because we usually format the spreadsheet to show two decimal places – but the 'fully-accurate' figures are retained by the spreadsheet and used in the calculations. The problem then is that the numbers look OK, but they do not appear to add up correctly, as shown in Fig. 5.2.

Fig. 5.2 Rounding errors

	Raw data, perhaps the result of a calculation	Displayed to 2 decimal places	Rounded to 2 decimal places	Rounded down	Rounded up
Number 1	2.004	2.00	2.00	2.00	2.01
Number 2	2.004	2.00	2.00	2.00	2.01
Totals (not rounded)	4.008	4.01	4.00	4.00	4.02

Fortunately, spreadsheets have some built-in functions that deal very effectively with this excess precision. They are shown in Fig. 5.3 and, I think, speak for themselves. Usually, the simple ROUND function is adequate. Remember that sometimes instead of rounding to the nearest amount, you need to round up or down (are you buying or selling?).

By the way, you might come across the self-explanatory spreadsheet option *Precision as displayed*. As tempting as this is, I recommend against using it. This feature makes it too easy to lose control over the accuracy of your numbers.

I put 'fully-accurate' in quotes above, because – as staggering as this might seem – computers do not handle numbers too well. My spreadsheet works with 15 significant figures only. You can test yours by keying =2/3 into a cell and then increasing the number of decimal places (click repeatedly). I am sure that you remember from school that two-thirds is 0.66 *recurring* – the sixes go on forever. However, your spreadsheet will display 0.666666666666666700000....two-thirds to 15 significant figures only. This is usually not a problem for business arithmetic. If it does cause you a problem recording your profits, give some to me.

> 'A little inaccuracy sometimes saves tons of explanation.'
>
> **Anon.**

Get your rounding right

Take care not to round too soon. The following table shows how two times two can be anything between two and six. It is easy to introduce significant errors in just a couple of steps if your round in the wrong place. The numbers in the first column all round to two (and everybody knows that 2 × 2 = 4). But when the numbers in the first column are multiplied by themselves and the result is rounded, the answer comes out at anything between two and six. Worse, 1.45 rounded once is 1; or, alternatively, it rounds to 1.5 which rounds to 2 (see the 4/5 rule opposite).

Apply common sense to avoid both spurious accuracy (not enough rounding) and too much rounding. Generally, you need to do your analysis and forecasting using un-rounded numbers, and then round off each value before putting them in your financial projections.

This number, *n*	Rounds to	Multiply *n* by itself	Which rounds to
1.5	2	2.25	2
2.0	2	4.00	4
2.4	2	5.76	6

Fig. 5.3 Rounding

In this extract from a spreadsheet, the formulas are applied to cell A1. You can replace the numerical constants (1,2,10) in the sample formulas with any values you choose

	A	B	C
1	124.453		
2			
3	Formula	Result	Comment on displayed result
4	=INT(A1)	124	Rounds down to the nearest whole integer
5	=EVEN(A1)	126	Round up to the nearest even integer
6	=ODD(A1)	125	Round up to the nearest odd integer
7			
8	=CEILING(A1,1)	125	Rounds up to multiple of n (nearest 1 and nearest
9	=CEILING(A1,10)	130	10 in these examples)
10	=FLOOR(A1,1)	124	Rounds down to a multiple of n (nearest 1 and
11	=FLOOR(A1,10)	120	nearest 10 in these examples)
12			
13	=ROUND(A1,1)	124.5	Rounds to the nearest n decimal places (1 and 2
14	=ROUND(A1,2)	124.45	decimal places in this example)
15	=ROUNDUP(A1,1)	124.5	Rounds up, away from zero
16	=ROUNDUP(A1,2)	124.46	
17	=ROUNDDOWN(A1,1)	124.4	Rounds down, towards zero
18	=ROUNDDOWN(A1,2)	124.45	
19			
20	=MOD(A1,2)	0.453	Remainder after dividing by n (2 and 10 in this
21	=MOD(A1,10)	4.453	example)

▶ When numbers talk

The problem with numbers is that there are too many of them. If you were to list the salaries paid to each person in a large company, or the price of each item in its catalogue, we would probably be here until long after dark. However, if you identify the highest, lowest and average amount (perhaps by department or category of product) this creates an instant picture of the situation:

◆ the average identifies the mid-point, and

◆ the highest and lowest values reveal the range or *spread*.

For example, you have a good idea of my price list if I say *that the average price of one of our widgets is $100; the cheapest is $85 and the most-expensive is $250.*

Such descriptive *summaries* are very important. By the time we reach the end of this book, you will be using them to manage risk – so bear with me for a moment. You might find the next couple of pages a little heavy going – but only because of the silly jargon. If you get lost, well, you could just trust me and use the calculator on this book's website.

> To see quick summaries in your spreadsheet, select a range of cells, right-click on the status bar along the bottom of the window, and choose an option. For example, if you choose **Sum**, the total of the selected values will be displayed in the status bar.

▶ Order from chaos

Summary measures such as totals and averages are good ways to bring order out of chaos. As you might expect, spreadsheets have useful functions built-in (see Fig. 5.4).

Let me give you a real-world example. A manufacturer of school equipment measured the heights of a large number of kiddies. Jordan, who did the survey, wrote down the observations, sorted them into order, grouped them into bands of 1 cm (about $4/10$ of an inch), and used a spreadsheet to draw the chart in Fig. 5.5. The average height, as you can see, was 100 cm, and the range of observations was between 85 and 115 cm. Maybe you have guessed that Jordan fixed the results to make it easy for us to interpret. The *distribution* of the measurements is shown in the chart.

It happens that Fig. 5.5 illustrates a pattern that you will come across time after time – or you would if you went around appraising things and drawing graphs. Whenever you have a large number of items that are subjected to many independent influences, you tend to find this bell shape. It is so common, that it is known as the *normal distribution*. Most values are clustered around the midpoint, and there are fewer observations as you move away from the middle. When you have a chunk of data that you want to analyse, ask yourself if it might be normally distributed. If it is, you can apply the tricks I am about to describe.

What is not normal?

Distributions that do not have the *normal* bell shape include those without a large number of independent influences (e.g. the range of salaries in a small department might be symmetrical, but they will probably be flat), and an occasional very high or low reading will *skew* a distribution (e.g. the pattern of salaries in your company might be knocked sideways by the remuneration paid in the accounting department).

Fig. 5.4 Descriptive functions

In this extract from a spreadsheet, the formulas are applied to the first row (cells A1:G1), and in a couple of instances also use the values in cells A2 or B2.

	A	B	C	D	E	F	G
1	1	3	3	5	6	7	17
2	2	0.1					
3							

	Formula	Result	Comment on displayed result
4			
5			
6	= AVERAGE(A1:G1)	6	The 'best' and most-commonly used average – it is called the arithmetic *mean* in math-speak.
7	= MODE(A1:G1)	3	The most-frequently occurring value – useful for categories that you cannot add up, as in 'our most popular colour is blue'.
8	= MEDIAN(A1:G1)	5	The middle value, when all values are ranked in order – useful because it is not affected by extremes, and 50% of values fall on either side of it. The median salary is a good yardstick against which to measure yours.
9			
10	= COUNT(A1:G1)	7	The number of values
11	= MIN(A1:G1)	1	The smallest value
12	= MAX(A1:G1)	17	The largest value
13	= LARGE(A1:G1, A2)	7	The nth largest value (e.g. 2nd largest in this example)
14	= SMALL(A1:G1, A2)	3	The nth smallest value (e.g. 2nd smallest in this example)
15			
16	=PERCENTILE(A1:G1,B2)	2.2	The value at the nth percentile (e.g. 10th in this example). It makes more sense with a large dataset. To see percentiles in action, rank the data in order and chop them up into 100 parts (i.e., with 500 observations, each percentile would contain five values). The values in each part form one percentile. The values on the boundaries are the percentile values. It often helps to discard the top and bottom percentile or two to get rid of outlying extremes.
17	=STDEV(A1:G1)	5.3	The standard deviation (see text)

Note that these formulas do not require the data to be sorted into size order before use.

Fig. 5.5 It's normally like this

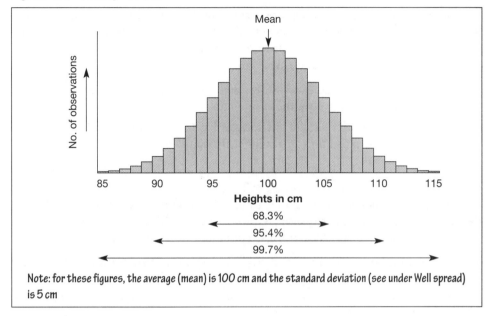

Note: for these figures, the average (mean) is 100 cm and the standard deviation (see under Well spread) is 5 cm

Well spread

The *range* (85 to 105 in this example) is a useful measure of spread, but it can be influenced by an extreme outlying value. For example, the range of values 1, 3, 3, 5, 6, 7, 17 is distorted by one extreme (17). One solution is to line up all the figures in numerical order, and chop off, say, the top and bottom few percent of readings (see *Percentiles* in Fig. 5.4).

A better solution is to use a handy measure with an appalling name – the *standard deviation*. This is nothing more than a simple indication of how closely some values are bunched around their average. It is little known, because it is horrible to calculate by hand. With a spreadsheet, it is as simple as any sum could be (as shown in Fig. 5.4).

For a *normal* distribution, the following rules of thumb *always* hold true:

◆ About two-thirds (68%) of the values are within one standard deviation of the average (i.e. one-third immediately below and one-third immediately above the mean).

◆ 95% of the observations are within two standard deviations of the mean.

◆ Almost all (99.7%) of the values are within three standard deviations of the mean.

You can see this very clearly if you inspect Fig. 5.5.

Now you know everything

You can probably see that if there are precise percentages associated with 1, 2 and 3 standard deviations, there must also be exact proportions directly related to any other number, such as 1.64 standard deviations. There are just two more bits of gobbledygook, to dispose of and then I can let you in on the big secret:

◆ To avoid the cumbersome expression *number of standard deviations*, statisticians call this a *z-score* (i.e. the 1.64 mentioned above).

◆ To make it clear which part of the range of values is under consideration, the extremes are known as *tails* (see under *Scary words, simple logic*).

Normal use

At last we have reached the important part: If you know the mean and standard deviation of a normal distribution, you know everything that there is to know about it. How do find out these things? I am about to explain three ways.

1 **Use the calculator on this book's website.** You input the mean and standard deviation of your figures and pose a question (such as *what percentage of these children are taller than 110 cm?*, or *how many widgets are underweight?*) and the calculator will tell you the answer.

2 **Look it up.** There is a handy lookup table in Fig. 5.6. You can enter the table from a percentage or a value (via a z-score). For example, if you want to know the maximum height of 99% of the children, find 99% in the first column, read across to see that the associated z-score is 2.33, and convert this to a height of 111.6 cm as shown in the table. In other words, 99% of children measured were 111.6 cm or less in height. A more detailed look-up table can be downloaded from this book's website.

3 **Work it out.** You can use the spreadsheet formulas starting with the letters NORM to find z-scores, percentages and so on. The sample spreadsheet will show you how the formulas work, if you really want to know.

Scary words, simple logic

Normal distribution. The pattern you find in when you measure things which are subject to a wide range of independent influences (e.g. heights or weights of a random selection of people).

Mean. The average of your observations.

Standard deviation. A measure of how widely the observations are spread out around the mean (e.g. 99.7% are within 3 standard deviations of the mean in either direction).

Z-score. The number of standard deviations (3 in the previous definition).

One-tail. The measurements at one end of distribution (i.e. greater than 3 standard deviations from the mean).

Two-tails. The measurements at both extremes (less than 3 standard deviations below the mean and greater than 3 standard deviations above it).

Fig. 5.6 Normal percentages and scores

Enter this table with a percentage (first four columns) and read off a z-score, or enter it with a z-score and read off a percentage. The example shows how to convert backwards and forwards between the observed or required values and z-scores.

Percentage of observations in one tail		Percentage of observations in two tails		z-score (i.e. number of standard deviations)	Examples below are based on Fig. 5.5 where the Mean is 100 cm and the standard deviation (SD) is 5 cm
					Required value = mean ± (z × SD)
Left	Right	Between extremes			For 99% in first column, z is 2.33
50.0	50.0	0.0	100.0	0.00	Value = 100 ± (2.33 x 5) = 100 ± 11.6:
66.7	33.3	33.3	66.7	0.43	
75.0	25.0	50.0	50.0	0.67	99% of observations are more
85.0	15.0	70.0	30.0	1.04	than 88.4 cm
90.0	10.0	80.0	20.0	1.28	99% are less than 111.6 cm
95.0	5.0	90.0	10.0	1.64	
97.5	2.5	95.0	5.0	1.96	z = (observed value ± mean) ÷SD
97.7	2.3	95.4	4.6	2.00	For a reading of 110 cm:
99.0	1.0	98.0	2.0	2.33	z = (110 - 100) ÷ 5 = 2
99.5	0.5	99.0	1.0	2.58	
99.9	0.1	99.8	0.2	3.09	Find 2 in the right hand column and read across to see that 97.7% of readings are less than 110 cm and 2.3% are greater than 110 cm*

* Note also, that where z = ±2.33 (i.e. mean ± 10), you can say 95.4% of observations are between 90 and 110 cm, and 4.6% are less than 90 or more than 110 cm.

When it is worth weighting

Sometimes simple averages are not enough. Let me give you an example. One way of arriving at a forecast for next year's sales is to ask a panel of experts. If you hold them all in equal regard, you can simply take the average of their predictions. However, if one of them is particularly erudite, you might want to give extra weight to her views.

Figure 5.7 shows this in action. Alex, Bob, and Chris predict that sales of a new product will be 1,000, 2,000 and 3,000 respectively. The simple average of these is 2,000. However, you think that your expert Alex is twice as likely to be right as either of the other two, and that Bob's views carry slightly more weight than Chris's. Accordingly, you allocate weights of 50%, 30% and 20% to their views and multiply out as shown in the illustration. On this basis, the *weighted average* of your expert's opinions is 1,700. More weight has been given to the views of the pessimists (accountants please note).

This technique of weighting is useful in many situations, such as dealing with several products, salaries, services and so on. Obviously, you can use any weights that make sense to you. Just ensure that they add up to 100%.

Fig. 5.7 Weighting the experts

	A	B	C	D		D
1				Forecast		Formulas in
2		Forecast	Weight	x weight		Column D
3	Alex	1,000	0.50	500		=B3*C3
4	Bob	2,000	0.30	600		=B4*C4
5	Chris	3,000	0.20	600		=B5*C5
6	Totals	6,000	1.00	1,700		=SUM(D3:D5)

Note: weights of 50%, 30% and 20% have been converted to proportions by dividing each one by 100. This makes the arithmetic simpler, as explained in Chapter 6: How money grows.

Comparisons

Suppose you were given two sets of figures for take-home pay shown on the left in Fig. 5.8. How would you analyse them? These are the figures which are illustrated on pages 61 and 62 – which should give you your first clue. You could easily use your spreadsheet to create revealing charts.

Another handy trick is to use a spreadsheet for some simple analysis. Columns D and E show the simplest comparison (e.g. that in 2000 the accountant's pay was more than $22,000 greater than that of the cleaner – or, looking at it from the other angle, the cleaner's pay was less than 10% that of the beanie's). The absolute changes (columns F and G) and percentage changes (columns H and I) are instructive, as are the index numbers (columns J and K). We will talk more about percentages in the next chapter. First, take a look at index numbers.

Indexing

Index numbers are nothing more than ordinary numbers on a standardized basis. Usually a value of 100 is chosen as the base, and all other numbers are expressed as a percentage of that base. To convert any number to an index:

1 Select a base (the year 2000 in the example) and note the actual value ($25,000 for the beanie).

2 Divide every figure by the base value and multiply the result by 100.

This removes the effect of scale, and allows direct trends and relative movements. There is a catch. Two indexes will always converge at the base (where they both equal 100 – the year 2000 in this example). You can see this clearly if you look back at the charts on pp. 62–3, *The beanie is caught/overtaken/lags*.

Fig. 5.8 Comparing pay

	A	B	C	D	E	F	G	H	I	J	K
1		Dollars		Differences		Dollar change from one year earlier		Percentage change over previous year		Index, 2000=100	
2	Year	Beanie	Cleaner	US $	%age	Beanie	Cleaner	Beanie	Cleaner	Beanie	Cleaner
3	1994	19,000	1,304	17,696	6.9					76	56
4	1995	20,000	1,434	18,566	7.2	1,000	130	5.3	10.0	80	62
5	1996	21,000	1,578	19,422	7.5	1,000	143	5.0	10.0	84	68
6	1997	22,000	1,736	20,264	7.9	1,000	158	4.8	10.0	88	75
7	1998	23,000	1,909	21,091	8.3	1,000	174	4.5	10.0	92	83
8	1999	24,000	2,100	21,900	8.8	1,000	191	4.3	10.0	96	91
9	2000	25,000	2,310	22,690	9.2	1,000	210	4.2	10.0	100	100
10	2001	26,000	2,541	23,459	9.8	1,000	231	4.0	10.0	104	110
11	2002	27,000	2,795	24,205	10.4	1,000	254	3.8	10.0	108	121
12	2003	28,000	3,075	24,925	11.0	1,000	280	3.7	10.0	112	133
13	2004	29,000	3,382	25,618	11.7	1,000	307	3.6	10.0	116	146
14	2005	30,000	3,720	26,280	12.4	1,000	338	3.4	10.0	120	161

Sample of cell formulas: =B14-C14   B14-B13   =B14/$B$9*100

=C14/B14*100

=((B14/B13)-1)*100

Index numbers are very good for examining relative movements – but you need to see the underlying figures (e.g. salary) to judge the absolute relationship between two amounts.

Relatives and absolutes. Note the dollar signs in the formula =B14/$B$9*100. When you copy functions into new cells (e.g. by using the fill handle, see Fig 4.1), the functions are updated to maintain the relative relationships with other cells – except that cell references prefixed with $ signs are not changed.

In this example, we want every figure in column J divided by the value in cell B9 – hence the absolute reference to B$9 (the relative relationship with column B is unchanged). When you are entering or formulas, press F4 one or more times to insert the $ signs. Try it and you will see what I mean.

Ten hard questions to ask or be asked

1 Are amounts stated with too much or too little precision for the purpose?

2 Have numbers been rounded correctly (e.g. has an amount been rounded up when it should have been rounded down)?

3 Were numbers rounded at the correct stage of a calculation (e.g. were calculations performed on rounded numbers when they should have used un-rounded values, or vice-versa?).*

4 Have calculations that were copied across or down a spreadsheet used the correct relative or absolute cell addressing?

5 Are the correct summary measures used? Is it the right average? Do extreme values distort a range?

6 Do weighted averages use realistic or correct weights?

7 Has the correct distribution been used? Has it been assumed that the *normal* applies, when in fact the distribution is squared or skewed?

8 Is the fact that two series of index numbers converge at the base misleading?

9 Is the correct type of chart used (e.g. do not use a pie chart to show trends over time)?

10 Is the chart misleading (e.g. compressed or inverted scale, data points omitted, etc.)?

*A famous ruse in the early days of computers was to pay (e.g. salaries) with amounts rounded down, charge (e.g. the payroll account) for the sum of the amounts rounded up, and pocket the difference – which could amount to thousands when applied to a large volume of transactions.

What's next?

This chapter has looked at a collection of techniques which help with examining and reporting. Some of them, such as charts, rounding and summarising, are used throughout this book and, no doubt, your work. The normal distribution is relevant to risk assessment which we review in Chapter 23. Weighting and index numbers are all around us – in stock market indices, some exchange rate indicators, many economic series such as inflation, and industrial production, and – notably – the financial analysis which is the main topic of this book.

Moreover, in the next chapter we will build on what we have just covered, by moving on to consider the arithmetic of investment and finance. This has wide ranging applications and will, as you will see, help you make better management decisions.

6

how money grows

'Mathematics is a game played according to certain simple rules with meaningless marks on paper.'

David Hilbert

▶ Chapter survival toolkit

▶ Overview

This chapter reviews the arithmetic of finance. We look at the relationships between proportions and percentages; growth, interest and discount rates; interest/discount rates, risk, and the present and future value of money. These are deeply intertwined, and they are critical elements in decisions about money when time is involved. They are also important for many other management issues, including growth in profits and inflation. The chapter concludes by looking at many practical applications of these relationships – and previews their use in assessing financial instruments and projects.

▶ Prerequisites

If you want to be able to perform the calculations introduced in this chapter, you really need to be on top of the spreadsheet basics and associated jargon introduced in Chapter 4.

▶ Mastering the arithmetic of money

After reading this chapter, you should be able to answer the following questions:

1 What is the relationship between percentages and proportions? Why is it useful?

2 How do percentages and proportions relate to growth?

3 What are simple and compound interest rates? What are their relationship to percentages and proportions?

4 What is the relationship between interest rates and discount rates?

5 What is the time value of money? How do interest rates and risk come into this issue?

6 What are the present and future value of money?

7 What are net present value and the internal rate of return?

8 How do you apply the foregoing to simple financial investments, loan repayments, discounts and rent-or-buy problems?

9 How do you apply the foregoing to financial markets and project assessment – the details of which are discussed in Chapters 19 and 21?

10 What do growth and inflation have in common?

> 'Algebra and money are essentially levellers; the
> first intellectually, the second effectively.'
>
> **Simone Weil**

▶ Jargon watch

Math-speak	Financial-speak
Percentage	Interest rates, discount rates, hurdle rates
Proportion	Simple interest, compound interest
Power	Conversion periods
	Present value
Beanie-speak	Future value
Sinking fund	Net present value (NPV)
Annuity	Internal rate of return (IRR)
	Discounted cash flow (DCF)
Economics-speak	Yield
Inflation	

▶ Investment arithmetic

This chapter is about the arithmetic of finance and investment. I hope this excites you. If instead it makes you feel nervous, let me reassure you. Talk of percentages, compound growth rates and discount rates might seem terrifying to some, but, if so, blame the educational system. These are actually simple concepts and they have the delight of being unarguable – back to one apple plus one apple is indubitably two apples. Moreover, the concepts presented here are the key to understanding investments. And who does not want to make one apple into ten apples or more.

Actually, if there is one theme for this chapter it is *relationships* – such as the relationships between:

1 proportions and percentages
2 growth and interest rates
3 interest rates and discount rates
4 interest rates, risk and time
5 the present and future value of money.

We shall examine each of these duos (OK, number 4 is a trio) and see how they relate to each other. They are all inextricably interwoven. Moreover, as you will have deduced by now, they are critical elements in decisions about money when time is involved. I nearly forgot to mention that we will see how to use our good friend the spreadsheet to do the calculations, so the arithmetic is not going to be too taxing.

The chapter concludes by looking at the practical applications of these relationships to the assessment of simple financial investments, loan repayments, interest rates, discounts for early payment, rent-or-buy problems, and so on. In later chapters we will apply the same arithmetic to assessing financial instruments and project plans.

▶ Interesting growth rates

▶ Watch those digits

Percentages need careful watching:

♦ If you boost sales by 10% a year for 10 years, the overall increase will be 160%, not 100%.

♦ If you boost prices by 50%, and then cut them by 50%, they end up 25% below where they started from.

♦ If your credit card company charges you 3.5% a month interest, this grosses up to a penal rate of over 50% per annum.

▶ Of money, percentages and proportions

We are all familiar with percentages and proportions from everyday dealings with money. Nevertheless, I am going to state the obvious:

> If something grows by x%, it has to shrink $x / (x + 100)$ to return to the starting point.
>
> For example, $1,000 increased by 25% = $1,250. The inverse is $25 / 125 = 20\%$; $1,250 less 20% is $1,000.

♦ **Proportions.** One cent is 0.01 of a dollar.

♦ **Percentages**. One cent is one *percent* (1%) of a dollar.

Proportions and percentages are identical except that percentages are 100 times bigger than proportions. A percentage is a proportion x 100; the decimal point is pushed two places to the right. This simple relationship is the key to the arithmetic of growth and investment. Read this paragraph again if you were not paying full attention.

One example will illustrate the point. A gizmo retails at $200 plus 15% value added tax or sales tax, which takes the total price to $230. If you know any two of these figures, you can calculate the third – a common requirement in business. The important thing to note is that, expressed as *proportions*, the tax rate is 0.15 and the tax-inclusive price is 1.15 of the pre-tax price.

♦ The total tax is $200 × 0.15 = $30.

♦ The tax-inclusive price is $200 × 1.15 = $230.

♦ The pre-tax price $230 ÷ 1.15 = $200.

♦ The tax rate is $30 ÷ $200 = 0.15 or ($230 ÷ $200) – 1 = 0.15.

You can substitute any two amounts and any percentage in the above, and apply the same reasoning to any situation involving percentages. Next, we will see how the same logic applies to growth rates.

Easy growth

Proportions make it easy to calculate growth rates. Take the earlier example of sales growing by 10% per annum for over a decade. This is the same as saying that sales should rise (be multiplied) by 1.10 each year. For arguments sake, assume that the starting point was sales of just $1. The sales targets for each year are as follows:

Year one: $1 × 1.10

Year two: $1 × 1.10 × 1.10

Year three: $1 × 1.10 × 1.10 × 1.10.

There is no need to go on. It is obvious that by year 10 the multiplier for sales is 1.10 multiplied by itself 10 times. Another way of saying this in math-speak is '1.10 to the power of 10'. Needless to say, there is a spreadsheet function that does this calculation painlessly:

Formula	Example	Result
=POWER(number, power)	=POWER(1.10,10)	2.594....

This reveals the answer to our little sum. In plain English, it tells us that at the end of 10 years, sales should be 2.594 times higher (i.e. one dollar of sales today should be replaced with $2.59 of sales in 10 years). If you take away the original $1, you should see that sales should be higher by a factor of 1.59, or 159%.

This same arithmetic applies to any growth rate over any period. The other example above was of a credit card company charging 3.5% a month interest. This is a growth situation also, since each month more interest is charged on the interest which has already accumulated. The spreadsheet formula is =POWER(1.035,12) which gives the answer 1.51, (i.e. 51%.). A few more examples are shown on p. 80. This formula, and some similar ones, can be used to solve growth rate and interest rate problems, as I will explain next.

> 'Time is that quality of nature which keeps events from happening all at once. Lately it doesn't seem to be working.'
>
> **Anon.**

Proportions and percentage calculations

	Generic Amount 1 changes to Amount 2	Example 1 200 grows to 220	Example 2 200 shrinks to 180
Step 1 Find Amount 2 as a proportion of Amount 1	Amount 2 / Amount 1	220/200 = 1.10 *220 is 1.10 times 200*	180/200 = 0.90 *180 is 0.90 of 200*
Step 2 Find Amount 2 as a percentage of Amount 1	Multiply the previous result by 100	$1.10 \times 100 = 110\%$ *220 is 110% of 200*	$0.90 \times 100 = 90\%$ *180 is 90% of 200*
Step 3 Find proportionate change	Subtract 1 from the result at Step 1	1.10 – 1 = 0.10 *220 is higher than 200* *by a factor of 0.10*	0.90 – 1 = –0.10 *180 is lower than 200* *by a factor of 0.10*
Step 4 Find percentage change	Multiply the previous result by 100	$0.10 \times 100 = 10\%$ *220 is 10% greater* *than 200*	$0.10 \times 100 = -10\%$ *180 is 10% smaller* *than 200*

Why growth matters

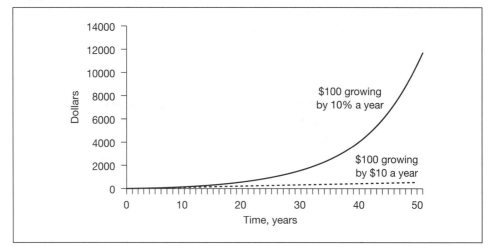

Compounding the issue

Simple interest rates do not provide any compounding. For example, if you put $100 in a special savings account and once a year you are sent a cheque for $5, the **principal** amount remains unchanged at $100.

However, if instead the $5 interest was added to the principal – **compounded** – then in the second year you would receive interest in the interest – **compound interest** – of $5.25. As discussed above, this can make quite a difference. Financiers, who are seldom stupid, sometimes pay simple interest on deposits, but *always* charge compound interest on loans.

Clearly, the frequency of interest payments affects the result. For example, 10% per annum compounded monthly pays more interest than 10% per annum compounded once a year, as the following table shows:

Interest paid:	Number of conversion periods	Quoted annual interest rate, %	Effective annual interest rate, %	Value of $1,000 after one year
Annually	1	10.00	10.00	1,100.00
Half-yearly	2	10.00	10.25	1,102.50
Quarterly	4	10.00	10.38	1,103.81
Monthly	12	10.00	10.47	1,104.71
Daily	365	10.00	10.52	1,105.16

The periods for which interest accrues and is paid are known as **conversion periods**.

Use the spreadsheet POWER function to convert quoted interest rates into effective rates or use the calculator on this book's website.

The time value of money

A bird in the hand

If in an uncharacteristic fit of generosity, your accountant offered you a $100 bonus and told you that you could choose whether to take it today or in one year's time – no strings attached – which would you choose? Obviously, you would grab it now with both hands. You do not need telling twice that money in your possession now is worth somewhat more than the promise of the same amount at some future time. There are two main reasons.

If interest rates have risen from 10% to 12% they have increased by two **percentage points** – or by 20%. The first is a unit, the second is a rate of change. Bankers, who often make money by taking advantage of very small changes in interest rates, refer to 1% as 100 **basis points**. For example, half a per cent is 50 basis points.

1 **Risk.** You would probably never see the $100 next year if, say, next week your bean counter was run over in the car park (possibly several times, by a disgruntled employee).

2 **Interest**. If you took $100 today and put it in the bank at 5% interest, you would be $5 better off in a year's time (100×0.05), compared to waiting for the cash. Accordingly, you might argue that you would want a promise of considerably more than $105 in a year's time to make it worth the risk of fore-going the cash handout today.

If you can see the logic of these two points, you are up to speed with everything there is to know about the concept of dealing with problems involving money, risk and time. Should you buy or lease? Is it worth paying early for the discount? How do you compare two projects with differing terms or rates of return? The answers to all the questions and more are found by the same logic – the linking factor is the rate of interest. I will explain more about this in a moment.

If you make the bold but generally acceptable assumption that a bank account is a completely safe place to put your money, then obviously the return on everything you do in business should be greater than the rate of interest you would earn from the bank. Otherwise, you would grow richer by putting your money on deposit and sitting on the beach. Moreover, the return from a business venture should not just equal, but should be significantly greater than, the rate of bank interest – otherwise the deal is simply not worth the risk.

> 'Money often costs too much.'
>
> **Ralph Waldo Emerson**

▶ Present and future value

Beanies deploy three bits of jargon to describe the relationships between money and interest rates. Taking the figures from the previous example:

> Interest rates and discount rates are the same thing with different names.
>
> ● Future value = present value plus **interest**.
> ● Present value = future value less **discount**.

◆ **Present value** is money in your hand today (e.g. $100).

◆ **Future value** is the worth of some amount in the future ($105).

◆ The **interest rate** or **discount rate** links the two (5%).

As with most financial analysis, if you know two of these things you can work out the third. The relationship is as follows. It helps to understand this, but do not get too hung up on it because there are spreadsheet formulas to do the sums.

Future value = present value × interest rate

$$\$105 = \$100 \times 1.05$$

Note how the interest rate is represented as a proportion, as discussed above. This is exactly the same arithmetic as the sales tax discussed above. Now, suppose we are dealing with more than one year. You will know from *growth rates*, above, that you multiply out by the interest payments. For example, for two years, the arithmetic is:

$$FV = \$100 \times 1.05 \times 1.05$$
$$= \$100 \times 1.1025$$
$$= \$110.25$$

Present and future value illustrated

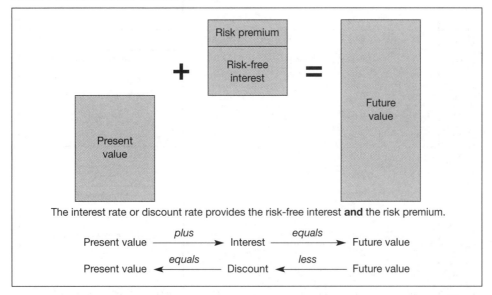

You can, of course, use the spreadsheet POWER function which we met above. However, as you guessed, spreadsheets have three specific functions built-in. You get at them by choosing *Insert/Function* and then clicking on *Financial*. They are PV, FV and RATE. I am sure you can work out which is which. Figure 6.1 shows them in use. It also includes an example (worked out the long way) of $100 invested at 5% pa interest for 20 years. A couple of things need explaining.

1 Present and future value calculations assume that there are flows in both directions. In other words, $100 flows out of your grasp at the beginning and $265.33 flows back in at the end. For this reason, the present value is entered as a negative amount. If you were borrowing, the initial value would be positive and the future value would be negative. It makes no difference to the numbers. The amounts and rates are the same whether you look at a transaction from the point of view of the lender or the borrower.

2 The formulas can also be used when you have a regular stream of identical payments (as you might do with a lease contract or pension plan), in which case the *payment* option in the formulas is completed, but another value (usually the *rate*) is left blank.

Fig. 6.1 Linking the interest/present and future

	A	B	C	D	E
1	Period	Interest/ discount rate	Interest $	Cumulative value $	
2	0			100.00	**Present value**
3	1	0.05	5.00	105.00	=PV(rate, periods, payment, FV, type)
4	2	0.05	5.25	110.25	=PV(0.05,20,,265.33,0)
5	3	0.05	5.51	115.76	$100.00
6	4	0.05	5.79	121.55	
7	5	0.05	6.08	127.63	
8	6	0.05	6.38	134.01	**Discount rate**
9	7	0.05	6.70	140.71	=RATE(periods, payment, PV, FV, type)
10	8	0.05	7.04	147.75	=RATE(20,,-100,265.33,0)
11	9	0.05	7.39	155.13	5%
12	10	0.05	7.76	162.89	
13	11	0.05	8.14	171.03	
14	12	0.05	8.55	179.59	
15	13	0.05	8.98	188.56	**Future value**
16	14	0.05	9.43	197.99	=PV × compounded interest rate
17	15	0.05	9.90	207.89	=100 * POWER(1.05,20)
18	16	0.05	10.39	218.29	$265.33
19	17	0.05	10.91	229.20	
20	18	0.05	11.46	240.66	=FV(rate, periods, payment, PV, type)
21	19	0.05	12.03	252.70	=FV(0.05,20,,-100,0)
22	20	0.05	12.63	265.33	$265.33

Notes:

The calculations require the interest rate *per period* as a proportion but it makes no difference whether these are months, years, or any other time span. Divide the annual rate by the number of periods in a year before plugging it into the formulas. Thus, for a one-year span you could use:

◆ an interest rate of 0.05 ÷ 4 for 4 periods – 5% per annum compounded quarterly;

◆ a rate of 0.05 ÷ 2 for 2 periods – 5% per annum compounded half-yearly; or

◆ 0.05 for 1 period – 5% per annum paid once at end of year.

The argument *type* indicates when interest is compounded: at the start (type=1) or end (type=0) of each period. This is usually set to 0 because you have to leave cash on deposit for a while before any interest is added – indeed, if you omit this value, the spreadsheet assumes a value of 0.

Bumpy trends

The calculations which we have just met cannot be applied when the amounts of the inflows and outflows vary from period to period. However, there are two variations that can be used. They are known rather pompously as *net present value* and *internal rate of return*. Let me introduce them and then explain about the *discount rate*.

> The practical application of net present value and the internal rate of return, and the choice between them is discussed in Chapter 21.

Net present value

The *net present value* of any future stream of income is essentially the amount of money that you would need to put in a bank deposit today at a given rate of interest to generate the identified cash flows. For example, if you project the pattern of spending and income that a project is expected to generate, calculate the present value of each future cash amount and sum the results, you arrive at the overall *net present value* of a project (sometimes called the NPV). The projects with the highest net present value usually get your money.

You will have guessed that spreadsheets perform this calculation painlessly. See Fig. 6.2. As you can see from the example, you can have payments and receipts dotted around. You are not constrained to just one outlay or a series of regular receipts. Watch though, that at different interest rates – more properly called the *discount rate* – different projects become more attractive because of the varying valuations of future income and payments. You might want to try changing the discount rate in cell B3 (the spreadsheet can be downloaded from this book's website) to see what happens to the net present value.

Internal rate of return

The alternative to using net present value is a measure named the *internal rate of return* (also called variously *IRR*, *discounted cash flow*, *DCF* and *yield* – and you thought that your marketing people were bad at naming things). The *internal rate of return* is simply the compound interest rate that links the present and future. Think of it as the interest rate that a bank would have to charge if it were to make you a loan (the project cost) that was going to generate the predicted future stream of repayments (the returns). Since we are dealing with the future, the interest rate is more properly called – you've got it – the discount rate. In this case, the projects with the highest internal rate of return are the top picks – so long as the rate exceeds a predetermined level discussed in a moment.

Spreadsheets do the sums for you, as shown also in Fig. 6.2. Note that if the rate in cell B3 had been set equivalent to the internal rate of return of 25%, the net present value in cell B1 would be zero. Try it.

Fig. 6.2 Net present value and internal rate of return

Net present value
Cell B1 displays the
NPV because it
contains this formula ⟶ =NPV ((B3) , (B5:B14))

Internal rate of return
Cell D3 displays the
IRR because it
contains this formula

Dummy

=IRR; ((D5:D14) , (0.1))

	A	B	C	D	E	F	G	H
1	Net present value	976						
2							Memo	
3	Rate	10.00%		25%			Cumulative	
4								
5	Period 1	−1000		−1000			−1000	
6	Period 2	80		80			−920	
7	Period 3	300		300			−620	
8	Period 4	400		400			−220	
9	Period 5	−200		−200			−420	
10	Period 6	100		100			−320	
11	Period 7	400		400			80	
12	Period 8	800		800			880	
13	Period 9	1000		1000			1880	
14	Period 10	1000		1000			2880	
15								

Why the dummy (top right)? The spreadsheet uses this as a starting point and performs an iterative trial-and-error process until it arrives at the correct value or gives up.

▶ Selecting a discount rate

Choosing the discount rate is not quite as simple as it might at first appear. Obviously, you might use bank interest rates as the discount rate, but this will not really take allowance of your actual costs of capital and the risks involved. In Chapter 19 we will look at calculating the cost of capital, and in Chapter 21 we will discuss the way to use this to arrive at the appropriate rate to use for corporate projects.

▶ Putting it to good use

The calculations concerning the present and future value of money are valuable aids to financial decision making. The following examples illustrate their practical application. Note that in all the examples, the interest rate is expressed as a proportion (e.g. 5% is entered as 0.05) and it is assumed that interest is compounded once a year. The sample spreadsheet for this chapter shows the formulas in use and includes some more complex examples.

▶ Sinking funds

A situation might arise where you want to set aside a lump sum to replace a machine in five years' time (although this might not be the best use of a cash surplus – see Chapter 19). For example, suppose you know that you will need to spend $50,000 in five years' time, and interest rates are 5% per annum. You can probably see that you need to find a *present value* that equates to the required *future* amount. Use of the spreadsheet formula in Fig. 6.1 would reveal that you should put $39,176.31 on deposit today at 5% per annum interest to produce $50,000 in five years' time.

Formula	Result
=PV(rate, periods, payment, future value, type)	
=PV(0.05, 5, ,50000,0)	$39,176.31

If, alternatively, you want to set aside a regular amount each year for five years to produce the lump sum, you can use a variation on the arithmetic. Logically, there are five separate future value calculations, which together add up to $50,000 – that is, five separate growth rates as shown on the left of the following table. Fortunately, there is a spreadsheet formula to do the work, as shown in action on the right. Either approach produces the values in the middle column – which shows how each annual amount would grow with the addition of compound interest.

Formula =PPMT(rate, period, number of periods, present value, future value)		
Basic arithmetic	Result	Formula
9,048.74 × 1.05 × 1.05 × 1.05 × 1.05	10,998.80	=PPMT(0.05,5,5,,50000)
9,048.74 × 1.05 × 1.05 × 1.05	10,475.05	=PPMT(0.05,4,5,,50000)
9,048.74 × 1.05 × 1.05	9,976.24	=PPMT(0.05,3,5,,50000)
9,048.74 × 1.05	9,501.18	=PPMT(0.05,2,5,,50000)
9,048.74	9,048.74	**=PPMT(0.05,1,5,,50000)**
Total	50,000.00	

The basic arithmetic on the left and the formula on right each produce the figures in the middle column.

The table reveals – if you look closely – that you would have to set aside $9,048.74 a year at 5% per annum interest to save $50,000 over five years. In fact, you need only to use the formula at the bottom-right of the table to find the desired figure. I will explain why.

These time-value calculations assume that interest is paid at the end of each period. In this example, final amount is put on deposit at the very end of the five years, and so does not have time to earn any interest. It is included in the calculation for one period only, which explains the 1 used in the formula. In other words, to use PPMT to find any principal amount, enter 1 for the period. In any such calculations, if you want to allow for the final amount earning interest, add one period (in this example, instead of 5 use 6). Note also that the formula is multi-purpose, and present value is left blank because it is not relevant in this instance.

▶ Finance up front

Take a variation on the previous example. Imagine that you have a project which needs finance of $10,000 a year for five years. What lump sum would your financiers have to put on deposit now at 5% per annum to allow you to draw down this annual cash requirement? Hands up if you spotted that you can use the present value formula in Fig. 6.1, as follows:

Formula	Result
=PV(rate, periods, payment, FV, type)	
=PV(0.05, 5, 10000, ,0)	$43,294.77

▶ One person's loan …

You will recall that one person's loan is another's investment. If your financiers wanted to borrow the $43,294.77 required in the previous example, how much would they have to pay back over five years at 5% per annum? Go to the top of the class if you said $10,000 a year. It is exactly the same situation as just discussed, but viewed from the perspective of the lender rather than the depositor. Of course, in reality, the interest rate charged to the lender would be higher than the interest rate paid to the depositor. The difference between the two – the spread – is how bankers traditionally made their money (these days, they tend to charge outlandish fees for everything as well).

▶ Repayment schedule

Spreadsheets provide a useful formula for determining the repayment schedule for loans where the amount and interest rate are known. Perhaps you want to borrow $50,000 at 5% per annum repayable in equal instalments over five years. The following formula shows that the annual repayment is $11,548.74.

Formula	Result
=PMT(rate, periods, present value, future value, type)	
=PMT(0.05, 5, 50000, ,0)	$11,548.74

Obviously, the average annual interest charge is $1,548.74 (since the other $10,000 of the repayment is reducing the principal) and the total interest charge is $1,548.74 × 5. If you divide each of the five repayments by the appropriate interest factor, similar to the PPMT example above, you will find, of course, that less of the principal is repaid in the early periods – when most of the payment is going to cover the interest. I have done it for you in the spreadsheet that you can download from this book's website.

▶ Awards and scholarships

Now suppose your altruistic board of directors decided to make an annual award of $10,000 to the most promising widget scientist. At first glance it might appear that you would need to put an enormous amount on deposit to guarantee this payment (known as a *perpetual annuity*, if you want to know). However, when you realize that the annual payment is no more than the interest on the lump sum, it becomes clear that the amount required is not so large. If interest rates were 10% per annum, the required deposit would be $10,000 / 0.10 = $100,000. If interest rates halved, the amount required would be $10,000 / 0.05 = $200,000. Simply divide the lump sum by the interest rate. This is not hard.

▶ Discount for cash

Business suppliers frequently offer a discount of around 2% for immediate payment. Is this good value? The trick is to annualise the rate and compare it with other rates. Typically, such discounts entail you parting with your cash about 15 days faster than you would otherwise. On this basis, there would be 24 conversion periods in a year, so the equivalent annual rate is 24 × 2% = 48% per annum (this is simple, not compound, interest). In effect, your supplier is borrowing from you at 48% a year for 15 days, and then using the cash to pay for the goods. If you have surplus cash earning less than this (it would be highly unusual if it was earning more), accept the discount with both hands. If you would incur interest charges yourself, then if they are less than 48% you should also take the discount. In effect you would be borrowing, say, from your bank at 10%, and on-lending at 48% a year.

So, is it good practice for you to offer your debtors similar discounts for early payment? It certainly would be if you have a cash flow crisis. It might also be worthwhile if you can get a better rate on these amounts receivable that you can on a similar value of payables. In effect, you might make money by borrowing from your clients and lending to your suppliers – although, of course, if you are not a bank this is not your business.

▶ Rent or buy?

You will frequently have the option of buying, say, machinery or office equipment – or leasing. You can find out which is better value by putting both streams of payments onto the same basis.

For example, you can buy a computer server for $5,000 or lease for $250 a month for two years. The outright purchase option has a present value of, well, $5,000. At a discount rate of 12% (a convenient 1% per month) the PV calculation reveals that leasing has a present value of just over $5,310. Leasing is slightly more expensive. If your costs of capital (see Chapter 19) are more than 12% per annum leasing might be more competitive. Do not forget that leasing also has cash flow advantages, and there might be warranty or maintenance benefits as well.

The comparison just discussed assumed that the computer had no residual value. If you own the leased computer at the end of the period, residual value makes no difference – since in both cases you end up with an asset with the same future value. For example, if you judge that the computer will have market value of $1,500 after two years, this effectively adds a present value of about $1,000 to both calculations – leaving the relative merits much unchanged. You will have noticed that the PV calculation has a payment ($250) and a future value ($1,000) slot which we have not used before now. This example is as follows:

Formula	Result
=PV(rate, periods, payment, FV, type)	
=PV(0.01, 24, 250,1500,0)	$6,492.20 (lease)
=5000 + PV(0.01, 24, 0,1500,0)	$6,330.78 (buy)

▶ Growth and inflation

A moment ago we touched on growth rates. Inflation – a general increase in prices – is simply a manifestation, albeit usually unwanted, of growth. Accordingly, the same arithmetic applies. For example, if inflation is 5% a year for three years, the overall increase in prices is $1.05 \times 1.05 \times 1.05$ or 15.8%.

Inflation erodes the value of money. Unadjusted prices – the amounts that you and I pay in the shops – are known as current prices. Prices adjusted to remove the effects of inflation are known as real or constant prices. For example, if inflation is running at 5% per annum and a company raises its prices by 7%, the real increase is 7 – 5 = 2%.

Governments produce various indices of prices – the retail price index, consumer price index, wholesale price indices, and various GDP deflators – which, as discussed in Chapter 18, can be used to convert any price trends into constant prices. The table on p. 274 shows how you can divide through by a price index to create a constant price index.

▶ Ten hard questions to ask or be asked

1 Are percentage changes calculated from the correct base, and are their inverses stated correctly?

2 Is the interest rate simple or compound?

3 How often is interest paid, or added to the principal amount?

4 Is like being compared with like (e.g. are interest rates *effective*)?

5 If the time periods are different, has proper account been taken of the time value of money for the unmatched period?

6 Are residual amounts/values properly accounted for?

7 Is the most appropriate interest, discount or hurdle rate being used as a yardstick?

8 Has inflation been correctly factored in to the calculations?

9 When calculating net present value, what happens if you change the discount rate?

10 Is the business taking/rejecting and offering discounts as appropriate?

▶ What's next?

With most of the arithmetical basics out of the way, we can now move on to look at how you keep track of your corporate spending and revenue. The next chapter, which should be easier going, introduces financial record keeping and money management.

7
keeping score

> 'Everything is vague to a degree you do not realize till you have tried to make it precise.'
>
> **Bertrand Russell**

▶ Chapter survival toolkit

▶ Overview

This chapter is about keeping financial records and physically controlling spending. These are the nuts and bolts of managing the numbers. The analysis comes later. To make it easy to introduce bookkeeping, I have approached it from the angle of an entrepreneur starting a new business. This is probably where you are if you have an overwhelming interest in posting your own transactions. However, even if you are working in a big corporation supported by teams of beanies, I hope you will at least skim the bookkeeping section and gain an understanding of debits and credits, double entry accounting, and the chart of accounts. Please take particular note of comments about passing transactions through the bank account – a topic to which I will return in the next chapter.

▶ Prerequisites

None, except perhaps the ability to spend money.

▶ Mastering bookkeeping basics

After reading this chapter, you should be able to answer the following questions:

1 What are debits and credits? Why do they infer the opposite to what you might expect?

2 What is double entry accounting? Why is it important?

3 What is a chart of accounts?

4 What are assets, liabilities, and equity?

5 What are income and revenue accounts?

6 How do you classify spending and receipts?

7 What are balance sheets and profit and loss accounts/income statements?

8 What is a trial balance? When would it be useful?

9 How would you select a PC-based accounting system?

10 How would you set up an electronic accounting system?

> 'Money was never a big motivation for me, except as a way to keep score. The real excitement is playing the game.'
>
> **Donald Trump**

> ▶ **Jargon watch**

New beanie buzz words
Chart of accounts
Fiscal year
Conversion date
Assets and liabilities
Owners'/shareholders' equity
Contra accounts
Sales, cost of sales, operating expenses

Retained earnings, dividends/owners'
   drawings
Debits and credits
Double entry accounting
Journal, ledger, trial balance

Beanie-speak previously encountered
Balance sheet
Profit and loss account/income statement

▶ Managing the numbers – literally

This chapter introduces the rudiments of financial record keeping. This is essential groundwork for understanding where the money comes from and where it goes. Of course, the topic has immediate practical applications if you are an entrepreneur, particularly if you are starting a new business, because you may well keep the books yourself. But even, or especially, if someone else is doing it for you, you need to understand what they are doing and why. Knowing these basics helps unlock many of the mysteries of what is possibly the world's second-oldest profession.

To try to give life to the topic, I have approached it from the point of view of an entrepreneur starting a business and maintaining financial accounts. The principles are the same for a one-person business or a huge multinational. The only difference is that in larger companies there will be a team of well-paid bean counters keeping the books using costly computer systems. If you wish, you can steal a march on them with some snappy low-cost software.

▶ A brief history of bookkeeping

The first bean counters recorded quantities by making notches in tally sticks. The sticks were then split in two and each party to the transaction kept one slice. Later, the two slices could be brought back together and compared to ensure that, shall I say, no mistakes were made. Today, tally sticks have been replaced by computer accounting systems, and the notches have evolved into a concept called double entry accounting. End of history lesson. I did say it would be brief.

▶ First buy some shoes

Suppose for the moment that you start a new business with a small number of clients who each pays you handsome fees – maybe for consulting services, software development or perhaps sculpturing. You will be quite busy enough without wanting to spend much time dealing with the rather important matter of keeping financial records. Here is a secret. The best way of ensuring that your records are accurate is to insist that every transaction passes through your bank account (even petty cash, of which more in the next chapter).

Every time you write a cheque or make a deposit, write the full details on a sheet of paper – pre-printed vouchers are available for this – staple any supporting documents to it, and drop it in a shoebox. Auditors, who delight in watching over your financial well being, prefer the vouchers to be pre-numbered consecutively. Any spoiled vouchers or spoiled cheques should be cancelled and retained so there can be no dispute over their fate. Once you get beyond being the only employee, you should require two signatures on all cheques and appoint someone to review and authorize the vouchers.

Many new or small business owners give the contents of this shoebox to their tame beanie once a week and let the pros worry about posting records, processing salaries, paying tax, and so on. If you want to stay on top of your finances, you might want to get hold of an accounting system for your PC and keep your own records, even if you still pass on the shoebox and let your accountant handle all the nasty, fiddly stuff.

Cheque voucher

Date:	Account:		Cheque no.
15 Jan	Bank account #1		123012
Payee:			Amount:
Happy Pencils Inc.			$24.50
Details			Amounts $
Office stationery – pens and paper			24.50
Total			24.50
Prepared by:		Authorized by:	
ABC		DEF	

▶ Selecting an electronic tally stick

If you are going to keep your own financial records, you need a software accounting system. Today's lower-end packages offer big-company functionality for just a few hundred dollars. Do not make the mistake of buying a specific package because your bean counter uses it. I know an entrepreneur who did, and ended up with a totally incomprehensible white elephant. Financial bods operate in a different universe. Anyway, if you later engage a new accountant, are you going to switch software as well?

When making a selection, be guided by reviews (e.g. on the Internet). There are many systems from which to choose. Peachtree seems to be a favourite of many accountants, QuickBooks claims the largest market share, while I admit a personal preference for MYOB.

Most of the popular packages are surprisingly easy to use and lead you through the bookkeeping process fairly painlessly. With such software the production of financial statements is a breeze – and you have the added bonus that you can also use it for other finance-related tasks such as payroll, invoicing and inventory management.

▶ Getting started

Perhaps the hardest part is getting started. When you first install and use an accounting package, it will ask you to make choices which may appear baffling. Here are some hints about the four tricky options:

1 **Chart of accounts.** You will have to select a chart of accounts (discussed next). Accounting packages come with dozens of charts tailored for various businesses (hairdressers, bricklayers, genetic engineering). The choice can be bewildering. Do not worry. Just select one close to your type of business. Eventually, you will find that you have deleted most predefined accounts and added many new ones.

2 **Allow changes.** You will be asked if you want to allow changes. Strictly speaking, accounting entries should never be amended directly. Auditors are allergic to that white correction fluid. If an error is discovered, the original transaction should be reversed by posting a second transaction which is the exact opposite of the incorrect one, and then the correct details should be posted as a third transaction. In fact (don't tell your accountant that I said this), if you are the only person using the accounting package, you will want to be able to totally erase silly mistakes. Accordingly, initially, set up the system to allow changes. As soon as you are comfortable with the system, switch off this option.

3 **Financial year.** The system will want to know your financial or fiscal year (accounting period). This will probably be the calendar year or maybe your tax year. It is rarely the 12 months commencing on the date on which you started business. Financial years are usually determined by tax considerations.

4 **Conversion date.** The final difficult question will be 'what is your conversion date?' This is simply the date on which you convert from your previous accounting system to the new one. If you are dealing with a new business, the conversion date is the first day of the first month in which you want to start keeping records.

The chart of accounts

An *account* is a list of related transactions (date, description and amount) in date order. I do not need to explain this. I am sure that you are familiar enough with your bank account or credit card statement.

For business accounting, all spending on rent is recorded in an *office rent account*, all spending on paper and pencils in an *office stationery account*, and so on – all very straightforward. A list of all of a company's accounts, by category, is known as a chart of accounts. A very short extract from a typical chart of accounts follows. Note that for ease of reference, each account is allocated an arbitrary identification or account number. Take a quick glance and then I will explain what it means.

Tetrylus Inc., chart of accounts (extract)

Acc. No.	Account	Normal balance
Assets		
1-1001	Petty cash	
1-1002	Bank account #1	Debit
1-1005	Accounts receivable (trade debtors)	
1-1015	Allowance for bad debts	Credit*
1-1200	Inventory (stock) of widgets	
1-1400	Prepayments (short-term)	Debit
1-1501	Fixed assets – computers	
1-1601	Accumulated Depreciation – computers	Credit*
Liabilities		
2-1001	Loans maturing within one year	
2-1005	Accounts payable (trade creditors)	Credit
2-1204	Accrued expenses (short-term)	
Shareholders' equity		
3-1001	Paid-in capital	
3-1002	Additional paid-in capital	Credit
3-1105	Treasury stock	Debit*
3-2000	Retained earnings	Credit
Sales revenue		
4-1001	Sales of widgets	
4-1002	Sales of software	Credit

---

* These are contra accounts – in that they have the opposite balance to that usually found in the group. Do not worry, I will explain this later on (see, for example, p. 115).

Cost of sales		
5-1001	Purchases of widgets	Debit
5-5001	Production line staff wages	
Operating expenses		
6-1002	Office staff salaries	Debit
6-3003	Office rents	
6-4006	Office stationery	
6-5001	Depreciation of computers	
6-9105	Professional audit fees	
Other income		
7-1001	Interest received on bank deposits	Credit
Other expenses		
8-1001	Interest paid on bank loans	Debit

▶ Categories defined

The above extract is very short. A typical chart would include dozens or hundreds of accounts. You will have noticed that the chart of accounts is split into categories – assets, liabilities, equity, sales, cost of sales, operating expenses, and other income and expenses. Let me explain first what the categories include.

Assets. Asset accounts record the value of things you own. They may not be in your possession yet. For example, when a client owes you money for products or services already delivered, this is classified as a trade debt (UK jargon) or account receivable (US terminology). The outstanding amount is not income until it is received, so it is temporarily recorded as an asset. Key asset accounts include cash, inventory, debtors/receivables, prepaid expenses, fixed assets, and refundable deposits paid. Do not be stressed about these terms if they are new to you. I will cover them all as we go along.

Liabilities. These represent money you owe to other people – credit from suppliers (trade credit/accounts payable), bank overdrafts and loans, other accrued payments (i.e. due but not paid) and other loans and advances.

Equity. At the end of the day, after all liabilities have been settled, any money remaining belongs to the owners of the business. For a sole trader, this is known as owner's equity. For a company, the owners are the shareholders, and their share is known, logically, as shareholders' or stockholders' equity. The equity accounts show the score at any one date – how much is owed to the owners from their original investment *plus* retained earnings *less* any accumulated losses.

Sales/cost of sales. These accounts record revenue from sales, and spending directly related to a unit of sales (raw materials, components, factory rent and wages, consultants' salaries which can be directly attributed to a specific job, and so on). See operating expenses (next paragraph) for more details.

Operating expenses. Spending which cannot be directly ascribed to sales is recorded as an operating expense. This includes directors' and administrative salaries, office rent, telecoms, most computer costs, bank charges and audit fees, and so on.

Other income. These accounts are set up to record any income which is not part of a business's main operations – such as interest on stock market investments or gains resulting from exchange-rate movements (assuming that the company is not incorporated for the purpose of financial trading).

Other expenses. You can guess that these include costs which are not part of the company's main operations – the red ink version of *other income*. (Red ink is traditionally used to record losses.)

▶ The scorecard

The classification scheme just outlined helps you to keep tabs on the financial state of your business. As I will explain as we move along, by looking at your asset and liability accounts you can measure the financial scale of your empire and be appraised of any and all commitments that are looming. As you can probably see, the difference between assets and liabilities is the net worth of the business – the owner's equity.

The balance sheet. Assets, liabilities and equity accounts remain in existence all the while a company is in business – in much the same way that your bank account exists so long as you are a customer of the bank. Every new transaction affecting assets, liabilities or equity accounts is added to their running tallies. If you write down the totals (balances) on these accounts at any moment in time, you can see the net balance of assets less liabilities. This summary is known creatively as a *balance sheet*. It is discussed in more detail in Chapter 15 and subsequent chapters.

Profit and loss account. The other accounts – sales, cost of sales, operating expenses and other income and expenses – show you how much you have spent or received in a given period. At the end of each fiscal year, the totals of each of these accounts are summarized and the net balance reveals your profit or loss for the 12 months. This summary is known – you guessed – as a *profit and loss account* (UK) or *income statement* (US). This is so important that all the chapters between here and the one on the balance sheet, and many after, deal with this topic.

Retained earnings. When the net profit or loss has been calculated, accounting entries are passed zeroing each of these accounts, and the net total is transferred to an equity account known as *retained earnings*. As already mentioned, the profit belongs to the owners. Some of it may be paid out to them as *dividends* (*owners' drawings* in the instance of a sole trader). By examining the retained earnings account, you can see the sum total of all profits ever earned by the business and not paid out to the owners or tax authorities. This represents finance for the business which is self-generated.

> 'If winning isn't everything, why do they keep score?'
>
> **Vince Lombardi**

Notching the tally stick

Back to the problem in hand. Recall that you have been making vouchers for all your spending and receipts, and dropping them into a shoebox. At regular intervals, say, once a week, you have to confront the paperwork. Start by dealing with the cheque vouchers. Open up your computer accounting system, click on the button that offers the opportunity to post cheques, and key in the date of the transaction, first cheque number, payee, and amount. So far so good. Now you have to identify on what you spent the money. If the payment was, for example, office stationery you would select that account, probably click to enter the details, and click OK.

The computer system will immediately perform the double entry accounting (i.e. notch both sides of the tally stick), by crediting your record of your *bank account* and debiting your *office stationery* account. Yes, you did read this

Cheque transaction, 12 Jan

Credit bank account:			
Account	Bank account #1	**Date**	12-Jan
Payee	Happy Pencils Inc.	**Cheque no.**	123012
Description	Paper and pens	**Amount $**	24.50

Charge to:			
Account no.	Account name	**Debit $**	**Credit $**
6-4006	Office stationery	25.50	–

Debits and credits

The word debit is derived from debt (an amount owed to you). When you put money into a bank account, you are actually making a loan to the bank. Accordingly, your company accounts show this as a debit. Similarly, withdrawals from the bank are credits in your accounts. If you can remember this, you will be able to work out how every other transaction is posted. Just start by thinking about what would happen on the bank side of the transaction (even if the transaction did not involve the bank) and it will all fall into place.

Clearly, **expense** accounts such as *rents*, *stationery*, and *accountant's fees* will normally have debit balances. Perhaps less obviously, **asset** accounts including *cash at bank* and *plant and machinery* will also normally have debit balances (follow the logic – credit *bank*, debit *machinery*), while **liability** accounts such as *loans from banks* and *credit from suppliers* will have normally credit balances (debit *bank*, credit *loans*). It should perhaps be self-evident that **revenue** accounts relating to sales have credit balances (debit *bank*, credit *sales*).

correctly. Withdrawals from a bank account are treated as credits and deposits are debits. It says the opposite on your bank statement because in the statement the bank is looking at your account from its own perspective; naturally, bankers put themselves first.

Note that when you post your transactions, some cheque payments might be matched by more than one credit. For example, it is not unusual for the monthly rent cheque to cover office rent, heating or air-conditioning and water. You post this by splitting the credit into three (non-equal) parts. Accounting software lets you save this as a recurring transaction, which means that you do not have to key in the same breakdown again next month.

Cheque transaction, 1 Dec

Credit bank account:			
Account	Bank account #1	Date	1-Dec
Payee	Prime Real Estate Inc.	Cheque no.	123006
Description	Rent for December	Amount $	9,990.00

Charge to:			
Account no	Account name	Debit $	Credit $
6-3003	Office rent	9000.00	–
6-3005	Utilities – power	900.00	–
6-3007	Utilities – water	90.00	–

A good technique is to set up records for suppliers, customers and so on in a sort of electronic card file. Then, when you post each transaction, you can record

---

Double entry accounting: preventing errors that no longer happen

The basic premise of double entry accounting is simple: every transaction is recorded twice, once as a credit and once as a debit. For example:

1 When you pay rent, you *credit* cash at bank and *debit* rents.

2 When you make sales, you *debit* cash at bank and *credit* sales.

3 When you take a bank loan, you *debit* cash at bank and *credit* bank loans.

When all the transactions have been cut into the electronic tally stick, so to speak, the two halves are compared. If they match (if the total of all credits equals the total of all debits) this means that the amounts were entered correctly – probably.

In fact, the checking principle is largely obsolete now that accounts are not written up by hand. With an electronic accounting system, you will enter each transaction once only and the computer will post it twice for you. However, as we shall see, double entry accounting is more than just a good idea from another age.

---

which vendor supplied the items and which customer or job they were bought for, if any. Later on, you can come back and see how much money you have spent with specific suppliers or how much one big-ticket sale actually cost you in terms of raw materials. This is useful for bargaining for discounts from vendors and analysing your performance.

▶ Assets, cost of sales, and expenses

When you post these transactions, you do need to give some thought to the intended use of the things you buy. Suppose you run a computer company and you purchased some blank CDs.

◆ If the CDs were for your own backup and archiving use, you would probably charge the **expense** account *computer sundries*.

◆ If they were for use in a job you were doing for a client, you would debit a **cost of sales** account.

◆ If you were in the business of burning CDs, you might regard them as part of your stock in trade, and charge an **asset account** such as *inventory*.

Most outlays tend to be plain expenses, otherwise the account to use is normally fairly self-evident. Cost of sales, inventory and other assets are discussed in more detail in Chapters 11 to 15.

▶ Liabilities, sales and equity

In the same way that there are various options for posting some disbursements, so it is with receipts.

◆ When you start up your business and receive a handy lump sum from an investor, you usually debit *cash at bank* and credit **shareholders' equity** – *paid-in capital*.

◆ If the receipt were a loan, you would credit a **liability** account such as *loans from bank*.

◆ By and large, you want most receipts to be credited to **sales** accounts.
◆ Very rarely, such as when you receive reimbursement of an overpayment to a supplier, you might credit an **expense** account.

Equity, liabilities, and sales are discussed in Chapters 13 and 15.

> 'Business is a good game – lots of competition and a minimum of rules. You keep score with money.'
>
> **Nolan Bushnell (Founder of Atari)**

The scorecard revisited

If you ask your computer accounting system to print a detailed *trial balance* for, say, the first month of your new business, it will produce a tidy list of all your accounts, showing the transactions during the month and the ending balance of each account. The terminology is a throwback to when daily transactions were written up by hand in *journals*, and totals were transferred to the *ledgers* (main books of accounts). At regular intervals, clerks would write down the balance of every account and check that the sum of all the debits equalled the sum of all the credits. Looking down this trial balance – your ledgers – will be instructive. You will find it gives you a good feel for what is happening in your business. The bank balance shows the net cash position. The trial balance shows you exactly where the money comes from and goes to.

▶ Financial statements

Another neat trick is to ask your accounting system for a profit and loss account (income statement) for a given period, and a balance sheet for the end of the period. These will be printed quickly and painlessly. They show a summary of all the accounts in your books, set out in a way which gives you a quick picture of the overall situation. They might seem a little alien right now, but we will come onto their interpretation in later chapters.

> 'I am interested in mathematics* only as a creative art.'
>
> **Godfrey Hardy**

* For mathematics read accounting

▶ Ten hard questions to ask or be asked

1 Do you separate and monitor responsibilities (e.g. does one person prepare cheques and vouchers and at least one other person verify and sign them?)? Could the person who is opening mail be pocketing cheques, money-transfer instructions, etc.?

2 Do you require two signatures on cheques, money-transfer instructions, etc.?

3 Is there a voucher for every payment and every receipt?

4 Are vouchers numbered consecutively and properly accounted for?

5 Are you identifying the vendor, client, job, project, etc. to which each transaction relates?

6 Are debits and credits correctly identified (i.e. in your accounts, money coming out of your bank account is a *credit*)?

7 Are outgoings correctly identified, as spending on inventory, deposits or other assets, cost of sales, refunds to clients, a repayment of liabilities or equity, other expenses?*

8 Are funds received carefully accounted for and correctly identified as sales, refunds from vendors, loans, equity, etc.?*

9 Does your accounting system permit subsequent, hidden changes which could be used fraudulently.

10 Will your accounting system produce a trial balance and financial statements on demand?

More on this in later chapters.

▶ What's next?

This super-fast run through of the basics of bookkeeping, right up to producing trial balances and financial statements, introduced many of the basic concepts of accounting in a real-world situation. Now is, perhaps, a convenient point to take a break. In the next chapter, we will go on to look at the timing of the transactions, managing bank accounts, petty cash, accounts receivable and cash flow. All important stuff.

managing money

'We were surprised how much our understanding of the business improved when we replaced cash accounting with accruals accounts, and the change was nowhere near as complicated as we feared it might be.'

A satisfied client

Chapter survival toolkit

▶ Overview

This chapter is primarily about keeping financial records and physically controlling bank balances, petty cash, expenses claims, collections, and cash flow. These are the nuts and bolts of managing the numbers. The real analysis comes later. Also introduced is a concept known as accruals accounting which helps with interpretation.

The information about controlling the bank and cash balances is important for everyone, most of all for managers. As soon as financial responsibilities are delegated, there is an increased risk of sticky fingers in the pie. Managers should be especially aware of ways that corporate funds might be abused.

▶ Prerequisites

You could perhaps read this chapter in isolation, but really it is a follow-on from the previous chapter.

▶ Mastering money management

After reading this chapter, you should be able to answer the following questions:

1 What is meant by bank reconciliation? Why is it so important?

2 Why is it important to use vouchers when keeping financial records?

3 What is the *imprest* system of cash management? What is so great about it?

4 How would you go about projecting your cash flow?

5 What are cleared and available bank balances?

6 How can you best manage expenses claims?

7 How do you anticipate bad debts? Collect efficiently from clients?

8 How do you avoid cheating? What are good rules for managing cash?

9 What is the difference between cash and accruals accounting? What is most useful for a manager?

10 How do you post accrued and prepaid expenses?

> 'If you don't have some bad loans, you are not in business.'
>
> **Paul Volcker**

▶ Balancing the books

It is time to discuss managing the numbers in a hands-on sense. The previous chapter began by stressing that you should arrange for all monetary transactions to pass through your bank account. This ensures that outlays and receipts are documented. It also provides a sort of double entry verification, in that you can check your records against the banks to ensure that all amounts are posted correctly by your company and by the bank. Let me begin by explaining how you reconcile these two sets of records. Then we will move on to consider managing petty cash, expenses claims, payments due from clients, and cash flow. Finally, I will introduce accruals accounting, which helps managers and entrepreneurs interpret the numbers which make business tick.

▶ Reconciling your bank

If you are in command of everything that flows through your bank account you have complete control over your finances – in a regulatory sense even if not from the perspective of understanding what is going on. We will dispose of any problems of understanding in future chapters.

All the paperwork we have done so far would not be any use without the final step – bank reconciliation. This is not about keeping your bank manager smiling. It is about making sure that you, your bosses and auditors are happy. When the bank statement arrives, it will almost certainly differ from the ledger balance (the balance in your accounting system). You need to find out why, and make any corrections that are necessary.

A sample bank statement, an extract from your records, and the reconciliation of the two are shown in Fig. 8.1. If you compare these you will see that two recent cheques (123034 and 35) have not yet been presented to the bank, and there was a $5,000 deposit which a generous client transferred to your account without notifying you. These items are noted in the reconciliation and explain the difference between the bank balance and your closing ledger balance. You will now locate details of the payment from the client, record that in your own accounts, and presumably send a receipt to the client.

Note that the previous reconciliation would have noted that two cheques (numbered 123012 and 123028) had not been not presented to your bank. These have shown up on this statement. They are checked off now, thus ensuring that each item is charged to your bank account once only. Banks make mistakes too. You need to watch them, as well as your own records.

Fig. 8.1 Bank reconciliation in action

Bank statement

Date	Description	Withdrawals	Deposits	Balance
8-Feb	Opening balance			63,024.50
8-Feb	123012	24.50	–	63,000.00
10-Feb	123033	46,000.00	–	17,000.00
10-Feb	Transfer TF23456	–	5,000.00	22,000.00
11-Feb	123028	500.00	–	21,500.00
11-Feb	123036	7,500.00	–	14,000.00

Bank reconciliation, 12 Feb

Balance from bank statement, 11 Feb	14,000.00
Less cheques not yet presented	
123034	(120.00)
123035	(100.00)
Less deposit not notified	
Client XY	(5,000.00)
Balance from ledger, 11 Feb	8,780.00

Reconciled by: ABC

Checked by: DEF   12-Feb

Ledger : Account 1–1002 Bank account #1

Date	ID	Item	Debits	Credits	Balance
		Balance b/f	–	–	62,500.00
8-Feb	123033	Widgets Internals Inc.	–	46,000.00	16,500.00
9-Feb	123034	Happy Pencils Inc.	–	120.00	16,380.00
10-Feb	123035	GAS Inc	–	100.00	16,280.00
11-Feb	123036	TSI Printing Ltd	–	7,500.00	8,780.00

Controlling cash

Is it realistic to suppose that every business payment will go through the bank account? What if you need to run out and buy some coffee or duplicate a few pages at a copy bureau? Well, there is a rather neat trick which allows you to pass even these tiny transactions through the bank account. The trick is known as the imprest system of accounting for petty cash, named after the old French word for loan. It works as follows.

The first step it to decide how much petty cash you will use between replenishments. A couple of week's worth of spending is usually about right. For the moment, forget about refreshing cash from cash sales and other sources. Such money should be paid into your bank account in its entirety to avoid confusion in the accounts.

Say you want a cash float of up to $100. On the day you start business, you write a cheque for this amount and put the cash in a locking box or drawer. At the end of the week when you empty your shoebox and pass on your transactions, you will credit cash at bank and debit petty cash. This will almost never change, as explained in a moment.

Cheque transaction, 15 Feb

Credit bank account:			
Account	Bank account #1	Date	15-Feb
Payee	Cash	Cheque no.	123056
Description	Establish petty cash float	Amount $	100.00
Charge to:			
Account no.	Account name	Debit $	Credit $
1-1001	Petty Cash	100.00	–

All raids on the petty cash drawer should be supported by a voucher – just as with withdrawals from the bank account. I suggested above that you could be a bit lax with bank vouchers and make up the accounts just once a week. This is not a good practice with cash. Keep a hardback notebook in the cash box and record details of each withdrawal as and when it is made. In fact, if you rule the notebook into columns, use one as a running total, and write the double entry (stationery, groceries, sundries, etc.) in one of the other columns, you are almost there.

> 'Numerical precision is the very soul of science.'
> **Sir D'Arcy Wentworth Thompson**

Petty cash book

Date	ID	Details	Post	Office	Tea	Other	Total	Balance	
15-Feb	123056	Establish float	–	–	–	+100.00	+100.00	100.00	S
16-Feb	PC001	Stamps	10.00	–	–	–	10.00	90.00	S
17-Feb	PC002	Stationery	–	2.50	–	–	2.50	87.50	S
17-Feb	PC003	Groceries	–	–	2.60	–	2.60	84.90	S
19-Feb	PC004	Stamps + Env.	15.00	2.50	–	–	17.50	67.40	S
20-Feb		Totals	25.0	5.00	2.60	+100.00	–	67.40	S
							Petty cash reconciled: ABC. 20 Feb		
20-Feb		Balance bf						67.40	
20-Feb	123059	Replenishment	–	–	–	+32.60	+32.60	100.00	S

Signature of checker and date

When the petty cash starts to run low, or on your chosen replenishment dates, you write a cheque to top up the petty cash to the original $100. If you had spent $32.60 since the previous refill, you put $32.60 back in this time. In this case you would rule off your notebook under the $32.60 worth of spending, start again in the notebook at $100, and post $32.60 worth of vouchers against the bank transaction as follows:

Cheque transaction, 20 Feb

Credit bank account:			
Account	Bank account #1	**Date**	20-Feb
Payee	Cash	**Cheque no.**	123059
Description	Replenish petty cash	**Amount $**	32.60

Charge to:			
Account no.	**Account name**	**Debit $**	**Credit $**
6–3503	Postage	25.00	–
6–4006	Office Stationery	5.00	–
6–4020	Office Sundries	2.60	–
	Totals	**32.60**	–

Your books will carry an asset account called *petty cash* with a debit balance of $100 almost for ever more, and all the petty cash spending is recorded against bank transactions. I think this is pretty neat. If you are going to admire bean counters for getting some things right, this is one of them.

Ten rules for managing cash

As soon as financial responsibilities are delegated, there is an increased risk of sticky fingers in the pie. You should be especially aware of ways that corporate funds might be abused.

1 Never permit alterations to a cheque. If you have signed against an alteration to the payee or amount, the cheque can be changed again.

2 Do not paint. This is the practice of inking over a figure that is badly written – painting provides an opportunity for further errors.

3 Cross cheques and mark them *account payee* to ensure that they go through the bank account of the payee.

4 Have all vouchers and cheques typewritten if possible to avoid misinterpretation.

5 Insist that all payments over, say, $25 are made by cheque – devious accounting staff have been known to make short-term use of company funds for a few weeks, between withdrawing money from the corporate bank account and paying suppliers in cash.

6 Review all contracts and agreements before signing cheques – it is not unknown for annual payments to be destined for your clerk's pocket initially, before being disbursed to suppliers in 12 monthly payments.

7 Maintain an approved list of suppliers; try to ensure that discounts destined for your company are not going into your purchasing clerk's retirement fund.

8 Watch that irregular payments to staff such as overtime and meal allowances reach the right people.

9 Do not permit payments to staff, especially travel expenses, to be paid from petty cash.

10 Pay as little as possible from petty cash – there will still be plenty of vouchers and it will be easy for irregular payments to slip through.

Managing expenses claims

One common problem area seems to be managing expenditure by employees. The matter comes under control relatively easily with proper procedures in place. Essentially, for each member of staff, decide whether they should have discretionary power to spend money on the company's behalf. If so, allocate limits on the amount of expenditure that they can authorize for each category of outlays. For example, a supervisor might have authority to spend up to $50 a month on stationery. A junior manager might be permitted to approve overtime within a certain ceiling. A senior manager may have power to undertake capital spending. And so on. Corporations often do this by department and job grade, although, as with any rules, it may be necessary to make sensible exceptions. The limits should preferably apply so long as overall spending is with certain pre-approved budgetary limits. This is discussed in Chapter 22.

Travel, accommodation and entertainment are always trouble spots – for both the manager and the spending employee. Individuals travelling on business are usually required to track spending, maybe convert it into the home currency, and list it by category and date to show that each day's spending in each category is within their authority. With the added complications of dealing with jet lag, tight and changing schedules, alien cultures, and spending on incidentals for which no receipt is issued, the traveller often loses track of all company outlays. Hands up all managers who have paid legitimate business expenses out of their own pockets and forgotten to claim it back.

For the traveller, the solution is to exercise self-discipline and write up notes at the end of each day. When abroad with a notebook computer or handheld organizer, the obvious trick is to maintain a spreadsheet with an extra couple of columns which facilitate currency conversions. Failing this, you may be able to visit an Internet café and keep notes on a password-protected area of a website – or send them to yourself by email. For the company, it may make sense to pay *per diems* – specific daily cash allowances, no questions asked, which dispense with the need for detailed expenses claims and sheaves of receipts. Either way, and especially for corporate entertainment, employees should at least be asked to sign an undertaking confirming that the spending was not lavish, was on company business and was in relation to an identified sale, client or project.

▶ Preventing bad debts

Not being able to pay the bills is a common killer. As we will discuss, it is possible to be making a profit and suffering a cash flow crisis at the same time. Accordingly, it is always important to try to bring in payments from customers as soon as possible after issuing invoices. For large credit sales, you may want to consult a credit agency before finalizing the sale, to see if the customer has a record of bad debts. You might also take an advance payment which covers a large part of your costs, so that you are risking mainly your profit. Offering discounts for early payment can be a strong incentive for clients to part with their cash, as discussed in Chapter 6. Charging interest on overdue accounts also helps bring tardy clients into line – but make sure that you charge interest in arrears or you might actually stall payment for an extra month. Beyond this, manage customer relations carefully and follow up promptly on *past due* accounts.

At regular intervals, say once a month, examine all outstanding accounts to see how overdue they are. The layout of the report you want to consider should look similar to the following *aging report*, except that there will be at least one line for each customer. Obviously, particular warning signs are clients with more than one past due account, and accounts which are very old. Also, keep your eye on accounts which are overdue because of undelivered goods, warranty claims, and disputes – they often give you warning signs about your own people.

A simple aging report

Accounts receivable						
				Past Due		
	Total	**Not past due**	**1–30 days**	**31–60 days**	**61–90 days**	**Over 90 days**
Total	150,000	120,000	15,000	5,000	–	10,000

No matter how careful you are in selecting clients and managing relationships, some debts always go bad. This is such a common problem that accounting for it is built into the beanie culture. Long before debts are finally *written off*, you will recognize that some may not be collectible. For example, if you conclude that that the $10,000 that is more than 90 days past due may never be paid, you would pass a bookkeeping entry as follows:

Bookkeeping transaction – allowance for bad debts, 31 Dec			
Account no.	**Account**	**Debit $**	**Credit $**
9–5045	Bad debts (Expense account)	10,000.00	–
1–1015	Accounts receivables contra	–	10,000.00

This has charged $10,000 against income, reducing net profit by $10,000. It has also credited an asset account *allowance for bad debts*. Recall that asset accounts usually have debit balance. The *allowance* is a *contra account*, meaning that it has the opposite balance to what you would normally expect. As a result, your net total of accounts receivable may be as follows:

Accounts receivable	$150,000
Less allowance for bad debts	10,000
Net accounts receivable	140,000

When you examine an aging report for the nth time and the same debt is still outstanding, you might finally make a management judgement that you should write it off. As painful as this is, you will have to credit *accounts receivable* and debit the *allowance for bad debts*, to wipe out the $10,000 asset. You do not have to charge an expense account because you did that when you recognized that the debt would probably not be paid.

However, if you were lucky and the account was paid, you would reverse the bookkeeping entry shown above and then debit cash and credit accounts receivable as normal.

Sometimes you can identify doubtful debts individually as described above. Once you have been in business for long enough, you will be able to say on the basis of past experience that, say, 2.5% of sales will turn into bad debts, or 1% of 1–30 days past due and 1.5% of receivables that are more than 30 days overdue. If you do not have a sufficient track record, you could examine the accounts of similar businesses (see Chapter 17) and estimate a percentage based on their experience. Your goal, of course, is to reduce the percentage as much as possible with effective credit management.

▶ Managing cash flow

Accounting systems are backward. That is, they are concerned primarily with what has already happened. Moreover, they do not build up cash reserves to meet commitments or warn you when you are about to experience a liquidity crisis (run out of cash). Accordingly, you have to make your own arrangements. This is not too hard. When you run through the process of planning and budgeting discussed in the following few chapters, you identify all your major commitments and you know what is coming.

Right now, since we are discussing the nitty-gritty of making payments, take a look at the following list of expected receipts and payments. It appears to project that the bank balance will remain healthy. However, if the client is a week late in paying, and goodness me this has been known to happen, the bank account will be $1,000 overdrawn within a few days. If possible, it would be prudent to defer the big payment to the supplier until the client's funds are safely in your possession. If the payments cannot be juggled, and the sales are late, you need to be ready to transfer from another account or make some other funding arrangements.

Cash flow projection for the week commencing 12 February

Date	Description	Receipts	Payments	Balance
Mon	Bank balance bf			84,000
	Supplier – AB		64,000	20,000
	Mobile phone bill		100	19,900
	Telephone bill		135	19,765
	Sales – Client BC	32,000		51,765
Tue	Wages		450	51,315
	Printing		5,500	45,815
Wed	Payroll taxes		130	45,685
	Social security		35	45,650
Thu	Courier		650	45,000
Fri	Supplier – CD		14,000	31,000
	Totals	**32,000**	**85,000**	

One question has to be asked. Does this schedule show the dates when you will write and receive cheques and authorize electronic payments – or the dates when they will hit the bank account? For cash flow management, you need to work with the dates when the transactions will actually be posted to the account by your bank. When your cheque is in the post, it hasn't been deducted from your bank balance.

A bank balance is not always what it seems. If the cash flow projection above was a bank statement, the **closing balance** on Monday was $51,765. Quite possibly, the **cleared balance** was $32,000 less, at $19,765, because until the remitter's bank has confirmed the validity of the transaction your bank will not let you spend the money. Payments are increasingly cleared instantly, or within 24 hours – but traditional cheque-clearing systems take 3–4 days, and cheques drawn on overseas banks can take 45 days or more to clear. If you have an overdraft limit, or some commitment to maintain a certain minimum balance, the **available balance** would be different again. For example, if the payment was not cleared, but you had a $10,000 borrowing limit, your **available balance** would be $29,765.

Cash versus accruals accounting

If you record all your transactions on the date that you write your cheques, you are operating a cash accounting system. An example is when you pay your office rental costs for a year in advance and record it all in your *office rents* account when the cheque is processed.

For management purposes, it is more instructive to charge one-twelfth of the total to rents each month during the year. You can then see more accurately what your costs and revenues were in any one month. In this example, when the payment is made you credit *bank* and debit the asset account *prepaid rents*. Then, each month for 12 months, you credit *prepaid rents* and debit the expense account *office rents*. The first step is to record the actual payment:

Cheque transaction, 3 Jan

Credit bank account:			
Account	Bank account #1	**Date**	3-Jan
Payee	Prime Real Estate Inc.	**Cheque no.**	123009
Description	Rent for 12 months	**Amount $**	36,000.00
Charge to:			
Account no.	**Account name**	**Debit $**	**Credit $**
1-1405	Prepaid rents	36,000.00	–

Then at the end of each month you can record the transaction that relates to that month:

Bookkeeping transaction, 31 Jan

Account no.	Account	Debit $	Credit $
6-3003	Office rents	3,000.00	–
1-1405	Prepaid rents	–	3,000.00

Bookkeeping transaction, 28 Feb

Account no.	Account	Debit $	Credit $
6-3003	Office rents	3,000.00	–
1-1405	Prepaid rents	–	3,000.00

... repeat every month March until November, and then ...

Bookkeeping transaction, 31 Dec

Account no.	Account	Debit $	Credit $
6-3003	Office rents	3,000.00	–
1-1405	Prepaid rents	–	3,000.00

If there had been no other transactions, at the end of the year the balance on pre-paid rents would be zero, the charges to office rents would be $36,000, and the bank balance would be $36,000 lower.

Similarly, if you know you have to make a payment in the future you can post an accruals adjustment. For example, if you receive a delivery of components with a generous three months to pay, you should immediately debit the account that records inventory of components and credit a liability account such as *accounts payable*.

Bookkeeping transaction, 10 Jan

Account no.	Account	Debit $	Credit $
1-1205	Inventory – widget components	46,000	–
2-1008	Accounts payable – widgets	–	46,000

Then when you make the payment, you credit *bank* and debit *accounts payable*.

Cheque transaction, 8 Feb				
Credit bank account:				
Account	Bank account #1	**Date**	8-Feb	
Payee	Widgets Internals Ltd	**Cheque no.**	123033	
Description	Cogs and sprockets	**Amount $**	46,000.00	
Charge to:				
Account no.	**Account name**	**Debit $**	**Credit $**	
2-1008	Accounts payable	46,000.00	–	

If there had been no other transactions, the balance on accounts payable would have returned to zero, the inventory account would show a balance of $46,000, and the bank balance would have reduced by the same amount.

This system of handling prepayments and accruals is known as *accruals accounting*. As far as possible, it *matches* payments and receipts to each other and to the most appropriate period. A market stallholder might use cash accounting. But nearly all corporate accounts are prepared using the accruals method. The naming is an excellent example of the beanie pessimism factor at work. It could just as easily have been called prepayments accounting, but it is knowing that you have to meet those accrued expenses that keeps your accountant awake at nights. Note that this is all bookkeeping. There is no attempt to build a cash reserve to help you make the actual payments. You have to plan your cash flow separately, as discussed above, and again later.

As well as prepayments and accruals, there are a few other accounting niceties involved in accruals accounting; notably, valuing and depreciating assets over their useful life (see Chapter 11) and valuing inventory (see Chapter 13).

▶ Is it material?

Clearly, you would not bother to treat spending on a pencil as a prepayment in order to show the expenditure in the accounts against the months in which you ground down the lead. The test should be *is it material?* If a transaction has an important effect on management or financial accounts, then accruals accounting should be used to the full. Otherwise, for insignificant payments and receipts, it is not worth anyone's time to try to make these adjustments. The same test of materiality applies throughout, as we shall see, to capital spending, budget and cost allocations, and so on.

Debts and taxation

An excellent example of beanie pessimism is the recording of trade debts and taxation. Accounts receivable are shown before tax because, after all, the tax is not actually owing to you. You are merely acting as an unpaid tax collector for the government. On the other hand, taxes are included in accounts payable so that they more accurately represent the amount of folding stuff that you will have to part with sooner or later.

Ten hard questions to ask or be asked

1 Are finance-related responsibilities properly separated and managed? (See *Ten hard questions* 1 and 2 from the previous chapter – I make no apology for repeating this requirement.)

2 Do you have sensible and well-documented rules controlling expenditure?

3 Do you use the imprest system for petty cash? Is it properly managed?

4 Are your bank accounts properly reconciled at appropriate intervals?

5 What were the cleared and effective balances on your bank accounts at 9 a.m. this morning?

6 Do you have an approved list of suppliers?

7 How often do you review the accounts receivable aging report?

8 Are there any overdue accounts which should be chased or handed to debt collection agencies?

9 How often is your cash flow projection updated? Is it used effectively?

10 If you are not using accruals accounting, why not?

What's next?

This chapter has looked at some crucial concepts in managing money. We will return to the bigger picture of cash management in the later chapters. For now, perhaps we are getting ahead of ourselves. In the next couple of chapters I want to look at how you forecast sales. Sales after all, are the key to cash flow. You will need to take off your beanie hat and fire up your spreadsheets again. Keep your feet planted in your management shoes, though, because you still need to apply judgement and common sense.

> 'Creditor, n. One of a tribe of savages dwelling beyond the Financial Straits and dreaded for their desolating incursions.'
>
> **Ambrose Bierce**

tracking trends

'I believe we are on an irreversible trend toward more freedom and democracy – but that could change.'

Dan Quayle

Chapter survival toolkit

▶ Overview

This chapter focuses on analysing trends – such as the path of monthly sales or quarterly production. This is perhaps the core of the book with regard to understanding the numbers. With the advent of spreadsheets this analysis is remarkably easy to do, and very instructive. It gives you a good feel for what is happening to your business.

It also helps you find relationships between your figures and other indicators. For example, you will be very much on top of your business if you can develop rules of thumb such as 'a 10% increase in spending on advertising boosts sales by 2% after two months' or 'our sales continue rising and peak eight months after the economy starts to enter recession'. For probably obvious reasons, this chapter is also essential reading before the next chapter, *How to forecast anything*. Later, in Chapter 22, we return to trends, but this time from the perspective of measuring them relative to the expected levels.

As you can probably infer, we are about to delve into the folds of spreadsheets again. I hope that you will try out the techniques on your PC as we work through the chapter together.

▶ Prerequisites

A basic familiarity with spreadsheets as covered in Chapter 4.

▶ Mastering trends

If you can cope with the following steps, you can analyse any trends:

1 Collect monthly sales figures for several years.
2 Identify blips cased by one-off special factors such as sales promotions.
3 Isolate the trend.
4 Look for a cyclical pattern.
5 Search for seasonality.
6 Recombine the patterns that you have identified and see how well they match the original sales figures.
7 If there is too much residual noise, work through the numbers again.
8 Now examine each pattern in turn and try to deduce what caused it.
9 Look for relationships with other indicators, internal (advertising, sales promotions) and external (activities by other companies, trends in the economy as a whole).
10 Based on the above, develop rules of thumb that help you understand *what if* ... for example, if you cut prices, if you increase advertising, if your competitors cut prices, if interest rates rise, etc.

> ► **Jargon watch**
>
> **Stats-speak**
>
> Cross-sectional data
> Time series, trend, cycle
> Residual noise
> Line of best fit
> Intercept
> r-squared
> Moving average
>
> **Economics-speak**
>
> Value, volume
> Seasonality
> Product life cycle
> Business cycle
> Leading indicator
>
> **Beanie-speak**
>
> Vertical analysis, horizontal analysis
> Ratio analysis

> 'Facts are stubborn, but statistics are more pliable.'
>
> **Mark Twain**

► Why analyse trends?

As an entrepreneur or manager, you are probably intensely concerned with ensuring that sales continue to rise year after year, or at worst stay steady; that inventory levels do not become too high or too low; that production is managed to keep pace with demand; or that some other indicators change in the right direction. If you are the chief executive you will be worried about all of these and more.

There are some handy tricks which help you analyse and manage trends. The techniques are definitely not onerous and they can be delightfully revealing. It is well worth spending a few minutes becoming familiar with them. Essentially, you are doing nothing more strenuous than looking for patterns, and it is surprising how well this can help you do your job.

There is the added benefit that once you have a feel for what has happened already, you are more than halfway to a decent forecast of what might happen in the future. This chapter, then, leads naturally into the next one: How to forecast anything. Given that business forecasting is usually about forecasting sales, sales are used as the examples here. You can, of course, apply the same techniques to any time series.

> 'Always draw your curves, then plot your reading.'
>
> **Anon.**

> ## ▶▶ Snapshots and time series
>
> In this chapter we are concerned with analysing trends over a period of time. This is known as **time series analysis** by mathematicians and statisticians and as **horizontal analysis** by bean counters. It is different from analysis of **cross-sectional** data, which is a snapshot on a given date – such as sales by region in March, or quality control rejects from batch 1306, etc. Our beanie friends call this **vertical analysis** or **ratio analysis**. It is discussed elsewhere, notably in Chapters 5, 18 and 19).

▶ Pursuing patterns

▶ Collecting the data

> **Values and volumes**
>
> Try to work with volumes (quantities) rather than values (costs or prices), to minimize the influence of monetary factors such as inflation and currency fluctuations.

The starting point for analysing your sales record, or any time series, is to collect historical figures for, say, each month or quarter, turn them into a chart, and look for patterns.

It is better to work with volumes (the quantity of widgets) rather than values (sales revenue) because volumes are not distorted so much by inflation, exchange rate movements, price changes and other monetary hiccups. Of course, money does affect volumes (e.g. a short-term price-cutting promotion generally boosts sales volumes). We will come to this later.

Clearly, the longer the run of historical data you can examine, the better the feel you will get for the numbers. A long run of numbers also assists when estimating the average effects of special promotions and seasonal influences.

In addition, a long run of figures helps you see where you are in the product life cycle. All products tend to go through the five stages shown in the Fig. 9.1: development, introduction, growth, maturity and decline. Generally, the objective is to maximize the growth stage and minimize the other phases, but this is a topic for another book. In the context of analysing and forecasting, if you know where you are in the life cycle, you will understand what has been happening, and what is most likely to happen. For example, there must be a very good reason to project a sudden increase in sales when a product is in decline, unless, perhaps, you have just introduced a product enhancement or cut prices.

> ## ▶▶ Products, services and no profit
>
> All the way through this book, the discussions tend to refer to products. This is convenient for descriptive purposes. Do not forget though that the word *product* stands in for product or service – or, in the case of a non-profit organization, a proxy such as admissions, cases, donations, etc.

Fig. 9.1 The product life cycle

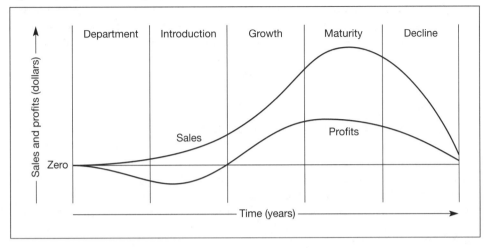

▶ Four patterns

Once you have collected and charted your data, there are three or four patterns you should expect to see (see Fig. 9.2). These are:

◆ an underlying trend;

◆ sometimes a cycle;

◆ usually a seasonal pattern;

◆ frequently, a series of special or one-off influences resulting from events such as price-cutting promotions; and

◆ residual noise that cannot be explained easily.

What to look for in your sales history

1 One-off influences
2 The underlying trend
3 Any cyclical factors
4 Seasonality
5 Residual noise.

If you collected enough figures, the trend would be the product life cycle (trends do not have to be straight lines). However, it is very rare to have enough figures to see anything like the whole life of a product. More often, the trend is just a part of the overall life cycle.

Sometimes you can discern all the patterns in the raw data – although not with any precision. So, you need to carve up the data to find them.

▶ Wielding the knife

How do you carve up your raw data to reveal the underlying patterns? Ideally you first estimate special influences such as the effects of price cuts and new product launches and then adjust the raw data to remove these effects. Then you could use a ruler to identify the trend, although we will look at some neat ways of using a spreadsheet to do this. Next, you can measure the difference between the raw data and the trend to get an indication of the cycle. You can use a smoothed cycle or moving average to estimate seasonality.

All this might sound a bit daunting, but spreadsheets provide some clever methods which make it easy. The sample workbook from this book's website and the following paragraphs walk step-by-step through the process. Figures 9.2 and 9.3 are extracts from the workbook. I recommend using the workbook because the figures are presented in easy steps rather than in one big scary heap. As always, when taken in small bites the analysis becomes very simple.

Step 1: The raw data

Figure 9.3 shows several columns of data. For time series analysis, it is easiest to work with columns rather than rows. In the example, dates are in columns A to C and the raw sales figures are in column D. Normally you can put the dates in just one column, but for the explanatory purposes of this book it was convenient to show the dates in three columns. Figure 9.2 and Chart 1 in the workbook show these sales figures visually. Recall that Chapter 5 explained how to produce charts using a computer.

Fig. 9.2 Four patterns revealed

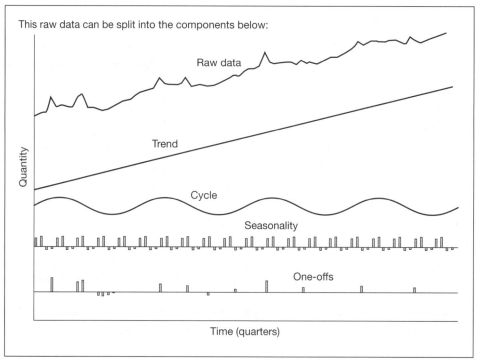

▶ Accounting for special one-off influences

Special one-off influences are distortions that you know about. They include the effects of price cutting promotions and experimental price hikes, the introduction of new lines and new models, sales at special events, and – of course – the effect on your sales of similar tricks by your competitors. In the example, one-offs include a price cutting promotion which boosted sales by 44 units in the first quarter of 2001, and catching up with a competitor's product modification which caused losses of 100 sales spread over the whole of 1986.

If you go back through your files, you may find that much of this is documented. If you ran a special sales promotion a couple of years ago, you probably identified exactly what it did for your sales (yes?). For example, if you expected sales in a previous August to be 550 units, but they were actually 660, you might have concluded that the promotion added 20% to sales. It is easiest to do this estimation at the time, while you are most aware of other influences. Later, you might forget that unusually sunny weather contributed to higher sales, while the promotion itself was not as effective as you told the boss.

Fig. 9.3 Data dismembered

This is an extract from the sample workbook, which steps through the analysis adding one or two columns at a time. Seeing them all at once as here might be a bit daunting.
Note: MA = moving average, SA = seasonal adjustment.

Period number   One-off influences   Sales less one-offs   Smoothed cycle   All Q1, All Q2, etc.

	A	B	C	D	E	F	G	H	I	J	K	L	M
1	Year	Qtr	No.	Sales	One-offs	AdjSales	Trend	Cycle	MA	SA	SA avg	Explained	Noise
62	1998	Q1	61	1152	0	1152	1109	1.039	1.014	1.025	1.025	1152	0
63		Q2	62	1183	0	1183	1119	1.057	1.028	1.028	1.020	1174	9
64		Q3	63	1224	54	1170	1130	1.035	1.050	0.986	0.980	1216	8
65		Q4	64	1181	0	1181	1141	1.035	1.057	0.979	0.974	1175	6
66	1999	Q1	65	1246	0	1246	1152	1.082	1.052	1.028	1.025	1243	3
67		Q2	66	1250	0	1250	1163	1.075	1.048	1.026	1.020	1243	7
68		Q3	67	1213	0	1213	1173	1.034	1.051	0.984	0.980	1209	4
69		Q4	68	1202	0	1202	1184	1.015	1.040	0.976	0.974	1201	1
70	2000	Q1	69	1254	0	1254	1195	1.049	1.021	1.027	1.025	1252	2
71		Q2	70	1240	0	1240	1206	1.028	1.007	1.022	1.020	1238	2
72		Q3	71	1193	0	1193	1217	0.981	1.002	0.978	0.980	1195	−2
73		Q4	72	1178	0	1178	1228	0.960	0.989	0.970	0.974	1183	−5
74	2001	Q1	73	1275	44	1231	1238	0.994	0.973	1.021	1.025	1280	−5
75		Q2	74	1228	0	1228	1249	0.983	0.966	1.017	1.020	1231	−3
76		Q3	75	1197	0	1197	1260	0.950	0.973	0.977	0.980	1201	−4
77		Q4	76	1200	0	1200	1271	0.944	0.971	0.973	0.974	1202	−2
78	2002	Q1	77	1270	0	1270	1282	0.991	0.969	1.023	1.025	1273	−3
79		Q2	78	1275	0	1275	1292	0.987	0.974	1.013	1.020	1285	−10
80		Q3	79	1268	0	1268	1303	0.973			0.980		
81		Q4	80	1283	0	1283	1314	0.976			0.974		

Sample Formulas in row 79:   =D79-E79   =F79/G79   =H79/I79   =D79-L79
                         =(F79*10.81)+449.19   =AVERAGE(H77:H81) =(G79*I79*K79)+E79

Column K is the average of all Q1s, all Q2s, all Q3s and all Q4s repeated every four cells all the way down.

A reusable workbook

You can reuse the sample workbook available on this book's website by keying in your own figures in columns D and E, and changing the dates if necessary. This will work for any quarterly data. For other frequencies (monthly, 4-weekly, etc.) you need to amend columns I and J as well.

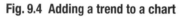

Step 2: Adjusting for one-offs

It is easy to adjust raw sales data for one-off influences. Simply key in your estimates of the effect of one-offs (into column E in the example). In the next column to the right, subtract one-offs from the sales data (e.g. in cell F2 key = D2-E2 then grab the fill handle and copy the formula down the column). The new column of adjusted sales volumes will be smoother than the original – compare Charts 1 and 2 in the sample workbook.

▶ Trends

About trends

The next step is to identify a trend. Sometimes this is easy. You could more or less lay a ruler on the raw data in the examples here and draw in a trend line by eye. If you shade in the areas between the actual sales and the trend, it immediately becomes obvious that when positioning the ruler you are trying to balance sales above and below the trend line (Fig. 9.4) – that is, you are trying to find the *line of best fit*. You can probably guess that there is a way to do this arithmetically. Before we try it, consider a small problem.

Fig. 9.4 Adding a trend to a chart

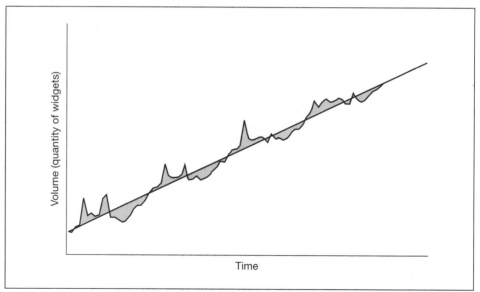

What if the trend is not linear? Recall that sales growing at, say, 10% a year trace an upwardly curved path (Chapter 6, p. 80). No problem. Growth trends can also be fitted using a computer. In fact, all manner of odd-shaped trends can be calculated – but this is rarely necessary. So long as you understand which part of the overall trend you are dealing with, you can generally fit a straight or growth trend to part of the time series. This allows you to get at the other patterns, but take great care if you extrapolate such short-term trends.

Step 3: Fitting a trend to a chart

At one time, fitting a trend demanded nightmare calculations. These days you do not even need to know the maths. You can simply plug the numbers into a spread-sheet, click a button, and view the results. Try the following, it will amaze you.

1 In the sample workbook, view Chart 2.
2 Right-click on the wiggly sales line on the chart and a pop-up menu will appear.
3 From this pop-up menu, select *Add Trendline* and a dialog box will appear.
4 Click OK.

The dialog box will close and the chart will miraculously contain a trend line, as in Fig. 9.5.

Fig. 9.5 Fitting a trend to a chart

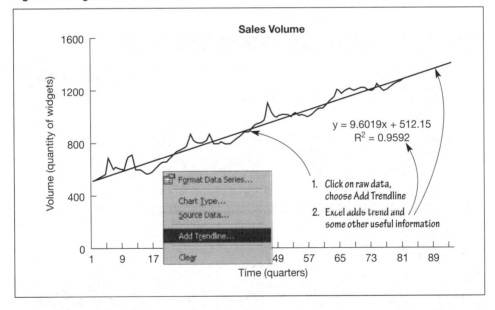

Trendline options

You probably noticed that the *Add Trendline* dialog box has some intriguing options (see Fig. 9.6). You can select these options before you draw a trend line.

Or afterwards you can right-click exactly on the trend, select *Format Trendline* and reselect from these options. They are discussed next.

Type. You can click on a little sketch to indicate the type of trend that you are looking for. You will find that for most business analysis you tend to work with linear and logarithmic trends and moving averages. More on this as we go along.

Options. The Options tab includes some very tempting stuff, as follows:

◆ *Trendline name* allows you to label the trend. OK, not an exciting start I grant you.

◆ *Forecast* is self-explanatory. It really does do what it says, but resist the temptation to throw down this book, click the option, and start writing up your sales forecast. There is more to come.

◆ *Intercept* can be ignored. The intercept is the sales volume on day zero – logically you would expect this to be nil, but it is unlikely to be so because of the way that the sales periods are numbered and various other gremlins. Leave this option unchecked and let the spreadsheet create a workable trend.

◆ *Display equation on chart* is self-explanatory in intent and important for analysis.

◆ *Display R-squared value on chart* is also very important.

Both these *Display* options are discussed in more detail below. For your own analysis, you will normally want to have these two options switched on. If you are presenting the figures to others, you may want to omit them.

Fig. 9.6 MS Excel's *Add Trendline* dialog

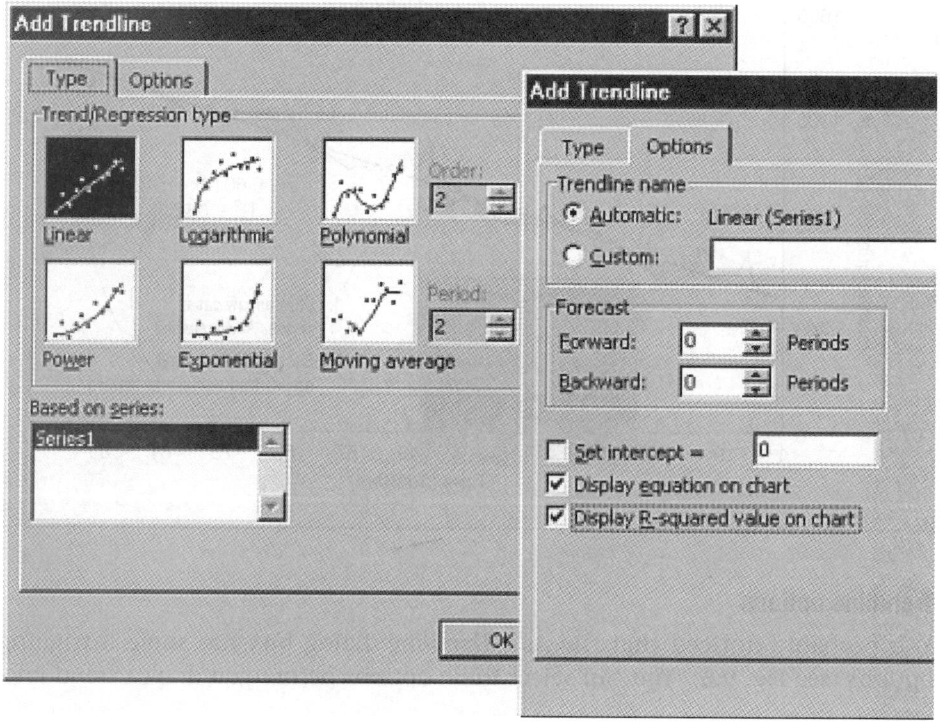

Estimating sales

The *Add Trendline* option that allows you to *Display equation on chart* (Fig. 9.6) does just what it says; it reveals the equation of the estimated trend line. It is important to know this. It allows you to calculate the value of the trend on any date. In other words, you could – but you won't yet – use it to put a number on sales for next year. The equation that the spreadsheet generates in the example here is (don't shudder):

$$y = 10.81x + 449.19$$

The computer is not bright enough to know that we are working with dates and sales values, so it replaces them with the shorthand notations x and y respectively. The equation says simply that if you multiply any date (x) by 10.81 and then add 449.19 you will find the trend of sales volume (y) on that date.

How do you multiply a date such as January? You cannot. But you can replace the dates with any sequence of numbers that is convenient. In the example, the dates are replaced with numbers 1 to 80, where 1 is the three-month period January–March 1983, 2 is April–June 1983, and so on through to 80 which represents October–December 2002.

In other words, for period 10, April–June 1985, the trend value for sales is 10.81 times 10 plus 449, or 557 widgets. For period 85, the first quarter of 2004, the trend predicts (and I use that word loosely) that sales will be 10.81 times 85 plus 449, or 1368 widgets.

There is a trend line, but is there a trend?

Suppose you flicked a wet paintbrush on a chart and produced an evenly splattered pattern of dots. If you then chose *Add Trendline*, your spreadsheet would obligingly draw in a line for you. However, it would not be very meaningful. Clearly, you need some measure of how well a trend line fits the data. This is exactly what the *Display R-squared value* option does.

R-squared (R^2) tells you how much you can trust the fitted line. It is a proportion. Multiply it by 100 to convert it to a more-understandable percentage. The r^2 in these examples (see Fig. 9.5) is 0.9792, or 97.92%. This is a good result which indicates that you that you can be about 98% confident that the trend line is a good fit. Generally, you can live with a value in the nineties. Anything less than about 90% calls the value of the trend line into doubt. Always examine r-squared when you fit a trend. By the way, statisticians call this the *coefficient of determination*; or r^2 with a lowercase r (but no one told Microsoft).

Step 4: Adding a trend to your data

Drawing a trend on a chart is visually informative, but it does not give you any numbers to work with. The easiest way to get at them is to enter the equation (see Figs 9.5 and 9.6) in the spreadsheet. In the example, you would key =(C2*10.81)+449.19 into cell G2 and then copy it down the column – and there is the trend line in numbers.

> **Advanced idea**
>
> Spreadsheets provide several approaches to fitting trends. I favour the graphical method described above because it is informative and easy. For simple trends you could bypass the chart, as follows, although you do not get a value for r-squared: In the Step 2 spreadsheet where column G is empty, select the data in column F, right-click and choose *copy*. Click on cell G2, right-click and choose *paste special*, *values*. Now select all of the data in column G (plus a few forecast periods if you wish) and choose *Edit, Fill, Series* then click *columns*, *linear*, *trend* and OK.
>
> You can also use the *trend* and *growth* functions (rendered unnecessary with the techniques described here) and the *LINEST* and *LOGEST* functions which provide additional information. If you are feeling brave, see the spreadsheet's *Help* file for more information.

▶ About the business cycle

The ideas of a trend, seasonality and special influences should be self-explanatory. The cycle is a persistent but less well-known external economic phenomenon.

Economies do not progress smoothly. They tend to follow a rhythmic path (depression, recession, recovery, boom), known as the economic, business or trade cycle. This typically repeats every five years or so, but the timing and   magnitude always vary. Think of it this way. When the economy is booming, firms will take on new employees and produce more. The employees spend their salaries and wages, creating more demand. Eventually bottlenecks and supply constraints such as labour shortages set in, limiting output. New investment will not be profitable or feasible. Economic growth (i.e. GDP or GNP) will peak. With less demand for investment goods, construction firms, machine tool producers and other capital goods manufacturers will cut back their labour forces. As a result, total consumer demand will fall and eventually recession will set in. And so on.

The cycle is perhaps more pronounced in the more-mature economies of the West, because less developed countries usually have much larger pools of unused resources on which to draw. However, no matter what your politicians may tell you, no government has succeeded in abolishing the business cycle. The truth of the matter is that their well-meaning tinkering usually contributes to it.

Leading indicators

Look for published leading indicators which try to predict turning points in the economy as much as 18 months in advance. Sounds useful? One caveat, interpret them with care because they are often revised as new information comes to hand.

Seeing cycles

If you can take a long enough run of data and isolate all other factors, you will almost certainly see a cycle in your sales figures. Ideally you want at least 10 years of monthly or quarterly data in order to find a couple of complete cycles. The problem is that you rarely have sales figures covering enough time periods to reach any viable conclusion. More often than not, you have to review the cycle at the national economic level, and make a sensible judgement about how this affects you.

A good newspaper will keep you informed (what better than the *Financial Times?*). If you want to go back to source, cyclical indicators are published by national governments, the OECD, and employers' organizations such as the Confederation of British Industry (CBI) or the German IFO labour institute.

Step 5: Isolating a cycle

When you search for a cycle in your sales figures, do so by removing the trend from the raw data and then smoothing the result. In the example, divide the adjusted sales figures by the trend (e.g., into cell H2 key =F2/G2 and copy this down the column). The values might look a bit odd. They are proportions. A number such as 1.051 indicates that the adjusted sales are 5.1% above the trend, while 0.98 indicates 2% below the trend. If you were to view this new column as a chart (chart 4 in the sample workbook) you would see the cycle, even though it's a bit lumpy. What you want to do now is smooth off the lumps and bumps with a moving average: in cell I4, key =AVERAGE(H2:H5) and copy this down to cell I79.

Moving averages

A moving average is just like any other average, but one applied to a time series. For example, a three-month moving average for February would be the figures for January, February and March added together and then divided by three. The moving average for March would be February to April's figures averaged, and so on. There is one important point to note about moving averages. Always use an odd number of periods and centre the average against the source data. This is why the first formula in the example went into cell I4, not I2.

This example uses an arbitrary five-period moving average. Really, using a multiple of four quarters would make better sense (each quarter would be included the same number of times) but an even number of periods cannot be centred. Also, the result is not ultra-smooth. But we can live with this – it works well enough to get useful results. (See Fig. 9.2 or Chart 4 in the workbook.)

Excel error

You should be aware that Excel will draw moving averages automatically, but it does not centre them properly. A useful exercise is to right-click on the unsmoothed series in Chart 4 of the sample workbook, and choose Add trendline, moving average. You will see clearly that the moving average curve which is added to the chart has the turning points in the wrong places. Nevertheless, experiment by changing the number of periods to see how moving averages over a greater number of periods give a smoother series, but with more data missing at the ends.

Using the cycle

There are three things to know about the business cycle. First, understand where you are in the cycle. You may not want to forecast continuing rapid growth in sales if the economy is starting to plunge into recession.

Second, determine the extent to which demand for your products and services is cyclical. You know the sort of thing: when times are tough businesses cut back on advertising expenditure and consumers spend less on luxury goods, but demand for staple foodstuffs will remain steady or may even rise as it displaces more costly gourmet trifles. How cyclical is the demand for your goods and services? Isolate the cycle as described below to find out.

Third, discern the extent to which you are in step with the cycle. For example, housing starts, companies' financial surpluses and share prices tend to peak up to 16 months ahead of the overall cycle. Consumer credit, car sales and manufacturing orders reach their zenith about six months ahead. Retail sales lead by about three months. On the other hand, job vacancies and average earnings tend to lag the cycle by three or four months. Interestingly, investment, order backlogs and inventories peak about a year after the overall cycle. Note that this is investment in the economic sense – spending money on factories, machinery and other assets with a life of more than a year. We discuss this in Chapter 11. Buying stocks and shares, which you and I often refer to as investment, is called *saving* by economists. Back to the point – draw your cycle on the same chart as the national business cycle and compare the timing of the two. This book's website has links to useful sources of economic data.

> The foregoing highlights the value of trying to discern cyclical patterns in your investment spending, order books and inventories. For example, if you find that you have tended to build unnecessary inventory in the months after a peak in economic activity, you can watch for the turn and reduce production sooner than usual. It is a tough call, and you will be actively contributing to the cycle, but you might find that you can manage your business more effectively when you track the cycle.

▶ Seeing seasonality

Seasonal factors affect a perhaps surprising range of goods and services. Obvious examples are sales of summer and winter clothing and sports goods, supplies to factories which shut for an annual holiday, travel bookings and greetings cards for annual festivals. You probably have a good feeling for the seasonality of your business already. Numerically, it is quite easy to estimate.

Step 6: Calculating seasonality

Possibly you have guessed that the lumps in the unsmoothed cycle are indicative of the seasonal pattern. To identify the seasonal factors, simply divide the unsmoothed by the smoothed cycle (e.g. in cell J4, key =H4/I4 and copy down). As with the cyclical indicator, the numbers are proportions.

For forecasting, you will find it useful to know the average seasonal adjustment factor for each month or quarter for the past few years. For January's seasonal adjustment factor, find the average of the January figures; for February's, take the average of the February figures and so on. This is simple arithmetic. The obvious, if tedious, way of doing it is to key in a formula such as this one which goes in cell

K2: =AVERAGE(J6,J10,J14,J18,J22,J26,J30,J34,J38,J42,J46,J50,J54,J58,J62,J66,J70,J74,J78). You need to do this only for the first four quarters. By cell K6, you can use =K2, which you can just copy down the column. Inspect the sample worksheet to see this in action.

Quick and dirty seasonality

Assume for the moment that you had no special promotions or other one-off influences last year. You can calculate the seasonal pattern for your monthly sales figures totals as follows.

1 Find the average monthly sales for the year (i.e. total annual sales divided by 12).

2 Now calculate each month's actual sales as a percentage of the average.

This is all. The percentages imply the seasonal pattern. For example, suppose February's sales were 10% below average and August's were 10% above average. If you are forecasting this year's sales at 500 widgets a month on average, you would expect to sell 450 in February and 550 in August. Sorry if we getting ahead of ourselves. We will come on to forecasting in a moment.

By the way, you can usually improve on this quick approach by using a linear trend or a moving average for each month in place of the simple average. Moreover, do remember that seasonal factors for just one year may not be typical of the underlying seasonality.

Timing of seasonal influences

There is a small problem with seasonality, which relates to the way that data is collected and compartmentalized. The influences on seasonality, including the weather and religious festivals, do not fall conveniently into step with the quirks in our calendars. Easter, the Chinese New Year and Muslim Eid are on different dates each year when marked in a Gregorian (Western) diary. February has an extra day every four years on the same calendar.

The bottom line is that you have to exercise a good dose of management judgement when calculating seasonality – as you do with all analysis. Do not accept the numbers that come straight off the spreadsheet. Question them and if necessary adjust them subjectively.

▶ Pulling it all together again

Step 7: Putting Humpty back together

The final step in analysing the patterns is to glue them back together and see if you end up with the raw data you started with. To do this, multiply together the trend, smoothed cycle and average seasonal adjustment factors, and add in special one-offs – in the example, in cell L4 key =(G4*I4*K4)+E4 and copy it down the column. If you estimate one-offs as proportionate influences on sales, which you might do particularly for forecast periods, you would multiply everything (eg, =G4*I4*K4*E4). The resultant figures in column L should be very similar to the originals in column D – but see *Noise*, below.

Noise

Note that when you reassemble your patterns, they will not recreate perfectly the original series. You will be left with some random values – noise – which cannot be readily explained (column M in the example, which is column D less column L). Time series analysis is not a perfect science. The best you can do is try to minimize the noise. It can alert you to one-offs and other factors which you have not identified fully, sometimes leading you to work though the numbers a second time and improve the analysis. (Chart 6 in the workbook compares the original and the rebuilt series and shows that our analysis is fairly accurate.)

Coffee time

We ran through the analysis looking at both the methods and the rationale for each pattern-hunting expedition. Now that you have dismembered and rebuilt the time series, it is a good time to sit back and look at what you have learned. Examine each pattern in turn, asking yourself what caused it and what it tells you. By now, you probably have a strong desire to project these patterns forward and produce a forecast. There is one more idea to review in this Chapter and then, I promise, we will get down to forecasting.

▶ Cause and effect

The foregoing discussion about patterns touched on cause and effect. During your analysis of special one-off influences, you probably hit on some relationships that you can use to good effect in the future. Try to find rules of thumb, preferably with timing built-in, such as 'a 10% increase in advertising in month one leads to a 2% increase in sales spread over months two and three', or 'a 5% cut in prices boosts sales by 10%'.

In addition, when you reviewed the cycle, you possibly found that events in the economy as a whole fed through to your bottom line in some predictable manner. With a bit of careful thought, you might identify all manner of relationships between your sales and published figures. Again, try to quantify the relationships in terms such as 'a 1% rise in consumer expenditure leads to a 5% increase in our sales commencing four quarters later'.

> **Turning points**
>
> You often have to make bold assumptions and guesses in order to arrive at workable rules of thumb. Sometimes, knowing about the turning points is almost as useful. If interest rates stop falling and start rising, or the dollar takes a dive, it might signify that you should run for an umbrella.

▶ Measuring relationships

If you have enough data, is it relatively easy to test these rule-of-thumb relationships and quantify their effectiveness. When we fitted a trend line we were looking for a relationship between sales and the passage of time. Spreadsheets also allow you to test the relationship between two or more time series. For example, suppose you manage a construction company and you notice that when interest rates fall your sales start to rise a few months later. Let me show you how to quantify this relationship and interpret the results.

▶ Ten hard questions to ask or be asked

1 Why does the trend slope the way it does? Is it really representative of what is happening?

2 Why can we/can't we see a cycle in our data?

3 What are the underlying causes of the cycle in our figures?

4 Are the seasonal adjustment factors correct?

5 Why is there such a big seasonal effect in this month?

6 Is there too much residual noise?

7 How reliable are these cause-and-effect rules of thumb?

8 Is this rule of thumb a genuine relationship, or a complete coincidence?

9 Have we thought about all the external influences which we might quantify?

10 Is there some external influence on our business that we have not identified?

Quantifying relationships

For this example using interest rates, open a new spreadsheet and into one column paste or key your monthly sales over several years and in the next column enter interest rates for the same periods. Average interest rates would be better, but if they are not available, rates on a given date each month are OK. It is better to remove extraneous factors, and use the cyclical component in your sales – or at least a series that has had one-offs and seasonal factors removed (sales less one-offs, multiplied by the seasonal adjustment factor).

> **Wide-ranging relationships**
>
> If you are really keen, you can have several columns of x values – interest rates, consumer spending, etc. and look for relationships between them all and your sales. Expand your selection for the results (E7 to F11 in the example here) to accommodate the extra returned values.

You also want to get the turning points side by side. If you think that the time lag between a change in rates and a blip in your sales is three months, you should select all the interest rates and move (drag) the selection back three rows. This way, changes in interest rates will be next to the change in your sales. You can inspect the effectiveness of this by quickly drawing a chart to see if the turning points match.

Then you would choose a group of cells in an empty area of the spreadsheet – say, E7 to F11 – and from the menu select *Insert, Function, Linest*. In the dialog that appears, you select the sales figures as the y values, interest rates as the x values, and then type in *true* for both *constant* and *stats*. Then, and this is where it is easy to go wrong, you do not press *OK*, but instead you press *Ctrl-Shift-Enter* (who dreamed up that one?). This covers the spreadsheet work. Now for the interpretation.

Interpreting the results

After entering the function described above, cells E7 to F11 will contain some useful numbers. The first row gives the values for the equation of a line – see *Estimating sales* above. The first entry in the third row is our friend r-squared. It is probable that this figure will be so low that you will not have any confidence in the estimated relationship – remember it should be well above 0.9 (i.e. 90%) to be of value. Regression (the statisticians' name for the analysis we have just done) rarely produces magnificent results in these general business situations. You can try moving the data (e.g. by 2 or 4 months instead of 3) to see if you get a better fit.

The next row down shows some values termed the F statistic and degrees of freedom. These are potentially useful – helping assess whether the any apparent relationship between the two series occurred by chance or not. Unfortunately, if you want to interpret them you will need statistical tables and a *quant* (a person who passes the time doing quantitative analysis with computers). It is much the same with the other numbers returned by the spreadsheet function. However, the simple equation and r-squared are enough to help you decide if the relationship you were looking for is quantifiable. A good test is to use the equation with past values of interest rates, see what sales values were predicted, and compare the equation for *forecast* with last year's sales. Would the predictions have been accurate or too wide of the mark?

Using the results

If in the example above you found a relationship which your judgement told you was worth using, you have to allow for timing differences caused by moving the interest rates series. In other words, with the four-month lag described above,

Fig. 9.7 Quantifying relationships

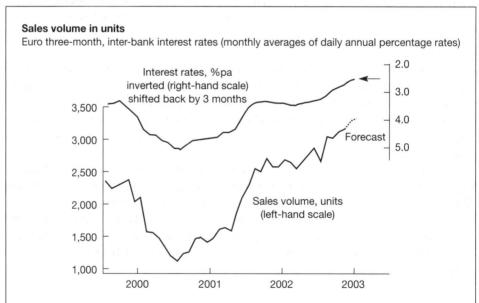

your estimated sales in April would be based on actual interest rates in January. Figure 9.7 illustrates this graphically. The calculations are available for download from this book's website.

Conclusion

The analysis covered in this chapter can help you find out a great deal about your operations, sales, market and industry. The really exciting part comes next when you combine this with your expert knowledge and produce a forecast.

> 'You can use all the quantitative data you can get, but you still have to distrust it and use your own intelligence and judgment.'
>
> **Alvin Toffler**

10

how to forecast anything

'Prediction is very difficult, especially about the future.'

Neils Bohr

▶ Chapter survival toolkit

▶ Overview

The content of this chapter should be self-evident from the title: How to forecast anything. Sales are used as the example, because forecasting anything in business usually boils down to forecasting sales and estimating everything else. The distinction between a forecast and an estimate is important. Also, it is usually easier to forecast in volume terms (quantities) rather than values. Accordingly, this chapter examines forecasting volumes. Subsequent chapters discuss quantities and the important topic of getting from quantities to revenues and net profit.

▶ Prerequisites

Time series analysis, as discussed in the previous chapter, plus a familiarity with spreadsheets as covered in Chapter 4.

▶ Mastering forecasting

If you can follow these steps, you can forecast sales:

1 Collect monthly sales figures for the most recent three years. [1]

2 Identify blips caused by one-off special factors such as sales promotions. [1]

3 Use a spreadsheet to identify a trend. [1]

4 Identify any seasonal pattern. [1,2]

5 Think about the economy, the industry, the market, the company and the products or services and then use judgement to estimate average monthly sales for the year ahead (i.e. project the trend judgementally).

6 Add in the seasonal factors. [2]

7 Add in an allowance for planned promotions and one-offs.

8 Recombine the figures to produce a forecast.

9 Identify cyclical effects. [3]

10 Identify cause-and-effect relationships which add rigour to your forecasting. [3]

Notes

1 The first four steps were covered in the previous chapter.

2 If you are certain there is no seasonal pattern in your sales you can skip steps 4 and 6.

3 If you have more time, you can analyse the patterns more thoroughly and look for the business cycle and cause-and-effect relationships that help add rigour to the forecasts.

> 'We are ready for any unforeseen event that may or may not occur.'
>
> **Dan Quayle**

So you need to forecast sales?

So, you need a sales forecast. How do I know this? Easy. Cooking up a forecast of anything in a business context nearly always boils down to forecasting sales volumes (i.e. quantity rather than value). Once you have this central number, everything else will be estimated, not forecast.

> **The secret**
>
> The secret of successful forecasting is to identify just one variable to forecast (usually sales) and estimate everything else based on that forecast.

For example, when the board of directors asks for a forecast of net income or net profit for next year, they are really asking you to forecast sales and then fit everything else into place around this key number. In a nutshell, once you have arrived at a figure for sales volume, sales values (the cash that changes hands) are a matter of simple arithmetic based on your pricing policies. Moreover, once you have predicted what contracts you will sign or how many units you will sell, you can work out the resources that are needed to make it happen – how many people, how many machines, how much raw material, and so on. You can put a price on these, subtract the total from sales value and there's the bottom line.

It is important to note the subtle difference between a forecast and an estimate. Frankly, forecasting requires a large measure of educated guesswork. Estimation requires only logic and simple arithmetic. The way this works will become clear shortly. When you have identified the one item that you need to forecast, you have cut away most of the guesswork and grey areas and structured your thinking. What is more, by linking all the other estimated numbers to the forecast, you can quickly see what would happen on a less – or more – optimistic scenario by amending the forecast and seeing how the changes ripple through the numbers. This chapter focuses on the forecasting; subsequent chapters cover estimating.

> ## Non-profit and cost centres
>
> The item you forecast will not always be called sales, but it will usually be an indicator of demand – in other words, a proxy for sales. If you are dealing with a non-profit enterprise, such as a charity, museum or cooperative society you might forecast donations, visitors, acquisitions, or the number of cases processed. For a government department, you might work with the number of applicants or permits. And so on. If you run a cost centre within an enterprise, you will base your numbers on the expected demand for your services or output (e.g. the number of research and development projects to be undertaken, or the quantity of desktop PCs to support). Usually, in such instances, the forecasting is done for you at the enterprise level and you have only to do the estimating.

▶ Wishes, targets or forecasts?

It is not at all uncommon for sales forecasts to become sales targets. A sales target is a key business objective and as such is often self-fulfilling. Your sales personnel will be working to meet their quota and, believe it or not, will often adjust their effort up or down to achieve the best result (for themselves mainly, which is not always the best result for the company). Accordingly, when you are forecasting you are frequently walking a tightrope, balancing what you have the capacity to sell or what you would like to sell against what you predict that market conditions will allow you to sell.

> 'How do you form your opinion about what a nasty event will be? Usually, you look at the past and assume it can't get any worse than it has been in the last 50 years.'
>
> **Mark Rubenstein**

▶ Multiple sales forecasts

Incidentally, from an arithmetical viewpoint, you will be lucky if you are forecasting just one item. You may have hundreds or even thousands of products. So far we have talked about forecasting just one central item – sales. This is more or less correct. In fact, you may need to make several sales forecasts and combine them into a grand total.

You do not usually need to go down to the level of forecasting sales for each individual product – unless they are *big ticket* (i.e. high-priced) or otherwise unique. It makes sense to work with groups of items that are subject to similar influences. Indeed this can actually

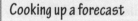

Cooking up a forecast

1 Analyse the patterns in your historical figures.
2 Look for cause and effect relationships which will help your forecast.
3 Throw in your knowledge of the market and stir well.

help to average out forecasting inaccuracies and make your predictions more accurate overall.

You can segment your sales forecasts according to types of product, category of buyer, geographic markets, and so on. For example, a computer outlet *might* forecast sales of business software, computer games, leisure software, and hardware as four separate categories. The key to successful segmentation is grouping together products and services which behave similarly under any given market conditions. This will become clear as you work through this chapter.

▶ History and knowledge

Take a look at Fig. 10.1, which charts sales figures over three years. Before you read on, grab a pencil and extend the lines to show what you think might happen to sales during the year ahead.

Fig. 10.1 Sales in three companies

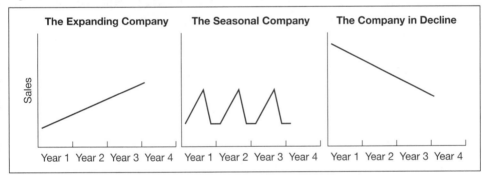

Now, suppose you were told the following facts. First, the Expanding Company's entire product line was just rendered obsolete by a miracle product released by a competitor. Second, the Seasonal Company has just replaced its winter and summer products with a single all-weather gizmo. Third, the Company in Decline has just won a huge government contract that will double sales. Does this change your projections?

We will not embarrass each other by discussing what you drew in and whether you changed it subsequently. (You should probably have said that you needed more information before you could make the forecasts – even after reading the three

'As far as the laws of mathematics refer to reality, they are not certain; and as far as they are certain, they do not refer to reality.'

Albert Einstein

facts.) True, quick and dirty forecasts sometimes rely almost wholly on projections – expecting more of the same. And managers frequently forecast almost on hunch – making educated guesses based on their perhaps subjective understanding of the situation. But the best forecasts combine both these methods; that is:

♦ the historical pattern in the numbers; and

♦ your knowledge about the environment (for sales, the environment encompasses the economy as a whole, competitors in the industry, the market, your business, the product, production plans, and so on).

▶ Patterns revisited

The previous chapter described pattern-hunting in some depth. If this is your first stop in this book it would be better to go back and review Chapter 9 before reading on. We will wait for you.

As always when reviewing numbers, do not forget the big picture. The patterns in Fig. 10.1 were very obvious, but you should always ask whether you are seeing the tip of the iceberg. The trend for the Expanding Company might be very different when viewed over 10 years (see Fig. 10.2).

Fig. 10.2 The tip of the iceberg

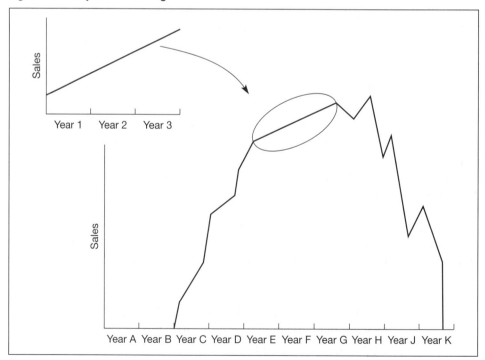

Clearly, the longer the run of historical data you can examine, the more of the iceberg you will see. This helps you put things in context. Of course, what happened five years ago might be largely irrelevant now, but even knowing this will help you make a better forecast.

What if there is no history?

Do not worry if you are forecasting for a new business or a new product or service without an apparent history. There is always somewhere to look for helpful patterns. Unless this is your first assignment, you will probably be able to dredge up an example from your past business experience. Moreover, your company may have broadly similar business areas or product histories which yield much information. If all else fails, you may be able to tell much by analysing your competitors' sales. But then you are doing that already. Right?

▶ Projecting pattens

Recall that we split the sales figures into one-offs, the trend, the cycle, seasonality, and noise. Forecasting with a ruler would assume no special one-offs and no noise in the year ahead, extend mechanically the other patterns, and then glue them all together. For a better-educated forecast you would apply your knowledge and understanding of the environment to the trend, cycle and one-offs before extending them.

The kick-off meeting

For forecasting involving teamwork, hold a kick-off meeting at which the underlying economic assumptions and corporate plans are specified or agreed.

As already mentioned, you may not be able to split the trend and the cycle – so you might treat them as one component. Seasonality is assumed to be a given. If you are tempted to amend the seasonal adjustment factors this means that either you are not comfortable with your assessment of them in the first place, or you are putting a one-off influence in the wrong place. We will return to patterns in a moment.

'There's little doubt that the Government figures are honest. The problem is that the things the numbers are supposed to measure cannot be determined with precision. ... Unless one is aware of the pitfalls ... the statistics can become extremely misleading.'

T.F. O'Leary, Jr.

▶ Applied knowledge

Once you have analysed the patterns in your sales as described in the previous chapter, you will have acquired a considerable understanding about what moves the numbers. If you are not planning to use cause and effect to forecast your sales, and even if you are, you need to review all the information you can collect about your sales environment and apply your judgement to projecting the trend. When reviewing the environment, it is logical to start with the big picture and work inwards towards your own office.

▶ The big wide world

Acting from the same script

The broad economic outlook is so important that the prospects are usually agreed at the corporate level before any round of forecasting and budgeting begins. This ensures that assumptions about the economy are acceptable to senior executives, and consistent across the enterprise.

Rather than making their own forecasts, organizations frequently rely on the opinions of the so-called experts. Their forecasts become your assumptions. There are many government, quasi-government, academic and private-sector bodies which publish economic forecasts. These are reported on the Internet and in higher-quality newspapers, sometimes with tabular presentations providing handy comparisons of several projections. If you are making the decisions or are tasked with setting the assumptions, you can use one of these forecasts, or a judgemental average of them. There are links to forecasts and economic figures on this book's website.

Your industry and market

If you are on top of your business you will already have a good understanding about the outlook for your industry. This may have been supplemented by your hard thinking about the economy. You might also want to revisit specialist industry-related journals for specific views on the prospects. You can clip useful articles and put them on file to support your forecast.

Economic assumptions – what is important for you?

- Interest rates
- Exchange rates
- GDP (home and overseas)
- Industrial production
- Inflation
- Average earnings
- Commodity prices (which?)
- Oil prices
- Employment
- Consumer spending
- Retail sales
- Fixed investment
- Tourism (it all depends what industry you are in!)
- And more…

If you do not mind me making a little plug, my book **The Economist Guide to Economic Indicators*** explains what all these figures are and how you can interpret them.

* (2003) 5th edn, Profile Books; Bloomberg Press

Obviously, you will review your competitors' strategies. Remember to include companies which are not currently in your industry, or not even in your market – yet. They might be next year. Look for surveys of buying intentions, or conduct your own market research. Again, remember that your sales could be affected by changes in demand for a product which does not appear to compete directly with yours.

> ### Expert witness
>
> Talk to trade associations, marketing consultants, distributors, re-sellers, suppliers and other business partners. What they are doing, and what they know about the market, can be a very useful input.

▶ Your company

Your forecasts also depend on your own corporate plans (production, product pricing, investment, etc.). Indeed, pricing policies are usually critical factors in forecasts. To some extent, the plans depend on the outcome of the forecasts. Accordingly, it may be necessary to conduct a round of planning and forecasting, review the results, make the tough decisions, and then repeat the forecasting on the basis of the revised plans.

How other companies forecast sales

From the ground up – by looking and asking. Sales professionals usually have a very close handle on their market, and order books can give a very clear indication of future business especially for products with long order-times such as building construction projects, aircraft and some software.

The numbers game – an arithmetical approach. So many cold calls will generate so many leads that will result in so many sales. When you know how many of each your sales people can process, and the size of your sales force, the rest is simple arithmetic. There is an example in Fig. 10.3.

Try harder – last year plus 10%. It is frequently tempting to forecast and set targets on the basis of last year's sales plus 10% or some other percentage. This can be very appealing, not least because it is based on what you know you can do, while at the same time stretching the organization. Remember though, that it is not very feasible to expect such exponential growth to continue indefinitely (see diagram in Chapter 6 Why growth matters on p.80).

Whatever you can manage – market share. An alternative to 'last year plus 10%' is to aim for 'x% of the market'. Your market share, of course, is your sales of, say, widgets as a percentage of total sales of widgets in a specific market during a given time period. Ideally you want this to be increasing over time. It is usually hard to measure, unless there are reliable industry-wide figures published without too much of a lag. Executives managing new products or new businesses frequently resort to market share for their forecasts ('if we capture 1% of the market our sales will be …').

> 'An economist is an expert who will know tomorrow why the things he predicted yesterday didn't happen today.'
>
> **Laurence J. Peter**

Fig. 10.3 Playing the numbers game

Tetrylus is a new business selling smart identity badges and tracking software. For consistency, the figures here are based on those in my companion book *The Definitive Business Plan* (2002, 2nd edn, FT Prentice Hall) but are presented differently. The basic sales forecast is contained in this spreadsheet – and built upon in the next and subsequent chapters of this book.

The company has projected the number of sales partners that it will be working with (row 7), the average number of sales that each partner will make (row 8), and the average number of components (a package of identity badges plus one software program) that will be included in each sale (rows 14 and 15). There is also provision for direct sales (i.e. not through partners) in row 10, but the executives have decided that they will pursue direct sales in forecast timeframe. With these figures, it is simple arithmetic to arrive at a forecast for sales volumes (rows 18 and 19). This spreadsheet also includes estimated sale prices (rows 34 and 35) from which gross sales revenue is calculated (see Fig. 13.6).

	A	B	C	D	E	F	
1	TETRYLUS Inc.						
2							
3	Sales projections, first five years						
4	Values in dollars						
5		Year 1	Year 2	Year 3	Year 4	Year 5	Notes
6	Channel arithmetic						
7	No. of channel partners	4	7	11	15	20	
8	No. of sales per partner	1	3	12	12	12	
9	Total no. channel sales	4	21	132	180	240	Line 7 × line 8
10	Direct sales	0	0	0	0	0	
11	Total no. sales	4	21	132	180	240	Line 9 + line 10
12							
13	Average volumes per sale						
14	Hardware	960	2,000	2,500	2,500	2,500	
15	Software	1	1	1	1	1	
16							
17	Total sales volumes						
18	Hardware	3,840	42,000	330,000	450,000	600,000	Line 11 × line 14
19	Software	4	21	132	180	240	Line 11 × line 15
20							
21	Cost of production per item						Reduction in year three
22	Hardware	25	23	12	11	10	reflects new production
23	Software	500	500	500	500	500	techniques made possi-
24							ble by higher sales
25	Channel price per item						volumes
26	Hardware	80	50	45	41	36	
27	Software	3,500	2,500	3,000	3,000	3,000	
28							
29	Mark up, %						
30	Hardware	220	122	275	275	275	((Line 26 / line 22) −1) × 100
31	Software	600	400	500	500	500	((Line 27 / line 23) −1) × 100
32							
33	Price per package						
34	Hardware	76,800	100,000	112,500	101,250	91,125	Line 14 × line 26
35	Software	3,500	2,500	3,000	3,000	3,000	Line 15 × line 27
36	Total	80,300	102,500	115,500	104,250	94,125	Line 34 + line 35

Note: Calculations are performed on <u>unrounded</u> figures to greater accuracy than is shown here. As with all illustrations in this book, the detailed spreadsheet is available for download at www.ManagingTheNumbers.com

▶ Making the forecast

By now, you have squeezed the patterns out of your sales records and decided how you are going to develop your forecast. It is time for some spreadsheeting. Begin by building a completely mechanical forecast, and then add in judgement or cause and effect. This is discussed next.

▶ Rulers only

Figure 10.4 shows the analysis from the previous chapter (Fig. 9.3), with most of the patterns projected mechanically into the future – for 2003 and 2004. This is the step-by-step approach (you can walk through it in the workbook that accompanies this chapter – see website):

Step 1: Extend the trend

In Chapter 9, the formula was calculated and keyed into column G. All you have to do is copy the formula down through the cells for 2003 and 2004.

Step 2: Extend the cyclical factors

The easy way to do this is examine the chart of the cycle, identify by eye which part of the cycle is missing in the forecast period, then copy the appropriate chunk of an earlier cycle to provide the projection (see Fig. 10.5). This is a bit simplistic, but it works. In the example, the projection requires the part of the cycle from 1997 Q3 through to the end of 1999, so select cells I60 to I69, copy them, then select cell I80 and choose *Paste Special*, *Values* (we want the values, not the formula).

Step 3: Extend the seasonal adjustment factors

These repeat every four periods, so it is just a case of copying the formula down through the forecast period.

Step 4: Extend the one-offs

There is some cheating here. If this were a purely mechanical forecast, there would be no allowance for special one-offs. However, assume that you have applied some judgement and estimated that price-cutting promotions will add 10% to sales in the third quarter of the two years ahead. Key in these judgemental figures in column E.

Step 5: Out with the glue

Finally, recombine the series to get the total forecast for sales volume. The formula is shown in Fig. 10.4.

This is all there is to it. There is no need to forecast the unsmoothed cycle and seasonal factors, while noise, by definition, cannot be forecast and as discussed is assumed to average out to about zero over time.

Fig. 10.4 Forecasting with a ruler

The top part of this table, down to about row 81 was developed in Chapter 9 – see Fig. 9.3.
Note: MA = moving average. SA = seasonal adjustment

	A	B	C	D	E	F	G	H	I	J	K	L	M
1	Year	Qtr	No.	Sales	One-offs	Adj Sales	Trend	Cycle	MA	SA	SA avg	Explained	Noise
58	1997	Q1	57	1053	0	1053	1065	0.988	0.965	1.024	1.025	1054	−1
59		Q2	58	1059	0	1059	1076	0.984	0.970	1.015	1.020	1065	−6
60		Q3	59	1049	0	1049	1087	0.965	0.990	0.975	0.980	1054	−5
61		Q4	60	1068	0	1068	1098	0.973	1.004	0.969	0.974	1074	−6
62	1998	Q1	61	1152	0	1152	1109	1.039	1.014	1.025	1.025	1152	0
63		Q2	62	1183	0	1183	1119	1.057	1.028	1.028	1.020	1174	9
64		Q3	63	1224	54	1170	1130	1.035	1.050	0.986	0.980	1216	8
65		Q4	64	1181	0	1181	1141	1.035	1.057	0.979	0.974	1175	6
66	1999	Q1	65	1246	0	1246	1152	1.082	1.052	1.028	1.025	1243	3
67		Q2	66	1250	0	1250	1163	1.075	1.048	1.026	1.020	1243	7
68		Q3	67	1213	0	1213	1173	1.034	1.051	0.984	0.980	1209	4
69		Q4	68	1202	0	1202	1184	1.015	1.040	0.976	0.974	1201	1
70	2000	Q1	69	1254	0	1254	1195	1.049	1.021	1.027	1.025	1252	2
71		Q2	70	1240	0	1240	1206	1.028	1.007	1.022	1.020	1238	2
72		Q3	71	1193	0	1193	1217	0.981	1.002	0.978	0.980	1195	−2
73		Q4	72	1178	0	1178	1228	0.960	0.989	0.970	0.974	1183	−5
74	2001	Q1	73	1275	44	1231	1238	0.994	0.973	1.021	1.025	1280	−5
75		Q2	74	1228	0	1228	1249	0.983	0.966	1.017	1.020	1231	−3
76		Q3	75	1197	0	1197	1260	0.950	0.973	0.977	0.980	1201	−4
77		Q4	76	1200	0	1200	1271	0.944	0.971	0.973	0.974	1202	−2
78	2002	Q1	77	1270	0	1270	1282	0.991	0.969	1.023	1.025	1273	−3
79		Q2	78	1275	0	1275	1292	0.987	0.974	1.013	1.020	1285	−10
80		Q3	79	1268	0	1268	1303	0.973	0.990		0.980		
81		Q4	80	1283	0	1283	1314	0.976	1.004		0.974		
82	2003	Q1	81	1377	0		1325		1.014		1.025		
83		Q2	82	1401	0		1336		1.028		1.020		
84		Q3	83	1520	135		1346		1.050		0.980		
85		Q4	84	1398	0		1357		1.057		0.974		
86	2004	Q1	85	1476	0		1368		1.052		1.025		
87		Q2	86	1612	138		1379		1.048		1.020		
88		Q3	87	1431	0		1390		1.051		0.980		
89		Q4	88	1420	0		1400		1.040		0.974		

The formula for cell D89 is =(G89*I89*K89)+E89

Based on judgement (see text)

The trend formula is copied down from cell G81

Cells I80 to I89 contain values copied-and-pasted from cells I60 to I69 (why? see text)

These SA factors repeat every four cells; the formula is copied down from cell K81

Fig. 10.5 Extending the cycle

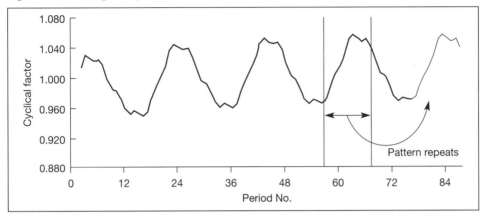

Ten hard questions to ask or be asked

1 Are we forecasting the right thing? Have we correctly identified what should be an assumption, estimate or forecast

2 What are the most important influences which are/are not within our control?

3 What if interest rates, exchange rates, economic growth, etc. are 1% higher or lower?

4 What if we cut prices by 10%? What if our competitors cut prices by 10%?

5 What if a competitor enters the market?

6 What if production constraints limit our output?

7 Why are there kinks in the projected patterns?

8 How do we expect to push up the trend so much in such a short space of time?

9 What is the worst-case outlook?

10 How accurate are the seasonal adjustment factors?

▶ Any advances

Despite the title of *Rulers only* for the previous section, it included the application of some judgement or rules of thumb in Step 4. If you believe that you should forecast some underlying changes in the trend or cycle, you would have to change the appropriate columns instead. If you have unearthed quantifiable cause-and-effect, or you are using good rules of thumb, you can use an equation as discussed in Chapter 9. More often than not, though, business forecasting is more judgemental.

Suppose that you conclude that all the applied knowledge factors reviewed above will have a net effect of boosting sales by about 10% above the historical trend over the next 12 months – this is about 2.4% a quarter compounded (see Fig. 10.6). Inspection shows that hitherto growth in the trend was about 0.8% a quarter. With a bit of simple arithmetic, we now project that the trend will

Fig. 10.6 Changing the trend

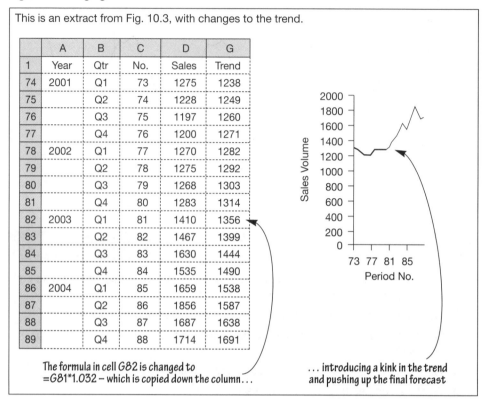

This is an extract from Fig. 10.3, with changes to the trend.

	A	B	C	D	G
1	Year	Qtr	No.	Sales	Trend
74	2001	Q1	73	1275	1238
75		Q2	74	1228	1249
76		Q3	75	1197	1260
77		Q4	76	1200	1271
78	2002	Q1	77	1270	1282
79		Q2	78	1275	1292
80		Q3	79	1268	1303
81		Q4	80	1283	1314
82	2003	Q1	81	1410	1356
83		Q2	82	1467	1399
84		Q3	83	1630	1444
85		Q4	84	1535	1490
86	2004	Q1	85	1659	1538
87		Q2	86	1856	1587
88		Q3	87	1687	1638
89		Q4	88	1714	1691

The formula in cell G82 is changed to =G81*1.032 – which is copied down the column...

... introducing a kink in the trend and pushing up the final forecast

expand by 3.2% a quarter – as shown in Fig. 10.6 and Step 6 in the workbook. This slightly changes Step 1 in *Rulers only* above, but there is no other work to do.

One warning. The new trend has a perhaps unrealistic kink. Either the extra 10% per annum growth is too optimistic, or you might want to use a growth rate smaller than 3.2% for the first few months of the forecast, so that the higher sales levels are phased in more gently.

▶ What if?

It is usually important, if not critical, to make one or more alternative forecasts to see what happens in a worst-case scenario (what if the economy enters recession? what if your competitors try to blow you out of the water?) and a best-case scenario (what if sales go through the roof?). At least having done the analysis and built the spreadsheet, there is not too much work involved in producing the alternative scenarios. The easiest way to do this is by making a duplicate of your spreadsheet and keying in some new numbers in the trend and/or one-off columns.

Among statisticians and beanies, what-if analysis is known by the mystical name of sensitivity analysis. This makes more sense if you think of it in terms of: 'what if interest rates rise by one percentage point?', 'what if sales demand rises by 1%?' and so on. We shall return to this in later chapters.

Best-case scenarios tend to get overlooked. How often have you heard someone say too many sales is a problem we would like to have and we will deal with if it happens. Nevertheless, your investors, board or senior managers might be cheered up if they see a realistic best-case outlook (do not hype something you cannot deliver). More important, it helps you to see what you are capable of and where bottlenecks and capacity constraints can occur. When you know the critical levels, you can monitor sales and react accordingly if warnings are triggered.

Are you sure?

You have now made a forecast for a series of specific future periods – be they weeks, months, quarters or years. Take any one of these; say, the third quarter next year. Are you sure that sales will be 1,687 units? Of course not. If pressed on the specifics, you are more likely to predict one of the following:

- 1,690
- 1,700
- 1,690 plus or minus 10 or 20
- 1,690 plus or minus 10%
- 1,660 to 1,700 with a central estimate of 1,687 (using the worst case and best case scenarios to define the range).

There are several important messages. First, build your spreadsheets so that you can amend one number and watch how the changes ripple through to the bottom line. Second, do not let your forecasts assume spurious accuracy just because they are based on detailed numerical analysis. And third, even though our spreadsheets tend to focus attention on very specific results, there are ways to capture the uncertainty – which I shall return to in Chapter 23 after getting a few other matters out of the way.

Conclusion

This chapter should have demonstrated that the spreadsheet work required for forecasting is remarkably simple. *Rulers only* produced what might be regarded as a central forecast (depending on what you know about the environment). The variation on the trend above could be looked upon as a best-case scenario. A little thought and a few more keystrokes would give the worrying worst case. Of course, these are quantities. The thing to do now is to convert them into a bottom line in money terms – which is what we do in the next few chapters. This is where estimating will come into play.

Presenting a forecast

1 Describe background.
2 Specify key assumptions.
3 Explain basis for forecast (projections, rules of thumb, cause and effect).
4 Preview the key factors.
5 Present the forecast.
6 Present alternative scenarios.
7 Answer tough questions.

11

counting capital

'To the accountants, a true work of art is an investment that hangs on the wall.'

Hilary Alexander

Chapter survival toolkit

▶ Overview

You may be pleased to know that the heavy spreadsheet work is over. From now on, we will use them for much simpler tasks. The next three chapters consider costs. This chapter sets the ball rolling by discussing the way that you account for long-lived assets – property, plant and equipment, as well as intangibles such as patents. The main emphasis is on analysing and understanding the main bookkeeping entries and the broad range of related management issues. We also see how to project capital spending into the future. Assessing investment projects and presenting capital budgets is saved for Chapters 21 and 22.

▶ Prerequisites

A basic familiarity with spreadsheets as covered in Chapter 4.

▶ Mastering capital spending

If you can answer these questions after reading this chapter, go to the top of the class:

1 Capital spending – what is it and why is it important? What is and isn't capital spending? What could be classed as capital spending, depending on the rules?

2 What is the difference between depreciation, amortization and depletion?

3 How do you *book* (record) capital spending and (a clue) how do you write off your spending on assets over their useful lives?

4 Are acquisition cost, useful life, maintenance costs, residual value and depreciation policy the key things you need to know to be able to write off capital assets?

5 What are the main depreciation policies? How do they work?

6 Do you need to maintain fixed asset registers and depreciation schedules?

7 Why don't accounting policies create sinking funds to replace expired assets?

8 How do you appraise asset values and make inter-company comparisons?

9 Why do managers, beanies, accounting regulators, tax authorities, insurance experts and sellers/buyers assess asset values differently

10 What is total cost of ownership? Why is it so important for managers?

> 'We thought we understood how carefully planned capital spending can boost productivity and save money in the longer term. But we quickly learned that investment in technology is ineffective without matching innovations in business processes.'
>
> **An entrepreneur**

> ## ▶ Jargon watch

New beanie buzz words

Capital expenditure, CapEx

Classes of assets: (1) fixed assets –
plant, property and equipment (PPE);
(2) intangible assets – intellectual property,
goodwill

Writing-down, by class of asset:
depreciation, amortization, depletion

Writing-down, techniques: straight line,
sum-of-the-years'-digits, double-
declining-balance, MACRS, units-of-
production, units-of-output, units-of-sales

Values: historic cost, book value, fair
market value, farm-gate value, replacement
value, residual value/salvage value,
accumulated depreciation

Other:

Revaluation surplus, depreciation schedule
Fixed asset register
Production costs, operating costs *

New financial terms

Finance lease, operating lease

New economic jargon

Cost of ownership, capital spending,
current spending

Previously encountered beanie terms

International Accounting Standards (IAS)

Assets

Equity

Retained earnings

Sinking fund

* First mention: not fully defined in this chapter.

▶ Accounting for the future

The previous chapter looked at forecasting sales. Now it is time to look at the cost side of the equation. Start by considering capital spending. Compared to other spending, capital outlays:

◆ often involve larger sums of money;

◆ are usually subject to a unique approvals process;

◆ generally do not immediately produce substantial income relative to their costs;

◆ are expected to produce future benefits; and

◆ receive special treatment in financial statements.

For these reasons, it is useful to discuss them seperately from other costs. We will look at how you account for them in general, and then discuss a whole range of related management issues. The main focus here is on the bean counting, which embraces financial accounting, tax accounting and – perhaps most important – management accounting. Elsewhere, we will discuss capital budgeting, investment and project appraisal (see Chapters 22 to 24).

> 'The important thing is never to stop questioning.'
>
> **Albert Einstein**

> ## Capital spending
>
> Capital spending is spending assets with productive lives of more than 12 months, such as plant, buildings, machinery, vehicles, computers, office equipment, fixtures and fitting, and intellectual property. Collectively, these are known as *fixed assets*. They do not have to be things you can touch and feel. They can also be intangible, as with software development by a computer company and goodwill on the acquisition of another business. Note that from a financial analysis and accounting viewpoint, mergers and acquisitions are treated in much the same way as any other major item of capital spending.

▶ Gone today, here tomorrow

If you spend a million on machinery that will be used over 10 years, how do you show it in your financial accounts? All other things being equal, if you charged the million to today's operational spending your profit and loss account would look rather sick this year, especially if you had not started using the machine. On the other hand, your profit and loss account would be very healthy next year when the machinery was producing output for no apparent outlay, other than perhaps the cost of feeding and maintaining it.

> You would be right in regarding your **inventory** as an asset, but it is not classed as a fixed asset. It is treated as a current asset – and discussed in Chapter 13.

Accordingly, it is usual and rational to divide the purchase cost of capital goods into several parts and charge them to operating costs over the life of the machine. For example, a $30,000 machine with a three-year life span and no residual value might be thought of as costing you $10,000 per annum for three years.

The exact way that you allocate the costs over time is specified by your:

◆ *depreciation policy* for physical assets;

◆ *amortization policy* for intangible assets; and

◆ *depletion policy* for natural resources.

Depreciation, amortization and depletion are different names for exactly the same thing – writing off costs over the working life of the asset. From now on, please take references to depreciation to include amortization and depletion as appropriate.

You can have a different depreciation policy for each category of assets (plant, machinery, office, etc.) or sometimes even for each asset. You will see how it works in a moment. Usually, it results in financial accounts which show assets at their historic cost or some other artificial book value.

Fixed asset arithmetic

Begin by looking at how a beanie would want you to account for fixed assets in, say, a monthly financial projection. Suppose that in October you acquire a squeezing machine for $120,000 cash; it has an expected life of five years (60 months), no residual value, and so you write it off in 60 equal instalments. The accounting entries are as follows:

Beanies and, by osmosis senior executives, tend to abbreviate the term capital expenditure to **CapEx**. The assets acquired are often known as **fixed assets** (even though they are not fixed in the physical sense). A subset of such assets is sometimes referred to as **PPE** – property, plant and equipment. The other major division is **intellectual property** – goodwill, patents, etc.

1 In October you debit *fixed assets – machinery* $120,000 and credit *cash at bank* by the same amount.

2 Every month commencing in November you debit $2,000 ($120,000 divided by 60 months) to the expenditure account *depreciation of machinery* and credit the asset account *fixed assets – depreciation of machinery* with the same amount.

Acquisition, 25 Oct

Acc no.	Account	Debit $	Credit $
1-1510	Fixed assets: machinery	120,000.00	
1-1002	Cash at bank		120,000.00

Depreciation, 30 Nov

Acc no.	Account	Debit $	Credit $
5-2210	Prod'n costs: depr'n of machinery	2,000.00	
1-1610	Machinery: accm'd depreciation		2,000.00

At the end of the first year:

◆ the (original) booked value is $120,000;

◆ the accumulated depreciation is $4,000 (two months' depreciation);

◆ the written-down, or net book value, is $116,000 ($120,000 *less* $4,000); and

◆ your production or operating costs for the year include $4,000 in depreciation.

If the only other transaction in the year was a $200,000 issue of shares, the financial transactions for September to December would be those illustrated in Fig. 11.1. Note how the balance sheet shows cumulative, end-month balances on asset, liability and shareholders equity accounts (you might want to refer back to the chart of accounts in Chapter 7), while the profit and loss account and cash flow statement both show totals for the month. Don't worry, I'll explain this in Chapter 15.

Fig. 11.1 Accounting for fixed assets

Extract from financial statements

Dollars

	Sep	Oct	Nov	Dec
Balance Sheet				
End month				
Assets				
Cash at bank	200,000	80,000	80,000	80,000
Fixed assets – machinery	0	120,000	120,000	120,000
Less accumulated depreciation, machinery	0	0	2,000	4,000
Net book value of assets	0	120,000	118,000	116,000
Total	**200,000**	**200,000**	**198,000**	**196,000**
Liabilities and shareholders' equity				
Paid-in share capital	200,000	200,000	200,000	200,000
Profit (loss), current year	0	0	(2,000)	(4,000)
Total	**200,000**	**200,000**	**198,000**	**196,000**
Profit & loss account				
Whole month				
Depreciation – machinery	0	0	2,000	2,000
Net profit (loss)	**0**	**0**	**(2,000)**	**(2,000)**
Cash flow				
Whole month				
Cash received from share issue	200,000	0	0	0
Acquisition of assets	0	(120,000)	0	0
Total for month	**200,000**	**(120,000)**	**0**	**0**
Net cash balance (cumulative)	**200,000**	**80,000**	**80,000**	**80,000**

This, essentially, is all there is to accounting for fixed assets. Although, in case you thought you were getting off lightly, there are some management issues that we should discuss. For the purposes of bean counting, the four main things that you have to consider, and which we will discuss below, are:

1 acquisition costs, including delivery, installation, etc.
2 expected life
3 expected residual value
4 depreciation policy.

> For tax purposes, depreciation in the year that you acquire an asset is often derived by some rule of thumb – such as 50% of whole -year depreciation regardless of the date on which the spending occurred.

Managing capital expenditure

▶ Does it hurt?

Capital spending can be tangible or intangible. It can be on machines that you can touch and feel, or items of intellectual property such as software development and registering patents – stuff that is much harder to physically hurt yourself with.

> ### What's not capital
>
> Under certain circumstances – especially if software is your business – you can treat software **development** as capital spending. Mostly, you cannot capitalize spending on **research**, start-ups, training and advertising, internally generated goodwill, brands, mastheads, publishing titles, customer lists and similar items.

Unlike most current expenditure, capital outlays are expected to produce benefits (and perhaps incur costs) in the future. These may be obvious and tangible, as with investment property or a clump press. Or the costs and benefits may be somewhat hard to measure, as in the instance of desktop computers for your beanies. Moreover, the future revenue and expenditure associated with assets may be straightforward (production machinery), or complex (as with mergers and acquisitions).

▶ Approvals

The approvals process, as with any other spending request, will require you to show why you need the sprocket grinder, flange flipper or whatever asset it is, and what costs and benefits will relate to its acquisition. The uniqueness of capital spending is that the benefits – and some of the costs – are not all immediate, but they will occur at sometime in the future. Capital budgeting and related topics are covered in Chapter 22. Remember to consider alternative approaches to acquiring one asset, which may include alternative production methods, outsourcing, and leasing (see below).

▶ Acquisition

> Under **international accounting standards**, if you can demonstrate that a website is capable of generating direct revenues by enabling orders to be placed, you can treat the **website development costs** as capital spending. A website intended primarily for promoting and advertising your products and services do not qualify.

For some assets, acquisition involves nothing more complex than taking delivery (passenger vehicles) or perhaps simple installation (plugging in a photocopier). For other items, such as a mainframe computer or a new building, acquisition may involve a separate project in its own right. Project management is discussed in Chapter 21.

Costs associated with bringing an asset into use can usually be treated as part of the capital outlay. These overheads can include delivery, installation, perhaps computer software, and other items which would otherwise be treated as consumption. For construction projects, international accounting standards permit you to capitalize borrowing costs.

▶ Expected life

You may find that your company has specific depreciation policies which arbitrarily define the expected life of certain categories of assets – such as two years for PCs. Many tax authorities define arbitrary lives for tax purposes. There may also be statutory limits, such as 20 or 40 years for buildings. Other examples are as follows. You do not have to use any of these periods for management analysis, but be prepared to defend your reasoning.

Machinery and equipment. Typical depreciation periods used in company accounts include three years for computers, five years for office equipment, 10 years for some industrial machinery, 20 years for a jumbo jet and 100 years for airport runways (I didn't think that this last example was reasonable either).

> New US accounting rules requiring companies to record at once any decline in the value of goodwill resulted in AOL Time Warner posting a world-record one-time charge against profits in 2002 – with a $54bn write-down in the value of AOL's purchase of Time Warner.

Fitting of premises. Spending on fittings that you cannot take with you – fixed partitioning, plumbing, cabling, decorating – is treated as freehold improvements (if you own the premises) or leasehold improvements (if you rent). Such spending is amortized over the shorter of the life of the fittings, the lease or the building.

Goodwill. Goodwill is the difference between the price you pay to buy another company and the net value of its assets. It represents the expectation of future cash flow that can be generated by, for example, trading on a name or location. Your accounts cannot show the goodwill value that you attach to your own company. But if you are taken over, the acquiring company can show your goodwill and amortize it over up to 20 years (longer if they can justify expecting financial benefits to continue to flow in). Note that the 20-year rule is an international accounting standard; it has been more common for companies in Europe to write off goodwill immediately on acquisition by charging it to shareholders' equity. (But see Chapter 19.)

Other intellectual property. The cost of acquiring patents, copyrights, trademarks and other licences is written off over their expected useful lives – which are often much less than the statutory protection afforded. A copyright, for example, generally lives for 50 years after the originator's death. Will the works have such a long life? You would probably write off the copyright on a fleetingly famous celebrity's novels over a much shorter period.

Start-up costs

Identifiable start-up costs for a new business – such as incorporation and professional adviser's fees and management costs – are often capitalized and written off over between two and five years, although international accounting standards require this to be treated as current spending.

▶ Running and maintenance costs

Fixed assets usually involve running costs and maintenance costs, which you will need to estimate for management analysis. These costs are usually entered as charges against profits in the periods when they are incurred, although in some circumstances you will be able to treat them as capital costs also and write them off over an extended period.

What does it really cost?

If you spend, say, $2,500 on a PC with software and a printer, and you boldly estimate a life of two years and resale value of $500, your financial accounts will show a charge against income of $1,000 a year. However, industry surveys estimate that the **total cost of ownership** for an office PC is anywhere from $7,500 to $15,000 a year after you take into account the costs of administration and support by the IT department and other unbudgeted costs.

Take another example, when your computer network goes down, it could be costing you hundreds of thousands of dollars an hour in lost productivity. I have seen figures somewhere showing that in the 1990s, network downtime cost American Express $170,000 a minute and brokerage house Charles Schwab $1 million a minute – and this is one of the costs of owning an asset that you would rather not own at that precise moment.

To get at the true costs and benefits of an asset, you have to brainstorm and identify all the obvious and not so obvious factors, which may stretch well across departmental boundaries. There is an upside for the cynical: every time that you spend $2,500 on a PC (which, obviously, you estimate will bring some economic benefits to your business area), you are making it $10,000 harder for your IT department to meet their budget.

▶ Residual value

As surprising as it may sound, accounting policies and common sense generally collide over the matter of estimating *residual values* – except that bean counters err on the side of caution and usually insist on writing book values down to zero within some given time period. In keeping with their reputation, they also prefer to call the residual value the *salvage value* because, well, it sounds rather more pessimistic. Use your knowledge of the market for similar assets, expectations of technological change, and other crystal-ball gazing to arrive at a reasonable estimate of what you can sell the asset for when you have finished with it.

If there are likely to be costs involved in the disposal of an asset at the end of its useful life, you probably have the option of including the estimated outlays in the 'depreciation' schedule or expensing them at the end of the period.

▶ Benefits

At last we come to the whole purpose of acquiring assets – to obtain a future stream of revenue. This may be explicit, as with production machinery, or highly intangible, as with PCs for administrative use. The rationale for acquiring an asset came out of your planning and forecasting process. So will the benefits. These are discussed more fully in Chapter 21.

▶ Depreciation

> In the US, both the Inland Revenue Service (IRS) and generally accepted accounting principles allow **declining-balance** depreciation – which the IRS calls Modified Accelerated Cost Recovery System (MACRS).

There are many ways to calculate depreciation. You may need to use one method for management analysis, another for financial reporting, and sometimes a third for tax calculations. This might sound a bit silly. The situation arises because tax authorities and financial accounting regulators do not always talk to each other, and both may have aims which differ from the manager's objective of estimating the strict economic benefits. If nothing else, this illustrates that there is no universally applicable way of estimating depreciation.

Let me explain three ways of calculating depreciation with a ruler. The first, the *straight-line* method introduced above, simply assumes an equal amount of depreciation in each year of the asset's life. The next two, which may sound off-putting but which are delightfully simple, are known by bean counters as the *sum-of-the-year's-digits*, and *double-declining-balance* depreciation. These are actually quite nifty techniques which *accelerate* (front-load) the depreciation. This is generally more realistic, given that the fastest drop in an asset's value usually occurs precisely when you are heaving it out of the showroom. The calculations are as follows, using as an example a $10,000 asset with a five-year life and no residual value (see Fig. 11.2):

◆ **Straight-line**. Divide the *depreciable base* (i.e. acquisition price less estimated residual value) by the number of years of expected service; e.g. depreciation is $10,000 / 5 = $2,000 a year.

◆ **Sum-of-the-year's-digits**. Number the years of useful life in reverse order counting down to one (e.g. 5, 4, 3, 2, 1). Find the sum $(5 + 4 + 3 + 2 + 1 = 15)$. Divide each year by the sum $(\frac{5}{15}, \frac{4}{15}, \frac{3}{15}, \frac{2}{15}$ and $\frac{1}{15})$ and multiply the *depreciable base* by these factors to find the depreciation. In the example here, depreciation in the first year is $10,000 \times \frac{5}{15} = $3,333. For the second year it is $10,000 \times \frac{4}{15} = $2,667 and so on.

◆ **Double-declining-balance**. Calculate the straight-line depreciation as above. Find the percentage depreciation in the first year, and double it $(2,000/10,000 * 2 = 0.4$ or 40%). Use this factor to calculate depreciation on the *outstanding balance*, but if the depreciation is less than the straight-line amount for the same period, use that amount instead, until the asset is completely written off. In this example, in the first two years the depreciation is 40% of the opening balance each year. However, in the third year, depreciation is higher when calculated using the straight-line method, so the straight-line figure is used.

Interpretation

These three depreciation methods discussed above are illustrated in Fig. 11.2. In each case, the depreciation is the figure which is charged against income (see the profit and loss account in Fig. 14.1), while the net asset value is the figure shown in the balance sheet. Depreciation is a pure bookkeeping entry and has no effect on cash flow.

Note that when using the double declining balance method, net profit is lowered by twice as much ($4,000) as it would be using straight line depreciation, while the value of assets on the balance sheet is only $6,000 compared with $8,000 using the straight-line method. Now imagine this scaled up for a company with millions or billions of dollars of assets. Depending on the depreciation method chosen, the financials can look very different even though the company's operations are fundamentally unaltered.

Of course, accelerated depreciation, as with the double declining balance method, lowers reported profits and therefore cuts, or at least defers, a tax liability.

> 'The general who wins the battle makes many calculations in his temple before the battle is fought. The general who loses makes but few calculations beforehand.'
>
> **Sun Tzu**

Fig. 11.2 Comparison of three depreciation methods

Dollars; depreciation is whole year; net asset value is end-year.

	Straight-line		Sum-of-years				Double-declining-balance (DDB)		
Year	Dep'n	Net asset value	Year	Factor	Dep'n	Net asset value	DDB calculation	Dep'n	Net asset value
0		10,000				10,000			10,000
1	2,000	8,000	5	5/15	3,333	6,667	4,000	4,000	6,000
2	2,000	6,000	4	4/15	2,667	4,000	2,400	2,400	3,600
3	2,000	4,000	3	3/15	2,000	2,000	1,440	2,000	1,600
4	2,000	2,000	2	2/15	1,333	667	864	1,600	0
5	2,000	0	1	1/15	667	0	518	0	0
Totals	10,000		15		10,000		9,222	10,000	

Error trapping: It hardly needs to be said that for any one asset, the acquisition costs less the residual value should equal total depreciation.

Back to the real world – units-of-production/output depreciation

If the depreciation methods outlined above seem artificial, it is because they are. A more rational approach is to pro-rata the depreciation according to the economic benefits that you expect to flow from an asset. For example, if you have a noisy machine that you estimate will punch out 20 million bottle tops in its lifetime and you predict that it will (or, with hindsight, you know that it did) produce 2 million in its first year of life, then depreciation for that period could be stated as $\frac{2}{20}$ of the depreciable base amount.

▶▶ Throw away your spreadsheet

Spreadsheets have built-in formulas for calculating depreciation. You will find them by choosing *Insert/Function* and then clicking *Financial*. The formula for straight-line depreciation (called SLN in spreadsheet-speak) is pointless because it takes longer to use than simply dividing the depreciation base by the number of periods. The formulas for declining balance (DDB and VDB – the V stands for variable) sort of work. DDB does not switch to the straight-line method, and so does not fully depreciate the asset. VDB will switch out of the declining balance calculation, but does its own straight-line over the remaining months (i.e. averages the remaining depreciation) rather than converting to straight-line over the *whole life* of the asset. The good news is that the formula for sum of the years (SYD) seems to work perfectly. You can try this yourself, or examine the spreadsheet for this chapter (downloadable from this book's website).

Of course, it does not always make sense to do it this way. For motor vehicles, desktop PCs, and many other items not associated directly with production you will probably have to go back to depreciating with a ruler.

If you develop computer software for sale, you may treat the development costs as capital spending, and then depreciate them over either the expected life of the software, or using a **units-of-sale** basis. For example, if you expected to sell 50 packages in total, and in the first year you sold 10, depreciation for the year would be $\frac{10}{50}$ of the development costs.

▶ Going with the herd

You should review your fixed assets at regular intervals, and if the fair market value is out of line with the book value you should consider revaluing them. Market values can often be assessed by professional appraisers or by comparison with similar assets, although this is not always possible. For consistency, if you revalue one asset, you should revalue all assets in the same category.

The evolving international accounting standards (IAS) permit the use of fair market value as an alternative to mechanical depreciation, although your national *generally accepted accounting principles* may not yet do so. In fact, IAS have controversially moved away from historic cost and actually *require* the use of *farm gate* valuation for biological assets such as livestock, agriculture and forestry products.

Four accounting entries for asset revaluations

1 Upward revaluations in assets should be credited to equity (revaluation surplus) unless reversing a previous charge to income.

2 Decreases in valuation should be charged to income unless reversing a previous credit to equity.

3 If the revalued asset is sold or otherwise disposed of, any remaining revaluation surplus either remains as a separate component of equity or is transferred directly to retained earnings (but not through the income statement).

4 If an asset's recoverable value falls below its book value, the decline should be recognized and charged to income (unless it reverses a previous credit to equity).

▶ Appreciating assets

There is no inverse of depreciation that can be applied to appreciating assets. In the past, land and buildings were usually recorded at cost and revalued upwards to reflect fair market values only in special exercises (such as when the CEO wanted to inflate income and the balance sheet). However, as mentioned above (see *Going with the herd*, above), international accounting standards permit regular revaluation based on fair market value.

▶ Replacing fixed assets

Depreciation is a bookkeeping entry created at a stroke of the accountant's pen. It does not establish a *sinking fund* or cash reserve for replacing an asset. If you wanted to do this, you would have to pass a separate set of entries – moving some of your profits from your bank account to a fixed-asset replacement fund each year. Then, of course, the cash in the fund would probably be earning less than your cost of capital and so it would be clawing down your overall return on capital employed (see Chapter 19). Such cash reserves tend to be the exception rather than the rule. You should decide if you need one using rational judgement and capital investment appraisal techniques (Chapter 21).

▶ Ten hard questions to ask or be asked

1 Are the book values of fixed assets representative of realizable market values?

2 What intangibles (such as brands, location and other intellectual property) exist which are not recorded as fixed assets?

3 Should this item really be regarded and booked as a fixed asset? Or is it an expense?

4 Have we taken correct amount of the acquisition and maintenance costs and residual values?

5 Are expected lives realistic?

6 Is the depreciation policy for each category of fixed assets appropriate?

7 Should we rent or buy?

8 Whar are the true costs of ownership?

9 Are insured values correct?

10 When comparing two asset-rich companies, is depreciation calculated on the same basis? (If not, adjust before comparison.)

▶ Other records

Fixed assets have a life of their own and pop up in all manner of company records. Aside from the financial statements detailed in Fig. 11.1, three other examples are included below. See also *Decision-making values*, below.

In summary

Your business plans, annual budget, financial statements and other relevant reports will include a summary of your fixed assets, along the lines of Fig. 11.3.

Fig. 11.3 Fixed asset summary

Fixed asset summary [extract] 2003

Book value, dollars

Category of assets	Opening value	Additions in year	Depreciation for year	Closing value
Machinery	0	120,000	4,000	116,000
Office equipment	0	72,000	5,000	67,000
Computers	0	48,000	3,000	45,000
...	...	...	...	...
Total	0	240,000	12,000	228,000

Note: Office equipment is depreciated over three years using the straight-line method.

Fixed asset register

Somewhere, often with the people that manage your facilities, you will find a fixed asset register. This might be combined with the depreciation schedule and kept in the bean counter's bottom drawer. Once a year, or more often if things are inclined to walk off the premises on their own, someone in a grey suit will climb over your production and operations people checking that a physical inventory of assets matches the register. (See Fig. 11.4.)

Depreciation schedule

For each asset, your accountant's depreciation schedule will show the original acquisition cost, depreciation to date, the current net book value – and probably estimates of current or replacement value for insurance purposes. (See Fig. 11.4.)

Fig. 11.4 Fixed assets detailed

This combines a fixed asset register with a depreciation schedule. It helps to open this list vertically and specify each asset that will be acquired (computer 1, computer 2, etc.) together with descriptive notes.

Fixed asset register and depreciation schedule [extract] 2003

Book value, dollars

		Sep	Oct	Nov	Dec
Capital outlays					
Machinery		0	120,000	0	0
Office equipment		36,000	36,000	0	0
Computers		0	24,000	24,000	0
...		...	...	...	...
Totals		**36,000**	**180,000**	**24,000**	**0**
Depreciation schedule	*Term**				
Machinery	60	0	0	2,000	2,000
Office equipment	36	0	1,000	2,000	2,000
Computers	24	0	0	1,000	2,000
...	...	...	...	...	...
Totals		**0**	**1,000**	**5,000**	**6,000**

*Term = number of months over which assets are depreciated, in this case using the straight-line method.

▶ Decision-making values

An excellent way to establish the actual or useful value of your fixed assets is to examine the summary, depreciation schedule and fixed asset register mentioned above. These all show the original cost, current book cost and the age of the assets. However, the written-down value is often way out of line with current or replacement values. You need to conduct a realistic appraisal to decide what is reasonable.

Market values. During your management review of the business, you will base decisions on market values. What is the underlying fair value of plant or machinery? Would it be better to sell it and use the proceeds elsewhere? Do you have competitive advantage because you have already written off the cost?

Insurance value. For your operational decisions, you will also have to decide whether to insure for current or replacement values.

▶ A new lease of life

It frequently makes sense to lease rather than buy. This reduces the up-front demands on your cash flow and is particularly helpful for new businesses. Chapter 6 explained the arithmetic of comparing outright purchase against leasing. There are two categories of lease:

- ◆ **Finance lease** – a lease where the risks and rewards of ownership are passed to the company using the things being leased to it.
- ◆ **Operating lease** – all other leases.

As the name implies, a finance lease is a sneaky way of financing an asset. In essence, it produces a liability (to pay for the asset) with the intention of hiding it off-balance sheet. Many countries, and now international accounting standards, have introduced the generally accepted accounting principle that requires finance leases to be shown on the balance sheet as an asset with a matching liability. The starting value on both sides of the balance sheet is the net present value (see Chapter 6) of the minimum lease payments. Depreciation is over the shorter of the term of the lease or the expected useful life of the assets. The excess of annual lease payments over the depreciation charge is charged to the profit and loss account as interest.

On the other hand, operating leases are just charged to the profit and loss account as an expense (such as 'computer leases').

International accounting standards

As you might expect, the International Accounting Standards Board has quite a lot to say about capital spending. The main standards relating to fixed assets are IAS 16 (plant, property and equipment), 17 (leases) and 38 (intangible assets). You can link to summaries of these from this book's website which, in turn, will lead you to the other relevant standards and interpretations.

▶ Looking ahead

Your required level of capital spending will become apparent as you work through your general forecasting, estimating and budgeting exercises, and your business and project planning. Basically, you are going to say 'I want to do XYZ, how will I do it?' By the time that you have decided how to do XYZ, you will know what capital assets you need to acquire, if any. When you know what you need to buy, you can account for it as already described in this chapter. An example is shown in Fig. 11.5.

Fig. 11.5 Projecting capital outlays and depreciation

	A	B	C	D	E	F	G	H	I
1		**TETRYLUS Inc.**							
2									
3		Capital outlays and depreciation, first six months							
4		Dollars							
5									
6			Month 1	Month 2	Month 3	Month 4	Month 5	Month 6	H1
7		**CAPITAL OUTLAYS**							
8	C-11	Office fitting	6,500	0	0	0	0	0	6,500
9	C-12	Office furniture	5,000	0	0	0	0	0	5,000
10	C-13	Office equipment	0	0	750	0	0	0	750
11	C-14	Telecoms equipment	0	0	0	0	0	0	0
12	C-15	Computers, etc.	20,000	1,500	0	1,000	0	0	22,500
13	C-16	Software	5,000	0	0	0	0	0	5,000
14	C-17	Motor vehicles	0	0	0	0	0	0	0
15	C-18	**Total capital outlays**	36,500	1,500	750	1,000	0	0	39,750
16									
17		**DEPRECIATION SCHEDULE**							
18	D-11	Office fitting	0	542	542	542	542	542	2,710
19	D-12	Office furniture	0	83	83	83	83	83	415
20	D-13	Office equipment	0	0	0	13	13	13	39
	D-14	Telecoms equipment	0	0	0	0	0	0	0
	D-15	Computers, etc.	0	556	597	597	625	625	3,000
	D-16	Software	0	208	208	208	208	208	1,040
	D-17	Motor vehicles	0	0	0	0	0	0	0
	D-18	**Total**	0	1,389	1,431	1,443	1,471	1,471	7,204

Note: The schedule is based on straight-line depreciation with no residual value over the following periods:

Item	Depreciation period
Office fittings:	The 12-month term of the office lease
Computers	Three years
Software	Two years
Other assets	Five years

Nine steps to projecting capital spending

1 Classify required assets according to purpose (plant, office, etc.).

2 Estimate their expected cost, delivery dates and payment terms.

3 Estimate useful life spans, residual values and other costs and benefits.

4 Determine the depreciation method.

5 Draw up a depreciation schedule commencing in the month after delivery.

6 Set the acquisition cost against your bank balance, offset by an increase in fixed assets.

7 Show the depreciation as an expense, matched by a charge against fixed assets.

8 Show insurance and maintenance costs as expenses, matched by withdrawals from the bank account.

9 Include the benefits of the assets (e.g. higher manufacturing output) in your other projections.

Conclusion

Counting the cost of capital is relatively simple in concept, perhaps more complex in terms of the management issues. I hope that you can see that these become simple to deal with when taken one at a time. As with every chapter, you might want to revisit the proficiency test and jargon watch in the chapter survival toolkit to see if you picked up the key points. Now we should move on briskly to assess other spending.

12

controlling costs

'In a competitive market we don't control the selling price. What we do control is the cost, and in the near term this reflects the efficiency and the effectiveness of our operations.'

An operations manager

▶ Chapter survival toolkit

▶ Overview

The previous chapter considered capital spending. This chapter moves on to look at various ways of classifying, analysing, interpreting and projecting costs of all kinds. The main thrust is the management of costs relative to the bottom line – net profit. Accordingly, we will mainly review costs on an accruals basis, as discussed in Chapter 8. By and large, this is the closest that accounting comes to assessing costs in the way that a manager needs to look at them. Activity-based costing – a relatively new buzz phrase for old logic – is also considered and extended.

▶ Prerequisites

It will help if you have read about the basic principles of financial record keeping (Chapter 7), seasonality (Chapter 9) and capital spending (Chapter 11). If you want to run the numbers yourself, you will need some familiarity with spreadsheets (Chapter 4). It also helps you to spot trends and patterns if you draw charts (Chapter 5).

▶ Mastering cost control

If you can answer the following questions after reading this chapter, you will be well placed to analyse and project costs:

1 Why do accountants and managers have various ways of classifying costs?

2 What do managers want to know about costs?

3 When analysing costs, should you focus on industry, product, geographic area or functional area?

4 Why divide functional costs into employee and non-employee costs?

5 How do you project costs?

6 When identifying production or operating costs, how do you account for capital spending and refundable deposits paid?

7 How can managers massage costs? Why would they do so?

8 As a manager, what tells you most about your costs: financial accounting, management accounting, cost accounting, or activity-based costing?

9 What is absorption costing? Is it accurate?

10 What is activity-based costing? Why is it important to managers?

> 'I don't pay good wages because I have a lot of money; I have a lot of money because I pay good wages.'
>
> **Robert Bosch**

> ## Jargon watch

Budding beans-talk

Trading costs, production costs, operating costs

Direct costs, indirect costs

Current spending

Income/revenue costs

Employee costs

Absorption costing

Activity-based costing

Contingency

Off-balance sheet*

Inventory costs/LIFO*

Provisions*

* First mention: not fully defined in this chapter.

Beans-talk already met

Cost of sales

Capital spending, capitalize

Fixed assets

Depreciation, amortization

Contingency reserve

Liabilities

Economics jargon from earlier pages

Seasonality/seasonal patterns

> ## Where the money goes

The previous chapter examined spending on fixed assets. Now I want to talk about how you analyse all other expenditure and how you analyse, interpret, project and manage costs in general.

> ### Costs in the financials

There are many ways of categorizing spending; but, for basic analysis, approvals, and reporting, beanies carve up costs as follows:

Seven ways of looking at costs

1 Production, trading, operating.
2 Direct, indirect.
3 Capital, current.
4 By category of product or service.
5 Geographic – by territory or region.
6 Functional – R & D, production, sales, etc.
7 Employee, non-employee.

1 **Production costs (cost of sales)** – current spending *directly* associated with sales, such as the acquisition of raw materials and the costs of production.

2 **Other operating expenses** – *indirect* current consumption; overheads such as the finance director's salary and other administrative costs which drain the bank balance whether you sell anything or not.

3 **Capital** – spending on assets with an expected life beyond the current accounting year, such as clump presses and aircraft.

4 **Other (non-operating)** – generally nasty stuff such as taxation and interest on loans.

> When accountants refer to current spending on production and operating overheads they sometimes say ' these costs should be **charged to income**' or refer to them as **revenue costs**. This may seem to be a contradiction in terms, but there you are.

We have already taken a look at capital spending, which feeds into production and operating costs. In this chapter we will look at costs in general and operating expenses in particular. In the next two chapters we will look at the cost of sales and other costs.

▶ Breaking it apart

As always, the key to dealing with any problem is to break it into little pieces. Your company structure may have achieved the first step already. The top level may be organized along one of the following lines:

1 Industry or product – soaps, aerospace, brands.

2 Geography – Spain, Europe, North-West.

3 Function – R&D, sales, etc.

Corporations are likely to move up this structural tree as their products and services become less homogeneous and the business grows – although the first two items on the list might be switched around. Basically, for forecasting and projection, you want to make these splits until you reach level three – activities organized by function. Then:

1 For each functional area, separate spending into employee and non-employee costs.

2 For each of employee and non-employee costs, separate spending into related sub-categories: salaries, overtime, premises, office, travel, and so on.

In a moment we will step through each of these items.

▶ Timing

You could analyse costs on a cash basis – when the spending took place rather than when the goods or services were consumed. However, for management review and financial reporting you will want to look at costs on an accruals accounting basis (Chapter 8). This moves you closer to matching spending and results. I have already introduced the method of passing the bookkeeping entries to achieve this. If you are recording your own financials on this basis, or if your bean counter or accounting department is doing it for you, your historical figures will be ready for review.

When you come to projecting costs, as far as possible try to match them to the relevant months. For example, for a bonus which is payable in December, you should record $\frac{1}{12}$ of the amount against each month of the year. For quarterly rent paid in January, show one-third against each of the first three months of the year. In Chapter 16 I will show you how to convert this bookkeeping into a cash flow forecast.

▶ When costs are not expenditure

Right now, we are trying to analyse and project the underlying spending which goes into profit or loss. Some outlays do not count as production or operating costs. We have already covered fixed assets – where the original outlay is treated as an asset and only depreciation is counted as expenditure against net profit.

Another obvious example is when you pay a refundable deposit when you rent a vehicle or office space. At some time in the future, this will be paid back to you (unless you trash the place, in which case the deposit really will become an expense).

Clearly you want to know about such payments, without recording them as expenses. Accordingly, when working through the costs figures, you should identify any spending which creates an *asset* and make a note of it in a separate spread-sheet table. In Chapter 15 you will record these in the balance sheet.

Similarly, keep an eye open for activities which do not involve spending now, but which might create a liability in the future – such as taxes. If the cost is *more likely than not* to occur, you will need to record it as a liability when you come to draw up a balance sheet. Other liabilities, such as possible adverse legal cases or environment clean-ups, should at least be noted for management review – and possibly there is a disclosure requirement. For the moment, just make notes. Later we will look at this in more detail.

▶ The certainty of taxes

Benjamin Franklin once said that the only two certainties in life are death and taxation. If so, the only certainty for a corporation is taxation, which is a bit distressing. By and large the Grim Reaper pays scant attention to companies (see *Debt restructuring*, Chapter 19). But taxes pop up all over the place and they need to be identified separately. For example, if you spend $110 on telephone bills and $10 is a sales tax, you should show $100 as a telecoms expense and $10 as taxation. This is particularly important with value added taxes – and other taxes where you can claim back all or part of the taxes you pay – because the tax may or may not be a cost depending on the level of your sales (see also *Debts and taxation* in Chapter 8). I know it is a certainly a pain to split all this spending into two parts, but remember that I am only the messenger.

▶ Employee costs

Employee costs are probably the easiest outlays to analyse and project. You have an unmistakably identifiable headcount (if not, go out and count them) and the associated costs are usually clearly defined and probably well documented. Employee costs go far beyond salaries and wages, as indicated in Fig. 12.1. You may also have other categories of expenditure, such as uniforms and – dare I mention it again – rice allowances.

Fig. 12.1 Twenty-four categories of employee-related costs

(*Read down, prefixing each item with the words 'employee-related'.*)

Direct	Benefits	Other costs
Salaries	Termination benefits	Recruitment
Wages	Pension plan	Relocation
Overtime	Rent allowances	Legal expenses
Shift allowances	Transport allowances	Training
Bonuses	Other allowances	Secondment
Employers' social welfare	Medical cover	Medical expenses
Employers' payroll taxes	Accident insurance	Professional subscriptions
Contract and temporary staff costs	Life assurance	Entertainment

You can use a spreadsheet to tabulate employee costs for the purposes of budgeting and financial reporting – see Fig. 12.2. It is a good idea to duplicate this table (use copy and paste) and then replace the monetary figures with percentages of the totals. Put a column into a pie chart for a quick visual representation of the breakdown. By reviewing the monetary amounts and the percentage breakdown, you get a good idea of where your employee costs hurt most.

Analysis of employee costs might be by functional or geographic area. When producing financials for a business as a whole, you will certainly need one table for staff involved in production (cost of sales) and another for other workers. To see how much any one employee costs you, you will make a table listing salary, overtime, bonuses, employers' social security contributions, and all the other employee-benefits and costs for that person. Your company's salary records will already have this information, but for management analysis you may want to include an apportionment of office costs and so on.

▶ Looking ahead

Your headcount projections follow naturally from your forecasts, estimates, budgets and business plans. When you know what you want to do, you can work out how many people with what skills you need to make it happen. Some of these may be on your payroll already. If you are starting a new business or expanding you will need to recruit. You will know from your existing payroll and your industry knowledge what packages of salaries and benefits you will need to provide. From here on it is simple arithmetic.

If you were paying attention, you will be aware that the spreadsheet you use to project employee costs is formatted similarly to that in Fig. 12.2. Essentially, for each item, enter $\frac{1}{12}$ of the annual total against each month, allowing for pay rises, amendments in social security rates and other changes. For some categories, you can use formula to calculate the amounts, such as when social security contributions are, say, 7.5% of salaries.

Fig. 12.2 Employee costs

	A	B	C	D	E	F	G	H	I
1		TETRYLUS Inc.							
2		Staff costs, first six months							
3		Dollars							
4									
5			Month 1	Month 2	Month 3	Month 4	Month 5	Month 6	H1
6		STAFF NUMBERS							
7		Directors/managers	3	3	3	3	3	3	3
8		Technical staff	2	4	4	4	4	4	4
9		Marketing staff	0	1	1	2	2	2	2
10		Administrative staff	2	2	2	2	2	3	3
11		Total	7	10	10	11	11	12	12
12									
13		STAFF COSTS							
14		Staff salaries							
15	S-1	Technical staff 1	5,000	5,000	5,000	5,000	5,000	5,000	30,000
16	S-2	Technical staff 2	5,000	5,000	5,000	5,000	5,000	5,000	30,000
17	S-3	Technical staff 3	–	5,000	5,000	5,000	5,000	5,000	25,000
18	S-4	Technical staff 4	–	5,000	5,000	5,000	5,000	5,000	25,000
19	S-5	Sales/distribution manager	–	–	–	5,000	5,000	5,000	15,000
20	S-6	Marketing assistant	–	2,500	2,500	2,500	2,500	2,500	12,500
21	S-7	Bookkeeping, etc	–	–	–	–	–	2,000	2,000
22	S-8	Receptionist/secretary	2,000	2,000	2,000	2,000	2,000	2,000	12,000
23	S-9	Messenger/security	1,500	1,500	1,500	1,500	1,500	1,500	9,000
24	S-00	TOTAL (sum S1 to S9)	13,500	26,000	26,000	31,000	31,000	33,000	160,500
25	S-11	Directors' stipends	10,000	10,000	10,000	10,000	10,000	10,000	60,000
26	S-13	Contract staff	10,000	10,000	10,000	10,000	10,000	10,000	60,000
27	S-14	Staff social security	1,763	2,700	2,700	3,075	3,075	3,225	16,538
28	S-15	Staff temporary	–	–	–	–	–	–	–
29	S-10	TOTAL DIRECT (11 to 19)	21,763	22,700	22,700	23,075	23,075	23,225	136,538
30	S-21	Staff pension fund	3,375	6,500	6,500	7,750	7,750	8,250	40,125
31	S-22	Staff termination fund	–	–	–	–	–	–	–
32	S-23	Staff rent allowances	–	–	–	–	–	–	–
33	S-24	Staff transport allowances	–	–	–	–	–	–	–
34	S-25	Staff other allowances	–	–	–	–	–	–	–
35	S-26	Staff group insurance	–	–	–	–	–	–	–
36	S-27	Staff medical insurance	12,000	–	–	–	–	–	12,000
37	S-28	Staff other benefits	–	–	–	–	–	–	–
38	S-20	TOTAL BENEFITS (21 to 29)	15,375	6,500	6,500	7,750	7,750	8,250	52,125
39	S-31	Staff medical expenses	–	–	–	–	–	–	–
40	S-32	Staff recruitment	–	–	–	–	–	–	–
41	S-33	Staff relocation	–	–	–	–	–	–	–
42	S-34	Staff legal expenses	3,500	–	–	–	–	–	3,500
43	S-36	Staff training	–	–	–	–	–	–	–
44	S-38	Staff entertainment	140	200	200	220	220	240	1,220
45	S-39	Staff sundry	–	–	–	–	–	–	–
46	S-30	TOTAL OTHER (31 to 39)	3,640	200	200	220	220	240	4,720
47	S-100	TOTAL STAFF (00+10+20+30)	54,278	55,400	55,400	62,045	62,045	64,715	353,883

Error trapping: The total for the first half year (reading down the right-hand column) should equal the sum of the six months (reading across the bottom row). Use the spreadsheet SUM formula to check. If these two totals are not identical, there is an error in your spreadsheet formula.

▶ Non-employee costs

Other costs, those not associated with employees, are generally fairly simple to analyse and project. Figure 12.3 lists over 50 categories of operating costs. You probably will not use all of these, but there may be other categories specific to your business.

Again, it is a case of working through the categories and examining the amounts in question. Figure 12.4 shows one way of classifying operating costs. Again, this might be for a function, geographic area, or the business as a whole. As before, you will probably want to duplicate this table and replace money amounts with percentages (of the totals) so you can get a better feel for where the money goes. Pie charts and stacked column charts can help you to visualize this. As with employee costs, when reviewing and projecting financials for a business as a whole, you will require one table for cost of sales and another for other costs.

Note that you do not include capital spending here – only depreciation for the period under consideration (see previous chapter).

Fig. 12.3 Fifty-plus other operating costs

(Read down under each heading.)

Marketing & sales	Occupancy	Office
Delivery, shipping, etc.	Dep'n, lease/f'hold improvements	Depreciation, furniture
Brochures and printing	Premises rental & taxes	Depreciation, equipment
Advertising	Heating and air-conditioning	Leased furniture
Direct mail	Electricity	Small equipment purchases
Exhibitions, seminars, etc.	Water	Stationery & printing
Promotional items & events	Security	Dues & subscriptions
PR, charities, community	Building repairs & maintenance	Books & periodicals
Other marketing & sales	Other occupancy	Other office

Communications	Computers	Travel & subsistence
Depreciation, telecoms	Depreciation, computers	Depreciation, vehicles
Telephone & fax	Leased hardware	Motor vehicle rental
Information services	Software licences	Motor vehicle expenses
Postage & courier	Software maintenance	Travel & subsistence
Messengerial	Computer consumables	Entertainment
Other communications	Other IT	Other TS&E

Professional fees	Other fees & costs	Other adjustments
Accounting fees	Insurance	Amortization, start-up costs
Audit fees	Bank charges	P&L on disposal of assets
Legal fees	Relocation costs	Bad debts & provisions
Other professional fees	Sundry expenditure	Contingency

PR = public relations, TS&E = travel, subsistence and entertainment.

Fig. 12.4 Operating costs detailed

	A	B	C	D	E	F	G	H	I
1		**TETRYLUS Inc.**							
2									
3		**Operating costs, first six months**							
4		Dollars							
5									
6			Month 1	Month 2	Month 3	Month 4	Month 5	Month 6	H1
7	E-11	Premises rental & taxes	1,000	1,000	1,000	1,000	1,000	1,000	**6,000**
8	E-12	Amort'n – lease improvements	0	542	542	542	542	542	**2,710**
9	E-13	Utilities	500	500	500	500	500	500	**3,000**
10	**E-10**	**TOTAL OCCUPANCY**	**1,500**	**2,042**	**2,042**	**2,042**	**2,042**	**2,042**	**11,710**
11	E-21	Dep'n – office furniture	0	83	83	83	83	83	**415**
12	E-22	Dep'n – office equipment	0	0	0	13	13	13	**39**
13	E-23	Small equipment	100	100	0	0	0	0	**200**
14	E-24	Stationery & printing	100	25	25	25	25	25	**225**
15	E-25	Dues & subscriptions	100	100	100	100	100	100	**600**
16	E-26	Books & periodicals	50	50	50	50	50	50	**300**
17	E-27	Other office	50	50	50	50	50	50	**300**
18	**E-20**	**TOTAL OFFICE**	**400**	**408**	**308**	**321**	**321**	**321**	**2,079**
19	E-31	Dep'n – coms. equipment	0	0	0	0	0	0	**0**
20	E-32	Telephone & fax	2,500	2,500	2,500	2,500	2,500	2,500	**15,000**
21	E-33	Information services	100	100	100	100	100	100	**600**
22	E-34	Postage & courier	250	250	250	250	250	250	**1,500**
23	**E-30**	**TOTAL COMMS**	**2,850**	**2,850**	**2,850**	**2,850**	**2,850**	**2,850**	**17,100**
24	E-41	Depreciation – computers	0	556	597	597	625	625	**3,000**
25	E-42	Depreciation – software	0	208	208	208	208	208	**1,040**
26	E-43	Other software licences	500	0	0	0	0	0	**500**
27	E-45	Computer consumables	50	50	50	50	50	50	**300**
28	**E-40**	**TOTAL COMPUTERS**	**550**	**814**	**855**	**855**	**883**	**883**	**4,840**
29	E-51	Product distribution	0	0	500	1,000	300	2,500	**4,300**
30	E-52	Brochures and printing	0	5,000	2,500	0	0	0	**7,500**
31	E-55	Promotional items	0	2,500	0	0	0	0	**2,500**
32	E-59	Other marketing	0	5,000	5,000	0	0	0	**10,000**
33	**E-50**	**TOTAL MKTG & SALES**	**0**	**12,500**	**8,000**	**1,000**	**300**	**2,500**	**24,300**
34	E-61	Depreciation – vehicles	0	0	0	0	0	0	**0**
35	E-62	Rental – vehicles	0	0	0	0	0	0	**0**
36	E-63	Motor vehicle expenses	100	100	100	100	100	100	**600**
37	E-64	Travel & subsistence	5,000	10,000	10,000	10,000	10,000	10,000	**55,000**
38	E-65	Entertainment	0	0	0	0	0	0	**0**
39	**E-60**	**TOTAL TS&E***	**5,100**	**10,100**	**10,100**	**10,100**	**10,100**	**10,100**	**55,600**
40	E-71	Audit fees	0	0	0	0	0	0	**0**
41	E-72	Legal fees	1,000	2,500	1,000	0	0	0	**4,500**
42	E-75	Other professional fees	0	0	0	0	0	0	**0**
43	**E-70**	**TOTAL PROF FEES**	**1,000**	**2,500**	**1,000**	**0**	**0**	**0**	**4,500**
44	E-83	Insurance	1,000	2,500	0	0	0	0	**3,500**
45	E-85	Sundry expenditure	100	100	100	100	100	100	**600**
46	E-86	Other	0	0	0	0	0	0	**0**
47	**E-80**	**TOTAL OTHER**	**1,100**	**2,600**	**100**	**100**	**100**	**100**	**4,100**
48	**E-100**	**TOTAL EXPENDITURE**	**12,500**	**33,814**	**25,255**	**17,268**	**16,596**	**18,796**	**124,229**

Note: Calculations are performed on <u>unrounded</u> figures to greater accuracy than is shown here. As with all illustrations in this book, the detailed spreadsheet is available for download at www.ManagingTheNumbers.com.

* Travel, subsistence and entertainment

▶ Non-employee costs in the future

As with employee costs, other costs are easy to project once you have determined your business needs. Start with a spreadsheet similar to Fig. 12.4 and work through it one row at a time. The projections will be based on logic.

Take a simple example. Suppose that you estimate that you will spend approximately $500 on stationery each month. Should you just enter $500 for each month? Or should you work out exactly what will be purchased in which months and arrive at a projection such as 534 for January, 405 in February, and so on? The answer is self-evident when you apply cost-benefit logic. How much work is required to arrive at the estimates – compared to the usefulness of the results. How large are the amounts in relation to the overall plan? What is the importance of capturing any erratic patterns?

For example, if you know that total expenditure will be tens of thousands of dollars a month and spending on fuel will vary by around $50 a month you can safely use the same amount for each month (the projected annual spend divided by 12). It would be pointless to spend a day trying to achieve an exact projection. On the other hand, if you expected outlays on fuel to vary by 50% a month you should use a closer projection for each month.

▶ Depreciation revisited

When you built up your capital spending plans you created a depreciation schedule. This gives you several ready-made entries for your cost tables. Just pull the depreciation figures into the production and operating cost spreadsheets. For example, leasehold improvements in the operating costs shown in Fig. 12.4 (line E-12) are copied directly from the depreciation schedule shown in Fig. 11.5 (line D-11). As you can see, the work you do early-on feeds into the later tasks. Forecasting becomes easier and easier as you progress.

▶ Precision projections

At this point, you might be saying that it is all very well for me to ask you to project costs, but more difficult for you to do. Well, in fact, there are some handy rules of thumb that you can apply. The obvious one – I hardly like to mention this – is to assess spending for the year and divide by 12. Other techniques are as follows:

1 **More of the same.** Sometimes, perhaps all too infrequently, you can take last year's spending, or perhaps the most-recent known monthly amount, and extend it (unaltered) into the future. This works well for lease contracts without escalation clauses and other spending where there is no seasonality or inflation. There may be predetermined step changes when, for example, an escalation clause in a lease contract kicks in.

2 **Fixed relationships.** Sometimes, one row has a simple proportional relationship to another. Rental contracts for office premises occasionally cover rent, heating or air conditioning, and water – each charged at a fixed rate per square

foot or metre of floor area. Aside from allowing for an annual rent review, each of these rows in the forecast is calculated in the spreadsheet as 'office area in square metres × rate-per-square-metre'. You can often calculate costs in relation to employee headcount. Might it be logical to project costs of computer printout paper at some fixed multiple of the number of accountants that you have?

3 **Steady rates of change**. When any alternative rational is absent, it may be legitimate to assume a steadily increasing (or, more rarely, decreasing) pattern, such as a 1% a month increase. Do not forget that this compounds. For example, a 10% increase each month is equivalent to 127% a year, not 120%.

4 **Seasonal pattern**. There might be a seasonal pattern that you can rely on. For example, you might project annual heating and air conditioning costs, and then allocate them among the months according to some observed pattern (11.0% of the annual total in January, 9.5% in February, 8.3% in March, and so on).

5 **Seasonal with steady change**. The effects of a steady rate of change and a seasonal pattern can be combined. A quick fix is to take a fixed change (i.e. + 10%) over the same month a year earlier.

Bad debts

If you give credit, or invoice after delivery, chances are you will have uncollectable debts. Accountants and other misunderstood professionals realize that their clients do not like to pay. These professionals frequently do not *recognize* their fees in their accounts until payment is safely in the bank. For the rest of us, a percentage of debts, or of debts over a certain age, is usually charged to operating costs as a provision for bad debts (see Chapter 8). Show this as:

◆ a charge (debit) entry in the operating expenses account (i.e. an extra line in Fig. 12.4).

◆ matched by a deduction (credit) to accounts receivable on the assets side of the balance sheet.

▶ Careful

When you are reviewing financials produced by others, watch for cheating. Figure 12.5 lists some tricks used – and watched for – by wily old dogs. More detailed examples include:

◆ **Inventory valuation**: such as using LIFO (*last-in first-out*) valuation where acquisition costs are falling in a high-tech business, to boost profits and minimize inventory shown on the balance sheet (see Chapter 13).

◆ **Depreciation**, amortization and depletion were discussed in Chapter 11. *Stretching the life of that new computer to ten years will make operating costs look much lower this year.* Similar tricks can be played with other accruals accounting techniques, including **capitalizing costs**: *we won't charge R&D outlays to the expenditure account, we will put them on the balance sheet as an asset.*

◆ **Leasing** was also touched on in Chapter 11. Other **off-balance sheet liabilities** are considered in Chapter 15. It is not unknown for companies to sell their inventories with an undertaking to buy them back when they are needed – creating cash in the bank and a hidden liability.

◆ **Provisions** for future payments to employees (such as pensions, redundancy and terminations pay) and bad debts are often covered by statutory regulations. Remember though that no money changes hands when the provisions are created by stroke of the bookkeeping pen – and when they are disbursed there is no entry on the profit and loss account.

◆ **Sub-contracting work or paying service fees** can shift money from one business to some other favoured firm. Moreover, since accounts show only payments actually incurred, outsourcing *increases* costs. The third party's fee will include a profit that would have been a *saving* if you had done it yourself. You cannot show *savings* in the profit and loss account – only actual spending.

◆ Finally, **timing errors** can build a useful cash reserve. Getting the seasonal pattern wrong was discussed a couple of pages back. Accruals accounting is another way that this can be achieved – an entry goes in the cash flow as a cost early on but, oops, it turns out that the cost can be treated as an accrued cost for a few months.

Fig. 12.5 Fourteen areas where managers massage costs

(Read downwards.)

Where no money changes hands

1 Inventory valuation

2 Depreciation

3 Amortization

4 Depletion

5 Provisions for payments to employees (e.g. termination costs)

6 Provision for bad debts

7 Contingency reserve

With identifiable spending

8 Capitalizing costs (R&D, interest on projects, etc.)

9 Leasing

10 Inflating or skimping on maintenance and repairs

11 Discretionary bonuses

12 Sub-contracting

13 Service fees

14 Timing errors

How to cut overheads at a stroke

Costs incurred in the factory – including administrative costs – are costs of sales, while office costs are usually operating expenses. This gives rise to a number of grey areas, especially in today's higher-tech industries. Where, for example, do you take the cost of personnel involved in watching quality? You will be able to make such decisions based on your understanding of your business.

Note, though, that sales costs are often accepted more or less as given ($x per item), while other overheads are subject to greater scrutiny. By *moving* spending into the cost-of-sales areas, managers can make their operating costs look leaner and avoid budget cuts. The message, obviously, is that all costs need the same careful examination and questioning.

Other income and costs

There is one more category to consider – the things which are outside of normal trading operations, such as interest, exchange rate gains and losses, investment income from equity stakes in other companies, and taxation. These are usually shown as 'after thoughts' in the profit and loss account – as explained in Chapter 14, which is also where I will review the related accounting issues.

I am sure that you are always asking how to cut the company's tax bill. It does not need to be said that you need to consider the tax implications of all financial transactions. Interest paid and received should be assessed in relation to cash balances – make sure that borrowing is controlled (Chapter 19) and that any idle balances are put to good use. Of course, the general principle is that companies should not speculate on the stock market or foreign exchange markets (unless, of course, this is their main business). Accordingly, you should take measures to limit the risks, discussion of which I will save for Chapter 23.

Looking ahead: a footnote

In the foregoing discussion, I outlined the way that you project employee and other spending. There is one footnote required. It is not really feasible to estimate all your future revenue and spending to the last penny. Rather than allowing slack in any specific item of spending, you should estimate each one as accurately as possible. It would be good if in the event over-estimates cancelled out under-estimates. In practice, under-shooting is rare. Accordingly, it is usual to build in a contingency which can be raided if necessary. Provided that outturn is less than the projection for total spending including contingency, you will have met your planning figures. The contingency is usually added at the end of the spending accounts, as summarized in Fig. 12.6. In this example, there is an allowance of 10% of total spending. Watch that contingencies do not become an excuse for excessive spending. If the estimates are basically last year's spending plus 10%, and there is another 10% contingency on top, you have effectively authorized a 20% surge in outlays.

'The accurate measurement of input costs is essential for determining whether the corporation earned a profit from its current activities. That determination was relatively straightforward when all receipts were cash and all expenses were cash costs. But, changes in balance-sheet valuations based on fragile forecasts have become a more important element in determining whether a particular corporate strategy was successful. And, as a consequence, cost estimation has become ever more problematic. But the principle of measuring profit as the value of output less the value of input is not altered by complexity of measurement.'

Alan Greenspan

Fig. 12.6 Being prepared – contingency planning in financial projections

	A	B	C	D	E	F	G	H	I
1		TETRYLUS Inc.							
2									
3		**Spending plan, first six months**							
4		Dollars							
5									
6			Month 1	Month 2	Month 3	Month 4	Month 5	Month 6	H1
7	S-100	Employee costs	54,278	55,400	55,400	62,045	62,045	64,715	**353,883**
8	E-100	Other expenditure	12,500	33,814	25,255	17,268	16,596	18,796	**124,229**
9	C-01	**Total op. costs**	**66,778**	**89,214**	**80,655**	**79,313**	**78,641**	**83,511**	**478,112**
10	C-02	Contingency	6,678	8,921	8,066	7,931	7,864	8,351	**47,811**
11	C-100	**Operating costs incl. contingency**	**73,456**	**98,135**	**88,721**	**87,244**	**86,505**	**91,862**	**525,923**

How managers assess costs

So far, we have discussed mainly the accountants' concept of cost allocation – with some lip service to economists. However, one of the most valuable assessments you can make is a review of costs by product or service. And for each item, you also need a breakdown by activity – development, production, sales, etc. You can then set these figures against revenues by product to see how your lines really stack up.

But how? Traditional cost accounting falls down in some areas. Its approach to *direct* product costs is fine, but it then assumes that *indirect* costs are allocated to products in some arbitrary way. The most usual method is to say that this product generates 20% of our revenue so we will assume that it *absorbs* 20% of our overheads. This is known as *absorption costing*. Clearly it is rather nonsensical. There may be minimal or huge overheads associated with one product – and completely the opposite situation with another. A better approach is *activity-based costing* – where you try to identify which overheads are associated with which activities. But even this falls flat on its face due to arbitrary inventory and depreciation valuations.

'To believe with certainty we must begin with doubting.'
Stanislaus I of Poland

▶ Common-sense costing

For management purposes, there is no better way to consider costs than to aggressively re-assess the financials, re-estimate inventory and fixed asset accounting, and apply logic and common sense to the allocation of costs.

Basically, try to make an accurate economic assessment of costs and benefits of your fixed assets, and the real cost of inventory. Use these figures in your management analysis in place of the bean counter's figures. Then take all of your spending and revenues – including bad debts, interest and tax – and try to allocate each dollar to a specific product. Remember to adjust these figures to get at the underlying picture. For example, if there were large bad debts relating to one product, and you honestly assess that there were special circumstances which will not be repeated, do not include all of the debts as costs of the product. You will build big spreadsheets based on a great deal of management judgement. But you will gain a good understanding of how each product shapes up.

At the end of the exercise, you want a list of products showing the profit from each one (sales less costs) and the margins (sales divided by costs). You will now see which product really does contribute most to your bottom line in cash terms, and which is most profitable in terms of the profit margin. You need to ask why these figures are as they are. For example, *why do we make such a big margin on this product, but it only generates a small part of our total revenue? Why does this product contribute so much revenue but at such a small margin?* Is there anything special about production, purchasing or sales techniques for the products with big margins which could be applied elsewhere? Can we concentrate on high-margin products and drop some with low margins? And so on.

▶ Ten hard questions to ask or be asked

1 Do you have a complete breakdown of costs by item for each functional area?

2 Are cost items correctly identified as spending on assets, cost of sales, overheads etc.?

3 Are taxes properly accounted for?

4 Is management analysis based on common sense costing?

5 Can you identify which costs are fixed, over what ranges, and which ones are variable?

6 Are spending projections realistic? Have seasonal factors been caught?

7 Is the timing of spending properly identified?

8 Is there proper control over spending, including items which are refundable (e.g. deposits, samples) and do such refunds end up in the company bank account?

9 Have bookkeeping entries been massaged (depreciation, inventory valuation, etc.)?

10 Is spending hunkydory (sub-contracting to whom? inflated or skimped maintenance, discretionary bonuses, etc.)?

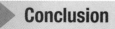

Conclusion

Careful assessment of quantities (e.g. headcount) and costs by category will give you a good feel for the way that the numbers stack up. Ratios, such as the margins just considered, are very valuable. We will return to these in Chapter 18. As for how you actually manage spending during the year, we will come on to this in Chapter 22. Next, though, I want to revisit sales and the directly associated costs.

> 'Everyone from bankers to venture capitalists to investors to bankruptcy courts is paying more attention to cash forecasts.'
>
> **Claudia Volk**

13

getting to gross profit

'The superior man understands what is right; the inferior man understands what will sell.'

Confucius

▶ Chapter survival toolkit

▶ Overview

Gross profit is sales less costs of sales. This chapter examines these costs arithmetically. It looks at product and production costs and inventory calculations – how you analyse, interpret and forecast them. It then pulls them together with the sales forecast you made back in Chapter 10 to arrive at gross profit. The next chapter brings in the other costs to arrive at the all-important figure for net profit.

▶ Prerequisites

If you were up to speed with the previous chapter, this one should be easy. When looking ahead, you will also need a sales forecast, which we discussed in Chapter 10.

▶ Mastering sales, production costs and inventory management

After reading this chapter, you should be able to answer the following questions:

1 What are sales revenue/turnover and the cost of sales?

2 How important is the concept of gross profit?

3 On what basis might you set prices?

4 What are the relevance of direct and indirect/fixed and variable costs?

5 What are product costs?

6 What is inventory?

7 How would you value inventory; what are the relative merits of specific costs, averaging, FIFO and LIFO?

8 How does inventory valuation affect your tax bill and the interpretation of financial reports?

9 How would you project your cost of sales and gross profit?

10 What bookkeeping entries are passed to record movements in inventory?

> 'A retail purchase is the last step in a long chain … that involves ordering, invoicing, sorting, loading and unloading, and shipping. Each step uses resources and creates potential mistakes, shortages or excess inventories.'
>
> **Martin Neil Baily**

▶ **Jargon watch**

New beanie words

Manufacturing account, trading account

Gross profit, gross sales, sales turnover

Profit margin

Pricing; cost-plus, value-based, mark-up

Inventory, stock-in-trade

Inventory valuation: specific unit costs/specific identification, averaging, FIFO, LIFO

New economics jargon

Price elasticity of demand, cross-elasticity, inelasticity

Unit costs

Beanie words taking an encore

Assets

Cost of sales

Contra

Direct costs, indirect costs, fixed costs, variable costs

Absorption costing

The bottom line near the top of the page

You will be pleased to know, I hope, that we are now moving on to look at how you arrive at gross profit. The arithmetic is no more complex than *sales revenue* less the *cost of sales*. However, if you thought that we had finished with our discussion of costs, think again. In this chapter, we will look more closely at the costs related to product or production costs and inventory. We will also look at pricing policies.

By the way, you will occasionally hear Americans refer to gross profit as gross *margin*. I think the idea is to avoid calling the figure *profit* – but for many of us margins are *ratios*. Gross profit is an important step on the way to net profit, but it is definitely not the bottom line. We will discuss the distinction between gross and net in the next chapter.

Tetrylus Inc.

Gross profit, year 5
Sales of hardware only

	US dollars
Sales	21 870 000
Less Cost of sales	5 832 000
Gross profit	**16 038 000**
Less Other expenses	4 038 000
Net profit	**12 000 000**

Sales revisited

Back in Chapters 9 and 10 you analysed and forecast sales volumes. It is time to pull those figures out of the hat and combine them with cost and pricing to analyse and forecast gross profit. I will start by discussing ways to project sales revenue.

▶ Pricing policies

Pricing policies may be determined by your corporate pricing strategy, market conditions, and the stage of the product life cycle (Fig. 9.1).

The price that you *could* charge depends on a concept that economists call *elasticity* (well, *price elasticity of demand* if you want the whole stretchy nine yards).

◆ Products that are price elastic are very sensitive to changes in price. Take a dollar off and sales will go through the roof. Add a dollar and sales will plummet. This is a situation where you might slash prices to achieve market penetration and win market share – but where the result might instead be price wars.

◆ *Inelastic prices* mean that it is hard to influence the level of sales by tinkering with prices – but on the other hand, you may be able to jack them up without seeing a fall in sales. In such instances, you might aim for quality, selling at a higher price to a smaller number of customers – skimming the cream off the market.

◆ *Cross elasticity* indicates the extent to which sales are influenced by the prices of competing products. If airfares rise, more people might travel by train.

Your knowledge of the market and trend analysis should give you a good feel for elasticity and how you can influence sales by changing your prices.

Corporate pricing objectives...

1 **Maximize current profits** – even if, for example, by cutting prices you damage longer-term profitability.
2 **Maximize current revenue** – perhaps by selling at a loss with the ultimate aim of increasing market share.
3 **Maximize quantity** – see above.
4 **Maximize profit margin** – by selling a lower quantity at a higher price.
5 **Quality leadership** – using price as a signal.
6 **Partial cost recovery** – better than nothing.
7 **Survival** – covering costs only.
8 **Status quo** – avoiding price wars.

... pricing strategy ...

1 **Cost-plus** – production costs plus a fixed mark-up.
2 **Value-based** – what the market will bear, perhaps on a client-by-client basis.
3 **Modelled** – using price points, signals of quality, subscription plans, etc.

... and discounting policies

1 **Trade discount** – for business partners who will generate sales for you.
2 **Quantity discount** – for customers who purchase in quantity.
3 **Cumulative quantity discount** – for customers and resellers who purchase large quantities over time but do not place large orders up front.
4 **Seasonal and timing discount** – such as off-season and weekend hotel rates and off-peak rate telephone charging.
5 **Promotional discount** – to boost sales in the short term.
6 **Cash discount** – for paying bills on time.

Sales volumes to values

When you have determined your pricing method, you will have either actual prices or mark-ups ready to feed into your projections. In the latter case, you can arrive at prices by applying the multiplier to costs. For example, if your costs of production are $100 and your mark-up is 10%, the price is going to be $110.

Once you know the price, multiply it by the volume to arrive at sales revenues. There is an example in Fig. 10.3, where in year five of the forecast period the company expects to sell 600 000 smart badges at $36 each. This would take total sales of these items to $21.9 million (i.e. 600 000 × 36 = 21,870,000), as shown in Fig. 13.1.

> British bean counters use the jargon **turnover** to mean gross **sales** revenue, and **stock**, or stock-in-trade, for **inventory**. Frankly the American terms sales and inventory are much less ambiguous.

Fig. 13.1 Gross sales

	A	B	C	D	E	F	
61	TETRYLUS Inc.						
62							
63	**Gross sales, first five years**						
64	Dollars						
65		Year 1	Year 2	Year 3	Year 4	Year 5	Notes: see Figs 10.3 and 13.6
66	**Gross sales**						
67	Hardware	307,200	2,100,000	14,850,000	18,225,000	21,870,000	Line 18 × line 26
68	Software	14,000	52,500	396,000	540,000	720,000	Line 19 × line 27
69	**Total**	321,200	2,152,500	15,246,000	18,765,000	22,590,000	Line 67 + line 68

Bookkeeping

Generally you record a sale net of any discounts. The exception can be where you offer a discount for cash. For example, if you make a $100 sale and the customer pays early, claiming a $2 discount, you probably record this gross by crediting sales with $100, and then posting a *contra* charge to sales – discounts. You could also post it net by crediting $98 direct to sales.

> **Reminder:** a **contra** account has the opposite balance to **usual**. For example, accumulated depreciation is an asset account with a credit balance (asset accounts usually have debit balances), while sales discounts is a sales account (which usually have credit balances) with a debit balance.

> 'Inventories can be managed, but people must be led.'
>
> **H. Ross Perot**

▶ Cost of sales

▶ What counts as cost of sales?

Cost of sales, sometimes perplexingly referred to as cost of goods sold, includes all the spending directly associated with the sales. A few examples should make this clear:

- For wholesalers, retailers and other resellers, costs of sales is essentially the price paid to acquire the goods or services that will be resold.
- For a software company, the cost of sales might be identified as $\frac{1}{100}$ of the cost of research and development directly associated with developing the product (if lifetime sales are expected to be 100 copies). Or cost of sales might be booked each month as $\frac{1}{24}$ of the cost of development, if the product is estimated to have a life of two years.
- In other manufacturing situations, the cost of sales is all spending directly attributed to production – raw materials, components, wages, factory overheads and so on.

The key word is *directly*. You could not run your business without your accountants (could you?), but although they create an operating expense, they are not a *direct* cost of sales. Only if you can directly match all or part of one item of sales to one unit of something can you class it as part of the cost of sales. Other outlays are known as, you guessed, *indirect* costs. To summarize:

- **Direct costs** are those outlays directly associated with a unit of a product – raw materials, components, factory overheads and so on.
- **Indirect costs** include all other spending which cannot be directly attributed to sales and production.

Sales commissions can be treated as cost of sales if their level directly relates to sales. Otherwise, they are an operating overhead.

As an example of a more complex cost-of-sales calculation, figures for a manufacturing concern are shown in Fig. 13.2. Note that the breakdown shows depreciation of machinery and not the acquisition cost of machinery, as explained and calculated in the previous chapter. The same applies to all capital spending.

'Corporation: an ingenious device for obtaining individual profit without individual responsibility.'

Ambrose Bierce

Fig. 13.2 Cost of sales

XYZ's Manufacturing Account

Year ended 31st December 2003

		US dollars
Raw materials		
Opening stock		50,000
Purchases		250,000
		300,000
Less closing stock		40,000
Cost of materials consumed		**260,000**
Production wages		150,000
Prime cost of production		**410,000**
Factory overheads		
Packers' wages	90,000	
Management salaries	110,000	
Administration salaries	50,000	
Rental and property taxes	100,000	
Electricity and water	12,000	
Maintenance of machinery	8,000	
Depreciation of machinery	10,000	
Depreciation of leasehold improvements	5,000	
Total overheads		**385,000**
		795,000
Less increase in work-in-progress		5,000
Cost of goods produced		**790,000**
Less increase in stock of finished goods in factory		10,000
Cost of goods shipped to warehouse		**780,000**
Less increase in stock of finished goods in warehouse*		30,000
Costs of sales		**750,000**

From the trading account.

▶ Product costs

It hardly needs to be said that you need to know the cost of one unit of your product. Apart from anything else, you will use this figure in your forecasts (see below). In keeping with true beanie tradition, this figure is not quite as obvious as you might expect. I will describe the calculations for a manufacturing business, because this involves all the elements you might encounter. The same logic applies if you are providing services, or reselling someone else's products, or making something that does not involve noisy machines (e.g. software development). For these other situations, the arithmetic is similar, but less complex.

For any one period, such as a year, the cost of producing one gizmo is derived by dividing total costs by the number of items. For example, if the $750,000 of activity in Fig. 13.2 produced 375,000 widgets, the costs associated with producing one widget are:

Unit cost = total cost of production ÷ volume of production

= $750,000 ÷ 375,000

= $2.

Incidentally, this is the *direct* cost of one unit. It does not tell you how to set your sales price, because production (and purchase) costs do not include operating overheads – and clearly you have to cover these in order to stay in business.

▶▶ | For broader analysis, you will want to *attribute* the portion of indirect costs (such as marketing) that has to be *absorbed* in the production and sale of each of your products. This was discussed in the previous chapter.

▶ How fixed is fixed?

The calculation above gives you a useful measure for one time period. You can take the analysis a little further by breaking spending into fixed and variable costs.

◆ **Variable costs** (such as raw materials or wholesale purchases) *vary* directly with sales volume.

◆ **Fixed costs** are *relatively* fixed in relation to production and sales. Factory rent will not vary, whether output is zero or running at maximum capacity. Machine costs might be fixed in relation to smaller quantities of output. If you lease machines which produce up to 100,000 units a month, your fixed costs related to the machines increase every time that production passes a 100,000 barrier.

Take a simple example. A gizmo manufacturer rents a factory, leases a machine, and employs a couple of people – all for $100,000 a year. These are the fixed costs of production. The variable costs, relating to materials and components, amount to a convenient $1 per gizmo.

◆ If the plant produces one gizmo, the cost of that item, and the total costs of production, are both $100,001.

◆ If production is 10,000 units, total costs rise to $110,000, but the average cost of each gizmo falls to $11,000.

◆ If production increases to 1 million items, total costs jump to $1,100,000, but average costs plummet to $1.10 per unit.

Clearly the average cost of one item depends crucially on how many are pumped out in any one period. Of course, real life is rarely as simple as this example. The machinery might be capable of producing a million gizmos each year, but what about the supporting cast? As output increases, the factory will probably need extra production or quality control staff, or more handling and storage space. If production exceeds one million, perhaps an additional machine will be required.

Fixed costs are only fixed over certain ranges of output. At various production levels, fixed costs ratchet up a notch.

▶ Production schedules

You can build a very interesting spreadsheet costing the resources required to produce at various levels of output. For example, for every increase of 100,000 units you might require one operative on the production line, each 300,000 extra units might require an extra packer, and so on. You can plug these figures, and the other costs, into a spreadsheet such as the simplified example in Fig. 13.3. This illustrates the *cumulative* cost at several levels of output. For example, for 300,000 units of production, total costs are $525,000 and the average cost per unit is $1.75. In other words, if sales are 300,000 units, you have to sell at a minimum price of $1.75 in order to cover product costs (but not overheads).

If you repeat this exercise including all other operating and overhead costs, you will see instantly the break-even selling price for any sales volume. But we are getting ahead of ourselves. More on this in Chapter 23.

'Profit in business comes from repeat customers that boast about your project or service, and that bring friends with them.'

W. Edwards Deming

Fig. 13.3 Product costs analysed

Units, millions	Costs, dollars					
	Production	Packing	Other fixed	Variable	Total	Average
0.1	20,000	15,000	150,000	100,000	285,000	2.85
0.2	40,000	15,000	150,000	200,000	405,000	2.03
0.3	60,000	15,000	150,000	300,000	525,000	1.75
0.4	80,000	30,000	150,000	400,000	660,000	1.65
0.5	100,000	30,000	150,000	500,000	780,000	1.56
0.6	120,000	30,000	150,000	600,000	900,000	1.50
0.7	140,000	45,000	150,000	700,000	1,035,000	1.48
0.8	160,000	45,000	150,000	800,000	1,155,000	1.44
0.9	180,000	45,000	150,000	900,000	1,275,000	1.42
1.0	200,000	60,000	150,000	1,000,000	1,410,000	1.41

Unambiguous inventory

Inventory is your stockpile of unsold raw materials, work-in-progress, finished goods and services that you intend to sell. You could, for example, have an inventory of computer software if this was your business. This is *trading inventory*. It is not what you have in your stationery cupboard (unless you are in the office supplies business) and it is not your stock of fixed assets (such as machinery and equipment).

Inventory

Products coming into your inventory in, say, July might not be sold until November. The acquisition is recorded in July, the product lives in your showroom or storeroom (and, incidentally, on the balance sheet) for five months, and then it is shipped out (at which time the appropriate amount is charged to cost of sales). Figure 13.4 shows the mechanics. This can become quite complex, when you have inventory of raw materials, components, work-in-progress and finished goods – for many product lines.

The book value of inventory can include shipping and handling costs. For work-in-progress and finished goods, you apportion raw material and production costs and overheads. Where warehousing is a significant factor – for example, when you are ageing wine and whiskey – those too can be counted as part of the cost of inventory.

However, the lags between acquisition (purchase or manufacture) and sales raise a timing problem. How do you value inventory if:

1 unit costs are changing over time; and

2 you do not or cannot *match specific units* of product to specific sales.

This is not as simple as it might sound. Four ways that bean counters cope are discussed next.

Fig. 13.4 Tracking inventory

	Jan	Feb	Mar	...
Volume, units				
...	...	...	...	...
Production (or purchases)				
Production volume, units	12,000	12,000	6,000	...
...	...	...	...	...
Inventory volume, units				
Opening stock	5,000	7,000	8,000	6,000
Add production	12,000	12,000	6,000	...
Less sales	10,000	11,000	8,000	...
End-month stock	**7,000**	**8,000**	**6,000**	
...	...	...	...	...
Sales				
Sales volume, units	10,000	11,000	8,000	...
...	...	...	...	...

▶ What's in store

There are various methods of valuing inventory, including the following:

1 **Specific unit costs** (also called **specific identification**) matches exactly the origin of each unit of your product and journey into, through and out of inventory. This is the purest method of valuation, but it cannot be used when units of your product are indistinguishable from each other (grain, paint, talcum powder).

> The International Accounting Standards Board prefers specific costs for inventory valuation. If this is not applicable, FIFO or weighted averaging can be used. The original standard also grudgingly allows LIFO. In May 2002 the Board proposed prohibiting this option – no decision had been made when this book went to press.

2 **Averaging** (also called **weighted averaging**) is where each unit of inventory is measured by:

   (a) *adding up* all the money spent acquiring inventory during the period (the value of the opening stock plus production/purchase costs); and
   (b) *dividing* the total calculated in step 1 by the number of items available for sale (opening quantity plus quantity purchased/produced).

3 **First-in first-out (FIFO)** tracks costs and assumes that the earliest items put into stock are the first ones removed. This is a situation where an accounting concept matches real-life common sense.

4 **Last-in first-out (LIFO)** tracks costs but assume that the latest items put into stock are the first ones removed. (Unfortunately, this is similar to my document filing system.)

When stock acquisition costs are rising (perhaps due to inflation), FIFO boosts the value of your closing stock. When prices are falling (such as with many high-tech items and some commodities), LIFO produces a higher valuation for the cost of goods sold and a lower value for closing stock. Figure 13.6 contrasts the effect of using FIFO and LIFO in a computer business where production costs are falling over time.

Companies sometimes use a mix of these valuation methods for various categories of inventory. By and large, the first two or three techniques are preferable for analytical purposes. The second two may be more advantageous for tax reasons. Higher costs results in lower gross and net profits. LIFO results in the lowest tax bill, and is popular in the US even though it is not accepted by some tax authorities (for example, in certain European countries) and some accounting standards authorities.

Clearly, inventory valuation is an example of where the books can be manipulated even when no money is changing hands.

Inventory issues for managers

1 Check the basis on which inventories are valued.

2 When comparing companies, especially when they carry large inventories, try to adjust onto the same valuation basis for consistency.

3 Large or rising inventories may indicate slackening sales or a build up of obsolete or obsolescent stocks.

4 Check for obsolete, damaged, spoiled, surplus and missing items.

5 Keep inventory as low as possible – it ties up cash that for the moment is not yet generating income.

6 Adequate opening and closing stocks do not automatically imply that you can meet demand during the month – if sales run ahead of production there might be an unacceptable delay in meeting orders.

7 Plan a buffer stock to meet unexpected changes in demand.

Looking forward

In Chapter 10 you forecast your sales. In this chapter you have calculated your product costs and looked at ways of valuing your inventory. Subtract these costs from sales to arrive at gross profit. It is this straightforward. Figure 13.5 shows a simple calculation, while Fig. 13.6 has a more complex example. The next chapter looks more deeply at controlling and analysing costs, while Chapter 23 considers the relationships between inventory, costs, and revenue.

Fig. 13.5 Simple arithmetic in a spreadsheet

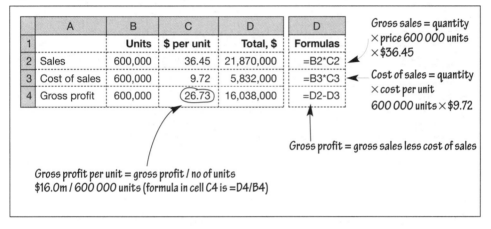

	A	B	C	D	D
1		Units	$ per unit	Total, $	Formulas
2	Sales	600,000	36.45	21,870,000	=B2*C2
3	Cost of sales	600,000	9.72	5,832,000	=B3*C3
4	Gross profit	600,000	(26.73)	16,038,000	=D2-D3

Gross sales = quantity × price 600 000 units × $36.45

Cost of sales = quantity × cost per unit 600 000 units × $9.72

Gross profit = gross sales less cost of sales

Gross profit per unit = gross profit / no of units $16.0m / 600 000 units (formula in cell C4 is =D4/B4)

'This year, we are asking you to reduce inventory assets. For instance, let's look at product flow. When a product in a certain process is suspended, most people would consider immediately moving that product to the next process. We should all realize that such action is actually the shortest move and that the accumulation of such actions could save billions of yen. ... The saved amount naturally contributes to savings. Thus, cash flow operation enables us to locate, collect, and effectively use "hidden" cash reserves within the workplace to stengthen the company and enrich our collective livelihoods.'

Masumi Fukuta

(President, Fujitsu Quantum Devices Limited)

Fig. 13.6 Playing the numbers game (2)

All of the figures here are calculated automatically from the first part of this spreadsheet, which is shown in Fig. 10.3. This spreadsheet also shows an example of the effects of using FIFO and LIFO to value inventory when production costs are falling.

	A	B	C	D	E	F	
38	TETRYLUS Inc.						
39							
40	**Sales, costs & prices, first five years**						
41	Dollars						
42		Year 1	Year 2	Year 3	Year 4	Year 5	Notes (see also Fig 10.3)
43	Hardware inventory volume						
44	Opening stock	0	1,160	1,160	1,160	1,160	Line 47, previous period
45	Additions (production)	5,000	42,000	330,000	450,000	600,000	Based on line 18
46	Reductions (sales)	−3 840	−42 000	−330 000	−450 000	−600 000	Line 18
47	**Closing stock**	1,160	1,160	1,160	1,160	1,160	Line 44 + line 45 + line 46
48							
49	Hardware inventory value (FIFO)						
50	Opening stock	0	29,000	31,900	49,880	87,232	Line 53, previous period
51	Additions (production)	125,000	945,000	3,960,000	4,860,000	5,832,000	Line 22 x line 45
52	Reductions (sales)	−96,000	−942,100	−3,942,020	−4,822,648	−5,756,043	Line 22 x line 46
53	**Closing stock**	29,000	31,900	49,880	87,232	163,189	Line 50 + line 51 + line 52
54							
55	Hardware inventory value (LIFO)						
56	Opening stock	0	29,000	29,000	29,000	29,000	Line 59, previous period
57	Additions (production)	125,000	945,000	3,960,000	4,860,000	5,832,000	Line 22 × line 45
58	Reductions (sales)	−96,000	−945,000	−3,960,000	−4,860,000	−5,832,000	Line 22 × line 46
59	**Closing stock**	29,000	29,000	29,000	29,000	29,000	Line 56 + line 57 + line 58
60							
61	TETRYLUS Inc.						((Line 46 − line 47
62							in previous period)
63	**Gross profit, first five years**						× line 22) + line 53
64	Dollars						
65		Year 1	Year 2	Year 3	Year 4	Year 5	
66	**Gross sales**						
67	Hardware	307,200	2,100,000	14,850,000	18,225,000	21,870,000	Line 18 × line 26
68	Software	14,000	52,500	396,000	540,000	720,000	Line 19 × line 27
69	Total	321,200	2,152,500	15,246,000	18,765,000	22,590,000	Line 67 + line 68
70							
71	**Cost of sales**						
72	Hardware	96,000	945,000	3,960,000	4,860,000	5,832,000	Line 18 × line 22
73	Software	2,000	10,500	66,000	90,000	120,000	Line 19 × line 23
74	Total	98,000	955,500	4,026,000	4,950,000	5,952,000	Line 72 + line 73
75							
76	**Gross profit**						
77	Hardware	211,200	1,155,000	10,890,000	13,365,000	16,038,000	Line 67 − line 72
78	Software	12,000	42,000	330,000	450,000	600,000	Line 68 − line 73
79	Total	223,200	1,197,000	11,220,000	13,815,000	16,638,000	Line 77 + line 78
80							
81	**Gross profit margin, %**						
82	Hardware	69	55	73	73	73	Line 77 / line 67
83	Software	86	80	83	83	83	Line 78 / line 68
84	Total	69	56	74	74	74	Line 79 / line 69

Note: Calculations are performed on <u>unrounded</u> figures to greater accuracy than is shown here. As with all illustrations in this book, the detailed spreadsheet is available for download at www.ManagingTheNumbers.com.

Record keeping for stockholders

The bookkeeping related to the issues in this chapter is simple enough when you have done it once. You guessed. I am going to run through an example. Begin by ordering and paying for a stock of widgets. Delivery and payment are usually separate, so for an order of 46,000 widgets at $1 each the transaction might look like this:

Delivery from supplier (46,000 widgets @ $1 each), 3 Jan

Acc no.	Account	Debit $	Credit $
1-1510	Inventory of widgets (asset)	46,000.00	–
2-1008	Accounts payable – inventory (liability)	–	46,000.00

Payment to supplier (46,000 widgets @ $1 each), 8 Feb

Acc no.	Account	Debit $	Credit $
2-1008	Accounts payable – inventory (liability)	46,000.00	–
1-1001	Cash at bank (asset)	–	46,000.00

Later, you might sell 40,000 widgets to an important customer for $1.50 each, as follows:

Withdrawal from inventory (40,000 widgets @ $1 each), 10 Mar

Acc no.	Account	Debit $	Credit $
2-1008	Cost of sales – widgets (cost)	40,000.00	–
1-1001	Inventory of widgets (asset)	–	40,000.00

Sale to customer (40,000 widgets @ $1.50 each), 10 Mar

Acc no.	Account	Debit $	Credit $
2-1008	Accounts receivable – widgets (asset)	60,000.00	–
1-1001	Sales – Widget Buyers Inc (revenue)	–	60,000.00

Payment from customer (40,000 widgets @ $1.50 each), 25 Mar

Acc no.	Account	Debit $	Credit $
2-1008	Acc'ts receivable – widgets (asset)	–	60,000.00
1-1001	Cash at bank (asset)	60,000.00	–

If there were no other transactions, accounts payable and accounts receivable would both have nil balances at the end of the period. Your assets would have increased by $20,000 (bank $14,000, inventory $6,000) reflecting a $20,000 gross profit, as shown in the following accounts. Of course, this is not the end of the story. You must have incurred other costs, which we will explore next.

Asset accounts

Bank balance

Date	Item	Debit $	Credit $	Balance $
8 Feb	Purchase of widgets		46,000	–46,000
25 Mar	Sale of widgets	60,000		+14,000
	Balance carried forward			+14,000

Inventory

Date	Item	Debit $	Credit $	Balance $
3 Jan	Purchase	46,000	–	+46,000
10 Mar	Sale	–	40,000	+6,000
	Balance carried forward			+6,000

Gross profit, Jan-Mar

Sales	$60,000
Cost of sales	–$40,000
Gross profit	**$20,000**

▶ Ten hard questions to ask or be asked

1 How price-sensitive is demand for the products? Are pricing policies (still) appropriate?

2 Are costs of sales properly identified?

3 Is revenue booked at the appropriate time period?

4 Do you have at your finger tips product costs at any given level of sales?

5 Which of your products has the lowest gross profit margin? The highest? Why?

6 Is inventory well managed and not bloated?

7 Is inventory valuation realistic? Is its realizable value different from the book value?

8 Does the inventory include any obsolete or damaged items?

9 Do you have appropriate controls over receipts from sales, refunds, etc.?

10 If comparing companies, are inventory valuation methods similar?

▶ Conclusion

This chapter covered quite a few concepts. I hope it was not too strenuous. Please look back at the chapter survival toolkit for a summary. The next few chapters develop the ideas, but I suspect that you will find them relatively easy going. In the next few pages we will examine the full profit and loss account, which reveals the true bottom-line for the business.

> 'Avarice, the spur of industry.'
> **David Hume**

producing a profit

'One out of every ten listed public companies [in the US] restated its earnings during the last five years.'

Paul S. Atkins
(Commissioner, U.S. Securities and Exchange Commission, 2002)

Chapter survival tookit

▶ Overview

You will be happy to know that the hard work has been done and this chapter should be very straightforward. It takes the revenue and spending discussed in the previous chapters, introduces a few new categories of spending and receipts, and brings them all together in the *profit and loss account* (or *income statement*). This shows the bottom line for the business, or, perhaps, the bottom *lines* since, believe it or not, there is more than one.

The profit and loss account is one of three key financial statements. The other two are the balance sheet and cash flow statement, which are covered in the next two chapters. Some introductory analysis and interpretation are discussed in this chapter, but the real secret of analysing the profit and loss account is found by taking it in combination with the other two financial statements. Accordingly, detailed analysis is deferred until Chapter 17.

▶ Prerequisites

You could probably read this chapter in isolation. If you coped well with the previous few pages, it will be especially easy going.

▶ Mastering profits

After reading this chapter, you should be able to answer the following questions:

1 What is operating profit? profit from ongoing operations? net profit?

2 What is comprehensive income?

3 Why distinguish between recurring and non-recurring non-trading income?

4 What is the difference between extraordinary and exceptional income?

5 Why are extraordinary events, discontinued operations and changes in accounting policies treated as unusual items?

6 Why is the classifiction of *other unrealized gains and losses* applied to bookkeeping gains and losses on foreign currency translations, investments and derivatives?

7 What are minority interests?

8 Why use earnings before interest, tax, depreciation and amortization (EBIT and EBITDA) when comparing companies?

9 Why distinguish between manufacturing, trading and operating accounts?

10 How would you use the figures from the previous few chapters to project net profit?

▶ Jargon watch

New beanie buzz words

Profit and loss (P&L) account/income statement

Operating profit, profit from ongoing operations, net profit

Extraordinary and exceptional items

Comprehensive income

Earnings before interest, tax, depreciation and amortization (EBIT and EBITDA)

Earnings per share (EPS)*

Minority interests

Foreign currency translation*

Beanie buzz words revisited

Depreciation

Inventory

Matching

Manufacturing, trading and operating accounts

Gross profit, cost of sales, operating costs

Investment bankers' buzz words

Derivatives*

Leverage*

First encounter: defined fully in later chapters.

'In America, the biggest financial disasters tend to be the result of individual greed leading to corruption – but in France they come about when you give very clever and ambitious technocrats the means to implement a vision.'

Paris banker (2002)

▶ Producing a profit

If you have followed the logic in the preceding few chapters, you have all the knowledge required to understand and create a profit and loss account and, indeed, a full set of financial statements. In fact, if you have performed your own calculations of sales and costs as described in the previous few chapters, you also have all the numbers that you need. All you have to do now is present them in the required format. In this case, you can more or less freewheel through the next few pages. This chapter describes the profit and loss account, what it is, how it is structured, what it shows, how to interpret it and how to project your own profits.

The world's biggest corporate blunders:

- AOL Time Warner racked up a record $99 bn loss in 2002 which included a record write-down of goodwill and other accounting adjustments.
- JDS Uniphase lost $51 bn in the second quarter of 2001.

Records in their own countries:

- Deutsche Telekom reported a loss of 24.5 bn euros ($24.6 bn) in the first nine months of 2002.
- UK mobile phone giant Vodafone made a loss of $13.5 bn ($24 bn) in the 12 months to end-March 2002.
- France's Vivendi posted a loss of $13.4 bn in March 2002.
- Australia's News Corp lost A$12 bn ($6.6 bn in the year to mid-2002, not including a A$3 bn loss arising on the foreign exchange translation of net assets of controlled entities.

(All figures in US dollars, unless otherwise stated.)

▶ The income statement, or profit and loss account

In a curious departure from the pessimism for which we have come to know and love bean counters, the American branch of their family has managed to give the profit and loss statement (P&L) an optimistic name. They call it an income statement, somehow ignoring the fact that it also includes costs – a lot of them too. Moreover, in the dismal days of the early millennium, when corporations around the world were announcing record losses, *income* statement might be considered a contradiction in terms. I stick with the term profit and loss because it seems less ambiguous, but the term income statement is increasing in popularity worldwide.

▶ P&L – what it is

A profit and loss account is exactly what it claims to be: basically, a record of sales, other revenues and costs, and gains and losses arising from ongoing operations. The bottom line in the P&L is the bottom line for the business: the net profit or loss.

The account does not include capital transactions, such as borrowing, investment and purchases of fixed assets, but it does show current income and costs (and, let me stress this, bookkeeping gains and losses) related to these items – interest, depreciation, and so on. The P&L is a statement of flows – the money which pours into and out of the business in a given period of time, be it a month, quarter, year or some other interlude. As far as possible, transactions are matched to the period of the account using the accruals system already discussed.

Getting to net profit

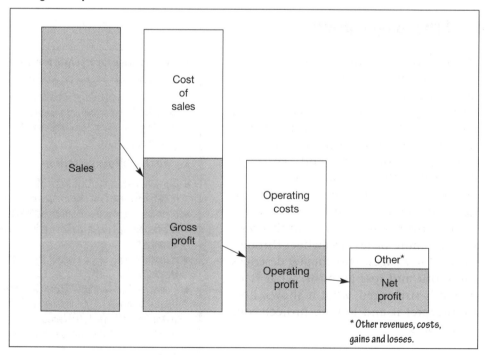

* Other revenues, costs, gains and losses.

▶ P&L – what it shows

There are several key balances struck in a profit and loss account, and it can be presented in various ways. The structure indicated in Fig. 14.1 highlights the key entries and balances as described next. Published accounts that you encounter probably will not spell out the entries in quite the way shown here. I have taken it step by step to highlight how the various subtotals are derived.

In the world's largest corporate scandal (well up to mid-2002 – it might have been outdone by the time you read this) the US telecoms giant WorldCom lied about making $3.85 bn of profits over 15 months, by booking expenses as capital investment – thus keeping them out of the profit and loss account.

When examining any financial reports, try to visualize how the entries were created. Always ask yourself *could they have recorded this differently*? Obvious areas ripe for window dressing are depreciation and inventory, but there is plenty of other scope for intentional or accidental trickery (e.g. see Fig. 12.5).

Fig. 14.1 It depends what you mean by profit

Tetrylus Software Inc.
Profit & loss account

US dollars millions

ID		2002
PL01	Sales	10.11
PL02	Cost of sales	(4.77)
PL03	**Gross profit**	**5.34**
PL04	Operating costs – sales and administration	(2.88)
PL05	Operating costs – depreciation, etc.	(0.80)
PL06	**Total operating costs**	**(3.68)**
PL07	**Operating profit (loss)**	**1.65**
PL08	Recurring non-trading net income	0.57
PL09	Recurring non-trading net expenditure	(0.29)
PL10	Other non-recurring non-trading net income	0.00
PL11	**Profit (loss) from continuing operations, before tax**	**1.94**
PL12	Provision for income tax	(0.02)
PL13	**Profit (loss) from continuing operations, after tax**	**1.93**
PL14	Unusual items	(0.00)
PL15	**Net profit (loss)**	**1.92**
PL16	Other unrealized gains or losses	0.59
PL17	**Comprehensive profit/income (loss)**	**2.51**

We are in beanie realm now, so this table and the next few show negative amounts in brackets – an accountant's trick to prevent you from overlooking minus signs.

Popular beanie acronyms are **EBIT** (earnings before interest and taxes), and **EBITDA** (ditto, and also before depreciation and amortization). These measures are good for comparing results from companies with differing financing structures (leverage), tax obligations, and depreciation policies.

Gross profit. You met with gross profit in the previous chapter: recall that it is *sales* less the *cost of sales*. For many companies, cost of sales makes up the major outlays.

Operating profit. Deduct operating costs from gross profit to arrive at the operating profit (or loss). This is, perhaps, the core of the profit and loss account. It is the net income which results from normal operations. In case you overlook its importance, given that it is swamped by the rest of the P&L shown here, remember that we have just spent several chapters reviewing these revenues and costs. The other items in Fig. 14.1 result from fewer transactions, but deserve special mention (as discussed below).

Profit from ongoing operations, before tax. Working down Fig 14.1, the next couple of entries show revenue, expenses, gains and losses which are not part of the company's normal operations but which nevertheless arise from its very existence. Such transactions include interest paid on loans, interest received on bank deposits and similar instruments, and investment income. For analysis, they can be classified as recurring or non-recurring, depending on whether they feature regularly in the accounts. I have shown them separately to emphasize the fact that recurring items can, loosely speaking, be expected to exert an ongoing influence on the bottom line.

Profit from ongoing operations, after tax. There is not too much to say about taxation, other than that your corporation will no doubt employ well-paid specialists to minimize the tax bill. Tax evasion is simple but illegal. Tax avoidance is legal, but complex. Taxes receive special attention in financials because no one much likes paying them – and reversing out taxes makes inter-company comparisons more reliable.

Do not confuse **extraordinary** items (one-offs such as the effects of natural disasters) with **exceptional** items (which result from the ordinary activities of the company but are large enough to require special attention).

Net profit. Maybe this should be called *net profit before comprehensive income*. It is the line struck in the profit and loss account after dealing with unusual items. These are things that are considered to have nothing to do with the normal performance of the business. They are income, expenditure, gains and losses arising from three events:

1 *Extraordinary items*, such as losses incurred due to flooding or other natural disaster.

2 *Discontinued operations*, such as costs and income which arise after a subsidiary has been shut down.

3 *Changes in accounting policies*, such as when the bean counter switches from LIFO to FIFO inventory valuation – see Fig. 13.6.

Comprehensive income. This is, shall I say, a fairly new innovation. It shows changes in a company's net wealth which result from three intangibles:

1 foreign currency translation adjustment (see Chapter 20);

2 unrealized gains and losses on available-for-sale securities;

3 deferred gains and losses on derivative financial instruments.

The total of these is shown in the example as other *unrealized gain and losses*. You will often see it referred to as *other comprehensive income*. In the past, these items were considered to be beyond management control and not part of income. They were buried in retained earnings on the balance sheet. Regulators have become concerned that such transactions were escaping the attention of shareholders and generally now require such *other comprehensive income* to be reported somewhere.

> **International accounting standards require** that the following items be identified separately in the profit and loss account:
>
> • revenue;
>
> • results of operating activities;
>
> • finance costs;
>
> • income from associates and joint ventures;
>
> • taxes;
>
> • profit or loss from ordinary activities;
>
> • extraordinary items;
>
> • profits from minority interest (see Chapter 15);
>
> • net profit or loss.
>
> Minority interests are net profits and net assets of a subsidiary that are not attributable to interests directly or indirectly owned by the parent.

You may find it as a line in the profit and loss account, as shown here. It may be presented in the *balance sheet*, in a separate *statement of other comprehensive income* (look in the notes to the financial statement) or it may be included in a *statement of changes in stockholders' equity* (see Chapter 15).

One more thing

International, and many national, accounting standards require *earnings per share* to be disclosed prominently on the face of the profit and loss account. This handy figure is defined and discussed along with other indicators of finance and investment in Chapter 19.

▶ P&L – what it means

You do not need me to tell you the importance of profits. As you are well aware, your salary and bonus may be directly liked to the earnings you help generate for the business. In the short term, profits also provide rewards for the providers of capital (i.e. in plain English, dividends for shareholders), social welfare which is channelled through the tax authorities and government (i.e. taxation), and sometimes charitable donations. In the longer term, retained earnings are ploughed back into the business to fund future operations and growth (see *Getting value*, Chapter 17).

From the point of view of assessing return on capital and the potential for future growth, you are going to be most interested in profit from ongoing operations (perhaps after subtracting net non-recurring non-trading income). The one-offs are deliberately singled out because in principle they affect this year only. If you are wondering why you did not receive a bonus, you might want to look at unusual items.

Manufacturing, trading and operating accounts

Depending on the amount of detail required and the nature of the business, a profit and loss account could be broken into several component parts. For example:

1 **A manufacturing account** such as in Fig. 13.2.

2 **A trading account**. This starts with *costs of good shipped to warehouse* (brought forward from the manufacturing account) and shows sales and distribution activities resulting in gross sales and gross profit.

3 **An operating account**. Finally, gross profit might be carried forward to a third account, the operating account, and adjusted for the other incomes and costs to arrive at net profit (or loss).

▶ P&L – looking ahead

If you are projecting profit and loss, and you have followed the examples in the previous few chapters, you have nothing more to do – other than bring the figures together in one table. This is so straightforward that I will leave any explanation to Fig. 14.2.

> 'Measures of profitability, however, can only be approximate. Although most pretax profits reflect cash receipts less cash costs, a significant part of profits results from changes in the valuation of items on the balance sheet. The values of almost all assets are based on their ability to produce future income. But an appropriate assessment of asset value depends critically on a forecast of forthcoming events, which by their nature are uncertain.'
>
> **Alan Greenspan**

Fig. 14.2 A sample profit and loss account

This is a simple summary of a projected profit and loss account. Sales and cost of sales are determined as shown in Figs 10.3 and 13.6. Operating costs are taken directly from Figs 12.2 and 12.4. The contingency is from Fig. 12.6. All of these tables would be assembled into one report, along with the balance sheet and cash flow statement (see Figs 15.4 and 16.2).

	A	B	C	D	E	F	G	H	I
1		**TETRYLUS Inc.**							
2		**Profit & loss account, first six months**							
3		Dollars							
4			Month 1	Month 2	Month 3	Month 4	Month 5	Month 6	H1
5	P-1	Sales	–	20,000	–	40,000	–	50,000	**110,000**
6	P-2	*Less:* Costs of sales	–	13,591	–	27,183	–	33,979	**74,753**
7	P-3	**Gross profit**	–	**6,409**	–	**12,817**	–	**16,021**	**35,247**
8	P-4								
9	P-5	*Less:* **Operating costs**							
10	P-6	Employee costs	54,278	55,400	55,400	62,045	62,045	64,715	**353,883**
11	P-7	Other expenditure	12,500	33,814	25,255	17,268	16,596	18,796	**124,229**
12	P-8	**Total operating costs**	**66,778**	**89,214**	**80,655**	**79,313**	**78,641**	**83,511**	**478,112**
13	P-9								
14	P-10								
15	P-11	**Net profit (loss) before contingency etc.**	**(66,778)**	**(82,805)**	**(80,655)**	**(66,496)**	**(78,641)**	**(67,490)**	**(442,865)**
16	P-12								
17	P-13	Contingency	6,678	8,921	8,066	7,931	7,864	8,351	47,811
18	P-14								
19	P-15	**Net profit (loss) before interest and tax**	**(73,456)**	**(91,726)**	**(88,721)**	**(74,427)**	**(86,505)**	**(75,841)**	**(490,676)**

Error trapping: As with every spreadsheet of this nature, you can check the arithmetical accuracy of your profit and loss account by comparing the horizontal total (the grand total of months 1 to 6 in the final row of this example) with the vertical total (the net total at the foot of the right-hand column). If the two figures are identical, everything is on track. If they differ, there must be a mistake in your formulas.

Ten hard questions to ask or be asked

1 Are expenses properly booked (e.g. not improperly hidden in the balance sheet)?

2 Is the breakdown between cost of sales and operating costs correct?

3 How signifcant is depreciation?

4 Is the *headline* net profit figure the most representative profit figure?

5 What exceptional and extraodinary items are in the account? What are the implications?

6 What is the orgin of non-trading income? How much is recurring? Why?

7 Are there any unusual items? Why? What are the implications?

8 Is there other comprehensive income? Why? What are the implications?

9 If there are discontinued operations, why?

10 If there has been a change in accounting policies, why?

What's next?

I hope that you agree that this chapter was relatively plain sailing across the duck pond. We will paddle on briskly to look at the other key financial statements and, ultimately, the detailed interpretation of them all taken in concert.

> '[Another] illusion played by some companies is using unrealistic assumptions to estimate liabilities for such items as sales returns, loans losses or warranty costs. In doing so, they stash accruals in cookie jars during the good times and reach into them when needed in the bad times. I'm reminded of one US company who took a large one-time loss to earnings reimburse franchisees for equipment. That equipment, however, which included literally the kitchen sink, had yet to be bought.'
>
> **Arthur Levitt**
> (Chairman, Securities and Exchange Commission)

15

building balance sheets

> 'It is puzzling, to say the least, that airlines can routinely operate without showing any planes on their balance sheet.'
>
> **Andrew Crockett**

▶ Chapter survival toolkit

▶ Overview

The previous chapter looked at the profit and loss account. This chapter reviews the balance sheet: a snapshot of what a business owns and owes, and it's net worth. Balance sheets are actually remarkably straightforward. They reveal a great deal of information about a company's financial status, but they are little more than a rearrangement of the categories of spending and revenue which we have already met. Indeed, since they are so simple, this chapter takes the opportunity to slip in a handful of new beanie buzz words. You should enjoy them.

▶ Prerequisites

This chapter follows on naturally from the previous chapter.

▶ Mastering balance sheets

After reading this chapter, you should be able to answer the following questions:

1 Why is the balance sheet important? Does it show financial flows or a snapshot of financial balances at a point in time? Could it be easily manipulated?

2 Assets less liabilities equals what? Who owns the shareholders' equity? What is net worth?

3 Why distinguish between short- and long-term assets? Is working capital measured by current assets less current liabilities? Why is working capital important?

4 How are fixed assets shown in a balance sheet? How is depreciation shown?

5 Could a company use a short-term loan to buy long-lived assets? Should it?

6 Why is some taxation deferred? Could this be an asset?

7 What is a provision? What is a contingent liability? Why should the balance sheet show provisions for probable obligations? Why should contingent liabilities be reported in the footnotes?

8 What is contributed capital? What is treasury stock? What are retained earnings?

9 Where are other unrealized gains and losses reported? What is comprehensive income?

10 How would you use the figures from the previous few chapters to create a balance sheet?

Balancing act

Balance sheets are the paper tigers of financial reporting. They are as easy to understand as the profit and loss account – perhaps easier – but they are widely feared and misunderstood. Do not worry. If you have made it this far, there is nothing to fear in this chapter. The balance sheet is a snapshot of the net wealth of an entity – showing (in summary) everything it owns and owes. This tells you a great deal about past performance and the potential for the future.

This chapter describes the balance sheet, what it is, how it is structured, what it shows, how to interpret it and how to project your own.

► Flows and snapshots

You will recall from the previous chapter that a profit and loss account (P&L) shows flows over time. You can add figures from two P&Ls, each covering, say, six months, to find the totals for the year as a whole.

In contrast, a balance sheet is a snapshot on a given date – say 30 June or 31 December. It is similar to the opening or closing balance on your bank statement; a statement of position at the close of business on one day. Logically, you cannot add two balance sheets. If you subtract one from another this will reveal the changes that took place between the two dates, but these are not total flows. As with the *bank statement* example, you would not know how much money came into and went out of an account between the opening and closing balances, only the net change.

▶ The balance sheet – what it is

A balance sheet is nothing more complex than a statement of position at a given date. The balance sheet lists all the money owned or owed to (*assets*) and owed by (*liabilities and shareholders' equity*) a business. I sense you were with me until I mentioned shareholders' equity. Basically, you always want assets to exceed liabilities. The difference belongs to the owners; it is the stake (equity) of the shareholders. As mentioned in Chapter 7, if a company were a person, shareholders' equity would be called *owners' equity* or *net worth*, as it is in a sole trader's accounts. Arithmetically, shareholder's equity always equals assets less liabilities. Or, to put it another way, assets equal liabilities plus shareholders' equity, as shown in this little diagram:

The balance sheet – assets equal liabilities plus shareholders' equity

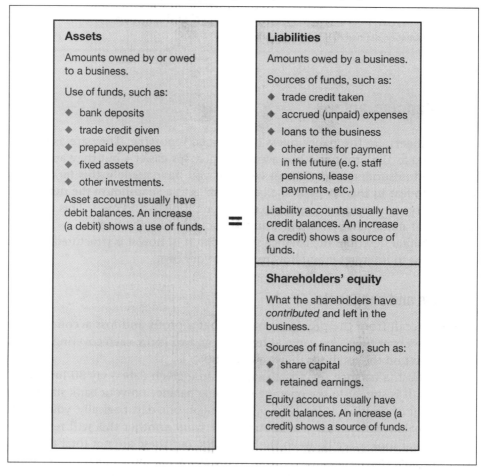

Assets	**Liabilities**
Amounts owned by or owed to a business.	Amounts owed by a business.
Use of funds, such as:	Sources of funds, such as:
◆ bank deposits	◆ trade credit taken
◆ trade credit given	◆ accrued (unpaid) expenses
◆ prepaid expenses	◆ loans to the business
◆ fixed assets	◆ other items for payment in the future (e.g. staff pensions, lease payments, etc.)
◆ other investments.	
Asset accounts usually have debit balances. An increase (a debit) shows a use of funds.	Liability accounts usually have credit balances. An increase (a credit) shows a source of funds.
	Shareholders' equity
	What the shareholders have *contributed* and left in the business.
	Sources of financing, such as:
	◆ share capital
	◆ retained earnings.
	Equity accounts usually have credit balances. An increase (a credit) shows a source of funds.

Let me stress once again that while a profit and loss account shows flows over a given period (say, one year), the balance sheet is a snapshot at the close of a given day (say, 31 December). You would be right in thinking that this leaves it open to some manipulation – a roguish practice known endearingly as *window dressing*. For example, cash balances might have been very different the day before or the day after. Keep this in mind when you look at financial statements.

▶ The balance sheet – what it shows

As indicated, every balance sheet has three sections – assets, liabilities and shareholders' equity. They may be laid out differently from the examples given here. More traditional accounts show liabilities/equity and assets side by side rather than vertically. You will not find this difference intellectually taxing.

Assets and liabilities may be classified into short and long term, and the entries are generally arranged in order of life expectancy. Regulators prefer (but do not usually demand) the specific identification of short-term assets and liabilities. Most companies do show current assets and liabilities and this certainly assists with analysis – the difference between the two is defined as working capital. The definition of short term may be in the notes to the financial statements, otherwise you can take it to be a year. The structure of a typical balance sheet is shown in Fig. 15.1. As with the profit and loss account, let me run through this financial statement starting at the top. This time, it is more useful to focus on the entries rather than the totals.

> 'It is one thing for a company to "cook the books" by fraudulently inflating revenue through phoney sales or inventing phantom inventory. ... But some of the recent accounting scandals have involved a different kind of activity – companies asserting aggressive interpretations of GAAP to justify financial statement treatment, such as capitalization of expenses or so called "true sales" off assets to off-blalance sheet entities to remove debt from the balance sheet.'
>
> **Paul S. Atkins**
> (Commissioner, U.S. Securities and Exchange Commission, 2002)

Fig. 15.1 In balance

Tetrylus Software Inc.
Balance sheet as at 31 December

US dollars millions

ID		2001	2002	Change
	Assets			
	Current assets			
A01	Cash at bank	1.33	0.67	(0.66)
A02	Inventory	0.00	0.00	0.00
A03	Debtors	1.90	1.20	(0.70)
A04	Investments	3.34	4.07	0.72
A05	Prepaid expenses	3.27	2.87	(0.40)
A06	**Total current assets**	**9.84**	**8.80**	**(1.04)**
	Long-term assets			
A07	Fixed assets	5.55	7.39	1.83
A08	*Less* accumulated depreciation	(0.94)	(1.74)	(0.80)
A09	**Net fixed assets**	**4.61**	**5.65**	**1.03**
A10	Other long-term assets	0.11	0.08	(0.02)
A11	**Total long-term assets**	**4.72**	**5.73**	**1.01**
A12	**Total assets**	**14.56**	**14.54**	**(0.03)**
	Liabilities			
	Current liabilities			
L01	Creditors	(0.44)	(0.16)	0.28
L02	Loans – short term	(1.03)	0.00	1.03
L03	Accruals	(1.05)	(0.69)	0.36
L04	Taxes payable	(2.14)	(2.12)	0.02
L05	**Total short-term liabilities**	**(4.65)**	**(2.96)**	**1.69**
	Long-term liabilities			
L06	Loans – long-term	0.00	0.00	0.00
L07	**Total long-term liabilities**	**0.00**	**0.00**	**0.00**
L08	**Total liabilities**	**(4.65)**	**(2.96)**	**1.69**
	Shareholders' equity			
E01	Paid-in share capital	(1.26)	(1.31)	(0.05)
E02	Additional paid-in capital	(2.39)	(2.70)	(0.32)
E03	Retained earnings	(6.52)	(8.40)	(1.88)
E04	Accumulated other comprehensive income	0.25	0.84	0.59
E05	**Total shareholders' equity**	**(9.91)**	**(11.57)**	**(1.66)**
	Total liabilities and shareholders' equity	**(14.56)**	**(14.54)**	**0.03**

Assets

Cash and bank deposits are the most liquid of assets – and, of course, they are used to pay the bills. As you have probably gathered, *transactional* bank deposits are regarded as synonymous with cash for the purposes of analysis. Time deposits are almost as good as paper money. Of course, any company should have enough liquidity to cover slumps in sales and other short-term crises.

Inventory includes raw materials, part-completed work-in-progress and finished items. The extent to which these can be turned into cash varies, as does the underlying true market value. Again, the notes to the accounts should provide more details. Look for the accounting policy (FIFO, LIFO, etc. – see Chapter 13). If inventory is growing faster than sales this might be a sign of a slowdown, and of obsolete or outdated stocks. The example has a nil entry for inventory because this software company does not record any in its accounts.

Trade debtors or **accounts receivable** represents money that will, or should, be collected from customers. The notes to the accounts should show long-standing debts and provisions for bad debts. If receivables are growing faster than sales, customers are getting slower in paying – a worrying trend?

Personally, I prefer the Americanism *accounts receivable*, which seems so much more positive than *debtors*. I have used *debtors* in this example for a simple reason. You can probably remember that a debtor owes you money which is rightly yours – so, *debtors* are on the *asset* side of the balance sheet, asset accounts have debit balances and an increase in an asset is a debit. Similarly you owe money to *creditors*, so they show on the *liabilities* side, liability accounts have credit balances and an increase in liabilities is a credit.

Prepayments are amounts paid in advance, such as rents or telecoms rentals. As you may know, they are often hard to recover. It may not be possible to turn them back into cash in a crisis, but providing the business continues to operate they are a measure of stored value.

Fixed assets were covered in detail in Chapter 11. The balance sheet will show the following:

◆ **Fixed assets at cost** – the total acquisition cost.
◆ **Accumulated depreciation** – the sum of all the depreciation that has been reported in the profit and loss account to date. Accumulated depreciation is a contra entry – in that it is a negative amount. The increase in *accumulated depreciation* (line A08) is the amount that shows as the *depreciation expense* in the profit and loss account (line PL05 in Fig. 14.1). Remember that we are using the term depreciation as shorthand for depreciation, amortization and depletion.
◆ **Net Fixed Assets** is the book value (i.e. at balance sheet date) of fixed assets after subtracting depreciation.

Plant property and equipment are usually shown separately from intangible assets. Remember that a company may have intellectual property of significant value (brands, position, reputation, competencies) which are not reflected in the balance sheet.

Also, note that certain fixed assets (e.g. machinery) may be easier to liquidate than some short-term assets (such as prepaid rents), and fixed assets often have a market value above book value. Look in the notes to the financial statements for more detail.

> **Deposits paid** are amounts paid in advance and are reimbursable in the normal course of events, such as when you vacate a leased office. There may be short-term and long-term deposits (e.g. reflecting the life of a lease) on either side of the balance sheet – depending on whether you have paid (assets) or collected (liabilities) deposits.

Liabilities

Trade creditors or **accounts payable** reflects loans from suppliers and business partners in the normal course of business. See the note after *trade debtors,* above.

Short-term loans are borrowing from banks and other lenders – repayable within 12 months. In the example here, the company has repaid all its borrowing between the two balance sheet dates.

> In December 2002 telecoms giant Cable & Wireless was criticized for not divulging a clause in its 1999 agreement with Deutsche Telecom, requiring that £1.5 bn of its £2.2bn net cash could be forced into an escrow account to cover tax liabilities.

Long-term loans represent more-structural borrowing – and should be matched against long-term assets (i.e. if short-term borrowing is being used to finance long-term assets there could be a funding crisis if loans are not renewed). We will return to this topic in Chapter 19.

> ## Deferred taxation
>
> As already discussed in Chapters 11 and 13, tax accounting may differ from financial accounting. (If only tax authorities and regulators would talk to each other.) As a result, differences can arise between *taxable profit* and *reported profit* or in the tax bases of certain assets or liabilities. These differences basically resolve themselves over time (e.g. when an asset is fully depreciated for both tax and reporting purposes). Accordingly, they are known as *temporary differences*. When temporary differences will result in a liability to pay tax in future years, the amount must be shown as a *deferred tax liability*. Conversely, if it is *more likely than not* that there will be a deductible amount in the future, this is shown as a *deferred tax asset*.

Provisions. Balance sheets may include an entry in the liabilities section for some contingent liabilities – *probable* future costs or losses where the timing or amount is uncertain – such as might arise under a contract. In the past, these were often referred to as contingencies, but the International Accounting Standards Board has tightened up the terminology. It refers to probable obligations as *provisions* and uses the word contingencies for *reasonably possible* or *remote* obligations and benefits which are not reported in the balance sheet (discussed below, see *Off balance sheet but not forgotten*).

Provisions should be charged to income (i.e. the profit and loss account) and accrued in the balance sheet if:

◆ there is an obligation arising from past events;

◆ it is probable that it will cause an outflow of resources; and

◆ the amount can be estimated reliably.

Shareholders' equity

Paid-in share capital is the book value of money raised by an equity issue. For example, if one million ordinary $1 shares were sold for $1.50 each, *paid-in capital* would increase by $1 million. The $0.5 million *excess over book value* would be listed as *additional paid-in capital*. This classification reflects regulations in some jurisdictions that companies must maintain a minimum level of capital (i.e., the *book value* or *par value* of paid-in capital) which cannot be distributed to shareholders. There may be more than one class of share capital (e.g., ordinary and preference shares). See Chapter 19 for more details.

Additional paid-in share capital. See paid-in share capital

Treasury stock. The example does not show treasury stock, but you will sometimes see a reduction in *contributed capital* (i.e. paid-in capital) under the heading *treasury stock*. This reflects the company's holding of its own stock repurchased in the open market (see Chapter 19). Treasury stock is a contra account because it will have a debit balance partially offsetting the normal credit balances on this part of the balance sheet.

Retained earnings is the name of a cumulative reserve built up by *not* distributing profits as dividends. Note that this is a bookkeeping reserve and the balance says nothing about cash reserves. Figure 15.2 shows the relationship between net profit and retained earnings.

Fig. 15.2 What they do with the profit

Tetrylus Software Inc.
Appropriation of profits/income

US dollars millions

		2002
AP01	Net profit	1.92
AP02	Dividends	(0.04)
AP03	**Retained earnings**	**1.88**

Row AP01 and AP02 can be found in the cash flow statements (Fig. 16.2, rows CF01 and CF20) and in changes in shareholders' equity (Fig 15.3, Lines CE04 and CE05).

Row AP01, net profit, of course, is also the profit and loss account (Fig 14.1, row PL15).

The net sum, row AP03 retained earnings, is in the balance sheet (Fig 15.1, row E03).

Other comprehensive income. You will recall that the penultimate line in the profit and loss account in Fig. 14.1 was a bookkeeping entry to cover *unrealized gains and losses* as at the balance sheet date. This amount is set against shareholders' equity as *other comprehensive income.*

▶ Statement of changes in shareholders' equity

If you have access to a full set of financials, there is nothing new in the statement of changes in shareholders' equity. However, in published accounts, it can reveal numbers which – traditionally at least – are not reported elsewhere.

Figure 15.3 shows a simplified presentation. If you can follow the logic, there is not much else to say. The changes represent:

1 **Change in contributed capital** – financing raised though share issues less funds disbursed repurchasing *treasury* stock.

2 **Retained earning** – which can be negative when there are losses.

3 **Dividends** paid out.

4 **Other unrealized gains and losses** (other comprehensive income).

All of these have been discussed already.

Fig. 15.3 How a company's wealth grows

Tetrylus Software Inc.
Changes in shareholders' equity

US dollars millions

		2002
CE01	**Balance as at 13 December 2001**	**9.91**
CE02	Common stock at par	0.05
CE03	Additional paid in capital	0.32
CE04	Net Profit	1.92
CE05	Dividend paid	(0.04)
CE06	Other comprehensive income	(0.59)
CE07	**Balance as at 31 December 2002**	**11.57**

The first and last lines in this table relate directly to the total of shareholders' equity in the balance sheet (Fig. 15.1, row E05).

▶ Off balance sheet but not forgotten

There are a number of items which do not appear in a balance sheet, but which nevertheless should be reported in the footnotes. These are often very revealing. The following items are not required in all jurisdictions, but they are mandatory under international accounting standards.

Contingencies. As mentioned above under *provisions*, *probable* future obligations should be included in the balance sheet, while r*easonably possible* or *remote* events should be disclosed in the notes. International accounting standards require disclosure as follows:

◆ **contingent liabilities** should be disclosed unless the possibility of an outflow of resources embodying economic benefits is remote.

◆ **contingent assets** should be disclosed if an inflow of economic benefits is probable.

Examples include bad debts, obligations related to product warranties and defects, obligations to repurchase assets that have been sold, guarantees for the debts of other enterprises, threatened litigation, claims, and so on.

Contracts and negotiations. Look in the footnotes for details of contracts and negotiations which might involve future obligations. Examples include leases, staff pension plans, and share option schemes.

Related parties. When a third party has control or significant influence over the financial or operating decisions of the company, the relationship should be noted – even if no transactions have taken place. Such relationships include parent companies, principal owners and significant investors (and their close family), entities under common control, and key management personnel.

Events after the balance sheet date. Significant events which occur between the date of the financial statements and their publication should be reported in the notes. Such *subsequent events* include bankruptcies of trading partners, catastrophe's such as fire or flood, the results of litigation, and gains or losses on marketable securities.

Other. A UK requirement, taken into International Accounting Standard No. 1, is that details of the company's place of incorporation, registered office, principal activities, immediate and ultimate parent company and number of employees should be stated.

▶ The balance sheet – what it means

Contemporary reporting and disclosure standards make current balance sheets more valuable than they were a few decades back. Remember to read the notes to the financial statements. Then read between the lines.

The previous few pages should have highlighted why each category of assets, liabilities and equity is important. However, there are other keys to unlocking the value of the balance sheet. One is the cash flow statement, considered in the next chapter. Other hints are included in the analysis and review of financials (Chapters 17 and 18). And the section on funding (Chapter 19) will help you to interpret loans and shareholders' equity.

▶ The balance sheet – looking ahead

Projecting a balance sheet is a logical progression from the forecasting and estimating that you have done so far. There is an example in Fig. 15.4 (see p. 234), which was derived as follows. First, remember that any *total* in the profit and loss account is a *change* in the balance sheet. Then work through the items in the balance sheet, but not necessarily in top-to-bottom order for reasons that the following notes will make clear:

1 The fixed assets and inventory entries in the balance sheet are taken from analysis conducted in Chapters 11 and 13. For example, spending of $1,500 on fixed assets was projected for month two, so the balance sheet total at the end of month two is $1,500 higher than the total at the end of month one.

2 Similarly, the entry for retained earnings *changes* by the amount of net profit in any one period.

3 Prepayments and accruals *change* by the amounts recorded as, well, prepayments and accruals adjustments. You will have derived these figures when passing bookkeeping entries to shift transactions from the date that cash changes hands to the relevant accounting periods (e.g. to record July's rent against July, and not against the month when you paid it – see accruals accounting in Chapter 8).

4 Deposits paid and taken *change* by the amounts disbursed and received in each period.

5 Accounts payable might be calculated in a similar manner to note 3 (which is the case in the example here). However, it is usually easier to project these as ratios. For example, if you receive the same average value of deliveries each week, if your suppliers give you 30 days' credit, and if you make one payment a month, payables will average one-half of one month's spending on supplies. On this basis, if your expenditure on materials, components, etc is $10,000 in January, payables at end of that month will be $5,000. Note that this is not a change, it is the *actual* figure which shows in the balance sheet at end-month.

6 Accounts receivable can be calculated using either of the two methods just described for payables. However, do not forget to make an allowance for bad debts (Chapter 8).

7 Other assets and liabilities (except cash, loans and share capital) are calculated on a similar basis to notes 4 and 5 above.

8 Cash, loans and share capital depend on your cash flow and financing policies. We will discuss these in more depth in Chapter 19. For the moment, pretend that share capital is fixed. One approach is to assume that cash balances remain at a level just sufficient to cover daily net cash requirements (perhaps some percentage of operating profit with depreciation added back in – because depreciation in the accounts does not involve spending real money), and loans increase or decrease by net cash flow over the period. Alternatively, you could assume that loans are fixed and let the cash balance change accordingly. You actually need more information – we will return to this after projecting cash flow (next chapter) and financing and investing (Chapter 19).

Error trapping

After passing all of the above transactions, perform some simple addition and check that the two halves of the balance sheet come to the same total (to labour the point, ensure that assets equal liabilities plus equity). Then reconfirm that retained earnings changes by the amount of net profit in the projected profit and loss account. If either of these two sums is in error, you have made a mistake, possibly a transcription error, and you need to work through your figures again.

'Like all human endeavours, accounting has its own internal politics and fads. A current fad is to run more and more transactions through the income statement, and to put on the balance sheet more and more human judgments, particularly about future values.'

Alfred R. Berkeley, III
(Vice-Chairman, The Nasdaq Stock Market, January 2003)

Fig. 15.4 Sample balance sheet

	A	B	C	D	E	F	G	H
1		**TETRYLUS Inc.**						
2								
3		**Balance sheet: first six months**						
4		Dollars						
5								
6			**Month 1**	**Month 2**	**Month 3**	**Month 4**	**Month 5**	**Month 6**
7		**ASSETS**						
8	B-1	Cash at bank	2,044	14,798	22,757	9,456	32,922	1,000
9	B-2	Accounts receivable	–	20,000	–	40,000	–	50,000
10	B-3	Deposits paid	2,000	2,000	2,000	2,000	2,000	2,000
11	B-4	Prepayments (rents)	11,000	10,000	9,000	8,000	7,000	6,000
12	B-5	Inventory	–	15,000	40,000	17,500	42,500	12,500
13	B-6	Fixed assets at cost	36,500	38,000	38,750	39,750	39,750	39,750
14	B-7	Less accumulated depreciation	–	(1,389)	(2,819)	(4,262)	(5,733)	(7,204)
15	**B-8**	**Memo: net fixed assets**	**36,500**	**36,611**	**35,931**	**35,488**	**34,017**	**32,546**
16	**B-9**	**Total assets**	**51,544**	**98,409**	**109,688**	**112,444**	**118,439**	**104,046**
17	B-10							
18	B-11	**LIABILITIES**						
19	B-12	Total loans	–	–	10,000	10,000	25,000	52,469
20	B-13	Accounts payable – hardware	–	10,000	–	22,500	–	30,000
21	B-14	Accounts payable – software	–	3,591	3,591	8,274	8,274	12,253
22	B-15	Accruals	–	–	–	–	–	–
23	**B-16**	**Total liabilities**	**–**	**13,591**	**13,591**	**40,774**	**33,274**	**94,722**
24	B-17							
25	B-18	**CAPITAL & RESERVES**						
26	B-19	Share capital	125,000	250,000	350,000	400,000	500,000	500,000
27	B-20	Unremitted P&L	(73,456)	(165,182)	(253,903)	(328,330)	(414,835)	(490,676)
28	**B-21**	**Total capital and reserves**	**51,544**	**84,818**	**96,097**	**71,670**	**85,165**	**9,324**
29	B-22							
30	**B-23**	**Total liabilities and equity**	**51,544**	**98,409**	**109,688**	**112,444**	**118,439**	**104,046**

Ten hard questions to ask or be asked

1 What did the balance sheet look like a day, week or month before this one was drawn up?

2 How is this one different from previous balance sheets?

3 What is the quality of assets? What could be liquidated, and at what market value?

4 How realistic are inventory valuation and depreciation policies? (See also *Ten hard questions* in Chapters 11 and 13.)

5 How strong is working capital – current assets less current liabilities?

6 What is the balance of total assets less total liabilities?

7 Are these significant near-term liabilities (accruals, taxes, loan repayments) which have to be met from cash flow?

8 What is off balance sheet? What contingent liabilities and assets are lurking?

9 What is the stucture of debt? What is the balance of short-term and longer-term loans?

10 What has happened to shareholder's equity (dividends, share repurchases, retained earnings)?

Conclusion

You may have entered this chapter with a certain apprehension about balance sheets. If so I hope that any misgivings were dispelled and you now see them as delightful companions in your quest for financial enlightenment. If you studied the foregoing section on projecting balance sheets, you will be anxious to read about cash flow. With this in mind, let us move briskly onwards.

watching cash flow

'Profits are an opinion, cash is a fact.'

Anon.

▶ Chapter survival toolkit

▶ Overview

This chapter covers the cash flow statement, the third of the three major financial statements (see also the profit and loss account and balance sheet covered in the previous two chapters). Cash flow is simply a rearrangement of the figures already encountered. Its simplicity can be judged by the shortness of the list of new beanie buzz words for this chapter. However, this is not to say that the cash flow statement is not important. It reveals sources and uses of corporate funds: how cash is generated by operations and financing and used in investing (but note that any one of these three sources and uses could reflect net inflows or outflows).

▶ Prerequisites

If you followed the path through the perious two chapters, you will be freewheeling downhill throughout this one.

▶ Mastering cash flow

After reading this chapter, you should be able to answer the following questions:

1 What are the main sources and uses of funds that are shown in the cash flow statement?

2 Can you list ten things that a cash flow statement reveals? Why are they important?

3 When might operations generate a deficit (negative cash flow)?

4 Why is it important that operations should generate a surplus (positive cash flow) in the longer run?

5 Do the three categories of investing activities relate to (1) fixed assets, (2) the acquisition of debt and equity of other enterprises, and (3) advances and loans made to or repaid by third parties?

6 Are the categories of financing activities (1) issues and redemption of equity, (2) issues and redemptions of debt instruments, and (3) other borrowing and repayments?

7 When is it easier to construct a cash flow statement directly from receipts and payments, and when is it faster to generate it indirectly by starting with net profit and working backwards? Are the end results the same?

8 Where are taxes shown in cash flow statements?

9 What is free tax flow?

10 How would you use the figures from the previous few chapters to project cash flow?

> 'Depreciation is usually the largest non-cash expense in financial statements.'
>
> **Anon.**

Cash flow

The cash flow statement is the third and final *major* financial statement (after the profit and loss account and the balance sheet). It is necessary because profit and loss accounts bear only a passing relationship to the money that actually changes hands. The cash flow statement focuses on, need I say, changes in liquidity – and incidentally reveals a lot more than just what is happening to the bank balance. Recall that the profit and loss account reveals profits. Take these two financial statements together and you have a remarkably good picture of profitability and liquidity. These are the prerequisites for overall success. In the long term it is not possible to run a business unless you have both.

This chapter describes the cash flow statement, what it is, how it is structured, what it shows, how to interpret it and how to project your own cash flow requirements.

▶ More revelations from the balance sheet

As mentioned in the previous chapter, balance sheets are snapshots. The differences between two balance sheet dates show the net change but not necessarily all of the activity that took place. The cash flow statement records these net changes, and by rearranging them into a specific classification it helps with the interpretation of corporate results.

▶ Cash flow statement – what it is

A statement of *cash flow* – or *sources and uses of funds* – explains changes in cash and cash equivalents during the period of the accounts (quarter, year, etc.). Cash equivalents are highly liquid instruments that are capable of being converted into known amounts of cash without notice. In the major accounting jurisdictions there is a requirement that the original maturity of the instruments should be less than three months.

Cash flow can be described *directly* by showing receipts from customers and payments to suppliers, employees, government, and so on (Fig. 16.1). It can also be derived *indirectly* by starting with net profit or loss and reversing out non-cash items (Fig. 16.2). This is how most corporations report cash flow, and this is the easiest approach when you are making your own forecasts and projections. In addition to showing how cash is generated, the cash flow statement also shows use of funds. This is essentially:

◆ Cash from operations
◆ *less* cash used in investing activities
◆ *less* cash used in financing operations
◆ *equals* change in cash balances.

The following diagram illustrates these sources and uses of funds. In the example shown, there is surplus cash generated from operations. Of course, there could instead be a deficit – which is often the case when businesses are in phases of start-up, growth, recovery, and maturity. Investing and financing could also reflect sources or uses of funds, depending on many factors.

Sources and uses of cash

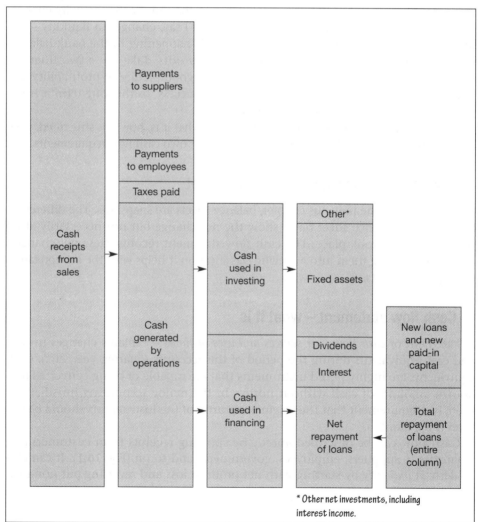

* Other net investments, including interest income.

Fig. 16.1 Direct cash flow

Tetrylus Software Inc.
Cash flow statement

US dollars millions

	2002
Cash receipts from sales	9.41
Cash paid to suppliers	(4.60)
Cash paid to employees	(1.88)
Cash generated from operations	**2.93**
Interest paid	(0.29)
Interest earned	0.57
Taxes	(0.02)
Net cash generated by operating activities	**3.19**

▶ Cash flow statement – what it shows

The cash flow statement is rather a nifty little document. Most financial regulators, including the International Accounting Standards Board, require that the statements classify cash flow into operating, investing, and financial activities.

Fig. 16.2 illustrates cash flow using the *indirect method*. The techniques for constructing these tables are discussed below. The content is self-explanatory, especially if you trace the sources of each entry back to the balance sheet (see the notes in the figure). Each of the entries has already been discussed under the heading *balance sheet,* above. Accordingly, these notes do not labour through the figures, but list what goes into each category and indicate typical disclosure requirements. Before we begin, two other points are worth noting:

1 Cash flows relating to taxes are usually disclosed separately within operating activities, as here, but they could be identified under one of the other headings.

2 Investing and financing activities that do not give rise to cash flows (e.g. non monetary transactions such as the acquisition of property by issuing debt) are excluded from the cash flow statement, but disclosed separately.

> 'If the cash is growing at a similar rate to net profit, the net income number hasn't been fudged.'
>
> **Anon.**

Fig. 16.2 Sources and uses of cash

Tetrylus Software Inc.

Cash flow statement

US dollars millions

ID		Source	2002
CF01	AP01	Net income	1.92
CF02	A02	Inventory	0.00
CF03	A03	Debtors	0.70
CF04	A05	Prepaid expenses	0.40
CF05	A08	Depreciation	0.80
CF06	A10	Other long-term assets	0.02
CF07	L01	Creditors	(0.28)
CF08	L03	Accruals	(0.36)
CF09	L04	Taxes payable	(0.02)
CF10		**Net cash generated by operating activities**	**3.19**
CF11		**Cash flow from investing activities**	
CF12	A07	Fixed assets	(1.83)
CF13	A04	Investments	(0.72)
CF14		**Net cash from (used in) investing activities**	**(2.56)**
CF15		**Cash flow from financing activities**	
CF16	E01	Paid-in share capital	0.05
CF17	E02	Additional paid-in capital	0.32
CF18	L02	Loans – short term	(1.03)
CF19	L06	Loans – non short term	0.00
CF20	AP02	Dividend paid	(0.04)
CF21		**Net cash from (used in) financing operations**	**(0.70)**
CF22	E04	Other	(0.59)
CF23		**Change in cash and equivalents**	**(0.66)**

This cash flow statement was created entirely from other financial statements. For example, the first entry is taken from row AI01 – row 01 in the appropriation of profits statement. The key to the letters is as follows:

AP = appropriation of profits Fig 15.2

A = assets in balance sheet – see Fig 15.1

L = liabilities in balance sheet – see Fig 15.1

E = shareholders' equity – see Fig 15.1

Cash flow from operating activities

This category hardly needs explanation. It is cash flow related to operating income, together with cash flow that is not shown under investing and financing activities.

Sources of funds

◆ Sales of goods and services
◆ Rental income
◆ Output value added tax and refunds of value added tax
◆ Other refunds of taxes and duties.

Uses of funds

◆ Purchases of goods and services
◆ Operating leases
◆ Payments to and on behalf of employees
◆ Input value added tax
◆ Income tax
◆ Other taxes and duties other than value added tax (e.g. sales taxes, import duty).

Cash flow from investing activities

Investing activities are the acquisition and disposal of long-term assets and investments not included in cash equivalents, as follows:

Sources of funds

◆ Sales of fixed assets (e.g. disposal of plant or real estate)
◆ Sales of other investments
◆ Dividends and distributions of profits
◆ Bond interest income
◆ Disposal of other long-term assets (e.g. sale of a patent).

Uses of funds

◆ Acquisition of fixed assets, intangible assets and other long-term assets
◆ Equity investments
◆ Debt investments.

Three categories for disclosure

1 Fixed assets
2 Equity or debt instruments of other enterprises (including acquisition or sale of subsidiaries)
3 Advances and loans made to, or repaid by, third parties.

Cash flow from financing activities

Financing activities are those activities that result in changes in the size and composition of the capital and borrowings of the enterprise, as follows:

Sources of funds

◆ Proceeds from issuing shares

◆ Proceeds from issuing bonds

◆ Receipts from loans taken and other borrowing.

Uses of funds

◆ Repayments of loans and other borrowings

◆ Payments of dividends or distributions of profits

◆ Financing costs

◆ Interest expenses

◆ Payments for finance leases

◆Repurchase of registered capital.

Three categories for disclosure

1 Issues and redemptions of equity

2 Borrowing and repayment of loans

3 Issues and repayments of debt instruments (bonds and notes).

▶ Cash flow statement – what it means

The cash flow statement reveals:

1 Cash earnings – the difference between net profits and the cash generated from income producing activities

2 How the business is using its funds

3 How the business is being financed

4 The need for outside financing

5 The company's ability to obtain financing

6 Where it is investing or divesting resources

7 How much it is investing for future growth

8 Its ability to generate future cash flows

9 Its ability to meet obligations

10 Its free cash flow (see below).

Cash flow from operations is a key indicator of the health of the company. As already mentioned, this figure is often negative when the company is growing (because cash is tied up in inventory and receivables, etc.). There is cause for concern if cash flow from operations is negative and the business is not growing, or if cash flow is negative for a prolonged period.

The cash flow statement also indicates how much is being invested for future growth. When interpreted carefully, this helps assess the ability of the firm to generate cash flows in the future. And, of course, the cash flow statement also reveals how the business is financed, which could be a major influence on the ability to keep trading – and could highlight inefficient use of capital. We will return to this in Chapter 19.

Free cash flow

One final point. A useful indicator is *free cash flow*. This is cash flow from operations less investments in operating assets. It indicates the cash available for acquisitions, repayment of debt, and distributions to shareholders.

Ten hard questions to ask or be asked

1 Are there any large or unusual items in the cash flow statement?

2 Is operating cash flow positive and growing? Is is greater than net profit?

3 Does operating cash flow cover net profit plus depreciation (i.e. consumption of capital)?

4 Does operating cash flow cover depreciation plus dividends? Investment plus dividends?

5 Does investment cash flow reveal significant purchases or sales of fixed assets?

6 Does investment cash flow reveal replacement of depreciated fixed assets?

7 Does investment cash flow reveal investment or divestment of subsidiaries?

8 Does investment cash flow reveal other investments or divestments?

9 Does financing cash flow show repayment of loans, or new borrowing?

10 Does financing cash flow show issues or repurchase of equity?

Cash flow statements – looking ahead

If you are with me up to here, and have produced your own estimates of revenues and costs, you have all the figures needed to produce your own cash flow projections. As you will already have spotted, there are two ways to do this.

1 You can extract the figures which involve exchanges of hard cash. This will generate a table similar to Fig. 16.1, although yours will be at a greater level of detail and have more rows.

2 Or you can take your forecast of net profit and reverse out the non-cash transactions.

The first method is so straightforward that I will leave it up to you. The second is slightly more complex, so I will cover it here. Essentially, go through your projected balance sheet and identify all the entries that relate to operations, financing and investments. Then build a spreadsheet which starts with net profit and lists the balance sheet changes. Add in a couple of totals, you have a cash flow projection similar to that in Fig. 16.3.

Fig. 16.3 Cash flow

	A	B	C	D	E	F	G	H
1		TETRYLUS Inc.						
2		Cash flow, first six months						
3		Dollars						
4			Month 1	Month 2	Month 3	Month 4	Month 5	Month 6
5	F-1	Net profit	(73,456)	(91,726)	(88,721)	(74,427)	(86,505)	(75,841)
6	F-2	Adjustments for changes in:						
7	F-3	Accounts receivable	0.00	(20,000)	20,000	(40,000)	40,000	(50,000)
8	F-4	Deposits paid	(2,000)	0.00	0.00	0.00	0.00	0.00
9	F-5	Prepayments (rents)	(11,000)	1,000	1,000	1,000	1,000	1,000
10	F-6	Inventory	0.00	(15,000)	(25,000)	22,500	(25,000)	30,000
11	F-7	Fixed assets	(36,500)	(1,500)	(750)	(1,000)	0.00	0.00
12	F-8	Depreciation	0.00	1,389	1,430	1,443	1,471	1,471
13	F-9	Acct's payable – h'ware	0.00	10,000	(10,000)	22,500	(22,500)	30,000
14	F-10	Acct's payable – s'ware	0.00	3,591	0.00	4,683	0.00	3,979
15	F-11	Accruals	0.00	0.00	0.00	0.00	0.00	0.00
16	F-12	Loans	0.00	0.00	10,000	0.00	15,000	27,469
17	F-13	Equity	125,000	125,000	100,000	50,000	100,000	0.00
18	F-14	Cash flow	2,044	12,754	7,959	(13,301)	23,466	(31,922)
19	F-15	Cumulative cash flow	2,044	14,798	22,757	9,456	32,922	1,000

▶ In pictures

It is instructive to chart the bottom line, *cumulative cash flow,* as shown in Fig. 16.4. This is the liquidity bottom line, which for managers is every bit as important as net profit – perhaps more so. For simplicity the sample curve is unrealistically smooth. Yours will bump up and down, reflecting seasonal pressures and other leads and lags between action and results. Remember that it charts the net changes in cash flow in each period. You need to allow for peaks and troughs during each month, quarter, etc. In other words, the figures here show the movements from month to month. For operational purposes, you will also need daily cash flow forecasts as discussed in Chapter 8.

Fig. 16.4 Cash flow crisis?

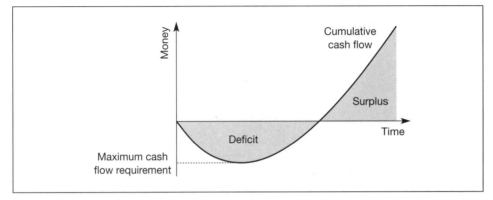

Cumulative cash flow presents a quandary for entrepreneurs and for managers who are responsible for the enterprise and business units. If there is a surplus, how do you use it? The answer is not necessarily obvious. If there is a deficit, how do you cover it? We will return to this in Chapter 19.

▶ What else to look for

If you are appraising someone's plan, question carefully the cash flow and the underlying assumptions. I have known executives who have deliberately massaged cash flow forecasts to make them look acceptable. Then, when the actual results were worse than 'expected', they went back to the management executive committee and asked for more – knowing that the boss would have to give them the money that would not have been approved at the outset. Genuine errors can happen. But deliberate cheating such as this suggests incompetence on both sides, and it usually ends in tears.

▶ There is more...

And this concludes our review of the financial statements. Except it doesn't. We have looked at the profit and loss account, balance sheet and cash flow statement in some depth. However, there are still a few more interesting odds and ends to examine, which we do in the next chapter and then we can pull them all together and review the financials as a whole.

reviewing reports

'How much easier it is to be critical than correct.'

Benjamin Disraeli

Chapter survival toolkit

▶ Overview

This chapter reviews all the information that you can expect to find relating to corporate financial statements. It looks particularly at annual reports and the myriad of commentary and tables that they contain. It also introduces two new financial statements: segment reports and value added statements.

▶ Prerequisites

You could probably read this chapter in isolation. However, an understanding of the previous few pages will help you to relate to the segment report and value added statement.

▶ Mastering financial reports

After reading this chapter, you should be able to answer the following questions:

1 What constitutes a full set of financial statements?
2 What is the main purpose of an annual report? The secondary purpose?
3 Which parts of an annual report are required by regulators?
4 Why might it be good for users if the operating and financial review is mandatory?
5 What does the auditor's report show?
6 Is it better to have an unqualified or qualified auditor's report?
7 What is a segment report? What does it show?
8 Will a company always report results for more than one geographical area? More than one industry sector or product line?
9 What size segment has to be disclosed when reporting under international accounting standards?
10 What is a value added statement? What does it show?

> 'Everything that is written merely to please the author is worthless.'
>
> **Blaise Pascal**

Published reports

Now is a good point at which to pull together the previous few chapters and look at what you might find in published financials. These might be formal reports to a regulatory agency, such as a quarterly report to the US Securities and Exchange Commission (SEC), or a glossy annual report aimed primarily at the public at large. The chapter starts by considering what you can expect to uncover in an annual report, because this is by far the best-known delivery platform for published financial data. We will also take a look at a couple of lesser financial statements, just to complete the set. In the next chapter we will get down to the analysis.

Collect the set

▶ It depends who you ask

By now, you probably know what a financial statement is. But what exactly constitutes a complete set of statements? It depends who you ask.

◆ For internal company use, a *cash flow statement, profit and loss account* and *balance sheet are often enough* – usually supplemented by some written explanatory information and perhaps some tables summarizing, for example, changes in fixed assets.

◆ For official reporting, it is increasingly mandatory to include *segment reports* (a slightly off-putting name for a breakdown of the numbers by territory and industry).

◆ For compliance with international accounting standards, you need all of the above plus a *statement of changes in shareholders' equity.*

Regulatory requirements for financial statements

They should:

- present a **fair view** of the company's finances;
- **comply** with accounting standards;
- present the company as a **going concern**;
- use **accrual** basis of accounting;
- be **consistent** in application of accounting policies;
- show **material** facts, immaterial amounts to be **aggregated** with amounts of a similar nature or function;
- not **offset** assets and liabilities or expenditure and income except where expressly permitted;
- provide **comparative** information when accounting policies are changed;
- be based on **substance over form**.

◆ For general publication, companies with a social conscience might include a *value added statement*. And then there is a collection of useful odds and ends such as the directors' report and auditors' report.

The main aim of public reporting was – and still is – to keep shareholders informed. However, corporate bosses soon realized that this obligation provided an excellent public relations opportunity. *Any publicity is good publicity.* Annual financial reports grew into weighty glossy brochures containing photographs of the smiling CEO, some meaningless blurb, and – tucked away at the back almost as an afterthought – the financials. Then the regulators started piling on rules and turning discretionary pitches into mandatory statements and certifications. Today, annual reports can be monsters. Many companies now send a lower-cost financial report to shareholders who do not ask for more. If you are looking at a company in depth, make sure you have the all-singing-all-dancing glossy report.

▶ Reading annual reports

Publication of an annual report marks the peak of a corporation's financial results cycle, combining mandatory financial statements with glossy public relations and marketing hype. The annual report is usually the most comprehensive document relating to the financials, but it is not necessarily the be all and end all. For example, in the US, reports submitted to the SEC contain information, such as biographies of directors, which you do not usually find in annual reports.

The best way to understand annual reports is to browse through a few. You can download some examples by visiting this book's website. You do not have to read them cover to cover. A quick scan of some reports online will be instructive. When you come to detailed study of an annual report, you may find that it is useful to start with the auditors report, primarily to establish the regulatory reporting basis for the accounts and the auditor's opinion. Glance over the financials, read the notes to the financials, work outwards from there, and then return to analyse the financials in detail. The main sections that may be included are as follows.

Chairman's statement. I could tell you now what it will say, even without knowing the company. Should be read with a cynical eye.

President/CEO/MD's report. This is usually more detailed than the chairman's statement but this is as much as I am prepared to say.

Review of the year. Probably written by the marketing department. Most, if not all, of the information will already be public knowledge by the time you see it. If this is your first real brush with the business, it might give you a useful overview of its more successful operations and perhaps its future plans. Given that the review is not required by regulators, do not expect it to be forthcoming about skeletons in the closet.

Directors' report. A more formal written report. It may contain a brief overview of the financials. Look for any disclosures or useful supplemental information.

Operating and financial review (OFR). This may be instead of or as well as, either or both of, the review of the year and directors' report. The important point is that this is increasingly becoming a requirement rather than an option. For example, the UK government's 2002 White Paper, *Modernizing Company Law*, proposed that an operating and financial review should be mandatory for large companies. If and when, it would probably be required to include the following:

◆ details of accounting policies which required the particular exercise of judgement in their application;

◆ details of where, and how, information from the financial statements has been adjusted for inclusion in the written report (often called 'pro forma information') together with a reconciliation back to the main financials;

◆ details of the measures that are used by the directors as key performance indicators in managing the business.

Auditor's report. This indicates the scope of the audit, the basis of the accounts (e.g. US GAAP) and, we hope, that the financial statements were found to comply with reporting regulations; that – in the words of the UK Companies Act – they give a *true and fair view* of the state of affairs of the company. When something wobbly is unearthed during the audit, the auditor's report will *qualify* the financial statements with suitable warnings. A *qualification* is perhaps reassuring, because you can be sure something will be done about the issues raised. The sceptics would say that *unqualified* reports are a worry because there might be something wrong that has not yet come to light. I have not checked them all, but I think that there were unqualified clean audits before all of the recent corporate accounting scandals (Worldcom, Enron, etc.).

> In a survey of over 1,000 Australian companies with balance sheet dates in July 2002, the Australian Securities and Investments Commission (ASIC) found that the accounts of 215 companies (that is, about 20%) had audit qualifications and/or *emphasis of matter* paragraphs. Six had audit qualifications relating to their continuation as going concerns. An *emphasis of matter* is required under Australian auditing standards to draw particular attention to matters disclosed in the notes of a financial report that are of particular importance to the company's future as a going concern.

Corporate governance statement. This is a new written report, prompted by various financial scandals. It essentially makes the directors put their hands on their hearts and confirm that they run the company properly, exercise prudence, and so on. Well, as long as they say they do I suppose it is all right. Such statements are often interesting for students who want to better understand the formal mechanics of running a business.

Financial statements. Financials at last. I will come back to these in a moment. They include:

♦ **profit and loss account** (discussed in Chapter 14)
♦ **balance sheet** (Chapter 15)
♦ **cash flow statement** (Chapter 16)
♦ **statement of changes in equity/comprehensive income** (Chapter 15)
♦ **segment reporting** (this chapter)
♦ **value added statement** (this chapter)
♦ **highlights for, say, five years** (this chapter).

Notes to the financial statements. If you ask me, this is the most interesting part, comprising a few pages of small print with various notes and required disclosures. In many reports it will contain some of the information listed above, under *financial statements*. It is always worth reading. The best way to appreciate the value of this section is to download an annual report or two and read the notes (see this book's website).

Highlights. One other table you might find is a five-year summary of key financial indicators – sales, operating profit, net assets, etc. The table will look similar to Fig. 17.1, except that the rows will be captioned differently. This may be outside of the regulated sections, and the numbers might not be directly comparable with the latest financials. Check the basis for the numbers (e.g. which measure of profit). Those selected will be as flattering as possible.

▶ Financial statements revisited

In case you forgot, let me remind you that the previous three chapters reviewed the profit and loss account, the balance sheet and the cash flow statement. When we were discussing the balance sheet we also looked at appropriation of income and changes in shareholders' equity. Bear with me while we run through the final couple: segment reporting and value added statements.

> 'All the news that's fit to print.'
> **Adolph S. Ochs**
> **(Former motto of *New York Times*)**

▶ Segment reporting

Major regulatory authorities require disclosure about financial results by region and industry – known in an off-putting way as segments. Segment reporting provides users of the financial statements with an idea of how, in the past at least, the company has allocated resources and earned profits.

Sample segments

Ericsson reports three industry segments and six geographic segments:

- Network systems
- Mobile phones
- Other.

- Western Europe
- Central and Eastern Europe
- Middle East and Africa
- North America
- Latin America
- Asia-Pacific.

The Boeing Company reports for four main industry segments:

- Commercial airplanes
- Military aircraft and missile systems
- Space and communications
- Customer and commercial financing.

Microsoft Corporation has three major segments:

- Windows platforms
- Productivity applications and developer systems
- Consumer, commerce, and other.

Royal Dutch Petroleum Company (Shell) reports five industry segments and four geographic segments:

- Exploration and production
- Gas and power
- Oil production
- Chemicals
- Corporate and other

- Europe
- Other eastern hemisphere
- USA
- Other western hemisphere

Safeway Inc. in the US has one major segment – retail grocery – accounting for over 98% of its sales and operations. The company reports two geographic segments: the US and Canada.

▶ The segment report – what it is

For financial statements, segments are the highest level of organizational units that report product and geographical information; that is, they are usually directly accountable to the CEO and board of directors. The basic principle is that only segments accounting for 10% or more of total revenues, assets or net profits must be disclosed, provided that at least 75% of consolidated revenue is explained through segment disclosures. Of course, a company operating almost wholly within one area (geographic or industry) may have no segments to report – see Safeway, above, for example. Segment reports contain an extract from the profit and loss account and balance sheet with some supplemental information, as noted next.

Segments may not sum to 100% of the total

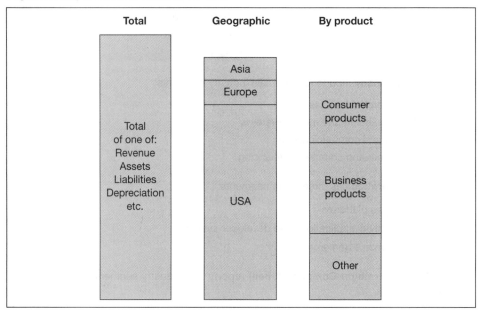

▶ The segment report – what it shows

International accounting standards require segment reporting by both product and service lines and by geographic lines. One basis will be defined as primary, the other as secondary. The following must be disclosed:

For primary and secondary segments:

◆ revenue, with external and inter-segment revenues shown separately

◆ book value of the segment's assets

◆ cost of acquisition of fixed assets

◆ the basis of inter-segment pricing.

In addition, for the primary segment only:

◆ net operating profit or loss before interest and taxes

◆ book value of the segment's liabilities

◆ depreciation and amortization

◆ non-cash expenses other than depreciation

◆ the share of profit or loss of equity and joint venture investments.

An extract from a segment report is shown in Fig. 17.1. Given that these figures are a subset of the financial statements already discussed, I do not think that you need me to elaborate on them here, but they are analysed extensively in Chapter 18.

Fig. 17.1 Segments exposed

Tetrylus Software Inc.
Business segments

US dollars millions

	1998	1999	2000	2001	2002
USA	2.35	2.98	4.02	5.76	8.11
Europe	0.43	0.49	0.65	0.81	1.39
Asia-Pacific	0.47	0.52	0.69	0.71	0.51
Other	0.00	0.00	0.00	0.01	0.10
Totals	**3.25**	**3.99**	**5.36**	**7.29**	**10.11**

▶ The segment report – what it means

The figures in a segment report may not sum to the totals in the main financial statements, because small segments do not have to be reported. Nevertheless, segment reports are useful sources of competitive information when you are assessing your rivals. It shows you where and how they are doing business. Apply the same tests to these figures as you would to the main statements to see which regions and lines are most and least profitable, and so on. As for your own segments, aside from applying the same analysis, you should also be asking which ones are missing – where could you be doing business but are not?

▶ Segment report – looking ahead

Given that figures by segment are merely extracts from the main financials, forecasting and projecting your own is straightforward. You should have the information to hand already. No doubt you have already analysed, forecast, and projected individually any segments that account for 10% or more of your business. Have you not?

Getting value

Another financial presentation worth considering is the *value added statement*. This is another way of looking at corporate performance. The value added statement attempts to measure the creation and distribution of wealth. Personally, I am a bit dubious about how wealth is created by, say, marking up the price of groceries before retailing them – but there you are. Economists rely on the concept of *value added* to measure activity. Consequently, the corporate value added statement is directly related to national income figures (such as GDP).

What did you do today?

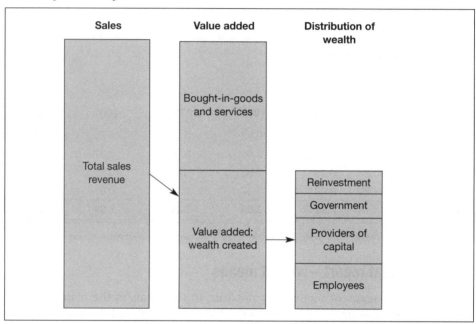

Value added statements are not an officially required component of financial reporting. Indeed, more often than not they are absent from published reports. Moreover, you cannot usually construct a value added statement without knowing the breakdown of costs and other figures at a level of detail which is not often found in published financials. Nevertheless, if the financials that you are examining do include a value added statement, or you have constructed one from your own accounts, you may find it useful.

Figure 17.2 shows an example. As you can see, there is not really any new information in the individual components, only in the presentation. Note that it shows how the wealth that has been created is shared out among employees, social welfare (i.e. via taxation), and the providers of capital (in plain English, bankers and shareholders) – and how much is reinvested for future growth.

However, you can derive some useful information by calculating various ratios (Fig. 17.2, right-hand column). For example, the number at top-right indicates that for every dollar of sales, 43 cents (i.e. 43%) is value added by the company.

The higher the number, the greater degree of vertical integration, or, to put it another way, the more the company produces for itself rather than buying-in from outside. You will also note that for every dollar of salaries, $2.30 of value is created. Another way of looking at this is to divide value added by the number of employees to reveal the average value added per employee. Imagine how much this figure would increase if all the deadweight in your organization was thrown overboard. Did anybody mention the accounting department?

Fig. 17.2 Value added

Tetrylus Software Inc.
Statement of value added

US dollars millions

ID	Source		2002	Ratio*
VA01	PL01	Sales	10.11	0.43
VA02	Note	Bought-in goods and services	(5.77)	(0.75)
VA03		**Value added**	**4.34**	**1.00**
VA04	PL08	Investment income	0.57	7.55
VA05	PL14	Other income (losses)	(0.00)	0.00
VA06		**Total wealth created**	**4.91**	**0.88**
VA07		Distribution of wealth		
VA08		Employees		
VA09	Note	Salaries, wages, etc.	(1.88)	(2.30)
VA10		**Total employees**	**(1.88)**	**(2.30)**
VA11		Capital providers		
VA12	PL09	Interest on loans	(0.29)	(15.09)
VA13		Dividends	(0.04)	(104.13)
VA14		**Total capital providers**	**(0.33)**	**(13.18)**
VA15		Government		
VA16	PL12	Taxes	(0.02)	(260.72)
VA17		**Total government**	**(0.02)**	**(260.72)**
VA18		**Reinvested for continuation and expansion**		
VA19	PL05	Depreciation	(0.80)	(5.42)
VA20	AP03	Retained earnings	(1.88)	(2.31)
VA21		**Total reinvestment**	**(2.68)**	**(1.62)**
VA22		**Total distribution of wealth**	**(4.91)**	**(0.88)**

Note: For this example, line VA02 bought-in goods and services is equivalent to the production and operating costs in the profit and loss account (Fig. 14.1, rows PL02, PL04 and PL05) excluding labour costs. Labour costs are shown in line VA09 above.

Sources beginning PL relate to rows in the profit and loss account (Fig. 14.1), while those commencing AP are found in the appropriation of profits statement (Fig. 15.2).

* For each row, the ratio is the figures in that row for 2002 divided into the value added ($4.34).

> ## Ten hard questions to ask or be asked

1 Is this report reliable? Is it covered by statutory reporting requirements? How much of it?

2 What other sources of information will provide useful data?

3 What does the commentary say? What can you read between the lines? What is not said?

4 What is buried in the footnotes? What are the implications?

5 Are the financials audited? What did the auditors say? Who were they?

6 What are the most important product lines? Why? What are the implications?

7 What are the most important industry sectors? Why? What are the implications?

8 What are the most important geographic sectors? Why? What are the implications?

9 Is the business dependent on any significantly large customers, areas, etc.? Why? What are the implications?

10 Where does the greatest value added come from?

> ## What's next?

This chapter looked at financial reporting as a whole. The main focus was on the annual report. Remember that you will find much interesting material in other reports, including reports to regulatory authorities (e.g. stock exchanges or securities and exchange commissions) and other published but unregulated reports and commentary. But beware that so-called pro forma (i.e. unregulated) financials can present a very different – and usually more rosy – picture from accounts prepared under generally accepted accounting principles. The next chapter looks more closely at analysing financial statements in concert. This is a very interesting topic and it will help you extract maximum value from any financials that happen to be lying around.

> 'In June [2002], we first required CEOs and CFOs to personally certify – in writing, under oath, and for publication – that their most recent reports filed with the [US Securities and Exchange Commission] were both complete and accurate ... with new rules requiring sworn certification of all future statements, executives are on notice that they had better know not just the bottom line, but how the company got there.'
>
> **Cynthia A. Glassman**
> (Commissioner, US Securities and Exchange Commission, 2002)

figuring financials

1
2
3
4
5
6
7
8
9
10
11
12
13
14
15
16
17
18
19
20
21
22
23
24

'Discovery consists of seeing what everybody has seen and thinking what nobody has thought.'

Albert von Szent

▶ Chapter survival toolkit

▶ Overview

The previous few chapters have covered all of the key financial statements, and a few incidental ones. The next few pages move on to look at how you analyse and interpret them together, and also how you compare published figures between companies. Accounting ratios and foreign currency issues are introduced here, and developed in the next couple of chapters.

▶ Prerequisites

Ideally, you should be up to speed with the previous four chapters before reading this one.

▶ Mastering financial analysis

After reading this chapter, you should be able to answer the following questions:

1 How do index numbers help you when interpreting trends in reported figures?

2 Three factors which make inter-company financial comparisons difficult are accounting policies, accounting periods and accounting currencies. Right or wrong?

3 How could you minimize the effects of inflation on reported financials?

4 What is the best way to measure a company's liquidity? What if cash flow forecasts are not available? Name three measures of liquidity that you could use with published financial statements.

5 How do turnover ratios provide a measure of the efficiency of a company's financial policies?

6 What is the major problem with using ratios which rely on figures from the balance sheet?

7 Why would you use index numbers to *common size* the profit and loss accounts of two companies? What does *common size* mean?

8 If a foreign company provided you with financials in its base operating currency and in a currency of your choosing, which set would you use to calculate ratios and trends?

9 If the net profits of a foreign company were unchanged between two years, and you translated them into another currency which depreciated by 10% during the same period, what would appear to have happened to the translated profits?

10 For what type of comparisons would you have to translate a foreign company's accounts into your own currency?

> ► **Jargon watch**

New beanie buzz words

Accounting ratio

Common size

Currency translation

Historical-cost accounting, inflation-accounting, hyperinflation

Current ratio, acid test, quick ratio, turnover ratios, return on capital employed, return on total assets

Overtrading, debt restructuring, bankruptcy*

New jargon from the economists

Deflator, deflate, current price, constant prices, real terms

New investment banker buzz words

Stock index, listed company, market capitalization*

*First encounter, explained fully in the next chapter.

Beanie buzz words revisited

Depreciation, inventory

Gross margin, gross profit, operating profit, profit and loss account

Assets, liabilities, working capital

Inflation accounting

GAAP

Encore for an economics term

Inflation

Numerical terms revisited

Cross-sectional data, trends, index numbers

Absolute, percentage, ratio

► Analysing the financials

Now that you have reviewed each of the main financial statements, it is time to look at how you combine the information in them to assess the status of a business. You might be dealing with your own financials, they might be provided by a business partner or they might be taken from published corporate reports. Generally, you will have the most information available from your own financials, and the least amount with published reports. Keep this in mind when you get down to the analysis.

This chapter reviews techniques for analysis, and then applies them all to some of the financial statements already encountered.

> 'There were at least ten levels of governance in the Enron case, and they all failed. This relates to the issue of excessive optimism: hard questions are not asked when things are going well.'
>
> **Wiliam R. White**
> (Economic Adviser, Bank for International Settlements)

▶ New ways of looking at the figures

So far, we have discussed the structure and content of financial statements. Now it is time to really *analyse* them. There are four key ways to look at the numbers:

◆ **As presented** – that is, you examine the underlying raw data.

◆ **Cross-sectional** – look at relationships between various numbers (e.g. current assets relative to total assets) – otherwise known as vertical analysis.

◆ **Trends over time** – otherwise known as horizontal analysis.

◆ **Comparisons** – with the industry average or key competitors.

Also, there are four ways of reviewing these. You can analyse:

◆ **Absolute values** – i.e. the raw data and increases or decreases in dollars.

◆ **Percentages.**

◆ **Index numbers.**

◆ **Ratios** – such as current assets as a percentage of total assets.

When you use the latter three analyses, you are ignoring absolute value to focus on relative values – beanies, ever ready with their own jargon, call this *common size analysis*.

▶ Analysis in action

The easiest way to explain the analysis is to walk through an example. The following notes use the figures for *sales by region* from the previous chapter.

Raw data

Tetrylus Software Inc.
Sales revenue by region

US dollars millions

	1998	1999	2000	2001	2002
USA	2.35	2.98	4.02	5.76	8.11
Europe	0.43	0.49	0.65	0.81	1.39
Asia-Pacific	0.47	0.52	0.69	0.71	0.51
Other	0.00	0.00	0.00	0.01	0.10
Totals	**3.25**	**3.99**	**5.36**	**7.29**	**10.11**

First, take a look at the raw data and see what you can deduce. The earliest and latest years are illustrated in Fig. 18.1. A chart often helps with interpretation. In these figures, it is immediately apparent that the US was by far the most important region in the latest year, while Europe lagged somewhat behind. In the earliest year, Europe and Asia-Pacific were roughly level pegging.

Fig. 18.1 Sales by region

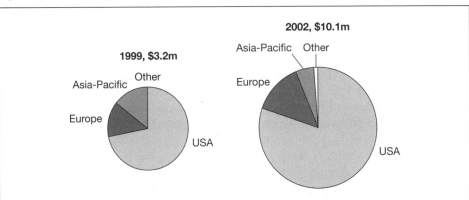

These pies were created in a spreadsheet as described in Chapter 5. Note that the areas (not the widths) are in the ratio 3.2:10.1. You can calculate the relative widths as follows. First, recall from your schooldays that the area of a circle is πr^2 – where r^2 is the radius (half the diameter) multiplied by itself, and π is the constant 3.14... Put another way, the spreadsheet formula for the radius is =SQRT(area/PI()) – where SQRT is the square root and PI is π. In other words, the radius of the pie on the left is SQRT(3.2/PI()) or 1.02, and for the pie on the right it is SQRT(10.1/PI()) or 1.79. Accordingly, the width of the pie on the right should be 1.79/1.02 = 176% the width of the one on the left. Got that?

Alternatively, use stacked bars to illustrate the situation. Not only will the spreadsheet do all the work for you, but you can show relative sales for all five years on one chart without over-crowding. Much easier.

You can also say something about the dollar amounts of revenue generated from each region. If you knew the average sale price by region, you could divide them into these revenue figures to find the underlying sales volumes, which would be very interesting (see Chapter 9).

Percentage of total

**Tetrylus Software Division
Revenue by region**

Percentage of totals

	1998	1999	2000	2001	2002
USA	72.3	74.6	75.0	79.0	80.2
Europe	13.2	12.3	12.1	11.1	13.7
Asia-Pacific	14.5	13.0	12.9	9.7	5.0
Other	0.0	0.1	0.1	0.2	1.0
Totals	**100.0**	**100.0**	**100.0**	**100.0**	**100.0**

Once the figures are restated on a percentage basis, it becomes much easier to quantify the importance of the US. In the most recent year, the US accounted for

80% of sales. This percentage has been climbing gently but steadily over the entire period under review. It is also clear that the proportion of sales in Europe tailed off slightly over the period, but recovered in the latest year. Sales in Asia-Pacific are in decline. One of the questions that you would need to look elsewhere to answer is *why have sales in Asia-Pacific dropped off?* Was it due to increasing competition or a deliberate attempt to target higher-priced markets elsewhere?

Note that sales in the rest of the world were less than $10,000 a year in the early periods, which rounds to zero (raw data). This was still large enough to show in many of the other tables here, which are calculated from the accurate raw data.

Dollar changes

Tetrylus Software Division
Revenue by region

Dollar changes

	1998	1999	2000	2001	2002
USA	–	0.63	1.04	1.74	2.35
Europe	–	0.06	0.16	0.16	0.58
Asia-Pacific	–	0.05	0.17	0.02	(0.20)
Other	–	0.00	0.00	0.01	0.09
Totals	–	0.74	1.37	1.93	2.82

When you can see the changes in dollars (or in whatever currency the accounts are reported), it is immediately obvious that total sales revenue has been growing steadily. The same applies to the growth in US markets. However, sales in Europe jumped up in the most recent period while those in Asia-Pacific actually fell.

Percentage change

Tetrylus Software Division
Revenue by region

Percentage changes

	1998	1999	2000	2001	2002
USA	–	26.8	34.9	43.3	40.8
Europe	–	14.0	32.7	24.6	71.6
Asia-Pacific	–	10.6	32.7	2.9	(28.2)
Other	–	90.9	52.4	337.5	614.3
Totals	–	22.8	34.3	36.0	38.6

The changes in percentage terms quantify the trends. It is immediately obvious that sales in the US did not grow as quickly in the latest period as they did in the year before. Why? The latest increase in sales in Europe is impressive, but the slow-down and then fall in Asia-Pacific could be significant. Sales in the rest of the world are so small that one extra sale can make a big difference in percentage terms.

Index numbers

**Tetrylus Software Division
Revenue by region**

Index, 1998=100

	1998	1999	2000	2001	2002
USA	100.0	126.8	171.1	245.1	345.1
Europe	100.0	114.0	151.2	188.4	323.3
Asia-Pacific	100.0	110.6	146.8	151.1	108.5
Other	100.0	190.9	290.9	1,272.7	9,090.9
Totals	**100.0**	**122.8**	**165.0**	**224.4**	**311.0**

Converting the raw data to index numbers highlights relative growth. It is clear that the trend in sales in Europe has not been far behind that in the US, except in 2001. Perhaps European sales did not so much jump in 2002 as falter in 2001 and then recover. Charts would help you spot the patterns in any of these tables. Indeed, Fig. 18.2 reveals these relative growth trends very clearly.

Fig. 18.2 Growth rates: Europe lags, Asia-Pacific slumps

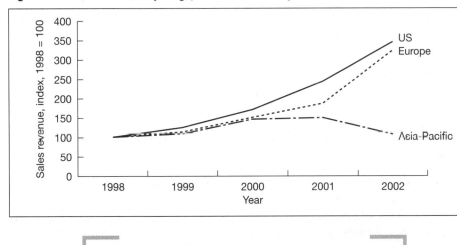

'The bank's accounts show its true position. The actual position is a little better still.'

Chairman, London and County Bank

Vertical and horizontal

Tetrylus Software Division Operating profit					
	1998	1999	2000	2001	2002
Reported, $m	0.39	0.48	0.78	1.15	1.65
Change, $m	–	0.09	0.30	0.37	0.50
Change, %	–	23.1	62.5	47.4	43.5
Index, 1998=100	100.0	123.1	200.0	294.9	423.1
Profit margin, %	12.00	12.02	14.54	15.77	16.32

This table shows a similar analysis of operating profit for the whole business. If you compare it with the sales figures, especially the index numbers, you can see that profits have been growing faster than sales. If you think about it, the implication is fairly obvious – the profit margin has been expanding (final row of the table; profit divided by sales revenue). The expanding margin might be the result of lower input prices, increased efficiency or a higher selling price. By bringing in a second series of numbers, we have extended the analysis considerably. Now, I do not know about you, but my first thoughts were: *this looks like a healthy profit margin, but how does it compare with other companies?*

Comparing competitors

Before comparing the sample company with another, it is as well to be familiar with a number of challenges. These include the problems of dealing with differing accounting policies, GAAPs, periods and currencies, and different operating environments. First, a overview of why these factors are important, then a real-world example.

Domestic environment. It always tricky to compare two companies, because the structure of their profit and loss accounts and balance sheets will differ according to their level of maturity, size, and industry. For example, younger companies may make lower profits while they are building market share, larger businesses have economies of scale, and supermarkets have lower gross margins than software developers.

Accounting periods. Fiscal years can produce an anomaly. If one business makes up its accounts for the 12 months to 30 June and another works on a calendar year basis, you could end up trying to compare results for two periods when operating conditions were very different.

Accounting policies. *Judicious* (and I use that word loosely) selection of accounting policies within one country's GAAP can change a company's bottom line significantly (see depreciation, Chapter 11, and inventory valuation, Chapter 13, for just two examples).

Accounting GAAP. However, if the same accounts are redrawn under another country's GAAP, the divergence can be even greater (see Chapter 2).

International environment. On top of this, cultural, institutional and other environmental factors can further magnify apparent variances. To take just one example, companies in the US, Europe and Japan are financed differently. Their varying use of short- and long-term loans and equity directly affects many indicators, not least those relating to debt and liquidity (see Chapter 19). Moreover, stock market investors clamouring for growth in earning and dividends heavily influence corporate policy in the US, while Japanese companies with a greater proportion of institutional and corporate shareholders can place stronger emphasis on building market share. And, for example, French and German companies have traditionally taken a more conservative approach to profits than their UK and US counterparts.

Accounting currencies. Finally, for the moment, currencies throw a potentially huge spanner in the works. Consider a foreign corporation with profits that are unchanged from year to year. Suppose that its national currency appreciates by 10% per annum against the dollar. Over, say, five years the company's net profit (converted into dollars) will appear to have risen by more than 60%, even though the company's performance was unchanged. There are other currency translation issues, which we will discuss in Chapter 21. For the moment, simply knowing that they exist is good enough.

> I am sure that you get the point. Comparing two corporations in the same jurisdiction is tricky enough. Measuring up companies across borders is a nightmare (more on this in Chapter 20).

One company, two currencies

Here are sales and profits figures for Indian software giant Infosys, prepared in accordance with Indian GAAP. The raw data are in rupees which of course cannot be compared directly with Tetrylus's results in dollars, but you can make good use of the percentage changes, index numbers and margins. Except perhaps for 2002, the growth rates and profit margins generated by Infosys seem to put Tetrylus to shame.

> 'In my opinion, the growing capacity for financial engineering and innovation in today's financial system tips the balance decisively in favour of principles-based standards. Detailed rules have become simply too easy to circumvent through what has euphemistically been called "aggressive accounting".'
>
> **Andrew Crockett**
> (General Manager of the Bank for International Settlements and Chairman of the Financial Stability Forum, 2002)

Infosys Technologies Ltd	1998	1999	2000	2001	2002
Sale					
Reported, Rs crore*	257.66	508.89	882.32	1,900.56	2,603.59
Change, Rs crore	–	251.2	373.4	1,018.2	703.0
Change, %	–	97.5	73.4	115.4	37.0
Index, 1998=100	100.0	197.5	342.4	737.6	1,010.5
Operating profit					
Reported, Rs crore	85.90	201.63	346.57	764.84	1,037.63
Change, Rs crore	–	115.7	144.9	418.3	272.8
Change, %	–	134.7	71.9	120.7	35.7
Index, 1998=100	100.0	234.7	403.5	890.4	1,208.0
Profit margin	**33.3**	**39.6**	**39.3**	**40.2**	**39.9**

*Rs crore = 10 million rupees; one crore = 10 million, a handy measure.

The following table shows the same data restated in US dollars under US GAAP. The absolute figures show that Infosys (total sales $550m in 2002) is a true giant compared with Tetrylus (2002 sales of $10 m). However, what is startling is the divergences between the Infosys indexes and margins based on rupees (e.g. profit margin 33% in 1998) and those for Infosys derived from dollar amounts (1998 profit margin of 18%).

Infosys Technologies Ltd	1998	1999	2000	2001	2002
Sales					
Reported, $m	68.33	120.96	203.44	413.85	545.05
Change, $m	–	52.6	82.5	210.4	131.2
Change, %	–	77.0	68.2	103.4	31.7
Index, 1998=100	100.0	177.0	297.7	605.7	797.7
Operating profit					
Reported, $m	12.38	22.87	60.50	137.52	178.55
Change, $m	–	10.5	37.6	77.0	41.0
Change, %	–	84.7	164.5	127.3	29.8
Index, 1998=100	100.0	184.7	488.6	1,110.7	1,442.1
Profit margin	**18.1**	**18.9**	**29.7**	**33.2**	**32.8**

The lesson

The clear message from the foregoing is that when analysing the performance of a company, you should prefer figures prepared in the operating currency (the *measurement* currency; rupees for Infosys). When comparing results for two companies with different measurement currencies, you have a dilemma. Where possible keep them in the original currencies but convert them onto the same GAAP and make further adjustments to bring accounting policies onto a similar basis. As already mentioned, analysts frequently use figures such as *earnings before interest, tax, depreciation and amortization* (EBITDA) to help minimize these problems – more on this below.

Another example

If you thought Infosys was big and successful, take a look at the sales, profits and margins for Seattle software colossus Microsoft, below.

Microsoft Corporation

	1998	1999	2000	2001	2002
Sales					
Reported, $m	15,262	19,747	22,956	25,296	28,365
Change, $m	–	4,485	3,209	2,340	3,069
Change, %	–	29.4	16.3	10.2	12.1
Index, 1998=100	100.0	129.4	150.4	165.7	185.9
Operating profit					
Reported, $m	6,585	10,010	11,006	11,720	11,910
Change, $m	–	3,425	996	714	190
Change, %	–	52.0	10.0	6.5	1.6
Index, 1998=100	100.0	152.0	167.1	178.0	180.9
Profit margin	**43.1**	**50.7**	**47.9**	**46.3**	**42.0**

A good question is how comparable is the businesses of Tetrylus with that of either Infosys or Microsoft? This query is especially valid, given the fact that these two giants have different markets and products. Obviously, by comparing various businesses, you can quickly assess relative performance, but you need to select the best benchmarks. Maybe you should compare each segment with the market leaders for that area or activity, rather than finding just one role model. It is also instructive to compare the company under the magnifying glass with the industry as a whole, and even an average for corporations in general. We will come on to this in a moment.

Comparisons extended

Just for the sake of extending the previous example, the following table compares profit and loss accounts for the three software companies. The figures in money terms are difficult to compare, given the different scale and currencies. But once the figures are converted into index form – *common sized* as beanies like to say – relative performance becomes very obvious.

For these examples, it is very likely that accounting differences result in differing treatment of expenses. Accordingly, the split between cost of sales and operational spending may be misleading. The allocation of costs between these two categories does not affect operating profits, but there are still divergences in the common size figures. There may be accounting differences, especially in the expensing and amortization of software development costs, which we should explore. Also interesting are the variations in the proportion of profit given up in income taxes.

Net profit for three companies

	Currency amounts *			Common size, Sales = 100		
	Tetrylus	Infosys	Microsoft	Tetrylus	Infosys	Microsoft
Sales	10.11	2,603.59	28,365	100.00	100.00	100.00
Cost of sales	(4.77)	(1,224.82)	(5,191)	(47.22)	(47.04)	(18.30)
Gross profit	**5.34**	**1,378.77**	**23,174**	**52.78**	**52.96**	**81.70**
Operating costs – sales and administration	(2.88)	(341.14)	(10,488)	(28.50)	(13.10)	(36.98)
Operating costs – depreciation, etc	(0.80)	(160.65)	(776)	(7.91)	(6.17)	(2.74)
Total operating costs	**(3.68)**	**(501.79)**	**(11,264)**	**(36.41)**	**(19.27)**	**(39.71)**
Operating profit (loss)	1.65	876.98	11,910	16.37	33.68	41.99
Non-trading net income	0.28	66.41	(397)	2.82	2.55	(1.40)
Profit (loss) from continuing operations before tax	**1.94**	**943.39**	**11,513**	**19.18**	**36.23**	**40.59**
Provision for income tax	(0.02)	(135.43)	(3,684)	(0.16)	(5.20)	(12.99)
Profit (loss) from continuing operations after tax	1.92	807.96	7,829	19.02	31.03	27.60
Unusual items	(0.00)	0.00	0.00	(0.03)	0.00	0.00
Net profit (loss)	**1.92**	**807.96**	**7,829**	**18.99**	**31.03**	**27.60**
Other unrealized gains or losses	0.59	0.00	(4)	5.80	0.00	(0.01)
Comprehensive profit/income (loss)	**2.51**	**807.96**	**7,825**	**24.78**	**31.03**	**27.59**

* Tetrylus and Microsoft US dollars millions, US GAAP; Infosys Rs crore, Indian GAAP.

As already mentioned, differences in financing, investment, tax and depreciation policies can obscure underlying performance. By reversing out these factors (i.e. calculating earnings before interest tax, depreciation and amortization – EBITDA), you arrive at the most directly comparable figures.

The market

Profit margins compared

Percentages, December 2002

	2002
Tetrylus	16.3
Infosys	32.8
Microsoft	42.0
The industry	12.4
The S&P 500 sector	18.3
S&P 500	30.7

Note: S&P = Standard & Poor's

As mentioned above, it is also instructive to compare a company against the average performance of a group of other businesses. Stock market indices helpfully provide such data. The table above shows the profit margin from the previous calculations, together with figures for an appropriate industry group, a sector and the market as a whole. The *industry* comprises similar companies in the *software and programming business*. The *sector* is a broader collection, including computer services, hardware and networks, and, as it happens, office equipment, scientific and technical instruments and semiconductors. I think I have already said that you need to make wise comparisons. The figure for the S&P 500 is an average for 500 companies in the Standard & Poor's stock market index.

Stock market indices

The shares of *listed* companies are traded on secondary markets, or stock markets (more on this in the next chapter). Every formal market has at least one published index of share prices. The best indices for analysis cover many companies and are weighted by market capitalization (see next chapter). These provide good industry and sectoral breakdowns. They include those published by Standard & Poor's in the US and the *Financial Times* in the UK. Links to these and other indices are provided on this book's website.

Did I mention...?

Now might be a good time for me to give you a little surprise. Thousands of commentators and analysts track the performance of companies whose shares are traded on the world's stock markets. Nothing beats reading an annual report for yourself. But you will be delighted to know that there are detailed commentaries and financial breakdowns readily available for a huge number of listed companies – including all manner of ratios. You will also find averages for industry groups and markets as a whole. You can find your way to these from – you guessed – this book's website.

Other analysis

I hope that these few notes have shown how easy it is to take a few figures and bring them to life. Figures 14.1 and 15.1 show further examples of the ratios and trends that we have discussed here. I am sure that you recall that Chapter 9 covered trend analysis in detail. It takes only moments to set up a spreadsheet to perform the calculations. Need I mention that there is an example on this book's website. One other important point that I want to discuss is inflation – then we will return to our discussion of ratios.

▶ Inflation

Tetrylus Software Division

USA revenue, rebased

	1998	1999	2000	2001	2002
Raw data					
USA revenue, $m	2.35	2.98	4.02	5.76	8.11
US CPI* 1982-84=100	163.0	166.6	172.2	177.1	179.8
Revenue index, 1998=100					
Current prices	100.0	126.8	171.1	245.1	345.1
Constant prices	100.0	124.1	161.9	225.6	312.9
Revenue, percentage change					
Current prices	–	26.8	34.9	43.3	40.8
Constant prices	–	24.1	30.5	39.3	38.7

* CPI = consumer price index (estimated for 2002)

Inflation (introduced in Chapter 6), especially when rapid, can significantly distort the figures. For example, if inflation is 10% a year, and sales revenue increases by 6%, sales have actually slipped by 4% in *real terms*. Accordingly, in times of high inflation, you might want to adjust data to remove the effects of general price changes and get at the underlying trends.

The optimum approach is to find a published indicator of inflation which is relevant to the figures under review. For example, the consumer or retail price index (CPI or RPI) might be relevant if you are dealing with a consumer goods company. A better alternative would be the consumers' expenditure deflator, which is a better weighted average than CPIs and RPIs. You will also find GDP and industrial production deflators, which include price indices relevant to specific consumer, industry, government and overseas trade sectors. Check also for indices of raw material and wholesale prices. There is more information on this book's website.

The table opposite uses the US consumer price index to *deflate* the sales revenue figures for the USA. The *current price* index is exactly the same sales index as previously calculated. The *constant price* index is revenue divided by the consumer price index and re-based to 1998=100. Obviously, given that inflation was not negative, the rate of growth in sales is slower in real terms. Such adjustment provides an alternative view of the numbers and can be quite useful.

Inflation accounting

In times of high inflation, conventional *historical cost* financial statements become increasingly difficult to interpret. For example, assets are shown in accounts at their acquisition cost less depreciation – and the net book value more rapidly falls out of line with rising market prices. Depreciation charges are not adequate to provide for asset replacement, and, indeed, future capital requirements become difficult to predict.

However, no one has managed to find a generally acceptable alternative to historic cost accounting. With the exception of some South American countries, which have experienced severe hyperinflation and have more-willingly embraced inflation accounting (current cost accounting), beanies cling to tradition. The US and UK flirted with inflation accounting in periods of rapid price rises during the 1970s, but immediately lost interest in the idea when price stability returned.

International accounting standards allow the revaluation of historical data during periods of hyperinflation – defined broadly as a doubling in the general price level in a three-year period – and require gains or losses resulting from the restatement to be disclosed separately in the profit and loss account. When hyperinflation has passed, the most recent restatement of values becomes the basis for the return to historical cost accounting.

▶ Some key indicators

As promised, it is time now to run through some key ratios and other relationships. Others are discussed in the next chapter. As you read the following paragraphs, remember the warnings about the problems with comparing competitors.

▶Liquidity

You will be well aware by now that profit does not equate directly to cash in the bank. There are no better measures of liquidity than detailed cash flow projections. Unfortunately, these are not going to be made available in the published statements of your competitors and other companies of interest. As an alternative, liquidity ratios can be used as an, albeit *historical*, indication whether the business is likely to be able to meet its *future* financial obligations as they fall due.

Working capital

> Current assets *less* current liabilities

The net of total assets and liabilities is known as working capital and is used as a proxy for cash requirements. Obviously, too much working capital implies wasted resources which claw down the return on capital. On the other hand, a company will have a painful cash flow crisis if short-term liabilities, such as trade credit and salaries, rents, etc. cannot be met. The expectation is that these costs will be met from short-term assets, primarily bank deposits, sales of inventory and receipts from trade debtors. The flaw in this argument is that even though assets may be classified as short term, some, such as refundable deposits and work-in-progress, cannot be converted into cash with ease. Moreover, the picture is distorted by inventory valuations (see Chapter 13). The acid test eliminates some of these difficulties.

> A company is said to be *overtrading* if it is operating with too little working capital. In this situation, accounts payable accumulate and ultimately the company may be forced to restructure or default (see *Debt restructuring* in Chapter 19).

Current ratio

> Current assets *divided by* current liabilities

The current ratio provides a guide for interpreting whether working capital is adequate. If it is less than 1, current liabilities exceed current assets. It looks as if the business cannot meet its daily commitments. A figure of 2 used to be a safe rule of thumb (current assets are twice current liabilities) but 1.5 is often acceptable.

Acid test (quick ratio, liquid ratio)

> (Current assets *less* stocks) *divided by* current liabilities

As discussed under *working capital,* inventory can be difficult to turn into cash, and interpretation is clouded by variations in inventory valuation methods. These issues are disposed of by the acid test, which eliminates inventory from the calculation. As a result, cross-company comparisons are also more valid. A ratio of 1 is a useful rule of thumb – but businesses that buy on credit and sell for cash (e.g., food retailing) may have acid test ratios as low as 0.2. This shows how careful you have to be when interpreting ratios.

Defensive interval (no-credit survival interval)

> (Production and operating costs excluding depreciation)
> *divided by* cash and equivalents *times* 365

This reveals the number of days a company could survive by living off cash in the bank. It is roughly the same thing as asking how long you could survive without income. However, it does exclude accounts receivable, inventory and other assets which, one would suppose, might be liquidated during a crisis.

▶ Profitability and operating efficiency

There is no need for me to tell you that profitability and efficiency are closely watched, although remember that maximizing profits might not be a critical short-run objective.

Profit margin

> Operating profit (before tax, interest, etc) *divided by* sales

This indicates the profit per dollar of sales. A low figure is not necessarily bad – for supermarkets it can fall to 1% – check against inventory and receivables turnover, asset value, gross profit margins, etc and the industry average. A figure below the industry average might indicate low prices and/or high costs. A high figure might attract competitors.

Return on capital employed

> Operating profit (before interest and tax)
> *divided by* (total assets *less* current liabilities)

Return on total assets

> Operating profit (before interest and tax) *divided by* total assets

These returns are clearly important as a measure of the company's operating efficiency. A low return on assets or capital employed (very similar, given the relationship between balance sheet entries) suggests a candidate for disposal – or bankruptcy in the next economic downturn. If the return is below the cost of loans, additional borrowing will *reduce* earnings per share. This measure provides a good yardstick for assessing new ventures – if their return is below it, it will be clawed down.

Turnover of (working) capital

> Sales *divided by* capital employed

Turnover of working capital measures sales per unit of capital. It shows how efficiently capital is being used to generate sales. A low ratio (sales are low relative to capital) tends to suggest that the capital is not being used profitably. At the other extreme, a very high ratio of sales to working capital warns of *overtrading* – inadequate working capital which could put creditors at risk. Watch also that a growing ratio might indicate that plant and machinery is not being kept up to date (depreciation is reducing the capital base and making the ratio look better).

Receivables turnover (trade debtors to sales)

Accounts receivable *divided by* sales

This shows credit allowed to customers – or, to put it another way – the speed at which debts are collected. If payment is collected by the end of the month following delivery, receivables will run at about 12% of sales. (Multiply the ratio by 365 to find the average number of days it takes to collect debts (based, remember, on one balance sheet date).) A high figure might indicate sloppy financial control. A reduction might suggest better control – or a desperate need for cash. Factoring (selling) debts also reduces the figure. Note by the way, the small inconsistency introduced because receivables includes sales tax or value added tax, while sales do not (see Chapter 8).

Payables turnover (trade creditors to sales)

Accounts payable *divided by* sales

This indicates the amount of trade credit that a company is allowed by its suppliers. Watch trends over time – an increase might indicate a rise in trade credit necessitated by cash flow problems. Other measures used include:

◆ **Receivables to inventory** – which shows what proportion of stocks is financed by suppliers (exceeds 100% in food retailing).
◆ **Debtors to receivables** – where sudden big changes can also give early warning of cash-flow pressures.

Inventory/stock turnover

Cost of sales *divided by*
average inventory (half the sum of opening *plus* closing stock)

This shows how fast inventory is moving through the business. A high turnover indicates healthy, saleable and liquid inventory with lower demands on cash flow (or maybe there are stock shortages!). A low average turnover suggests overstocking and dated merchandise (or stockpiling to meet seasonal demand). Calculating the average from only two days a period is highly dangerous if those are not representative days. I am sure that companies would not manage their inventory levels on those dates to influence this ratio.

▶ Other

There are many other similar indicators which are of great interest and value, including the key debt and investment indicators that are discussed in the next chapter.

Ten hard questions to ask or be asked

1 Can you take the figures at face value, or do you need to adjust for national GAAP, accounting policies, etc.?

2 How do the latest financials stack up?

3 What do the trends over time show?

4 Do the indicators of liquidity suggest that there is adequate cash flow?

5 What do the indicators of effciency tell you? Is the business well managed?

6 Do you need to adjust for inflation? Is the company operating in an area with high inflation?

7 If the accounts have been adjusted for inflation, has the correct deflator been used?

8 How did the company perform relative to competitors? The industry as a whole? The entire market?

9 When comparing companies, are you comparing like with like?

10 What are the effects of variables such as depreciation policies, inventory valuation, taxation etc.?

Conclusion

I do not know about you, but I quite enjoyed that. We covered a lot of ground together, but the going did not seem too tough. The techniques just discussed can be applied to any financials, and, in many instances, to other figures are well. Moreover, you can quickly build a spreadsheet (did anyone mention this book's website?) to crunch the numbers and lead you to more learned understanding and better decisions. Indeed, most of the little tables in this chapter can be arranged into one spreadsheet for rapid review.

'The difficulties of judging earnings trends have been intensified by revelations of misleading accounting practices at some prominent businesses. ... Businesses concerned about the impact of possible adverse publicity regarding their accounting practices on their access to finance could revert to a much heavier emphasis on cash generation and accumulation.'

Alan Greenspan

19

financing and investing

'The public be damned! I'm working for my stockholders.'

William H. Vanderbilt

Chapter survival toolkit

▶ Overview

This chapter takes a rather interesting journey through sources and uses of finance, and – the flip side of the coin – investment. Apart from anything else, it will help you decide how to use a cash surplus or how to finance a deficit. It should also be useful if you are making investments in other companies, from either a corporate viewpoint or as a personal investor.

▶ Prerequisites

You could probably read this chapter in isolation. If you coped well with the previous few pages, it will be especially easy going.

▶ Mastering financing and investment

After reading this chapter, you should be able to answer the following questions:

1 Name three sources of each of short-term, medium-term and long-term finance.

2 What are debt instruments? What sets them apart from other borrowing? Why would a company borrow by issuing bonds? Who would lend the funds to the company?

3 What happens to the market price of a bond if interest rates fall?

4 What is equity? Does it have to be repaid? Where is it traded? What is a stock split? How much money would a stock split raise for the company?

5 Why might share prices move even when nothing fundamental has changed at the issuing company?

6 How do you use share prices to value a company? Why is the price earning ratio important?

7 How could one company attain control over another?

8 How could one company use an investment in another to cook the books?

9 Which involves greater risk for an investor (all things being equal), debt or equity? Why is equity more costly than debt for the company receiving the funds?

10 How would you calculate your cost of capital?

> 'If you owe the bank $100 that's your problem. If you owe the bank $100 million, that's the bank's problem.'
>
> **J. Paul Getty**

▶ Jargon watch

The following list might look lengthy, but it is relatively straightforward.

Investment banker's buzz words first encountered

Equity:

Joint stock company

Capitalization

Share/stock capital: authorized, issued, paid, paid-in, par, stock split

Shares/stock: common, ordinary, preference, preferred, redeemable, cumulative

Dividend, dividend cover, payout ratio

Earnings per share (EPS)

Price earnings ratio/multiple (PE, PER)

Debt instruments:

Debt, bonds, debentures, loan stock, junk bonds, coupon, zero coupon, debt service

Debt, equity, et al.:

Capital: seed, venture, risk, injection capital, fixed, growth

Factoring, hire purchase

Leverage, gearing, interest cover, debt-service ratio

Overtrading, borrowed up, restructuring, Chapter 11, bankruptcy

Return on: investment (ROI), equity (ROE), capital employed (ROCE), assets (ROA)

Fundamental analysis, technical analysis

Cost of capital; capital asset pricing, beta, market/systematic risk, specific risk

Credit rating; debt rating

In with the big boys:

Markets: secondary, stock, bond market

Merger, acquisition, joint venture (JV); subsidiary, associate

Credit rating, AAA, triple A, AA, etc.

New beanie buzz words

Consolidation, one-line consolidation, equity method, cost method, merger accounting, pooling of interests accounting, cost accounting

Beanie buzz words revisited

Fixed assets, leasing, amortization

Asset, liability, net asset value, book value, net worth, contingent liabilities

Cash flow

Profit margin

Operating costs, retained earnings

Contingent liabilities

Encore for economists/investment bankers' buzz words

Time value of money

Interest: simple, compound, effective

Net present value, discount rate, hurdle rate

Index numbers

> 'Business is other people's money.'
>
> **James Gillray**

The financing imperative

Every business needs financing, even when at first glance it might appear that funding is unnecessary. For example, if you are retailing goods and do not pay the supplier until after you have collected from your clients, you are using *trade finance*. If you have a cash surplus which you use to buy the gizmos, you are financing your operations from *retained earnings*. And so on.

It is important that financing is efficient, which usually means low cost. The choices are not always as obvious as they might appear. Moreover, there are two angles to this topic. First, there is the matter of raising finance through equity and loans, and finding the optimal balance. Then there is the investor's viewpoint to consider. An investor's objectives might be primarily related to savings and capital gains – or the motives might be connected with joint ventures, control of subsidiaries, mergers, acquisitions and so on. As you have probably guessed, there are quite a few items on the agenda.

> A record $382 bn in assets went into bankruptcy in the US in 2003, including WorldCom, which at $104 bn was the largest bankruptcy in history.

In this chapter, we will run through the main sources of finance, paying special attention to comparison of debt and equity; introduce yardsticks which you can use to measure debt and investment; and conclude with a few key issues relating to management decision making about these topics.

What's in a name?

◆ *Seed, venture, start-up, adventure, risk* and *injection capital* are various names for the cash needed to get a business off the ground.

◆ *Working capital* is money used to pay for inventory, salaries, and other production and operating costs.

◆ *Fixed capital* is money locked up in fixed assets such as buildings and equipment.

◆ *Growth capital* is cash targeted specifically to fund expansion.

Sources of finance

The following is not exhaustive, but it identifies the major sources of finance. Debt and equity are discussed in more detail in a moment.

Sources of short-term finance

Trade credit from suppliers and trade partners. This helps finance inventory, either on terms (e.g. 90 days to pay) or a consignment basis (you pay the supplier only when you sell the goods).

Factoring. This is where you sell your invoices at a discount (maybe 90% of face value or less) and the factoring company takes full responsibility for collecting from your client. Factoring unlocks value from your invoices, but can be expensive and might damage your relationship with your customers if the factoring company is heavy handed. Note that accepting even a 5% discount on invoices which would normally be collected within 30 days amounts to paying 80% per annum interest.

Bank overdrafts or loans. These can be very flexible, although banks usually require security over specific assets – occasionally invoices or inventory but often more-tangible plant, property or equipment.

> **Loans** might be provided by banks, finance or credit companies, or even private investors. Government and some non-government agencies, and private foundations may also offer loans, research grants, and other endowments.
>
> Look to government agencies for export credit guarantees. See also the notes on foreign trade finance in the next chapter.

▶ Medium-term finance

Leasing. This is where you make staged payments for the purchase or rent of plant, property or equipment. Recall the difference between operating and finance leases (Chapter 11).

Hire purchase. This is broadly similar to leasing. A finance company buys an asset, hires it to you for a monthly fee, and transfers ownership to you at the end of the contract.

Medium-term loans are usually for a specific purpose, over a fixed period, with a pre-determined rate of interest and, usually, secured against plant or property.

▶ Long-term finance

Long-term loans. These are similar to medium-term loans, but probably secured by a mortgage over land and property.

Corporate bonds or **loan stock.** This is borrowing by a company, where the *paper* is traded on secondary financial markets, at a fixed interest rate (*coupon*) and with fixed repayment. Such borrowing may be secured against specific assets – a *debenture* is an unsecured bond.

> **Employee share ownership plans** can provide an efficient source of finance which helps build employee commitment: employees buy shares for cash or by deduction from their salaries: the company contributes in shares. Either way the money stays in the family. Whether options should be set against profit or carried on the balance sheet was a hot regulatory topic at the start of 2003.

Equity. Shares issued by a company; not repayable. Discussed below.

▶ Demanding debt

The trade credit, loans, and bonds mentioned above are all forms of debt. The most important point is the obvious: debt is repayable (for all intents and purposes, equity is not). Moreover, lenders are very demanding. They are concerned mainly with security and cash flow. They usually lend to borrowers who *own* more than they *owe* and who can prove that they can definitely afford to pay it back. That is, corporate borrowers need assets and cash flow. The main cost is the interest payment. There will also be arrangement fees and commissions which you should factor into your costing. I will come on to this in a moment.

▶ Debt instruments

Corporate notes and bonds are simply forms of debt which can be traded in secondary markets. For example, a major corporation might make a *$500 million issue of 10%, 10-year loan stock*. This means that the company raises about $500 million from, probably, many lenders, and is committed to paying $50 million per annum in interest for 10 years and to buying back the bonds for $500 million at the end of the period. Note that for the company, this is simple interest; it is not compounded. Investors who buy these bonds can sell them at any time that they can find a buyer. The price will reflect the interest rate on debt which investors perceive have comparable risk. OK, I will explain.

Pricing

The starting point for **interest rates** is the rate at which bankers will lend to the lowest-risk borrowers. In the US this is known as the **prime rate** for obvious reasons. Elsewhere, the term **base rate** is common. Higher-risk borrowers will pay prime or base rate plus 2% points, or 3%, or 10% or whatever. The granddaddy of money-pricing yardsticks is the London interbank offered rate (**LIBOR**), and you will hear mention of many other IBORs, including the unpronounceable **EURIBOR**.

If you bought $10,000 of 10% long-dated bonds, you would receive a fixed $1,000 a year in interest (*the coupon*). If interest rates for similar debt halved to 5%, you would be able to sell the paper for double what you paid for it – because the $1,000 annual coupon amounts to 5% of $20,000.

However, as the bonds approach maturity, the market price moves towards the redemption value. No one would pay $20,000 even for 10% interest if in a year's time they would have to give up the bonds for a mere $10,000. This is the *time value of money* at play (we first met this in Chapter 6).

The basic rule of thumb is that if interest rates or the perceived risk fall, the market value of bonds rises. If interest rates or the perceived risk rise, the value drops. There is no cash flow effect for the company, except that if interest rates move while the issue is first being arranged, the initial proceeds may be different from the face value. Otherwise, the interest payments and redemption will be unchanged (but see *Debt restructuring*, below.)

Variations on a theme

Bonds may be *unsecured* (except that they rank above share capital for repayment in the event that the company fails), or secured against fixed assets, usually land and buildings. *Zero coupon bonds* are issued at a discount to the redemption value. Junk bonds are highly speculative – see *Credit rating*.

Credit rating

Companies such as Moody's Investors Service and Standard & Poor's publish credit ratings for many corporations. Prime credit worthy businesses are rated AAA (referred to as *triple A*). The second tier is rated AA; upper-medium risk companies are rated A, and the lower-mediums are BBB (Baa under Moody's classification). Anything lower than this is classed as *junk* – highly speculative in ability to meet financial obligations. Clearly, the higher a company's ratings, the lower the perceived risk and the lower its cost of borrowing. Quite aside from financing issues, if you are about to do significant business with another company you might want to check its credit rating.

Enticing equity

The joint stock companies formed to finance seafaring adventures in the 1500s were such a success (not least because of the vast riches plundered by buccaneers) that the concept was rapidly extended to more mundane ventures. The principle is simple. When a large number of investors contribute capital, their individual risk is spread, the company receives the finance it needs, but the investors still share the rewards. These *shareholders* are actually part owners of the company, but they delegate the day-to-day running of the business to the directors. Shareholders with large blocks of shares, or acting in collusion with other investors, exercise influence or control through their ability to hire and fire directors – which at least ensures that captains of industry keep looking over their shoulders.

There is no statutory obligation for a company to distribute profits (as dividends). Moreover, the company does not have to repay the capital unless it ceases operations. If this does happen, shareholders have (only) the pickings after assets have been sold, and the employees and debtors have been paid off. Shareholders *can* unlock their investment by selling their shares in the secondary stock markets, but the price they will receive depends only on what someone else is prepared to pay. These secondary transactions do not affect the company's finances directly, except that the directors are under constant pressure to perform well so that the share price rises. Indeed, ordinary investors usually buy shares for the expected increase in value (the capital gain), rather than the dividends.

> PizzaExpress' share price soared by over 24% in one day in December 2002 on renewed talk of takeover bids – pushing the company's market capitalization to £237m.

Why are share prices important?

If you purchased 100% of a company's shares, you would own it outright. Accordingly, the share price (multiplied by the number of its shares) indicates the market value of a company – its *market capitalization*. Of course, you would be hard pushed to buy the company for that price, because as soon as other investors saw you buying up the share capital they would guess what was going on and try to get in on the action.

In mid-2001, Irish biotech giant Elan's share price plummeted by 52% in one day – triggered by rumours, later confirmed, of dubious accounting techniques. The most spectacular crash in Irish corporate history, it accounted for a 16% fall in the Irish ISEQ market index. The market capitalization of Elan fell from $22 bn to under $1 bn.

▶ What determines share prices?

How do investors decide what to pay for shares? All other things being equal, you would suppose that investors are buying into a going concern and that they want it to stay that way (but see *asset strippers*, below) If so, the price indicates the value that they put on the future stream of profits that the company is expected to generate. These profits, in turn, depend on many factors including the following *fundamentals:*

1 The earning ability of the company's net assets – both tangible (plant property and equipment) and, possibly more important, intangible (patents, brands, position, reputation). This may bear little relationship to their book value, given the way that beanies do their sums (see especially Chapters 11 and 13)

2 The ability of top management, although remember that they can always leave or be replaced.

3 External conditions (the economy, competitors, technological change, etc.).

Incidentally, in case you are talking to investment bankers, the extent to which the price of a company's shares move with the market is known as market or **systematic risk**. The way that a corporation's performance affects its share price is known as **specific risk**.

If there was no new information from the company for a period of time, the share price would still bump around due to changes in investors' perceptions of external conditions. This is why the announcement of a smaller than expected increase in industrial production or a larger than predicted fall in employment can send stock markets tumbling. And, conversely, why surprise good news can make share prices surge.

With all this externally induced turbulence, how do you tell what is happening to the underlying price of a company's shares? You compare it with similar corporations, the average for its sector (e.g. the retail companies share index), and the market as a whole (e.g. using market indices such as the S&P 500 or the all-share index) – see this book's website.

Technical analysis

By the way, market psychology and even computer trading programs can move share prices significantly. Technical analysis tries to predict such movements. Its proponents claim that if share prices break some trend line, or form certain patterns (such as two small peaks around one big one – called a *head-and-shoulders*), the next major move can be forecast. Given that such events may cause technical analysts to shout *buy* or *sell* in unison, their prophesy might be little more than a self-fulfilling contribution to market sentiment. However, if it works for them, who am I to argue.

Unlisted but not unloved

A company with shares trading on a recognized stock exchange is said to be *listed* or *quoted*. An *unlisted* or *unquoted* company will not have a published market-determined share price. How can you value such companies? The easy way is to estimate what the share price would be if the company was listed.

The key is the *price earnings ratio/multiple,* which is profit per share as a multiple of the share price. For example, many companies trade at a price earnings multiple of between 10 or 20. This implies that when you buy an ordinary share you are acquiring a stream of profits equivalent to 10 to 20 times the price you pay. Put another way, if net profit is a healthy $1 billion, this suggests a valuation of $10 billion to $20 billion. Technology companies, where present profits are taken perhaps oddly as a promise of exorbitantly higher earnings in the future, traded at outlandish price earnings ratios in excess of 600 during the dot-com boom which itself peaked in 2000.

Accordingly, if you take the price earnings ratio of an appropriate listed company, and multiply it by the unlisted company's net profit, you arrive at an estimate of the value of the unlisted company. For example, if you examine two or three similar companies and see that their average price earnings ratio is about 12, and your company's net profit is $10 million, its value could be estimated at $120 million. If it happens that a similar company has been taken over recently, you might be able to use that as the model. Of course, you need to be careful about comparing like with like, but I know that I can leave that to your judgement.

Other valuation techniques

There are other ways to value a company. Let me mention two.

1 *Brew the beans*. One way is to project the net profit for, say, the next 10 or 20 years and work out the net present value at an appropriate discount rate. Net present value is discussed in Chapter 6. This might be especially relevant if you were considering acquiring a majority stake and putting in your own management.

2 *Strip the assets*. Alternatively, you could perform your own calculation of net asset value. Essentially, you work through the balance sheet valuing each asset and liability at, say, its market price (as opposed to book value) and work out how much money you would have left (if any) if you closed down the company, sold its assets, and settled its debts. This is how asset strippers make their money. Of course, the assessment does not have to be an open-market valuation. You might be thinking about acquiring a company because you consider that its patents, brands or other assets would be much more valuable when combined with your own resources.

▶ Other issues about equity

To avoid confusion, let me highlight the distinction between *authorized, issued* and *paid (paid-in* or *paid-up)* capital.

Authorized capital indicates the maximum amount of shares that could be sold, and their book value. A company's *memorandum and articles of association*, its *bylaws*, will identify its authorized capital. This could be specified as, say, 10 million ordinary shares of $1 each, meaning that the company can issue up to 10 million shares, at – wait for it – any price it chooses. If you were awake when we discussed balance sheets, you will recall that a company might sell its $1 shares at $1.50 each. In such a case, $1 would be recorded as paid-in capital and $0.50 as additional paid-in capital. Shares may never trade at their face value, or par value ($1 in this example), which is an arbitrary number. Shareholders can vote to change the structure and amount of a company's authorized capital.

Issued. A company might not issue all of its shares if, for example, it requires less capital than it could raise by selling all of its shares.

Paid. A company might issue *partially-paid* shares. For example, if a $1 share was issued for 60 cents, its holder would have a liability to pay the remaining 40 cents on demand or on a predetermined date. An investor's maximum liability as a shareholder is the par value of the shares held.

> ▶▶ Note that many governments and licensing authorities stipulate minimum levels of paid-in capital, with the basic aim of protecting creditors. Specific industries (e.g. financial institutions) are often subject to special regulations, for similar reasons. Stock exchanges have more severe requirements for full listing. Business partners and association may also have conditions. For example, travel agents cannot belong to their international association (IATA) unless their capital exceeds certain amounts.

Stock splits

When the price of a traded stock rises too far, the directors might ask shareholders to approve a stock split to make the shares seem more appealing to new investors. A split is when the company, say, divides each share in half to double the number outstanding. For example, if a company has 10,000 shares issued, and each share is trading at $100, then after a 2-for-1 stock split, there will be 20,000 shares outstanding at $50 each. The total value of all shares, and each shareholder's percentage of the total, remains unchanged. Stocks can split two for one, three for two, five for one, or any other creative combination.

Variations on a theme

The core of a company's share capital will be *ordinary shares,* also known as *common stock.* Companies also issue *preferred stock* to encourage investment.

> International accounting standards require companies to classify as debt **redeemable preference stock** where redemption is mandatory.

Preferred stockholders may not receive dividends, but they have to be paid a preset amount of dividends for the period in full before ordinary shareholders can receive theirs. Moreover, if a company ceases trading and there are funds left to repay shareholders, preferred stockholders are paid off ahead of ordinary shareholders. *Cumulative preferred stock holders* are also at the head of the queue for unpaid dividends for prior periods. Holders of *convertible preferred stock* can switch it into ordinary stock under predefined terms.

Well, with all these benefits, you would expect that there was a catch. There are two. Preferred stock holders rarely have voting rights, which helps directors to sleep easier. And while there is usually a floor on dividends, there is also a ceiling. You have to give some benefits to ordinary shareholders.

Dividend policy

If there is one area where directors manage the numbers, it is with dividend policies. There are large variations between industry sectors and between companies. Commentators perceive that dividends are an indicator of the health of a business. This raises two issues for the board.

First, should dividends be paid at all? For example, US tech firms have tended to retain cash for investment; their shareholders have taken profits as capital gains. Indeed, it is argued that tech firms who do pay dividends are admitting that they have used up their opportunities to reinvest for future growth. However, when Microsoft announced its first ever dividend in early 2003, the company justified this on the grounds that it no longer needed to retain cash to defend itself against antitrust allegations. Its also showed support for President Bush's proposed tax relief on dividends. (Oh, and by the way, it meant that Chairman Bill Gates was to receive a cool $100 million in tax-free dividend income.)

The second issue is that if dividends are being paid, the trend should be *smooth:* stable and, perhaps, growing. Announcement of cuts in dividends can be disastrous. For example, the share price of US telecoms giant AT&T slumped from a high of $60 in 2002 to under $20 after the company announced an 83% reduction in its dividend payout as it tried to pare its $3 billion annual interest costs and $63 billion debt. (See also *dividend payout ratio*, below.)

▶ Debt and equity compared

What difference does it make whether funding comes from debt or equity? Debt is a burden – repayments of principle and interest drain cash flow. Equity does not necessarily involve parting with any cash – even the dividends can be deferred until better cash flow days. Moreover, equity investors accept higher risk in exchange for better returns in the future. This means that you can persuade them to swap their cash for your shares when the bankers are sucking in their breath and shaking their heads. But while the cash flow effect of equity is far less painful, the overall cost is actually greater than that of debt.

Debt and equity compared

Debt	Equity
Lenders are risk averse	Equity investors accept higher risk
No loss of ownership	Involves giving up some ownership
No explicit loss of control	May reduce control
Interest payments are mandatory	Dividends are optional
Interest payments are an expense	Dividends are a distribution of equity
Debt has to be repaid	Equity does not have to be repaid
Increases demands on cash flow	Exerts small demands on cash flow
Reduces cost of capital	Increases cost of capital
Increases return on equity (other things being equal)	Reduces return on equity (other things being equal)

▶ Why equity costs more than debt

Why is the cost of equity greater than the cost of debt? The short answer is that equity is more risky and so the borrowing cost is higher. Follow through these simple arguments:

1 Equity investors are looking for a *return on equity* that is greater than the rate of interest that they could earn on a lower-risk investment.
2 Corporate debt is secured against assets and cash flow, so such debt must have a lower risk than the company's equity.
3 Therefore, logically, a company's equity must produce a higher return than the interest rate that it pays on its debt.

Put another way, companies can increase their *return on equity* by *leveraging* it and using it to help them borrow at a lower cost.

When the proportion of debt relative to equity increases, the overall cost of capital falls. If you earn the same profits with a lower amount of equity capital, the return on equity (profit divided by equity) must increase.

▶ Debt restructuring

A company with a cash flow crisis may have to re-negotiate or reschedule loans and other contractual agreements, raise additional share capital and sell assets in order to ensure survival. This is known as *debt restructuring*, even though it may involve equity. In the US, a corporation may voluntarily file for *Chapter 11* protection, which freezes all outstanding financial claims and lawsuits against the company while it continues operating and reorganizes financially. The alternative might be forced or voluntary liquidation, which is what happens to erring companies in most other countries.

Analysing debt

In the previous chapter you saw how ratios can be used to analyse financial statements. As promised, here are some more ratios. Indicators of debt reveal information about *solvency* – whether a business is borrowing too much or whether it could borrow more.

Leverage (US) or gearing (UK)

> Debt *divided* by equity

This indicates the extent to which a company is dependent on debt or equity. Analysts calculate this simple sum in various ways, which can affect comparisons The best way is to define debt is as interest-bearing liabilities (loans) plus preference shares; and equity as ordinary shareholders funds. Also, it is better to use market values rather than book values.

Low leverage/gearing indicates a low reliance on debt – finance is mainly equity – which suggests a greater likelihood that the company can borrow more if necessary. A highly geared/leveraged company has a higher reliance on debt, which could lead to a cash flow crisis.

Debt to net worth

> Total debt (liabilities) *divided by*
> tangible net worth (shareholders' equity less intangible assets)

This compares what is owned with what is owed. A high ratio indicates that creditors' claims exceed those of the owners. For example, a ratio of 2 indicates that liabilities are twice the size of tangible net worth. In this case a business is *borrowed up* and its ability to raise more debt is in question.

Debt-service coverage (interest cover, times interest earned)

> Operating profit (before interest and tax) *divided by*
> annual interest payments

This is another way of looking at gearing/leverage. It is also a measure of a company's ability to meet its interest on borrowings. The higher the ratio the more likely it is that the business will be able to pay interest on (i.e. *service*) its debt. A figure of at least 3 is usually considered safe, and would be a good sign for a company wanting to borrow more. A figure of below 1 indicates a high risk of default or bankruptcy.

Contingent liabilities

Contingent liabilities *divided by* shareholders' equity

Recall from Chapter 15 that contingent liabilities are possible liabilities that do not show on the balance sheet. Contingent liabilities that are large in relation to equity could seriously undermine financial stability if they materialised into payments due.

▶ Investment indicators

Return on equity

Profit (after tax) *divided by* owners' equity

Alternative measures of return (return on assets and return on capital employed) are significant for the *business manager*. But this one, return on equity, is critical to *shareholders*. It is their bottom line.

Earnings per share (EPS, net income per ordinary share)

Profit *divided by* number of ordinary shares

The profit attributable to each ordinary share (i.e. after tax etc.) is one number that you cannot compare between companies directly – it depends on the number of shares issued. But the trend over time is often regarded as critical. As already discussed, for many companies steady long-term growth in earnings per share *is the* central objective. Calculate earning per share as net profit (including minority interests) after tax *less* dividends on preference shares.

International accounting standards require basic *(undiluted)* and *diluted* net income per ordinary share to be stated with equal prominence on the face of the profit and loss account. Diluted EPS reflects potential reduction of EPS from options, warrants, rights, convertible debt, convertible preferred, and other contingent issuances of ordinary shares.

Price earning (ratio/multiple) – PE/PER

> Market price of ordinary shares *divided by*
> earnings per ordinary share after tax

The price earnings ratio indicates the number of years' earnings acquired when you buy one share. It reflects the market's expectation of future earnings growth – and as discussed is a crucial measure of the value of a company.

Dividend cover (payout ratio when inverted)

> Earnings per share *divided by*
> net dividend per share

Dividend cover indicates how many times the dividend is covered by profits. A high cover (low payout ratio) suggests that profits are being reinvested for future growth – and that there is sufficient margin to ensure that dividends will remain stable. The opposite suggests that dividends might disappear in a downturn.

Net asset value (NAV, market to book)

> (Ordinary) shareholders' equity *divided by*
> number of shares issued

Note that shareholders' equity is equal to assets less liabilities; i.e., the net asset value. Net asset value indicates the proportion of the share price that is represented by assets (albeit at book value) – the other portion of the price therefore reflecting expectations about profits. The alternative is market capitalization to book value (how much it would cost you to buy all the company's shares – and how much you would get back if you sold all the assets and settled all liabilities). These indicators reveal exactly what the market thinks about the value of the company's future income stream.

Return on investment

The term *return on investment* (ROI) is used loosely.

- The ROI for **lenders** is the interest that you pay them.
- **Equity investors'** ROI is measured by *return on equity* (ROE) – since, of course, their investment is the company's share capital.
- As the **business manager**, the ROI that you are interested in is *return on capital employed* (ROCE) or *return on assets* (ROA).

Fig. 19.1 How returns vary

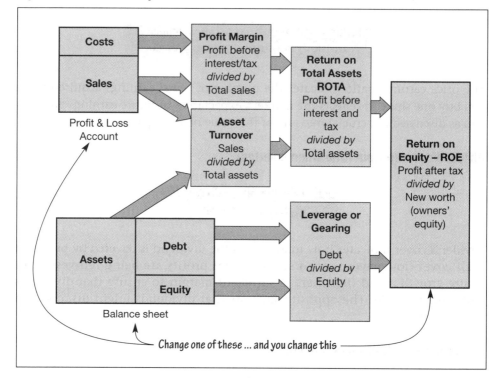

The way that the objectives of company management and of investors hang together is illustrated in Fig. 19.1. The connection between the two sides of the diagram is self-evident. Vary one number in the profit and loss account or the balance sheet, and this must result in a change in the return on equity. However, if you follow the logic through – and remember that assets equal liabilities (debt) plus equity – you can see how the following classic relationship holds true:

Profit *divided by* Sales	×	Sales *divided by* Assets	×	Assets *divided by* Equity	=	Profit *divided by* Equity

Or, essentially:

Profit margin	×	Asset turnover	×	Leverage	=	ROE

Thus, increase any one of the terms on the left (profit margin, asset turnover or leverage) and you increase return on equity. Believe it or not, some companies actually manage these indicators specifically.

► Mergers, acquisitions and joint ventures

Companies cooperate for many reasons. Joint ventures range from shared assets (e.g. oil pipelines), through jointly controlled operations (as with the Airbus consortium), to shared control of a third entity. Equity investments range from a few shares purchased to show commitment to a supplier or distributor, to outright acquisition in order to acquire control of assets or market share, or a merger which replaces two companies with one new enterprise. A company might also make loans to another, usually to promote some mutual interest. You can assess such opportunities using the techniques discussed elsewhere in this book, especially in Chapter 6.

Accounting for such mergers, acquisitions and joint ventures, varies significantly across jurisdictions, although, as you have guessed, there is a slow move towards convergence. The aim of regulators is to prevent manipulation of accounts. For example, under cost accounting rules, an investor might use its power to defer payment of dividends thereby avoiding reporting its share of the associate company's net profit; while merger accounting rules have permitted true acquisition costs to be hidden.

The following list is a rough and ready overview of international accounting standards. It defines the classification of business combinations and cooperation, and the applicable accounting policies. The list is arranged in order of priority and the first one of these to apply to a particular situation is the definition to be used:

1 **Subsidiary** – company owns more than 50% of the equity of another. Financial statements should be **consolidated**, showing combined totals for each category of assets, liabilities, incomes and expenses. Intra-group balances and transactions and resulting unrealized profits must be eliminated.

2 **Joint venture** – a contractual arrangement, with jointly controlled operations, assets or entities (one partner may manage the venture, but neither/none has absolute control). Financial statements should show assets, liabilities, expenses and revenues arising from the joint venture (proportionally for shared assets); for jointly controlled entities, use proportionate consolidation or the equity (see next) method.

3 **Associate** – company owns between 20% and 50% inclusive of another's shares. Financial reporting should use the **equity method** (*one line consolidation*) where investments are shown initially at cost and subsequently adjusted for the investor's share in the net assets of the associate; and the profit and loss account shows the investor's share of the associates net profits.

4 **Investment** – company owns less than 20% of the shares. Reporting should use the **cost method** where investments are shown as an asset at cost; and dividends are reported in the profit and loss account as investment income.

If you think this seems too straightforward, you are right. For example, merger accounting (used where no clear acquirer can be identified) was prohibited by the US and Canada in 2001, and is not allowed by other countries, but was still permitted by the International Accounting Standards Board (IASB) and the UK. In

December 2002, amid charges of pandering to the US, the IASB proposed changes including the following for business combinations:

◆ Universal application of acquisition (purchase) accounting and the dropping of merger (*pooling of interests*) accounting.

◆ Intangible items to be recognized as assets separately from goodwill.

◆ Identifiable assets acquired, and liabilities and contingent liabilities assumed, to be measured initially at fair value.

◆ No amortization of goodwill or intangible assets with indefinite useful lives; instead they should be tested for impairment at least annually.

Visit this book's website for an update on the story.

Transfer prices and cost centres

Transactions between related entities provide scope for creative accounting. First, *transfer prices* can be set selectively. By selling goods, services, or intellectual property at a knock down price, profits are transferred to the buyer. Similarly, inflated expenses are sometimes charged to other entities in order to tranfer profits in the other direction. There are a number of possible objectives, including minimizing tax liabilities (with dubious legality) and supporting a subsidiary. Of course, tax authorities and accounting regulators demand realism in *transfer pricing*. In addition, companies frequently charge business units with a share of head office costs, turning the subsidiary entity into a cost centre for tax or other reasons.

▶ The cost of capital

There are two good reasons for knowing the exact cost of each of the various financing options. The first is so that you can choose between them. The second is that that you know overall the rate or return you need to beat (the *hurdle rate*) in order for any project to be successful – I will come back to this in the next chapter.

Estimating and comparing the cost of various types of debt is a breeze when you use the spreadsheet formula explained in Chapter 6. For a borrower, there is an inflow

'Although many of the proposals are consistent with standards issued in Canada and the United States during 2001, the IASB has drawn on requirements in other jurisdictions when it believed a higher quality solution existed. This project is a good example of how convergence can and should work – for instance, the [US Financial Accounting Standards Board] has agreed to reconsider its own standards ...'.

Sir David Tweedie,
Chairman of the International Accounting Standards Board (IASB), on the December 2002 release of proposals to amend standards of accounting for business combinations

(the principal amount of the loan) and a series of outflows (any arrangement fee and commission, interest, and the repayment of the principal). You can plug these values into a spreadsheet to standardize and compare interest rates. As already indicated, you can do much the same sums with leases, hire purchase and rental agreements.

It is slightly more tricky to value equity. The simplest way is to project future dividends per share allowing for growth, treat the current stock price as the inflow, and again use a spreadsheet to determine the rate of interest that ties these amounts together.

An alternative is known grandly as the *capital asset pricing model*. To cut a long story short, we can arrive at a cost of capital (a pseudo-interest rate) by starting with the interest rate on risk free investment and marking it up by the return required to compensate for the risk of holding shares in a specific company. The risk factor of investing in any one company is known as its *beta*. This measures the extent to which a company share price moves relative to the market. For example, if share prices on average rise by 1%, the share price of a company with a beta of 1.5 will rise 1.5%, while the share price of a company with a beta of 0.5% will rise by, you guessed, only 0.5%. You will be delighted to know that industry analysts calculate and publish betas for companies quoted on the world's major stock markets. You can access these through this book's website (where there are also calculators that you can use to estimate the cost of capital for equity and the effective interest rate on debt).

Multiply your beta by the average stock market rate of return to arrive at the risk premium. For example, if the market is paying 5% more than government securities and your beta is 1.6, your risk premium is 8% (5% × 1.6). If the coupon on government securities is 7%, the required rate of return on your equity (i.e. your cost of equity capital) is 7% + 8% = 15%.

The overall cost of capital reflects gearing – the mix of loans and equity. For example, if 80% of your capital is equity, you pay 12% on your loans and your required rate of return on equity is 15%, your cost of capital is:

Loans	20% of 12%	=	2.4%
Equity	80% of 15%	=	12.0%
Total (weighted average)		=	**14.4%**

'[The Europeans] see options [as] an unfair competition and need to pull us down to their own miserable levels of opportunity and performance. Europe has tried and failed to use options to motivate innovation and spread ownership. Unable to unleash the creative power of their own economies, Europeans, particularly bureaucrats, are appalled at the willingness of American workers to accept low wages and willingly work 50 and 60 hour weeks in return for a sliver of ownership in their own business. Using "convergence of accounting standards" as a political grail, they plan to lower America to their own pitiful level of innovation and labour mobility.'

Alfred R. Berkeley, III
Vice chairman, The Nasdaq Stock Market, arguing against
the expensing of employee stock options, January 2003

▶ Other management issues

By now it should be clear that you can put the cost of all financing options onto the same basis, line them up and, starting with the cheapest one, select those which give you the lowest cost financing package. Would that life were that simple. As you already know, too much debt can sink the ship. You need at least enough equity capital to weather the cash flow storms.

Another issue which I quietly omitted to mention in the previous paragraph is taxation. In general, a company's tax bill is not affected by dividends, but it is reduced by debt interest payments (which are expensed). This does not affect the relative cost of debt instruments – they all have the same net tax effect. But it does impact on comparison of debt with equity and other financing options such as leasing.

> Generally, short-term borrowing should be used to finance short-term assets. The logic is inescapable. If you use, say, a bank overdraft or six-month loan to finance the acquisition of a fixed asset, such as a clump press or a factory, you could be in big trouble when the loan expires if it cannot be renewed – or if the terms are considerably more adverse. To a lesser extent, long-term finance should be used with caution for funding near-term cash needs. You would not want to fritter away a loan on short-term benefits if you then had to repay it back for the next 30 years.

▶ Ten hard questions to ask or be asked

1 Does the business have a credit rating? What is it? Does your industry knowledge suggest that the rating might be incorrect?

2 What do market analysts (fundamental or techical) have to say about this company (or, if it is not listed/tracked, about similar companies)?

3 How does the capital structure look?

4 Should the business be factoring, leasing, or otherwise refinancing?

5 How are the results of subsidiaries, joint ventures, associates and other investments accounted for? Is this realistic?

6 Are the figures realistic, or do you need to adjust them?

7 What is the true cost of capital? How does this affect your view of operations?

8 How does the business measure up using indicators of debt?

9 What do the investment indicators look like?

10 If comparing two companies, are you comparing like with like?

▶ Moving on

We have covered a great deal of ground in this chapter. I hope that it provided food for thought about using a surplus or financing a deficit. Remember that cash in the bank claws down your return on investment (ROI). As discussed, the largest ROI should come from minding your own business. If ultimately you can earn more by putting the money in a bank, you might as well sell the business and sit on a beach. But you are not going to do this. The next chapter picks up the theme nicely for two reasons. First, it discusses how you manage the numbers while building an international business. Second, it introduces some new forms of finance associated with foreign trade. See you there.

20

business across borders

'Money speaks sense in a language all nations understand.'

Aphra Behn

Chapter survival toolkit

▶ Overview

This chapter looks at how you *manage the numbers* of international business. The following few pages review the arithmetic and jargon of foreign exchange, the risks of doing business overseas and how you can minimize them, the finance of foreign trade, and the problems of dealing with financial transactions and accounts in foreign currencies.

▶ Prerequisites

You can read parts of this chapter in isolation, but you need an understanding of financial statements (see especially Chapters 14, 15 and, perhaps, 18) to get the most out of it. Chapter 2 might also provide a useful refresher on international accounting standards.

▶ Mastering international business

After reading this chapter, you should be able to answer the following questions:

1 Would it be good or bad if you were doing business across borders and your currency appreciated against the foreign currency? What would happen to the foreign currency price of your products? Would your purchases in foreign markets appear cheaper or more expensive?

2 How could you use a trade-weighted exchange rate in your daily work?

3 Can you name four ways of dealing with the risks of exchange-rate movements?

4 Can you name four currency market derivatives which help minimize exchange-rate risks?

5 How does trade credit lower risks? What is an export letter of credit? An import letter of credit? A standby LC?

6 What bookkeeping entries would you pass at year-end if you had uncovered receivables in a foreign currency, and the exchange rate had moved against you?

7 What is the difference between currency conversions and currency translations?

8 What freedom do managers and beanies have when selecting exchange rates? How can this affect bookkeeping entries?

9 Why do you need to include an exchange-rate gain or loss when translating financial statements from one currency to another?

10 How would you decide whether foreign operations were integral to your business? How would this affect translation of the financial accounts?

> 'Before everything else, getting ready is the secret to success.'
>
> **Henry Ford**

▶ **Jargon watch**

New international banking jargon

Foreign exchange, forex, spread, bid, offer/ask, big and small figures, point, pip, ticks, margin, swap rate/swap point

Fixed and floating rates, dirty float, appreciation, depreciation, revaluation, devaluation

Effective exchange rate, trade-weighted exchange rate, special drawing right (SDR)

Parity, purchasing power parity

Covered, uncovered, netting, matching, hedging, derivatives, forward rate/contract, futures, options, swap, foreign exchange swap, currency swap, interest rate swap, basis swap, cross-currency interest rate swap

Sovereign credit rating

Trade credit, documentary credit, letter of credit (LC), standby LC, packing credit, shipping guarantee, trust receipt, bill of lading

Derivatives

New beanie buzz words

Exchange rate gains and losses, currency translation, foreign exchange book rate, integral foreign entity, non-integral/foreign entity

Beanie buzz words revisited

Comprehensive income, unrealized gains and losses, current

Mathematician's mumblings revisited

Significant figures

▶ **New markets**

In this new global village you will be left behind if you do not think internationally. The most competitive businesses sell into new markets across borders, look to different cultures for new ideas, and source goods and services from suppliers in lower-cost economies. There are new opportunities to grasp and new risks to manage.

We have already discussed the internationalization, harmonization and convergence of accounting principles and the implications for reporting responsibilities (Chapter 2). In this chapter, we will look at *doing the numbers* associated with doing business across borders. The prime focus is managing transactions: the arithmetic of foreign exchange as well as recognizing, minimizing and hedging currency risk. We will also discuss ways of handling the financial accounts of foreign branches and subsidiaries, the complications of managing overseas business units, and the translation of financial accounts from one currency to another.

Some questions to ask before doing business across borders

Note: in each case the follow-on questions include *what is the cost?* and *what is the time frame?*

1 Will we need new people? Or will our existing people require retraining or additional language skills?
2 Do we need to modify or amend our products? For example, do they need to operate at a different voltage, or have new electrical or telecoms plugs and sockets?
3 Do we need to comply with product regulations or obtain type approval (e.g. European CE rating)?
4 Do we need to produce marketing material, specifications or manuals in a new language?
5 Do we need new packaging?
6 How will any goods be shipped?
7 What currency will be used for the transaction?
8 How will payment be made?
9 Will any country or currency be involved other than those of the two parties to the transaction?
10 How much might exchange rates move between the dates when the price is agreed and the payment is made?
11 Should we use forward cover or some other hedging mechanism?
12 Will we need permission from any government body before we can conclude the transaction?
13 Could any government impose or amend their exchange controls in a way which would alter the amount of, or delay or prohibit, the payment?
14 Are we required to obtain customs clearance or any other authorization for delivery?
15 Is there any sales, value added, income or other tax or duty which will affect the cost of the transaction?
16 Will our overseas buyer be required to withhold tax on any payment made to us?
17 Do we need, or can we obtain, any guarantee that goods or services will be delivered and payment will be made (e.g. export credit guarantee, letters of credit)?
18 Can or should we insure against specific risks of cross-border business?
19 What other risks should we try to quantify?

▶ Doing the numbers

There is no need to mention that if you are doing business across borders you proably need to manage foreign currency issues. Each day, an average of $1 trillion changes hand in the *foreign exchange markets*. There is no formal trading floor, as there are with stock exchanges and cattle markets. Currency trading takes place 24 hours a day between bankers over telephone and computer links (good business for telecoms providers).

Forex dealers have a rich jargon of their own. Fortunately, you will be spared much of this because you will typically transact with your bankers or specialist currency brokers and they will communicate with the forex people. However, for your protection, buzz words are highlighted in the following pages.

The price of someone else's money. It is as well to cover the basics first. Starting right at the beginning: exchange rates are the price of one country's money in terms of another. For example, when you see that the dollar is 1.10 *to the euro*, this means that one euro will buy $1.10. Put simply, €1 = $1.10. Commentators sometimes refer to this as the euro/dollar rate, which is a trifle misleading. Avoid confusion by identifying clearly the *denominator* currency with a value of one; the euro in the example here.

Currency conversions. To convert an amount from, say, euros to dollars, multiply by the dollar-per-euro rate. If you have 2 million euros and the rate is €1 = US $1.10, the dollar amount is €2 million × 1.10 = $2.2 million. Alternatively, if you have dollars, divide by this rate to find the euro equivalent: $2.2 million ÷ 1.10 = €2 million.

Inverted rates. Divide into one to find *inverse* or *reciprocal* rates. If €1 = US $1.10 then one dollar will buy 1 ÷ $1.10 euros; i.e. $1 = €0.91.

Cross rates. If you know two rates you can calculate a third. For example, if one euro will buy $1.05 or ¥125, then obviously you could swap dollars for yen (or vice versa) at a rate of $1.05 = ¥125 (assuming for the moment that there are no transaction charges). Divide both sides by the required denominator to find a per-dollar or per-yen rate. For example, dividing through by 1.05 gives the answer $1 = ¥119.05, as shown in the following table. Incidentally, since one yen will buy less than one US cent, it is conventional to quote rates per 100 units of the Japanese currency.

	A	B	C	Formulas in column C
1	**If you know these exchange rates:**			
2	Dollar per euro	€1 = $	1.0500	
3	Yen per euro	€1 = ¥	125.00	
4	**You know these inverse rates:**			
5	Euro per dollar	$1 = €	0.9524	=1/C2
6	Euro per 100 yen	¥100 = €	0.8000	=1/C3
7	**And these cross rates:**			
8	Dollar per 100 yen	¥100 = $	0.8400	=C2/C3*100
9	Yen per dollar	$1 = ¥	119.05	=C3/C2

Appreciation. When an exchange rate gets numerically larger, the denominator is getting *stronger* and the other currency is *weakening*. For example, if the rate leapt from €1 = $1.00 to €1 = $2.00, the euro would have *appreciated* by 100%. Obviously, the dollar would not have *depreciated* by 100% or it would have zero value. To find the second currency's movement, invert the rates first. In this example, the dollar has plunged from $1 = €1.00 to $1 = €0.50; a 50% depreciation.

Countertrade

In some 15% of world trade, no money changes hands. Instead, the parties resort to countertrade such as barter where, for example, one company pays in widgets for another entity's cogs and sprockets. Variations include the creatively named offset, buyback, tolling and switch-trading.

Obviously, these are popular when foreign exchange restrictions and other regulations limit the scope for conventional business. Countertrade might lead you into new territory dealing in some new goods or commodities. The most important point, for your own financials and when examining others, is to check that valuations are realistic and that the associated costs are well covered.

Dealing with dealers

The dollar dominates. Currencies are frequently quoted in terms of one US dollar. Sterling is an exception: a hangover from the days of pounds, shillings and pence, when it was easier to quote the decimal-dollar per one British pound. The euro has also managed to carve itself a niche as a base currency.

Spreads, bids and offers. For general use, exchange rates are usually specified to about five significant figures with two or four decimal places. See Fig. 20.1. Dealers quote rates as two numbers, such as $1.0554–1.0555 to the euro. This indicates that dealers are *bidding* to buy dollars (in exchange for euros) at $1.0555 and *offering* (or *asking*) to sell dollars for $1.0554. The *spread* between the *bid* and *offer/ask* indicates the *market-makers'* profit. You can easily identify which is the bid and which is the offer by checking which way round makes them money (or, more important, costs you money). Watch that sneaky bankers and brokers also add on a commission charge – allowing them to quote a good rate and then take part of it back.

Fig. 20.1 Sample foreign exchange rates

Rates per 1 euro
Average are averages of closing rates on working days.

	Annual average			End year		
	2000	2001	2002	2000	2001	2002
Australian dollar	1.5889	1.7319	1.7376	1.6770	1.7280	1.8556
Canadian dollar	1.3706	1.3864	1.4838	1.3965	1.4077	1.6550
Hong Kong dollar	7.1971	6.9855	7.3750	7.2578	6.8723	8.1781
Japanese yen	99.47	108.68	118.06	106.92	115.33	124.39
New Zealand dollar	2.0288	2.1300	2.0366	2.1120	2.1215	1.9975
Singapore dollar	1.5923	1.6039	1.6912	1.6126	1.6306	1.8199
Swiss franc	1.5579	1.5105	1.4670	1.5232	1.4829	1.4524
UK pound	0.6095	0.6219	0.6288	0.6241	0.6085	0.6505
US dollar	0.9236	0.8956	0.9456	0.9305	0.8813	1.0487

Source: Bank of England

Big and small, pips and points. Dealers, being lazy, normally shout out the last two digits only – known as the *small figures* or *points*. The smallest figure is a *pip*. For the rate in the previous paragraph they would quote the rate as *fifty-four-fifty-five;* bewildering for the uninitiated. The amount to the left of the points, the *big figures*, are taken as understood.

The euro

A dozen European currencies were consigned to the history books on 1 January 2002 when the euro replaced the notes and coins of many western European countries.

The European Central Bank in Frankfurt has published several pages of gobbledygook decreeing that euro rates should be quoted to six significant figures, that there should be no rounding in conversions, and that inverse rates should not be used when converting between national currencies. This last point is to avoid rounding errors. For example, to convert from the French to the German currency before they were wiped out, you would have converted from the franc to the euro and then from the euro to the mark. The same will apply when other countries ditch their own currencies in the future. For the record, and in case you have any old agreements in the deceased currencies, *the irrevocably fixed conversion rates between the euro and the currencies of the member states adopting the euro are:*

1 euro	=	40.3399	Belgian francs
	=	1.95583	German marks
	=	340.750	Greek drachma
	=	166.386	Spanish pesetas
	=	6.55957	French francs
	=	0.787564	Irish pounds
	=	1,936.27	Italian lire
	=	40.3399	Luxembourg francs
	=	2.20371	Dutch guilders
	=	13.7603	Austrian schillings
	=	200.482	Portuguese escudos
	=	5.94573	Finnish marks

At the time of writing in early 2003, Britain, Denmark and Sweden were the only European Union (EU) members outside the euro; and 10 other countries were about to join the EU. It is likely that the euro-bloc will enlarge in time.

Trade-weighted exchange rates

Governments and research bodies publish *effective exchange rate* indices which are based on the relative importance of competitor-country's manufacturing sectors. For example, approximately two-thirds of the UK's trade in manufactures is with the dozen countries that use the single currency, so the euro has a 65% weight in sterling's *trade-weighted index*. The implication is that, for example, a 10% change in the sterling-euro rate would be similar to a 6.5% movement in all currencies against the pound (all other things being equal, as economists love to say).

As published, trade-weighted indices may not be all that useful for you – apart from giving you a general picture of the external situation. However, if you do business in several currencies, you can create your own trade-weighted exchange rate. The calculation is similar to that for the SDR (see p. 312), where weights reflect the relative importance of each currency in your foreign currency spending or revenue figures. Changes in the rate will indicate how exchange rates are affecting your foreign sources and markets overall. You could include your own unique trade-weighted valuation in your financial reports – allowing you to make observations such as *exchange rate movements alone would have added $X million to our overseas earnings last month....*

The immediate effect of exchange-rate movements

Events	Your own currency strengthens against the other country's	Your own currency weakens against the other country's
Effect on your company		
You are sourcing products or services	Favourable. You can buy more for the same price	Unfavourable. Prices rise
You are making sales in foreign markets	Unfavourable. Your product costs more	Favourable. Your product costs less
You have other income from overseas	Unfavourable. Remittances to you are worth less	Favourable. Remittances to you are worth more
Effect on your customer		
Your customer is receiving sales or other income from overseas	Unfavourable. Customer's income falls	Favourable. Customer's income rises
Your customer is sourcing from abroad	Favourable. Customer's costs fall	Unfavourable. Customer's costs rise
Effect on your suppliers		
Your suppliers are sourcing from abroad	Favourable. Supplier's costs decline	Unfavourable. Supplier's costs rise
Effect on your competitor		
Your competitor is selling in foreign markets	Questionable.* Competitor's sales decline	Questionable.* Competitor's sales decline
Your competitor is receiving other income from overseas	Favourable. Competitor's income declines	Unfavourable. Competitor's income rises
Your competitor is sourcing overseas	Unfavourable. Competitor's costs are lower	Favourable. Competitor's costs rise

* It may be good or bad if your competitors are receiving income from overseas and their base currency appreciates, pushing up their prices for foreign customers and reducing the value of remittances received from overseas. In principle it helps your relative position, because it squeezes their cash flow, cuts profits and reduces their funds available for investment. However, it may mean that they compete more aggressively against you at home.

How do exchange rates happen?

Where do currencies go when they are left to find their own levels? No one knows exactly. You would think with all these economists and computers around there would be an exact explanation. But there you are. Of course, as with any price set by the markets, the key factors are supply and demand.

Logically, you would expect that if you can go shopping in any country, you will choose to buy from the one with the lowest prices. Demand for that nation's cash, to acquire its goods and services, will push up its currency rate until its price advantages are eroded. To quantify this, and look at it from another angle, if US inflation is 4% and Canadian inflation is 3%, the US dollar will have to fall by 1% to restore *purchasing power parity* (assuming that inflation actually measures the relevant internationally traded basket of goods and services).

However, life is not this straightforward. The major global *financial flows* are not trade related – they reflect capital funds slopping around the world's financial markets in search of the *best* investment returns. Best, in this context, means optimization of the risk-reward duo, taking account of financial, economic, monetary, political and other conditions and expectations. Thus, in the longer-term exchange rates may be trying to adjust so that there is purchasing power parity between nations, but, in the shorter term, volatile capital flows can and often do cause wild swings.

> For managed currencies, appreciation and depreciation are known as **revaluation** and **devaluation**.

Floating. Of the world's 170 or so currencies (they change so fast – it seems as if there were a dozen more at the start of the millennium), significantly less than one-third are determined directly by market forces. These include the US, Canadian and Australian dollars, the euro, the Japanese yen, Swiss franc, Britain's pound, and other major monetary units which dominate trade and international payments. Historically, the exchange rates for these currencies were *fixed* by governments and central bankers – which is why they are now referred to as *floating*. Central banks sometimes intervene to smooth out extreme peaks and troughs – giving rise to the expression *dirty floats*.

Fixed, with the market's consent. The majority of less developed countries fix their rates to varying extents, either with *managed floats* or by *pegging* their units to the dollar, the currency of another trading partner, or – most popular – a basket of currencies. This might give a semblance of certainty, but beware. Central bankers who try to stem the forces of supply and demand often find that the dam breaks and the currency comes plunging down under the pressure of pent up market forces. Make sure you are not standing in the way. This is a fitting point to discuss ways to cover your corporate exposure to foreign currency risk.

Sovereign risk and exchange control

You will recall from the previous chapter that credit rating agencies grade companies according to their perceived creditworthiness. It hardly needs to be said that before doing business with a major foreign corporation, you may find it useful to review its credit rating. It is also worth noting that the rating agencies grade the creditworthiness of whole countries. When you are reviewing the risks of doing business across borders, these ratings may help you assess the economic and political risks of a new venture. Apart from anything else, a country with severe economic problems may be more likely to impose or extend foreign exchange controls restricting or prohibiting the exchange of currency between residents and non-residents.

SDRs

The International Monetary Fund (IMF) and some other international organizations use the special drawing right (SDR) as their unit of account. This pseudo-currency was created as a reserve asset in 1969. Originally based on the value of gold, since 1974 it is calculated as a weighted average of several currencies. The current composition came into effect on 1 January 2001, and the basket is reviewed every five years.

SDR calculation
1 January 2003

Currency	Weight		Exchange rate per US$		US$ equivalent
Euro	0.4260	×	1.0418	=	0.4438
Japanese yen	21.0000	÷	119.2200	=	0.1761
Pounds sterling	0.0984	×	1.6019	=	0.1576
US dollars	0.5770	×	1.0000	=	0.5770
SDR (total)					1.3546

SDR1 = US$ 1.3546
US$1 = SDR 0.7382

Coping with uncertainty

Clearly, exchange rate movements can lead to surprise gains and losses. For example, if you are dollar based and you sign a contract for €900,000 on the day that $1 = €0.90, you would expect to receive a cool one million dollars. But if the rate moved to $1 = €1.00 by the date you were paid, you would net only $900,000. There are four ways of dealing with this sort of situation:

◆ speculation
◆ netting
◆ matching
◆ hedging.

▶ Do nothing – or speculate

You could just live with exchange rate uncertainty, hope that rates move in your favour, and juggle your cash flow by delaying or accelerating payments and receipts to try to take advantage of exchange-rate movements. However, unless you are a currency dealer this is not what you are supposed to be doing. Strictly speaking, it may even be *ultra vires* – beyond your authority as defined by your company's *memorandum of association* or *bylaws (the objects clause* of this important document defines what business you are in, such as software development, retailing specific goods, etc.). You might make currency gains by accidental or deliberate speculation, but the costs can be considerable and the outcome is, of course, not predictable with certainty.

▶ Netting

If your company has enough overseas dealings, you may be able to net out receipts and payments in each currency. In the previous example, if the costs of running your operations in Europe were €900,000 in the period under consideration, you could keep the euros from the sale and use them to cover expenses. It is rather unlikely that you will be able to do this all the time. Where you can, you remove or minimize exchange rate risks. Significantly, there is little or no financial cost other than the opportunity cost of perhaps not having funds available at a different time, place or currency.

▶ Matching

If you do not have foreign currency revenues and costs to net out, you could always create them. In the example given above, you could borrow euros when you sign the contract and clear the loan when you are paid. The interest payments on the loan are the price you pay for increased certainty. If the inverse applies, and you need to cover expenses due at a future date, you could covert the cash into the required currency and place it on deposit in the money markets or at a bank. It might appear that interest received on the deposit converts the exchange rate risk into a gain.

> Covering risks by matching or taking out forward contracts is known as **hedging** – as in **hedging your bets**.

However, of course, you would normally expect that company funds will generate a bigger profit than that which could be earned by putting the money on deposit – otherwise, why are you in business (this idea was discussed in the previous chapter).

▶ Hedging

Netting and matching are ways of *hedging* your bets, but the financial markets provide several *derivatives* of spot exchange rates which provide structured opportunities for avoiding or minimizing risks. The key derivatives are:

- ◆ forward rates
- ◆ futures
- ◆ options
- ◆ swaps.

Forward contracts

Financial institutions generously provide a form of matching for you. Well, I was joking about *generously*, because they will charge you for it. This is how it works. You take out a *forward contract* to exchange euros for dollars (for the example introduced above) on a given date in the future. Essentially, your bank borrows euros today, sells them immediately for dollars, and puts the dollars on deposit. On the settlement date, the bank gives you the dollars and repays the loan with your euros. The cost to the bank is the difference between the interest paid on the loan in euros and the interest earned on the dollars. No one takes an exchange rate risk and the cost is related to relative interest rates (note: not to currency rate movements). Forward rates are quoted for 30, 60, 90 days and so on up to two years.

More dealer-talk. Forward exchange rates are usually quoted as *margins* on the *spot* rate, because the forward element does not jump around as much as spot rates. The margin, also known as *swap rate* or *swap points,* may be at a *premium* or *discount,* depending on relative interest rates. In the following example, the dollar is quoted at 1.0470–1.0475 to the euro, euro interest rates are higher than dollar interest rates, and so the six-month forward rate is at a discount which can be termed as follows:

◆ $0.0078–0.0065, or

◆ 0.78 to 0.65 cents, or

◆ 78 to 65 points.

If the margin is at a premium, add it to the spot rate to arrive at the forward rate, or if the margin is standing at a discount, subtract it from the spot rate. In the example, the spread is €1 = $1.0392–1.0410.

Forward exchange rates

	Bid	Offer
US interest rate, 6 months, %	1.2500	1.3750
Euro interest rate, 6 months, %	2.6250	2.7500
Spot exchange rate, €1=$	1.0470	1.0475
Margin (+ premium/ – discount)	–0.0078	–0.0065
Forward exchange rate, €1=$	1.0392	1.0410

Generic formula:

$$\text{bid margin} = \frac{\text{spot rate} \times \text{annualized interest rate differential}}{1 + \text{annualized euro interest rate}}$$

Example:

$$\text{bid margin} = \frac{1.25 \times (0.0125 - 0.0275) \times 182/360}{1 + (0.0275 \times 182/360)}$$

$$= -0.0078$$

Suppose you have just signed a deal where you will receive €1 million in six months. If you had the euros in your hand right now, you could sell them for $1.0470 million (bid column, third figure down – easy isn't it). The forward rate guarantees you $1.0392 million (bid column, final figure). The cost is the difference of $7,800, plus, sorry to say, any commission payable to your bankers. Apart from any performance guarantee (a bank might require security that you will honour the transaction) no money changes hand until the forward settlement date.

Futures

In principle, currency futures contracts and their pricing are the same as forward contracts. The main differences are that futures are standardized in size, quote mechanism and settlement dates, and they are traded on a regulated exchange (such as the Chicago Mercantile Exchange) by *open outcry* similar to, but perhaps not quite as civilized as, a schoolboys' auction. The minimum price movement is a *tick* (essentially a *pip,* see above). The costs are brokerage fees and any *margin* required upfront to cover the final settlement.

Options

Currency options provide the buyer with the right, but not the obligation, to buy (*call*) or sell (*put*) a specified amount of a foreign currency on a given date in the future. The great advantage of this is that it caps the downside risk, but still allows you to take advantage of favourable currency movements. There is a cost, of course, which is the premium that the *writer* will charge for accepting the risk.

Swaps

The term *swap* means different things to different people. Here is one set of definitions.

1 A *foreign exchange swap* is a spot sale (or purchase) of currencies combined with a simultaneous forward purchase (or sale) of the same currencies. This is essentially what we discussed above.

2 *Currency swaps* are similar, but – inevitably – a little more complex. Essentially, they allow a corporation with recurring cash flows in a foreign currency, or one seeking financing in a foreign country, to eliminate exchange rate risk. Originally, the swap would take place directly between two companies, each with borrowing advantages in the market that the other wanted to tap. For example, a US company might borrow in dollars, while a European company would borrow in euros. They would then swap funds and repayment obligations. The US corporation would acquire the newly-borrowed euros (converted into dollars in the spot market) – and then use a future stream of revenue in euros to repay the euro loan. Within the past decade or so, currency swaps have developed to the point where a company can deal with a financial intermediary, rather than another company; where the principal might not be exchanged until maturity; and where only the price differential changes hands.

3 *Interest rate swaps* are not directly related to foreign trade, but it is convenient to mention them here. They involve an exchange of debt service obligations, but only in one currency. A company might exchange fixed for floating rate interest payments, often called simply a *swap*; or exchange maturities (e.g. three for six months) or tenors (e.g. a rate linked US dollar prime rate for one linked to US dollar LIBOR – see Chapter 19) in what is known as a *basis swap*.

4 *Cross-currency interest rate swaps* are a mix of the two swaps just outlined.

Clearly, you value these using the techniques for analysing exchange rates and interest rates discussed previously (see this chapter and Chapter 6).

Trade finance

The international departments of commercial banks have developed some nifty, and perhaps costly, techniques for financing foreign trade. The best known of these require the presentation of key documents (see inset) and as a result they are known loosely as *documentary credits, letters of credit* or *LCs*. The shorthand term *DC* is sometimes used, but this has a different meaning in the US.

When a bank issues a letter of credit, it is guaranteeing to release payment on presentation of the specific documents. Incidentally, about 50% of all letters of credit are delayed or rejected by pernickety bankers because of sometimes trivial discrepancies in the documents. The key LCs, and some other examples of the numerous forms of trade finances are as follows:

Key documents of foreign trade:

- detailed invoice;
- bill of lading (a sort of shipping list providing terms of carriage, proof of ownership and a receipt from the shippers);
- insurance certificate;
- inspection certificate/s;
- customs papers.

- *Import letters of credit* guarantee that a supplier will be paid.
- *Export letters of credit* guarantee that you will receive payment for your sales.
- *Standby letters of credit* provide a guarantee in case one party cannot fulfil contractual or financial obligations.
- *Packing credit* finances the exporter's inventory against the documentary evidence of the order.
- *Shipping guarantees* allow importers to take possession of the goods immediately upon arrival.
- *Trust receipts* are issued by importers undertaking to hold goods in trust for the bank, pending sale.

Your bankers will advise you about their services and the associated costs. You can convert these prices into effective interest rates (see Chapter 6) for comparison and cost estimation – and build them into your projections when assessing the viability of a transaction.

'It is impossible to forecast exchange rates in the volatile world of the float.'

Anon.

Booking foreign currency transactions

You will recall that during the lag between invoicing and being paid, the amounts outstanding are recorded as accounts receivables. Suppose you invoice an overseas client for €1,000, and record this as an account receivable of $1,100 (i.e., €1=$1.10). If, at your end-year reporting date the rate has moved to €1=$1.08, and by the payment date it is at $1.05, you would record this follows:

Bookkeeping entries		
1 When invoice is raised Memo: rate is €1=$1.10; receivables are $1,100	**Debit $**	**Credit $**
Accounts receivable	1,100	
Global widget sales		1,100

Bookkeeping entries		
2 At reporting date Memo: rate is €1=$1.08; receivables total is now only $1080	**Debit $**	**Credit $**
Exchange rate losses	20	
Accounts receivable		20

Bookkeeping entries		
3 When payment is received Memo: rate is €1=$1.05; receivable now only $1050	**Debit $**	**Credit $**
Bank	1,050	
Exchange rate losses	30	
Accounts receivable		1,080

Note that the second transaction is an unrealized bookkeeping loss (no money changes hands) and you reduce accounts receivable by the amount of the unrealized losses. The third transaction reflects the actual payment and actual loss.

The balance on the *Exchange rate gains and losses account* is set against net profit – as shown in Fig. 14.1. Note incidentally, that if your generous bankers deduct, say, $40 in transfer fees and commissions – you would post this as an additional debit to your *Bank charges and commissions account*. These charges are considered to be an operating expense and accordingly they are charged *above the line* against operating profit.

Similar currency gains and losses can occur with other transactions, including deposits and loans, as discussed next.

Currency translations

So far, we have been dealing with foreign currency *conversions*. Interesting problems arise with foreign currency *translations*, where no money changes hands but book-keeping entries and financial statements are restated in a different currency. We touched on this in Chapter 18 (see *Comparing competitors*). Let me give another example which shows how unavoidable errors and discrepancies can arise.

▶ Sleight of hand

A subsidiary records payments due to its parent company (but does not necessarily make the payments) in March and August. At the rate applicable on the dates of the entries, a total of $100 million was owed to the parent company. See following table.

However, the transactions are probably not booked at the spot exchange rate applying on the transaction date. Companies which handle a large number of transactions frequently use a fixed *book rate* for a given period, such as a month or a year. This rate is usually fixed *in advance* based on recent observations.

For example, the rate to be used here might be that in force on 1 January. If so, these payments would have been booked at $90 million (lower than 'actual'). Alternatively, the beanies might have seen the euro appreciating and projected a rate of €1 = $1, (i.e. *parity*) – in which case the transfers would have been recorded at $95 million (still too low). On the other hand, if they were making up the accounts at the end of the year with the benefit of hindsight, they might legiti-mately have used the end-year or, better, the annual-average rate. If so, the payments would have been overstated by as much as $6 million.

	Exchange rate €1 = $	Euro transfers €m	Dollar equivalents $m
Transactions			
25-Mar	1.01	15	15
31-Aug	1.06	80	85
Total	1.05 *	95	100
Conversion of total at other rates			
1-Jan	0.95	95	90
31-Dec	1.12	95	106
Annual average	1.08	95	103

The average exchange rate €1 = $1.05 was found by dividing the dollar total by the euro total – it is a weighted-average.

This illustrates how accidental or judicious selection of exchange rates can influ-ence the numbers. You have to be especially careful in watching what other people do in this regard.

▶ Translating financial statements

Another occasion when the choice of exchange rates introduces problems is when translating a complete set of financial statements. There are two major problems:

1 Many differing exchanges rates can, and usually do, apply. There would be a blue moon in the night sky if the financial statements balanced neatly after translation. A balancing entry – *translation gains or losses* – has to be added to the accounts. This is discussed in a moment.

2 The value of the figures can become questionable. Suppose your South American branch acquires a building for the equivalent of $100,000. If the exchange rate depreciates by 20%, has the dollar value of the building fallen to $80,000? It can hardly be exported. What if inflation over the same period was 20%?

Single or multiple rates

In the simplest form of currency translation, all figures in financial statements are transformed from one currency to another at the spot exchange rate on, say, the balance sheet date. This is easy and consistent, but inaccurate. The revenues and expenses took place during a period when exchange rates might have been moving considerably. One solution is to use a second exchange rate, an average exchange rate for the period, to translate the flows. An example is shown in Fig. 20.2.

With a single rate, all relationships and vertical ratios are maintained. With a dual rate, the figure used to translate the amount of retained earnings is different for the balance sheet and the profit and loss account. Accordingly, you have to fudge the accounts and include an *exchange rate gain or loss* as indicated in the example. In this illustration, comprehensive income (profit) in euros has been boosted by 5% even though nothing fundamental has changed. The discrepancy could be much larger, which shows how careful you have to be when interpreting comprehensive income. It also reinforces the importance of calculating ratios using the accounts in the original measurement currency (as discussed in Chapter 18).

Four methods of translating accounts

There are four common methods of translation, two of which are all but obsolete. They are:

Current/non-current. Current assets and liabilities are translated at the current rate and non-current assets and liabilities at the applicable historical rates. Flaws include valuing inventory at current exchanges rates and long-term debt at historical rates. These are practices which could distort the underlying position considerably. Now you know about it, forget it.

Temporal. This translates cash, receivables, payables, and assets and liabilities carried at present value using current exchange rates, and all other assets and liabilities at historical rates. Formerly used by the US, among other countries, this is similar to the next re-measurement technique, by which it has been replaced. You can disregard this technique also.

Fig. 20.2 Translation mischief at work

Tetrylus Software Inc
Balance sheet

As at 31 December

	Reported $m	Exchange rate, $1=€	Translated, €m
Assets			
Current assets	8.80	0.95	8.36
Long-term assets	5.73	0.95	5.44
Total assets	**14.53**		**13.80**
Total liabilities	**(2.96)**	0.95	**(2.81)**
Shareholders' equity			
Total paid-in capital	(9.65)	0.95	(9.17)
Retained earnings	(1.92)	–	(1.73)
Accumulated other comprehensive income	0.00	–	(0.09)
Total shareholders' equity	**(11.57)**		**(10.99)**
Total liabilities and shareholders' equity	**(14.53)**		**(13.80)**

Tetrylus Software Inc.
Profit & loss account

12 months to 31 December

Sales	10.11	0.90	9.10
Cost of sales	(4.77)	0.90	(4.30)
Gross profit	**5.34**		**4.80**
Total operating costs	(3.68)	0.90	(3.31)
Operating profit (loss)	**1.65**		**1.49**
Recurring non-trading net income	0.27	0.90	0.24
Net profit (loss)	**1.92**	**0.90**	**1.73**
Other unrealized gains or losses	0.00	–	0.09
Comprehensive profit/income (loss)	**1.92**		**1.82**

Notes

1 The simplified financial statements assume no retained earnings in the previous year, so that the net profit shows directly in the balance sheet (i.e. zero retained earnings brought forward plus retained earnings for the year equals accumulated retained earnings of $1.92 million).

2 The balance sheet is translated at the (fictitious) end-year exchange rate of $1 = €0.95, except for retained earnings and comprehensive income, see notes 3 to 5.

3 The profit and loss account entries are translated at the 12-month average rate of $1 = €0.90.

4 The balance sheet entry for retained earnings is therefore the translated net profit of $1.73 million (retained earnings bought forward, zero).

5 An adjusting entry of €0.09 million is shown under accumulated comprehensive income – foreign exchange translation gains/losses – in order to make the balance sheet balance.

6 Comprehensive profit/income is boosted by 5% (0.09/1.73) at the stroke of a key/pen.

Monetary/non-monetary. You can probably guess that this technique translates monetary balance sheet entries at current rates and all other assets and liabilities at historical rates (the valuation on acquisition or revaluation). It is required by US generally accepted accounting principles (GAAP) when records are not maintained in the *functional currency* (i.e. the home currency of the principal entity).

Current rate. This translates all assets and liabilities at the rate of exchange that is current on the balance sheet date. Arguments in its favour include maintaining the ratio between debt and the assets it is used to acquire. It is prescribed by US GAAP when the functional currency is the foreign currency.

The new standard

International accounting standards distinguish between foreign operations which are integral to the business of the parent and other foreign entities. Whether or not a foreign entity is integral to the parent requires some judgement. General rules that signify that the foreign entity is **not** integral to the reporting company include:

1 autonomy of the foreign entity;

2 no more than a low proportion of its transactions are with the reporting company;

3 activities are financed primarily from its own resources or borrowing;

4 labour and other costs are settled in its own currency;

5 sales are not principally in the reporting company's currency;

6 reporting company's cash flows are not directly affected by foreign operations.

In either case, income and expense items are translated at transaction rates. In practice, this usually means an average of end-month exchange rates – which can be an extremely inaccurate measure.

Foreign operations which are integral. The monetary/non-monetary method of translation is used. Two points should be noted. Inventories are translated at the exchange rate in effect at the date of acquisition or, if revalued, at the date or revaluation. Depreciation is translated using the currency rate at the date of acquisition or revaluation – which affects the figure that goes into the profit and loss account. Differences arising on translation of monetary items are set against net profit, except that net investment in a foreign entity is reported in equity until disposal of the asset or liability.

Other foreign entities. The current rate technique is used and translation differences are taken directly to equity. In the instance of hyperinflation (defined in Chapter 18), income and expense items are translated at the exchange rate current on the balance sheet date.

> 'Derivatives trading is shifting risk to the dumbest guy in the room.'
>
> **Merton Miller**

Ten hard questions to ask or be asked

1 Are there overseas markets which we should be tapping? If not, Why not?

2 What exchange rate was used (e.g. current spot, yesterday's rate, end-period, average)?

3 What could move the exchange rate? Is the rate floating, fixed, dirty?

4 How will this transaction/position be affected by a 1% change in the exchange rate?

5 Is this transaction/position covered (matched, hedged, etc.)? How? At what cost?

6 Have there been exchange rate movements which affect the underlying position but which are not reflected in the accounts?

7 Could there be any unexpected taxes, duties or other levies?

8 Are there any foreign government regulations which will limit our freedom of action? Could new laws or regulations be introduced?

9 Are all the documents in order? (There is a 50% chance that they are not.)

10 Do we really understand the new culture that we will be dealing with?

Conclusion

This quick run-through of currency-related issues was intended to stimulate your thoughts. The arithmetic of foreign exchange is not difficult, and most of the issues which will arise have both a quantitative and a judgemental aspect. The first step is you use your management skills to decide what you need to do or what is going on. Then you apply simple numerical logic to create, compare or value the results. After this, you may need to return to your management skills to help you interpret your results or conclusions.

> 'The new electronic interdependence recreates the world in the image of a global village.'
>
> **Marshall McLuhan**

21

appraising projects

'An expert is someone who knows some of the worst mistakes that can be made in his subject, and how to avoid them.'

Werner Heisenberg

▶ Chapter survival toolkit

▶ Overview

This chapter pulls together most of the preceding chapters and explains how to use the information gained so far to appraise and select projects. It also reviews techniques for planning and managing projects. The next chapter continues the financial control theme by looking at budgetary controls, which, of course, can and should be applied to project management.

▶ Prerequisites

You could read this chapter in isolation. However, Chapter 5 will remind you how to create charts using spreadsheets. Chapter 6 will help you understand the calculations. Chapters 9 and 10 will help with project forecasting. The other chapters preceding this one will help you with the financial aspects of project planning.

▶ Mastering projects

After reading this chapter, you should be able to answer the following questions:

1 What are the weaknesses of using payback and return on investment to assess projects?

2 Why would you use internal rate of return (IRR) or net present value (NPV) to assess projects? Which is better? When can't you use IRR?

3 What factors are not taken into account by metrics such as IRR and NPV?

4 What is critical path analysis? What does it tell you?

5 What is PERT? What does it tell you?

6 What is a Gantt chart? How can you create one using a spreadsheet's floating bar chart?

7 What is Prince 2? Can you use it instead of techniques such as CPA and PERT?

8 What is the hurdle rate? How do you set it? Why is it higher than the cost of capital?

9 How do you choose between multiple projects with differing cash flows and returns?

10 Why should you go on to read the next chapter on budgets after reading this one?

> 'Adding manpower to a late software project makes it later.'
>
> **Frederick Brooks**

> ► **Jargon watch**

New project management buzz words

Critical path analysis/method (CPA/CPM)

Program evaluation and review technique (PERT), completion time

Gantt chart

New beanie buzz word

Payback

New economics jargon

Opportunity cost

Economics jargon revisited

Inflation, constant prices

Beanie buzz words revisited

Return on investment (ROI), capital employed, assets, equity

Depreciation

Cash flow

Propeller-head terms revisited

Net present value, internal rate of return, hurdle rate, compound interest, cost of capital, risk premium

Normal distribution, standard deviation, variance, z-score

> ► **Project appraisal and management**

This chapter builds on the analysis covered so far in this book, by applying it to projects. The focus is on appraising, authorizing, planning and managing projects. Ensuring that they come in on budget is obviously critical, and this theme is continued in the next chapter.

A key identifying element of a project is its finite or temporary nature. It has a beginning and an end date (which themselves are targets) and could run for as little as a day or as long as years or decades. However, I am going to stretch a point and ask you to consider almost any business activity as a project. The techniques discussed here can help you with most issues related to *managing the numbers*.

Thus, a project in the current sense could be anything you spend money on, or which generates a future stream of revenue, or both. This covers most business activities, including installing a new computer network or clump press, undertaking R&D, acquiring investment property, building a power plant, undertaking a joint venture, or acquiring another company. In fact, you could look upon running a business as running many projects in tandem. The top-level project (running the enterprise) is really a *programme* but lets not worry too much about semantics in this respect.

Relevant analysis from previous chapters includes, well, pretty much everything: forecasting, fixed investment, costs, financial statements, return on investment, the cost of capital, oh yes, and using spreadsheets. Do not worry, though, if you have not read the previous chapters yet, you should still be able to make sense of this one.

▶▶ You are constantly forced to choose between alternatives. The cost of one is the *opportunity cost* of not doing something different. What you have to do is put the options onto the same basis and make a sensible comparison.

▶ Will it pay off?

How do you assess the financial viability of the proposed project? I am about to walk you step by step through the decision process, starting with the initial forecasting. Before I do, let me mention two yardsticks which are sometimes used – payback and return on investment (ROI). These are simple, but inaccurate. We will go on to discuss better measures later in this chapter.

▶ Payback

It is common to hear executives talk about payback – the amount of money that a project pays out and the speed with which it happens. *This project pays back 10,000 in 12 months.* By itself, this is not a very useful statement. However, a company with cash flow problems might become concerned primarily with making a fast return. This is one situation where payback might take precedence over value.

▶ Return on investment

Various measures of return on investment (ROI) were discussed in Chapter 19 – return on capital employed, assets and equity. The metric to use depends on your perspective (manager, lender, shareholder). Calculating these measures for historical periods is straightforward when using figures from financial accounts, as already indicated.

When looking ahead, a simplified measure of return on investment (capital employed) is frequently but misguidedly used to assess projects. For example, if a project costs $100 and pays back $10 this year and $40 the year after, the return on investment is 50%. The figure is sometimes annualized crudely by dividing it by the life of the project in years – giving a yearly return of 25% in this instance. Either way, simple ROI ignores the time value of money, compounding and risks. If the payback was $40 this year and $10 next year, the ROI in this example is unchanged, even though the risks are reduced.

'The first 90% of a project takes 90% of the time, the last 10% takes the other 90% of the time.'

Anon.

Measuring up projects

1 Forecast the expected cash flow from each project.

2 Choose an appraisal method – net present value or internal rate of return (which are explained in a moment).

3 Identify your cost of capital (how much does it cost you to fund the project?).

4 Assess the returns from the project (financial and other gains such as prestige or experience).

5 Assess the risk of the project.

6 Identify the hurdles that this project should clear to be considered acceptable.

7 Review comparative risks and returns on alternative projects.

8 Assess the opportunity costs of not using these resources for something else.

▶ Step 1: Make your cash flow forecasts

The first step is to draw up a cash flow forecast for each project. You need to estimate all revenues and expenditure and draw up a cash flow forecast (as discussed in Chapters 10 to 16). Figure 21.1 shows a brief summary showing the *after-tax* cash flow. Note that depreciation is added back in because it is a bookkeeping deduction, not a cash payment. Cash flow does, of course, include the actual capital outlays on fixed assets.

Fig. 21.1 Projecting a stream of income

**Project *Watchman*
Cash flow projection**

Dollars, millions

	Year 1	Year 2	Year 3	
Outlays	-10,000	-8,000	-5,000	...
Income	11,000	15,000	25,000	...
Net income, before tax	1,000	7,000	20,000	...
100% less tax rate	75%	75%	75%	...
Income after tax				
(excl. depreciation allowance)	750	5,250	15,000	...
Add back depreciation × tax rate	1,000	1,000	1,000	...
Net cash flow after tax	**1,750**	**6,250**	**16,000**	...

> **Inflation**
>
> You might make your projections in constant price terms (ignoring inflation). However, given that our real-world experiences relate to cash values that include the effects of inflation, it is probably more realistic to work in expected real-world prices. This makes observation and measurement easier.
>
> As an aside, the British government – and others – used to project and approve spending plans in constant price terms. As a result, nobody really knew what was going on because prices were changing all the time. For example, big pay increases were sneaked through because they did not change the approved volume figures (number of employees).

▶ Step 2: Choose the valuation technique

The key measures used for valuing projects are *net present value* and *internal rate of return*. I am sure that you recall meeting these oddly named metrics in Chapter 6.

Net present value is the current value of a project at a given discount (interest) rate. Watch though, that at different interest rates, different projects become more attractive because of the varying valuations of future income and payments. One decision that you do have to make is the correct discount rate to use. In fact, the discount is usually called the *hurdle rate* when applied to project appraisal. More on this in a moment.

The alternative, the *internal rate of return* is simply the compound interest rate that links the present and future. Think of it as the interest rate that a bank would have to charge if it were to make you a loan (the project cost) that was going to generate the projected future stream of repayments (the returns).

Choosing between twins

You can probably see that net present value and internal rate of return (IRR) are the same thing approached from different angles. The internal rate of return is quoted as a percentage figure that feels friendly. However, there are occasions when IRR is impossible to calculate (you might find this if you switch from negative to positive cash flows several times). Moreover, with internal rate of return, the reinvestment rate is the calculated IRR, whereas with net present value the reinvestment rate is the discount rate that you specify – which is superior. The metric you use might be dictated by company policy. If not, you pay your money and take your choice.

▶ Step 3: Identify the hurdle rate

The hurdle rate is a yardstick by which you judge a project proposal. If the proposal clears the hurdle, you can give it further consideration. In essence, each project has its own hurdle rate. These are based on the cost of capital, plus an allowance for non-profit-making projects, plus a risk premium.

> Some companies refer to the **hurdle rate** as the **discount rate** or **test discount rate**.

Cost of capital

We calculated cost of capital in Chapter 19. Usually, it is the overall cost which is relevant. Occasionally, you might want to view a project outside of the overall corporate investment picture, in which case you could use the financing costs applicable in that instance.

Non-profitable projects

In principle, any project has to return at least the cost of capital to be worthwhile. Sounds high? What if you undertake projects that do not add to your profits – such as that sparkly-new executive restaurant or an environmental programme – you need to earn more on the profitable projects.

For example, if your cost of capital is 14.4% and if just 85% of your spending is on profit-earning projects, they have to have to earn you at least 14.4% ÷ 85% = 17%. But even this is not the figure that the bank manager will be looking for. The hurdle is probably even higher than this.

Accounting for risk

Almost there. There is one more step. You cannot use the same hurdle rate for every project, because different projects have differing risks. Key factors are:

◆ **Gearing** – risks increase as the proportion of variable cash flows (e.g. sales) rises relative to more certain cash flow (e.g. the initial investment).

◆ **Revenue sensitivity** – risks are higher when projected cash flows are more volatile.

◆ **Timing** – the longer that it will take to produce revenue, the greater the risk.

This is where a touch of subjectivity comes in. You can assign different *betas* (see *Cost of capital*, Chapter 9) or different risk factors to various projects or classes of projects. For example, for low-risk activities you might add 3% to the 17% in the above example, to arrive at a hurdle rate of 20%. For high-risk undertakings, you might pump up the hurdle rate to 30% or 40%.

We have finally arrived at the hurdle rate. It is:

◆ the cost of capital

◆ *plus* an adjustment for non-earning projects

◆ *plus* a risk premium for the specific project (or project class).

Some companies draw up a matrix of risk premiums that they apply to various classes of project. You might like to do this to help classify projects according to risk, and to help achieve consistency now and in the future.

▶ Step 4: Comparing projects

So, you line up the projects and see which one gives the best return? Yes, and no. It is rarely quite so simple in real life. Figure 21.2 shows why. It illustrates two projects, code named Alpha and Beta, yielding 20% and 15% respectively. It happens that Project Alpha wins hands down. It requires an outlay of $1,000 only and returns 20%, whereas Beta requires double the outlay but returns only 15%. However, what if it was not so clear cut? Then you do your analysis at the margin.

Projects on the margin

You can consider Project Beta (Fig. 21.2) to be made up of two sub-projects: Project Alpha and Project Charlie. This new Project Charlie is simply the difference between the other two projects – cash flow in Project Alpha subtracted from cash flow in Project Beta. Thus, your choice is actually undertaking:

◆ option one – Project Alpha, or

◆ option two – a project with returns equivalent to Alpha *and* Charlie.

All you have to do is assess the returns from Charlie to decide if it adds to or subtracts from Project Alpha. In this case Charlie doesn't look too good, so Beta would probably be junked. Alpha comes first again.

Fig. 21.2 It's as simple as Alpha Beta Charlie

	Project Alpha	Project Beta	Project Charlie
Outlay	1,000	2,000	1,000
Return	1,200	2,300	1,100
Yield	20%	15%	10%

▶ Step 5: Making the decision

You are now ready to line up the projects and make a decision. Figure 21.3 shows six projects ranked according to their net present values at their respective hurdle rates. The hurdle rates reveal the degree of risk attached to each project – the lower the rate the safer the perception of the project.

In terms of net present value, Project 104 appears to be the most attractive; project 101 the least. If there were capital constraints that allowed spending of 250,000 only, probably the first five would be approved while project 101 would be axed.

Of course, this is not the end of the story. First, you will consider the extent to which projects and finance can be matched. You will also take into account the opportunity costs of these projects, intangible benefits such as prestige, and other factors including liquidity. The methodology shown here is a good starting point for rigorous analysis – before you apply your management judgement which is, after all, what you are paid for.

Fig. 21.3 Six projects ranked

Project ID	Costs	Hurdle rate, %	Net present value	Cumulative costs
104	40,000	19	90,000	40,000
100	50,000	15	80,000	90,000
105	100,000	40	70,000	190,000
102	10,000	22	50,000	200,000
103	30,000	36	40,000	230,000
101	100,000	25	30,000	330,000

What's wrong with metrics?

Project metrics such as internal rate of return and net present value:

1 do not take account of non-monetary factors, such as intangible benefits;
2 do not reveal the overall impact on the enterprise;
3 are more accurate for cost-cutting projects (because data is available) than for revenue-generating projects (where data usually has to be estimated).

▶ What if?

The results of project appraisal (net present value or internal rate of return) depend entirely on the estimates fed in. *Garbage in, garbage out* to put not too fine a point on it. Or rather, since you have followed the processes outlined earlier in this book, your inputs will be based on carefully considered analysis – but are they correct?

As discussed at the end of Chapter 10, a point-estimate (a single predicted value for cash flow in any specific future period) suggests a spurious degree of accuracy. Almost always, this value is your best estimate (best guess?) but given the uncertainty of predicting the future there *could be a range* of possible outcomes. You might, therefore, want to assess alternative outcomes. The tried-and-tested *worst case* and *best case* provide a range to work with. The risk assessment techniques discussed in Chapter 23 are rather good.

'Trust one who has gone through it.'

Virgil

Project planning

A little at a time

So far, I have assumed that a project is treated as one cohesive lump. In practice, you will want to try to break it into smaller units. The results of each stage will signal a go-no-go for the next one. For example, if you are trying to build a better mousetrap, you might treat it as several, smaller projects – a board, spring, a hinged-wire, etc. If you build a prototype board and it passes inspection, you go on to the next project – the spring. If that fails, you can still sell small cheese boards. If you assign a probability of success to each stage, you can work out the overall chance of succeeding before you start – I will return to this intriguing thought in Chapter 23.

> Project planning software, such as Microsoft Project, helps you to document the required activities at an appropriate level of detail, although it requires a little effort to learn.

How long will it take?

There is a saying that the expert is the one who says it will take longest and cost the most. We have dwelt extensively on costs, and will return to them. Let us chat for a while about estimating completion times.

Critical paths

For any one project, or sub-project, start by identifying the activities that have to be undertaken, and their inter-relationships. Start with the big picture and work inwards.

For example, our company is going to install a new network server. Major activities include preparing the site, installing the server, installing server software, testing, and so on. The first major phase, preparing the site, involves constructing a secure server room, a backup power generator, uninterrupted power supply units, electrical cabling, network cabling, and communications cabling. Each one of these tasks has its own set of activities. Constructing the secure server room includes selecting a contractor, obtaining building permits, undertaking concreting and carpentry, installing air conditioning, fire sprinklers and smoke alarms, and so on. Of course, each one of these jobs breaks down to a further level of detail.

> Remember, projects always run late, always come in over budget, and always undershoot the revenue targets. Why will yours be different?

Some of these activities can be carried out concurrently (e.g. building the server room and installing the generators outside), while others are consecutive (the room must be finished before the server can be installed). When you have estimated the duration for each of the consecutive activities, you can work out the shortest possible completion time for the whole project. Those activities which determine the overall timing are said to be on the *critical path*. This technique is known as *critical path analysis* (CPA) or *method* (CPM).

To help you identify the critical path, you can sketch tree diagrams which illustrate the activities. They branch when two or more activities are carried out consecutively, and eventually all the twigs come back together at the completion point. You can also illustrate this as a Gantt chart where the duration of each activity is indicated by the length of a horizontal bar (as in Fig. 21.4).

Spreadsheets to the rescue

You may be happy to know that spreadsheets can help with project planning. Figure 21.4 shows an extract from a worksheet with a selection of activities listed in the first column. The day on which the activities should start is in the second column, and the duration of each activity is in column C. Below the table is a chart, created with a few mouse clicks, as explained in the figure.

The good thing is that you can amend the figures in the table and watch the chart update automatically. For example, I wanted the installation of the generator to finish on the same day that the room was completed, so by changing the value in B4 I could move the bar until it was in the right place (much easier than subtracting 2 from 10). This makes it clear that the latest date for delivery of the generator is day 8. It could perhaps be delivered earlier than this.

Another point is that the cabling work *inside* the server room cannot begin until the room is finished. However, the networking cabling *outside* the room can start earlier – and we can see that it must start no later than day 7 to coincide with the completion of the electrical cabling.

By working through the activities, it becomes clear that building the room and fitting the electrical cabling are the two consecutive tasks which take the longest – they are on the critical path. The shortest possible completion time for this phase is 12 days.

Creating a project schedule

1 Estimate the duration of each activity.

2 Identify the activities on the critical path.

3 Start at the beginning, and work though the critical path, noting the start and end dates of each of these activities.

4 Start at the end, and work backwards towards the start noting the latest completion dates (and therefore the latest start dates) of all the other activities.

Fig. 21.4 Project plans illustrated

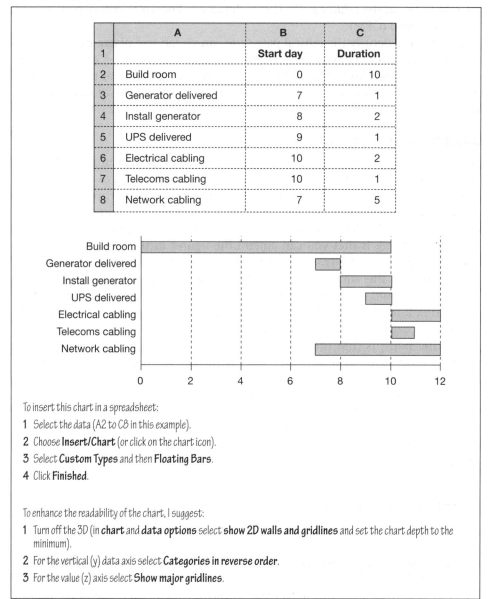

	A	B	C
1		**Start day**	**Duration**
2	Build room	0	10
3	Generator delivered	7	1
4	Install generator	8	2
5	UPS delivered	9	1
6	Electrical cabling	10	2
7	Telecoms cabling	10	1
8	Network cabling	7	5

To insert this chart in a spreadsheet:

1 Select the data (A2 to C8 in this example).

2 Choose **Insert/Chart** (or click on the chart icon).

3 Select **Custom Types** and then **Floating Bars**.

4 Click **Finished**.

To enhance the readability of the chart, I suggest:

1 Turn off the 3D (in **chart** and **data options** select **show 2D walls and gridlines** and set the chart depth to the minimum).

2 For the vertical (y) data axis select **Categories in reverse order**.

3 For the value (z) axis select **Show major gridlines**.

▶ Pert projects

Everybody knows that the biggest project overruns happen in the public sector. Accordingly, it should come as no surprise that the US Navy developed a system it calls program evaluation and review technique (PERT) to try to manage big projects. It may be more of a shock if I tell you that the system was developed in the 1950s. *Ah*, you say, *in that case I guess it doesn't work*. Well, actually, it is quite handy and it can work for you. Moreover, it was first used by the Navy to plan the massive *Polaris Project* and that one, believe it or not, came in ahead of time.

PERT tells you two things. The most likely duration of the project, and the probability of completing it by any given date. It works as follows.

Expected completion time

This is really easy. The predicted completion time is a simple weighted average of the most likely, best-case and worst case timescales, with twice as much weight given to the most-likely duration as the weight given to the extremes. For example, a project manager estimates that activity A (see Fig. 21.5) should be completed after 100 days, but that it might last for between 90 and 130 days. PERT predicts that the activity will actually take 103 days (column E).

The probability of being on time

The chances of completing the project in a given time is every bit as easy to calculate. Sorry that it involves some off-putting terminology. I will take it in three steps.

1 Perform a simple sum to find the *variance* of your estimates (column F in Fig. 21.5). This is of interest to mathematicians only, but we need it for step three.

2 Add up variances for all the activities in the project (cell F6).

3 Do something else as shown in cell G6. (Sorry, I could not bring myself to say *take the square root of the sum of the variances* – you can only say such things if you are wearing a tweed jacket and standing in front of an old blackboard using squeaky chalk.)

Anyway, we are just about there. We have two key numbers in Fig. 21.5. For the whole project, there is an expected completion time of 246 days with a standard deviation of 11.3 days. Recall from Chapter 5 that the *standard deviation* is a nastily-named measure of spread. Remember also that if you assume that the project will suffer from many random influences, you can also assume that the range of possible outcomes is *normally spread*. So there is:

◆ a 69% probability that the project will take between 235 and 258 days (i.e. 246 ± 11);

◆ a 95% chance that it will last between 223 and 269 days (i.e. 246 ± 23);

◆ a 99.7% likelihood that it will be completed within 212 to 280 days (i.e. 246 ± 34).

Or you could say that there is a 2.5% possibility that it will take more than 269 days (or less than 223 days) and so on.

It might have been hard work to get here, but I think that the results are useful enough to have made it worthwhile. In fact, we can take this a little further, but I will save the best for last (see z-scores in Chapter 23). One final point on this topic – do not forget that, as with all calculations, *garbage in, garbage* out. Make your estimates meaningful.

Fig. 21.5 PERT at work

	A	B	C	D	E	F	G
1				Duration			
2	Activity	Optimistic	Likely	Pessimistic	Expected	Variance	Standard deviation
3	A	90	100	130	103	44.44	6.67
4	B	30	50	80	52	69.44	8.33
5	C	82	90	105	91	14.69	3.83
6	Totals	202	240	315	246	128.58	11.34

=(B3+(C3*4)+D3)/6   =SQRT(F6)

=POWER((D3-B3)/6,2)

The first four columns are your figures.

Column E is a weighted average of the estimated durations

Column F is an intermediate step, which subtracts the most-optimistic from the most-pessimistic duration, divides by 6, and squares the result.

Column G is the square root of column F (for all rows including row 6)

For those readers with a statistical bent, 6 is the magic number in these calculations because the extremes are ±3 standard deviations either side of the mean. The expected completion time is modelled on the beta distribution. So now you know.

Reminder: The spreadsheets in this book are available for download from this book's website, **www.ManagingTheNumbers.com**.

▶ Small reversible steps

The final point that I want to make about project planning is perhaps the most important. When you come to the detail of the planning process, you should try to break the execution into small reversible steps.

You need to identify steps that you can measure, perhaps as little as a couple of weeks apart. These might be costs, revenues, quantities, user acceptances – anything that you can appraise or classify. The most-critical projects should have the most tightly defined triggers. In other words, if it is important and it is going even slightly wrong, you want to know about it, fast – as discussed next.

PRINCE 2

Prince (PRojects IN Controlled Environments) is the UK government's methodology for IT projects. First introduced in 1989, it was extensively revised and relaunched in 1996, and it is now widely used in both the public and private sectors in many countries. Suitable for managing projects of all sizes, it provides a structured approach encompassing best practices. However, it does not stipulate the precise methods to be used for managing risks, etc. Accordingly, it is best used in conjunction with other quantitative techniques, such as CPA and PERT (discussed in these pages).

Project management

Fig. 21.6 The general flow of project management

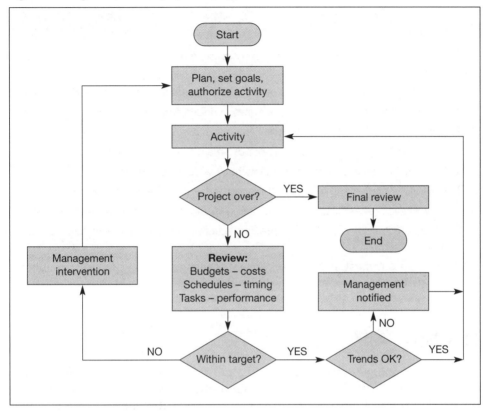

▶ Don't tell me what's right

It might be clear from the foregoing that the secret of successful project management is in the planning. Isn't this always the way. Once the project is running:

◆ Measure the progress of each step against the predetermined milestones according to a set time schedule.

◆ Proceed automatically to the next step if nothing is awry.

◆ If the results at any stage are outside of the predetermined range of acceptable values, intervene immediately.

You need to do two things as each checkpoint is reached. The first is to ensure that an exception report is triggered if any actual figure is outside the predefined acceptable range (management by exception – *don't tell me what's right, tell me what's wrong*) – in which case management intervention should be immediate. You can then reassess the plan, implement corrective action, approve new goals, etc. The second is to check the trend. For example, if one category of spending is moving a little closer to the upper limit each month, this might be an early warning signal that the limit is about to be breached. This is so important, that the next chapter is devoted to it.

Ten hard questions to ask or be asked

1 Have we really used to correct metric to measure to expected return on this project (e.g. ROI, IRR, etc.)?

2 How do we rank the importance of the outcomes (cost, features, timescale, etc.)?

3 The calculations are impressive, but are the underlying assumptions correct?

4 How did we choose the hurdle rate? Is it correct?

5 Do we really understand the range of possible returns? Accurately?

6 Have we considered all the risks? How have we covered them?

7 How did we arrive at the expected completion times? Are the ranges realistic?

8 Do we have the best metrics (quantity and quality) with which to measure progress?

9 What safeguards do we have to prevent *feature creep* (i.e. increases in the scope of the project)?

10 Who are our most experienced project managers? What do they say about this plan?

What's next?

Project methodologies can be applied to almost anything, from managing a one-day task to running a large enterprise. Similarly, budgeting techniques apply to the whole gamut of business including, as just indicated, project management. Accordingly, the next chapter should be read in conjunction with this one.

22

brilliant budgets

> 'Management by objectives works if you first think through your objectives. Ninety percent of the time you have not.'
>
> **Peter F. Drucker**

► Chapter survival toolkit

► Overview

This chapter discusses budgets. It explains how they are created and managed; how they provide a summary of expected activity, as well as a tool for management control, and a target against which performance is measured; and it emphasizes that while they are important for *managing the numbers*, they should not be taken as the be all and end all of financial control.

► Prerequisites

This chapter is similar to the previous one, in that you could read it in isolation; but, ideally, you should view it as a follow-on to everything discussed so far.

► Mastering budgets

After reading this chapter, you should be able to answer the following questions:

1 What is a budget? Can you name three key indicators that it provides once approved?

2 What is a rolling budget? What is a flexible budget? What is a cash budget? What is a capital budget?

3 What does a balanced scorecard track? How does this relate to budgets?

4 Are the figures in a budget guidelines or targets? Is it better to undershoot or over-shoot? What is a budget cycle?

5 For how many months does the budget cycle last? How many months spending are usually controlled by the budget plan?

6 Who should prepare the budget projections?

7 Should departments prepare their budgets in isolation?

8 How do managers control budgets during the year? How often should budget progress reports be produced?

9 What is an outturn? What is a variance? Do variances matter?

10 Give three key reasons why the outturn may vary from the plan?

> 'Management account reports . . . were longer than a CIA intelligence study – and just about as useful. We need reports that are short and sharp, readable and read. If employees understand the company's financial goals, then they'll understand how to get there.'
>
> **Simon Drakeford**

The budget bane

Budgets can be the bane of any manager's life. It always seems to be time to prepare next year's budget, report on progress or attend a meeting on some aspect of budgeting. Yet if you put a structure in place and get on top of the budget process, it can be quite simple and – dare I suggest – a useful exercise for all concerned. I suppose mentioning that it might become a pleasure would be going too far.

> This chapter is written from the assumption that you are preparing a budget as part of a larger, probably enterprise-wide budgeting exercise. If it happens that you are in charge of the overall budget process, just read the following from that perspective.

► Budgets, right or wrong

Budgets are simply short-term financial plans. They usually cover a 12-month period, although rolling budgets with no hard and fast start and end points are better. The best budget plans also contain at least a page or two of written explanation. (See, for example, Fig. 22.2.) Once approved, the plans become a summary of expected activity, a tool for management control, and a target against which performance is measured. This is where the problems arise.

These spending plans become limits – floors and, especially, ceilings. Managers can usually get away with some undershooting on expenditure, but overshooting is often a heinous crime. This conflicts directly with the best performance metrics, which should stretch the organization and encourage growth. Accordingly, it is important to maintain a common-sense approach to budgets and keep the good of the enterprise foremost in your thinking. Budget figures should not be taken in isolation. A *balanced scorecard* approach is required (see overleaf).

> 'Most of what we call management consists of making it difficult for people to get their work done.'
>
> **Peter F. Drucker**

▶▶

The balanced scorecard

As with so many management buzz words and phrases, the balanced scorecard is a popularized name for a common-sense approach which supplements financial controls with three other perspectives on performance (which should be measured by appropriate metrics):

◆ Financial. *How well do we manage costs*?

◆ Processes. *How strong are our core competencies*?

◆ Innovation. *Are we learning, improving, innovating*?

◆ Customer-related. *How is our performance perceived by our customers*?

▶ An overview of the budget process

Budgets typically run in an overlapping 18-month cycle, with the targets covering 12 months – frequently a calendar year. See Fig. 22.1.

Generally, senior executives set targets, preferably in a two-way consultation with managers (top-down, bottom-up). From these targets, operating plans are devised and financial projections are developed. There may well be a couple of rounds of, shall I say, negotiation and revisions before the plans are approved. The financial plans then become budgets.

Managers are usually required to report on progress at the end of each month, comparing actual spending (often called *outturn*) with the budget targets. Beanies term this process the *analysis of variance* to highlight the fact that they come from a different planet. There will probably be more detailed and more painful reviews every three months. Then, when the budget year has ended, there will be an extensive post-mortem. If you have ever been involved in a project or budget, there is no need to elaborate on the witch hunts that follow missed targets and the chocolate beans that are handed out in reward when targets are met.

Given that targets usually affect salaries and bonuses, and these figures themselves go into budgets, goals are frequently set for a 12-month period which is slightly ahead of the budget year. For example, when the budget year runs January to December, a manager may be rewarded (or punished) for his performance over the 12 months to the end of October or November.

'Dozens of times I have asked CEOs and other corporate leaders how they stay on top of their large, complex businesses: "How do you know what's really going on in your company?" Invariably, I receive the clear answer that they have five or six – maybe 10 or 12 – key business indicators that they track daily or weekly. These indicators tell them what they need to know about their company's current performance and near-term prospects. Without notes or preparation, most CEOs can tell you in just a few minutes exactly what these indicators are and what the current numbers are telling them.'

Peter R. Fisher US Under Secretary of the Treasury
(speaking to the Securities Industry Association, 8 November 2002)

Fig. 22.1 The budget cycle

This is an example of how the budget cycle plays out in one particular company and, no doubt, in countless others. There may be revisions to budgets during the year if things go wrong for the enterprise as a whole. In this common model, budgets are set in a top-down bottom-up process – a method in which managers are more involved in target setting is more likely to produce good results.

	2003 budget	2004 budget	2005 budget
July 2003	Detailed review of first six months feeds into 2004 target setting.	Senior executives set targets for 2004, such as production or sales of X, maximum spending of Y, headcount reduction of Z.	
August	Managers report seven months to end July.		
September	Managers report eight months to end August	Plans are communicated to managers.	
October	Detailed review of first nine months feeds into 2004 planning process	Managers prepare activity plans to achieve targets, cost their plans and draw up the financial projections.	
November	Managers report 10 months to end October	Managers present the financial projections, committees debate, plans are revised and eventually approved as budgets.	
December	Managers report 11 months to end November		
January 2004	Full and painful review of 2003 budget outturn	New budget year begins; 2004 budgets may be revised in light of 2003 outturn.	
February to June		Managers submit end-month reports showing performance relative to the budget. A more thorough review takes place in early April.	
July		Detailed review of first six months feeds into 2005 target setting.	
August to December		Managers submit end-month reports showing performance relative to the budget. A more thorough review takes place in early October.	New budget planning cycle begins. Senior executives set targets for 2005...
January 2005		Full and painful review of 2004 budget outturn	

Who prepares the budgets?

Usually each department head or business unit manager with spending responsibility prepares a budget. When all these separate budgets are aggregated, they will create a spending plan for the enterprise as a whole. For ease of reference, let me refer to *departments,* but treat this term as interchangeable with the *enterprise, division* or *business unit.*

Of course, the department head's own budget may be created by aggregating budgets which were prepared by subordinate managers. The budgeting process can – and probably should – ripple deeply into the organization. There is inevitably an element of centralization in bringing together the plan, but watch that central planning *per se* takes the initiative away from the individual manager and can be demoralizing and damaging.

MEMO

From: Secretary to Budget Committee
To: Department Heads
Date: 20 August 2003
Subject: **Annual budget – kick-off meeting**

Please attend the first budget meeting for 2004 in the main conference room at 14.00 on 27 August. Preliminary briefing material is attached, containing background material on the planning process and timetable, proposed roles and responsibilities, and provisional assumptions and targets. This should be read in conjunction with your copy of the five-year strategic plans …

AGENDA

Annual budget kick-off meeting, 27 August 2003

1 **Introductions** – who's who
2 **Budget overview** – purpose, scope, deliverables
3 **Roles and responsibilities** – who does what
4 **Timetable** – when each phase has to be completed
5 **Planning assumptions** – discussion and agreement
6 **Targets** – discussion and agreement
7 **Questions** – ensure everyone is clear
8 **Wrap up** – to restate major responsibilities, actions and deadlines

---

```
MINUTES

Meeting:        Budget Committee
Present:        See attached Annex A
Date:           27 August 2003
Subject:        Annual budget – kick-off meeting

1  Responsibilities were allocated as specified in Annex A
3  The timetable agreed is set out in Annex B
3  Responsibilities ...
```

Consistency

It hardly needs to be said that budgets need to be consistent across the organization.

- First, each budget must be prepared using the same expectations and assumptions. It would be rather pointless if Sales worked on the basis that some wonder product would go into the shops in July, while Manufacturing did not plan to start production until October. Similarly, you do not want the inconsistency of departments using differing exchange rates, interest rates or economic forecasts.

- Second, the headings on the financial budgets need to be consistent so that they can be aggregated. Essentially, you want a standard spreadsheet (*a budget pro forma* if you want to make it sound needlessly outdated and unfriendly).

If you are in charge of the overall budget process, you will want to produce and circulate a list of assumptions, a spreadsheet with instructions for completion, and maybe a standard framework for commentary.

```
MEMO

From:          Budget Coordinator
To:            Department Heads
Date:          15th September 2003
Subject:       Annual budget – Forms

Attached please find:
1  A spreadsheet workbook containing standard assumptions and budget framework.
2  A Word document with standard headings for your commentary.
3  A brief budget manual describing the process, defining expenditure
   categories, etc.

You are required to complete...
```

Setting assumptions and targets

Assumptions and targets for next year (the *budget year*) are usually set about halfway through this year, although they may be revised before or even during the budget year. The overall performance of the enterprise, and of individual departmental managers, will influence the new goals and objectives. It hardly needs to be said that those setting the standards need to stand back and see the big picture. If you want to explore this topic further, you might want to read the *Definitive Business Plan* (2002, 2nd edn, FT Prentice Hall) another one of my books.

> Cynical managers sometimes use **zero-based budgeting**. Essentially last year's figures are hidden and you have to draw up a budget from scratch. Might this be helpful? It does highlight that there can be benefits in asking hard questions such as 'Just because we are already spending this much on that, does it make it right?'

Ideally, all department heads should be involved in developing the strategic plans and then setting assumptions and collective targets. The individuals involved will be more likely to understand and support these parameters. Personal targets may be a more private matter. If you are a department head conveying the parameters to your subordinates you have a more difficult job ensuring their buy-in. Perhaps you can involve them when you are preparing your input before the targets and assumptions are set.

Developing spending plans

Once the targets and assumptions are agreed, they should be communicated in writing to department heads. Converting these into financial plans has been covered already (see Chapters 11 to 16). You may be relieved to know that if you drew up your own projections as you worked through the previous chapters you already know all about the forecasting and projecting associated with budgeting. The tables that you produce will take one of four forms, depending on what you do:

1 **Spending**. Every department contributing to the budget will draw up a table or tables of expenditure as shown in Figs 12.2, 12.4 and 12.6 – supplemented with a capital expenditure budget as shown in Fig. 11.5.

2 **Sales**. The sales department will also produce a sales budget, which will look something like an extract from Fig. 13.6.

3 **Production**. The production department will also generate product volumes and costs as in Fig. 10.3, with inventory numbers from Fig. 13.6.

4 **Financial statements**. All the above will be brought together in a budget at the divisional or enterprise level that follows Figs 14.2, 15.4 and 16.3.

In fact, smaller companies, subsidiaries and business units will more or less go straight to step four, although of course this will contain all the elements of the other three categories.

> 'It is a bad plan that admits of no modification.'
>
> **Publilius Syrus**

One forecast, four budget formats

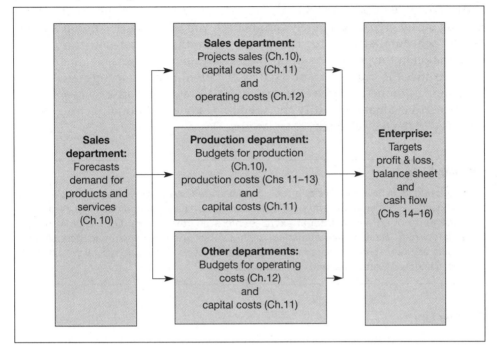

Flexible budgets

Production departments and, sometimes, other cost centres, often produce several budgets each based on a different level of production and sales. If in the event demand in, say, June is for 1.5 million units, the budget based on that level of activity will be the one that is used in that month for management control and measurement.

Cash or accruals?

Cash budgets or *cash flow budgets* contain spending and revenue projections on a cash basis. They are relatively simple to draw up and they provide an essential bottom line for treasury (cash) managers. However, budgets produced on an accruals basis provide superior management information. Accordingly, it is most useful to:

1 produce budgets on an accruals basis (see Chapter 8), and then
2 generate cash flow projections (see Chapters 8 and 16).

Capital budgets

For some reason, capital budgeting sounds more terrifying than budgeting. In fact, it is easier to draw up a capital budget, because the number of items involved is usually relatively small.

A capital budget is little more than a list of the fixed assets (computers, desks, earth-moving equipment) that you need to acquire during the coming year. Unless you are preparing a purely cash budget, you will have to draw up a depreciation schedule, at least for the first few months, so that you can include depreciation in the production or operating expenditure budgets.

Given that the acquisition of fixed assets often involves spending relatively large sums of money, it receives special attention often on a case-by-case basis. If you need to evaluate or justify the spending, some additional techniques are described in the next chapter.

Rolling budgets

Rolling budgets usually look five quarters ahead and are revised every three months – when a new quarter is added to the end of the plan. On the one hand, this can be seen as changing the terror of an annual budget exercise into a quarterly chore. On the other hand, mandatory re-forecasting (re-estimating) each quarter formalizes what managers should be doing anyway. There are no artificial breaks in the cycle due to the annual cut-off, and financial targets are smoother and less disconnected.

Commentary

Usually you will need to document the financials, although curiously I have seen organizations where financials were compiled by accountants who wanted the figures, not the rationale. Brevity is usually welcome, as long as you explain the key points. Put yourself in the position of the reader. See *Getting it approved* in this chapter.

Presentation, revision and approval

Be prepared to explain and defend your budget plans to a committee. If you are in a large or formal organization, and near the top of the budget process, you may need to make a PowerPoint or at least a whiteboard presentation. Otherwise, perhaps you will talk your colleagues through your written report. In either case, explaining the whats, whys and hows should take you through the process fairly smoothly.

Invariably, at first brush, there will be conflicting departmental activities, or aggregate spending will be too high, or the overall corporate plan will not be ambitious enough, or too ambitious, or whatever. Be prepared to revisit and revise your plan. Budgets frequently contain padding – room to make cuts up front if required or wriggle if the year turns out to be worse than expected. Watch for this in budgets passed up to you and, I guess, try to avoid doing it yourself. It is better to grade activities according to how essential they are – and to start cutting with the least essential if necessary.

Getting it approved

1 Remind them where you came in on target last year.

2 Explain where past misses were the result of extraneous factors (natural disaster, civil war, technology shift).

3 Make it clear how what you learned from last year's budgeting exercise will make this year's budget outcome better.

4 Explain how this budget helps work toward your department's long-term goals.

5 Teach the uninitiated – explain the benefits of doing X or using product Y.

6 Distinguish between essentials and nice-to-haves.

7 Walk them through it step by step.

8 Be ready to show that you have considered alternatives (outsource, buy or lease, full-time or contract staff) and chosen the ones with the best cost-benefits.

Timing

Do not tell anybody that I told you this, but there is a trick you can play with timing. If you are not sure when a transaction will happen, put it in an earlier month. Delaying the purchase until later might save an overshoot. If the spending is one-off (such as buying a filing cabinet), you have one-time reprieve. If it is repetitive or cumulative (hiring an employee, or starting a production line), a couple of months' delay could add up to a big saving by year end. Of course, the same applies to sales – if they start or increase earlier than expected then you could exceed your budget comfortably.

When things go wrong

According to the *Financial Times*, when US retailer K-Mart filed for Chapter 11 bankruptcy protection in 2002, investigators found that former management

'... aimed to delay or reduce payments to suppliers to avert a looming liquidity crisis ... senior managers imposed [on merchandising staff] "unattainable" targets for gross margins and financing from suppliers, demoting or transferring employees when they refused to incorporate "unrealistic" numbers into forecasts and reports. This top-down imposition of numbers led to the board receiving a substantially inflated forecast in the fourth quarter of 2001 ... [Moreover,] executives authorised spending $12m on new corporate aircraft, which was not in the company's budget. They also "abused an already generous corporate aircraft policy" by masking personal travel as store visits.'

Financial Times, 26 January 2003

I guess nothing like this happens in your business.

Fig. 22.2 A live budget

ANNUAL BUDGET

	A	B	C	D	E	F	G	H
1	ZXTY International							
2	Marketing Department							
3	Budget for calendar year 20xx							
4	Local currency							Year to
5		Jan	Feb	Mar	Apr	May	Jun	end June
6	Salaries	10,000	10,000	10,000	10,000	10,000	10,000	60,000
7								
8	Travel	5,000	5,500	4,000	4,500	4,750	5,000	28,750
9								
10	Total spending	400,050	410,150	385,450	433,000	453,200	399,750	2,481,600
11	Contingency	40,005	41,015	38,545	43,300	45,320	39,975	248,160
12	Total spending	440,055	451,165	423,995	476,300	498,520		
13	Cumulative	440,055	891,220	1,315,215	1,791,515	2,290,035		

	A	B	C	D	E	F
1	Marketing Department					
2	Outturn for January to June 20xx					
3	Local currency					
4		Jan	Feb	Mar	Apr	May
5	Salaries	9,986	9,986	10,125	10,125	10,125
6						
7	Travel	5,120	5,977	5,450	5,569	5,420
8						
9	Total actual	399,457	420,435	399,499	451,397	490,364
10	Contingency unused	40,598	30,730	24,496	24,903	8,156
11	Total actual	399,457	420,435	399,499	451,397	490,364
12	Cumulative, actual	399,457	819,892	1,219,391	1,670,788	2,161,152

	A	B	C	D	E	F	G	H	I
1	Marketing Department								
2	Budget report, June 20xx								
3	Local currency								
4		Month of June				Year			
5		Actual	Budget	Variance	Var, %	Actual	Budget		
6	Salaries	11,004	10,000	1,004	10.0	61,351	60,0		
7									
8	Travel	5,995	5,000	995	19.9	33,531	28,2		
9									
10	Total spending	458,204	399,750	58,454	14.6	2,619,356	2,481,6		
11	Contingency	58,454	39,975	-18,479	46.2	137,756	248,1		
12	Total spending	458,204	439,725	18,479	4.2	2,619,356	2,729,7		

Budget Commentary

This is the budget for the marketing department for the fiscal year 2004. It was prepared on the basis of the standard assumptions in Table 1 and the targets for 2004 set out in Table 2.

Overview

In order to meet our targets, we will need to recruit two new staff as indicated below. We shall also plan to attend the International Widget Trade Fair in Berlin for the first time and as well as the costs of …

A review by budget heading follows:

Due and subscriptions
No change from 2003

Marketing materials – brochures
In order to produce the substantial number of new brochures and flyers, we shall outsource all design and production to Quick Pzazz Ltd. This will add temporary costs of $25,000 to expenditure in the period February–May…

Managing a budget

Once the budget year is in full swing, each month you will be required to produce a summary comparing what did happen with what you expected to happen, and write a short commentary explaining the difference between the two (the *variance*, to use a word beloved of bean counters). It will be a rare budget that is spot on target all year. An extract from a monthly report is as follows:

Marketing Department
Budget report, June 2004

Dollars

	Month of June				Year to end June			
	Budget	Actual	Variance	Var, %	Budget	Actual	Variance	Var, %
Salaries	10,000	11,004	1,004	10.0	60,000	61,351	1,351	2.3
...	...	...	...		...	...	...	...
Travel	5,000	5,995	995	19.9	28,750	33,531	4,781	16.6
...		...	...	...	...	...	...	...
Total spending	**399,750**	**458,204**	**58,454**	**14.6**	**2,481,600**	**2,619,356**	**137,756**	**5.6**
Contingency	39,975	58,454	18,479	46.2	248,160	137,756	(110,404)	(44.5)
Total spending	**439,725**	**458,204**	**18,479**	**4.2**	**2,729,760**	**2,619,356**	**(110,404)**	**(4.0)**

Commentary
Spending for the year to date is still within target, although extra responsibilities resulting from the recent reorganization continues to exert upward pressure on the spending needs of the Marketing Department. The early recruitment of staff previously planned to start in August pushed up salaries ...

In fact, the manager responsible for this budget tracks it in a workbook containing three spreadsheets (See Fig. 22.3):

1 The first spreadsheet is the original budget – what was planned.

2 The second shows the actual transactions (the *outturn*) – what happened.

3 The third analyses the variances – where the reality diverged from the plan.

The third spreadsheet was used to produce the report above. It shows planned and actual spending in the month, together with the actual and percentage *variance* between the two. It also does the same for the year to date – the first six months in this example.

The three rows – salaries, travel and total spending – are illustrated graphically in Fig. 22.4. With such pictures, it is easy to spot what is happening. You can read the same information from the budget report (the lower spreadsheet). Taking each in turn:

◆ **Salaries**. Salaries were close to budget each month until June. Over the first six months they were just 2.3% above plan and even in June itself they were within what might be regarded as a reasonable margin of error – 10%. However, the sudden jump in June suggests an unexpected event – perhaps across-the-board pay awards or recruitment of an extra member of staff. This merits investigation.

◆ **Travel**. The percentage variances show that travel spending is running seriously over budget and needs investigation. Looking back at the raw data there is persistent overspending that should have been questioned already.

◆ **Total spending**. The summary shows that total expenditure in the year to June was 5.6% over the level of *identified* planned spending, but still within the overall plan including the 10% contingency. Spending in the month of June was over target.

> Watch for spending binges at near year end, when managers realize that expenditure is running under-budget and go on unnecessary spending sprees.

What does all this tell us? It indicates that percentages are more revealing than raw numbers. It shows that many questions can be raised by a quick perusal of the budget report. It highlights the fact that more information is needed. It is, incidentally, valuable to include volume figures – such as planned and actual headcount, number of units produced or sold, volume of inventory, number of contracts completed. Most important, you cannot make any decision without looking at both the spending and the revenue side of the equation.

If the extra spending is going into generating more sales it might be entirely acceptable and welcome. However, recall from Chapter 10 that it can sometimes be counterproductive if sales exceed their optimum level.

▶▶ Ten items in budget reports that might imply problems

1 Spending is on target, sales are not (or vice versa).

2 Variances that are, say, more than 10% above or below plan.

3 Deteriorating trends, even if totals are still well within targets.

4 Sudden, large changes.

5 Single items of expenditure that exceed corporate, departmental, personal or other spending limits.

6 Outlays on rental and leases that could be circumventing controls over capital spending and/or creating long-term liabilities.

7 Unhealthy increases in accounts receivable (credit to customers); aging accounts receivable – debts not being collected in a timely manner.

8 An increasing proportion of uncollected debts hidden within accounts receivable.

9 Other changes in balance sheet entries that do not relate directly to the expenditure reports (accruals and prepayments).

10 Commission, cost of sales, and other headings concealing payments ostensibly to agents or third parties – I have seen some very devious practices here.

See also Fig 12.5 *Fourteen areas where managers massage costs*.

As mentioned elsewhere, keep a close eye on trends, and especially trends in trends. Even if spending is well below target, if it is getting a little closer to the limit each month, this might indicate that it is on an almost irreversible slippery path towards an overshoot.

Fig. 22.3 Sample monthly budget health check

ZXTY International
Marketing Department
Budget for calendar year 20xx
Local currency

	Jan	Feb	Mar	Apr	May	Jun	Year to end June
Salaries	10,000	10,000	10,000	10,000	10,000	10,000	60,000
...		...	...	...	...	...	...
Travel	5,000	5,500	4,000	4,500	4,750	5,000	28,750
...		...		...		...	...
Total spending	400,050	410,150	385,450	433,000	453,200	399,750	2,481,600
Contingency	40,005	41,015	38,545	43,300	45,320	39,975	248,160
Total spending	440,055	451,165	423,995	476,300	498,520	439,725	2,729,760
Cumulative	440,055	891,220	1,315,215	1,791,515	2,290,035	2,729,760	

Marketing Department
Outturn for January to June 20xx
Local currency

	Jan	Feb	Mar	Apr	May	Jun	Year to end June
Salaries	9,986	9,986	10,125	10,125	10,125	11,004	61,351
...		...	...	...	...	...	...
Travel	5,120	5,977	5,450	5,569	5,420	5,995	33,531
...		...		...		...	...
Total actual	399,457	420,435	399,499	451,397	490,364	458,204	2,619,356
Contingency unused	40,598	30,730	24,496	24,903	8,156	(18,479)	110,404
Total budget	440,055	451,165	423,995	476,300	498,520	439,725	2,729,760
Cumulative, actual	399,457	819,892	1,219,391	1,670,788	2,161,152	2,619,356	

Marketing Department
Budget report, June 20xx
Local currency

	Month of June				Year to end June			
	Actual	Budget	Variance	Var, %	Actual	Budget	Variance	Var, %
Salaries	11,004	10,000	1,004	10.0	61,351	60,000	1,351	2.3
...		...	...	...		...	...	...
Travel	5,995	5,000	995	19.9	33,531	28,750	4,781	16.6
...		...	...	...		...	...	...
Total spending	458,204	399,750	58,454	14.6	2,619,356	2,481,600	137,756	5.6
Contingency	58,454	39,975	18,479	46.2	137,756	248,160	(110,404)	(44.5)
Total spending	458,204	439,725	18,479	4.2	2,619,356	2,729,760	(110,404)	(4.0)

Salaries within acceptable % variance but check if Marketing recruited above headcount budget in June or conceded big pay increases.

Total spending was high in June. Contingency for month was exceeded by 46% (worrying) BUT less than half the contingency for Jan–June was consumed (good) and overall spending is 4% below the total provision.

Travel is running over budget. Check and control or revise budget.

Fig. 22.4 Budget and outturn illustrated

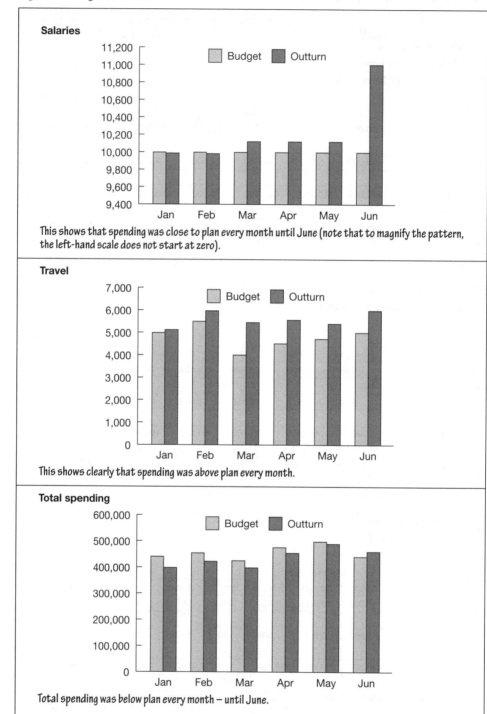

Salaries

This shows that spending was close to plan every month until June (note that to magnify the pattern, the left-hand scale does not start at zero).

Travel

This shows clearly that spending was above plan every month.

Total spending

Total spending was below plan every month – until June.

When things go wrong

There is perhaps nothing more common or more irritating than a boss who is hung up on spending figures. Overall performance should be more important than hitting a budget. And results are not usually measured by whether you are or should be spending $100 or $200 on telephone calls. So, as already indicated, take spending with revenue – and look at this in the light of overall objectives and constraints.

If spending is running over budget (or sales are down) this is when you will be pleased that you graded activities according to how significant they were in the overall scheme of things. You do not need to be told that the least essential items should be the first to be cut.

Three key explanations for variances

1 **Values**. You acquired the approved goods and services, but at a different price.

2 **Volumes**. You acquired more or less goods and services.

3 **Efficiency**. Volumes and values were as projected, but you did it better than expected.

The big review

Quarterly and end-year budget reviews should not go unmentioned. They should be essentially the same as every other monthly review. The quarterly reviews might provide an occasion for a little more brainstorming about what is happening and why. The end-year review is a good time to look back at the previous budget cycle and budget year. Ask what you can learn from events to make the next budget better still.

Should you bin the budget?

A majority of corporations and not-for-profit organizations use budgets as the main instrument of financial control, and often as a key measure of performance. In many cases, budgets have become onerous, bureaucratic burdens. Consequently, it is popular to criticize them and search for alternatives – which usually involve cost targets, activity-based costing, categorized investment appraisal, flexible or rolling budgets or a balanced scorecard approach.

The striking point about budgets and all of these so-called *alternatives* is that corporations should be using all these things in conjunction anyway. I do not know about you, but I would not want my performance to be measured on how well I controlled spending on office stationery alone. Moreover, I do not see how I could judge the success of things I manage using beanie bean-counting alone. But it is also clear that the big ducks upstairs need to plan and control company finances, not least cash flow. If there is a problem, it is not the concept of budgets, but their execution, which is in question. A budget is a useful tool if it is used sensibly, is as unbureaucratic as possible, and is just one of a range of measurements and controls.

Ten hard questions to ask or be asked

1 Why didn't I/we start the budget process a month earlier so that we could have met the deadlines?

2 Just because we are already spending $x on that, does it make it right?

3 Are these spending plans graded according to importance/expected returns?

4 If I had to hack out 10%, what would I cut?

5 Is our budgeting process too rigid? Should we use rolling and/or flexible budgets?

6 Are we consistent in format and assumptions across the organization?

7 Who set these targets? Does the manager who will have to operate within them believe in them?

8 Does the budget form part of a wider set of performance measures? If not, why not?

9 How well are we monitoring progress? What is the trend in the trend?

10 Did we complete an effective post-mortem and learn from the past?

What's next?

In the previous chapter we brought together the topics previously discussed, in a review of project appraisal and management. This chapter did a similar thing, looking at management control over the numbers. The next chapter looks at some additional techniques to help you make better decisions when managing the numbers.

23

making better decisions

'Human beings, who are almost unique in having the ability to learn from the experience of others, are also remarkable for their apparent disinclination to do so.'

Douglas Adams

1
2
3
4
5
6
7
8
9
10
11
12
13
14
15
16
17
18
19
20
21
22
23
24

▶ Chapter survival toolkit

▶ Overview

This chapter discusses decision-making methods which can be used under conditions of uncertainty and risk. The chapter starts by looking at three general techniques. It then reviews the important topics of break even and profit maximization, capacity planning, pricing, and inventory control.

▶ Prerequisites

Parts of this chapter stand alone. However, the following pages also build on everything preceding it in this book. One specific topic you may wish to refresh in your mind is the arithmetic of the normal distribution discussed in Chapter 5.

▶ Mastering more advanced decision-making techniques

After reading this chapter, you should be able to answer the following questions:

1 What is PMI? How would you use it when factors in a decision are hard to quantify?

2 What is expected payoff? Why would you use it in decision making when you can quantify the likelihood of various outcomes? Would you automatically opt for the highest expected payoff?

3 What is break even? Why is it important? To what period does it apply?

4 What is the margin of safety? Why is it important?

5 How does a break-even chart show you where profits are maximized?

6 Does capacity planning apply only to manufacturing? Why is capacity planning important for all businesses?

7 How can you calculate the minimum economic sales quantity and price? Why is it important?

8 How can you determine your optimum level of inventory? What is the re-order point? What is a buffer stock?

9 How can you use the normal distribution to quantify risk?

10 Which techniques discussed in this chapter cannot be supplemented with risk analysis using the normal curve?

> 'An approximate answer to the right question is worth far more than a precise answer to the wrong one.'
>
> **John Tukey**

Understand better, report better

Every manager is forced to take choices and make decisions based on imperfect information and uncertainty. However, if you can quantify the unknowns you move from uncertainty to risk – and, it has to be said, there are some neat techniques for handling risk. A few of the most useful ones are introduced in this chapter. We are also going to build on the previous pages by examining break even, profit maximization, pricing policies, capacity planning, and inventory control.

Tough decisions

You will frequently have to choose between competing options when you do not have all the facts, when the outcomes are uncertain, and sometimes when you cannot even quantify any or all of the forces in play. Start by considering three decision-making techniques: *Plusses and minuses* for situations which are hard to quantify, *expected payoff* for making decisions under risk, and the use of the *normal distribution* for quantifying risk.

Plusses and minuses

One way to analyse the factors that are hard to quantify is to use a plusses, minuses, interesting ideas (PMI) table. For example, you have in front of you a proposal to rework your company's website. Assume that it is a brochure site with no e-commerce benefits. You could draw up a little spreadsheet as follows, in which you create three lists of benefits, negatives and interesting points. You give each entry a subjective score on a scale of, say, –10 to +10. Note that there is not necessarily any direct association between the entries on any one row.

Plusses	Score	Minuses	Score	Interesting	Score
Will enhance image	8	Expensive	−4	May help attract new investment	7
Will demonstrate our use of latest standards	4	Will divert staff from other projects	−3	May reduce demand for printed brochures	2
Total	12	Total	−7	Total	9
Overall score (12 − 7 + 9)					14

Normally, of course, there would be many more rows. I have just used two to show the broad idea. The scoring helps you assess the relative importance of each factor and the overall rating of the project. The range of possible overall scores will be $\pm$ (10×2 rows) = ± 20. A relatively large positive figure, as here, indicates a 'go'. A negative result suggests caution.

Note that this technique was documented by Edward de Bono. His *six thinking hats*, although not a numerical technique, is interesting. See this book's website for a link.

▶ Expected payoffs

Now we should move on to consider decision making under risk – a situation where various possible outcomes *can* be quantified. Essentially, you estimate the likelihood of various outcomes and choose the one with the highest expected payoff. Let me give an example.

Suppose that the new website discussed above could have an e-commerce angle. You do not have any direct experience of Internet sales through your existing site, so you are not confident about the likely outcome. However, this does not stop you running the numbers and making a range of estimates.

Assume that you have four options (a site with a few test products for sale, a medium-size site, and a large catalogue site, or, of course, a site with no e-commerce angle). For simplicity, we will work with three possible levels of sales (low, average or high). By estimating the costs associated with developing, hosting, managing and promoting each size site, the numbers of hits and the proportions that will turn into sales, the net revenue from sales, and so on, we can arrive at the estimated net profit or loss associated with each option. These figures are shown in the body of the following table.

Row 4 shows the probabilities (expressed as proportions) that might be associated with each level of sales. For example, you might cautiously project a 50% chance of low sales, and only a 20% possibility of high sales. The right-hand column (column E) shows the expected payoff for each option. These expected payoffs are weighted averages of the rows, calculated as shown below the table.

> 'Is it better to have enough ideas for some of them to be wrong, than to be always right by having no ideas at all.'
>
> **Edward de Bono**

	A	B	C	D	E
1	Website decision table				
2	Net profit, dollars		Level of sales		Expected
3		Low	Average	High	payoff
4	Probabilities	0.50	0.30	0.20	
5	No e-commerce	–	–	–	–
6	Small site	7,500	15,000	100,000	28,250
7	Medium site	–10,000	25,000	175,000	37,500
8	Large site	–75,000	60,000	250,000	30,500

The formula in cell E6 is as follows:
=(B6*B4)+(C6*C4)+(D6*D4)
=(7,500 * 0.50) + (15,000 * 0.30) + (100,000 * 0.20)

Note: The combination of low sales and a medium or large site is expected to result in a net loss.

In principle, you select the option with the highest expected payoff – a medium-size site in this example. However, as you can see, the expected payoffs are very closely matched. My first instinct is to suggest opting for the small site for a couple of reasons. In absolute money terms, the expected payoff from the small site is not that different from the payoff from the medium site. Moreover, on these figures, there is a 50% likelihood that the medium site will make a loss. And, of course, it is often better to move ahead in small steps – in this instance, to obtain knowledge with a small site and build on that experience by expanding later.

In arriving at the net profit for each of the four options, you will have calculated the internal rate of return, or net present value. You should also take these into account when assessing the expected payoffs. The small site quite possibly also offers the highest expected payoff relative to the assets employed – further validating its selection as the best option.

By the way, the results of this analysis are very definitely not set in stone. If you alter the probabilities in the above table, the highest expected payoff can change. You can download the table from this book's website and try it.

Overall, the message is that expected payoff tables give you a useful framework for decision-making analysis, but are they are only one of the tools available. Let us move on to consider decision-making where the range of possibilities is viewed as continuous instead of being broken into discrete steps.

▶ Be certain about uncertainty

You know the routine. You have run the figures through your spreadsheets and produced a solid projection of sales, production, spending or whatever. You have presented the numbers to the board or management committee. All has gone well. Now it is time for questions. The first one: *how confident are you about this forecast?* This is where you could be torn apart by the ifs, maybes, and perhaps.

The problem is that you know, and they know, that your forecast is likely to be a bit out. However, it is fair to say that unless something drastic happens, the range of potential outcomes is likely to be clustered around your central estimate. The probability that the actual figure will be any given amount decreases as you move further and further away from the expected figure. For example, if your prediction is that sales will be $100 million, you might say that there is only a 15% chance that they will be below $95 million.

In many instances, you can assume that the likely outcomes for your forecasts are distributed normally – as illustrated in Fig. 23.1. (Look back at Chapter 5 if you need a refresher on the normal distribution.) Recall that if you know the mean and standard deviation of the normal, you know everything that there is to know.

For forecasting, the mean is simply your central expectation – $100 million in the example here. The standard deviation is a measure of spread. If you can make one other estimate you have an indication of the spread and so you can calculate the standard deviation. Here, we said that there is a *15% chance that sales will be below $95 million*. This is remarkably useful, because if you look back at Fig 5.6 you will see that approximately 15% of a distribution is below one standard deviation from the mean. In other words, one standard deviation is $100 – $95 = $5 million. (You could also have found the standard deviation by estimating that there was a 15% chance that sales would be above $105 million – because the normal is symmetrical).

Armed with the mean and standard deviation of your forecast or projection, you can assess the risk of any particular outcome. For example, if you are told that you will receive a handsome bonus if sales top $110 million, what are the odds of success? Well, this target is 2 standard deviations above the mean (i.e. the z-score is 2). If you refer to Fig. 5.6, you will see that there is a 2.3% chance of exceeding $110 million. Maybe you need to revisit your sales and marketing plan. You can apply this analysis to many business situations, as discussed below.

Fig. 23.1 The normal distribution

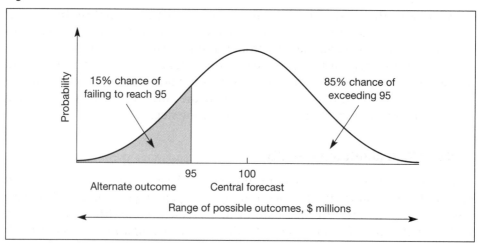

362

Break even

Even if you skipped the first 22 chapters of this book and started reading here, you will be aware that practically every business incurs costs even if it is not making any sales. There are *fixed costs* – rent, salaries, and so on – that have to be paid regardless. It hardly needs to be said that you need to know the level of sales you must achieve in order to cover these fixed costs, to avoid making a loss. The point at

Beanies describe the analysis discussed here at **cost-volume-profit (CVP)** or **profit-volume(PV)** analysis. **Break even** works for me.

which you are moving from loss to profit is known as break even.

To state the obvious, you break even when you just cover the costs of buying or making the product (variable costs) and other production and operating expenses (fixed costs). Here is an example. Suppose that you pay $80 a day in rental and other fixed costs, that you buy widgets for $1 each, and that you sell them for $5. Clearly, variable costs are $1 and *net revenue* is $4 per widget. You can probably see that you have to sell 20 widgets a day to break even – to cover your $80 fixed costs and the *variable* cost of sales. The twenty-first widget starts earning you net profit.

By the way, beanies refer to the $4 net revenue as the *contribution* to fixed costs and – ultimately – profits. If you divide the contribution by the sales price per unit ($5 in this example) you have the rather ugly named profit-volume ratio (0.80 in this example). In plain English, each dollar of sales is contributing 80 cents to the bottom line. If it is OK with you, I will refer to this price-volume thing as the *contribution ratio*. Accordingly:

Break even sales volume = fixed costs ÷ contribution (net revenue) per unit
= 80 ÷ 4 = 20 units

Break even sales value = fixed costs ÷ contribution ratio
= 80 ÷ 0.80 = $100

If your goal is to make a profit of $20 per day, you can deduce the target level of sales as:

Required sales volume = (fixed costs + required profits) ÷ contribution per unit
= (80 + 20) ÷ 4 = 25 units

Required sales value = (fixed costs + required profit) ÷ contribution ratio
= (80 + 20) ÷ 0.80 = $125

Of course, if you are operating at sales of $125 a day, and you wish to push up profits by, say $25 a day, you can rearrange the formula to this:

Change in sales volume = required change in profits ÷ contribution per unit
= 20 ÷ 4 = 5 units

As you can probably see, you can calculate break even for any period: a day, month, year, the life of a project, etc. If you have a monthly budget to meet, you may have to calculate these figures on a monthly basis. Generally, though, it is better to work with longer periods in order to average out seasonality, and deal with varying costs and prices over a wide range of sales and output.

▶ Break even illustrated

If you examine how your gross sales revenue rises as sales increase, you will find a curve similar to the one shown in Fig. 23.2. The more you sell, the more you earn. The curve flattens off because sales usually taper away as the market becomes saturated.

The chart also shows how costs increase with quantity. This curve starts above zero because of the fixed expenses that you have to meet even if you are not doing anything. The curve then slopes more gently than sales, reflecting the fact that prices exceed product costs (presumably!). However, the curve will turn upwards at higher volumes due to the quaintly named *law of diminishing returns* – you have to start employing more sales people who become more and more difficult to manage. ... Moreover, in some conditions, fixed cost will increase in a sharp steps. Recall from Chapter 12 that fixed costs are unchanged over a specific range. At certain quantities, there will be extra *fixed* expenditure on additional machinery, real estate, staff, and so on.

The point where the two curves cross indicates break even. This presupposes a perhaps unrealistic level of accuracy in the projections. If you are operating close to break even, you might want to use the normal to estimate the likelihood of staying out of the red, as outlined above.

Fig. 23.2 In the black?

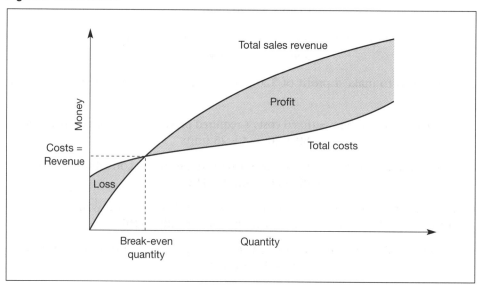

▶ Safety margins

The gap between actual or forecast sales and break even is known as the margin of safety. It reveals the extent by which sales can fall before losses are sustained. In the example here, where sales are $125 and the break- even sales value is $100:

Margin of safety ratio   = (sales – break-even sales) ÷ sales
= ($125 – $100) ÷ 100
= 25%

This shows that sales are 25% above the break even level. Put another way, they can fall by 25 ÷ (100 + 25) = 20% before you are in trouble. A useful number to know.

▶ Profit maximization

Given that profit equals sales less costs, you can also see from Fig. 23.2 that profits are maximized where the sales and spending curves are furthest apart. This point may be way off the chart to the right, although at some level profits and costs usually start to converge for the reasons mentioned above. The curves may even meet at a second, upper limit of break even.

Accordingly, by extending this analysis using cost and revenue projections as discussed in Chapters 10 to 14, you can identify your lower break even point, possibly your maximum profits, and maybe the upper limit on sales. The point where profits are maximized is perhaps the *optimum* sales and production level, depending on capacity.

▶ Capacity planning

When you are fully staffed and fully stretched and your machinery is processing the largest volume of products possible, you are operating at 100% of capacity. You will know what this volume is from the analysis in Chapter 13. Remember, though, that as with fixed costs, capacity is only fixed until you change it – you could, for example, close down a production line, or open a new factory.

Continuing with the previous example. Suppose you calculate that the largest number of widgets that you can turn over in a day is 100, due to limits on storage, packing, distribution, etc. (Capacity is not just about production.) You have just established that you break even at 20 widgets a day. Accordingly, break even is at a comfortably low 20% of capacity, as follows:

Break even capacity use   = break even sales volume ÷ capacity × 100
= 20 ÷ 100 × 100
= 20%

'Logic doesn't apply to the real world.'

Marvin Lee Minsky

Moreover, if you estimated that profits will be maximized at sales of 80 widgets, you know that your profit-optimized capacity utilization is $80 \div 100 = 80\%$. It happens that this squares away nicely with your actual optimum capacity use. It should do, because I made up the figures. I knew that in this example, if production rises much against 80%, machinery wears out more rapidly, replacement, maintenance costs and overtime pay soar (these were in the break-even analysis) and tempers fray. If your profit-optimized capacity use is significantly out of line with your actual optimum capacity level, you need to revisit your production and operating plans.

However, there is little point in setting up your organization to produce at the optimum level for the resources you can deploy, if your sales machinery or the market cannot keep up. Sales may never reach the profit-maximizing optimum of 80 units in this example, because there is not enough demand or because your competitors move into your lucrative market. Clearly, you need to pull all the factors at play into balance in your forecasting and planning.

▶ Marginal likelihood of shutting down

Would you sell your products for less than they cost? Does this sound likely? Unless you had some very special reason for wanting to make (or, at least, to accept) a loss you will sell one more widget only if the revenue from that sale exceeds its cost to you. But what, exactly, is the cost?

Recall in the above example that you buy widgets for $1 each and sell them for $5 and you have fixed costs of $80 a day.

If you sell just one widget in a day, *your total*, *average* and *marginal costs* are $81. If you sell two widgets, *total costs* edge up $82, *average total cost per widget* slips to $42 and the *marginal cost per item* plummets to $1.

Marginal cost is the expense associated with selling one more item (the *incremental* cost, or in beanie-speak, the *differential*). In this example, the total cost will rise steadily, the average cost will continue falling, and the marginal cost of every widget after the first one will remain fixed at $1. Except that it won't. At some point the marginal cost will start rising due to limited supply of widgets or the additional costs of employing staff, renting more space, trucking more widgets – the *law of diminishing returns* nearly always rears its ugly head sooner or later.

At sales of 40 widgets a day the *average total cost* has slipped to $3. Suppose that rationing pushes up the amount that you have to pay for the forty-first widget to $4 (and your buying costs per unit will continue to increase thereafter). Marginal cost has gone back above average cost, so average cost must rise. This is obvious if you think about the way that an average is calculated.

If you were to plot these trends, you would see a chart similar to Fig. 23.3. You will spot two key figures:

Fig. 23.3 Shut down or expand?

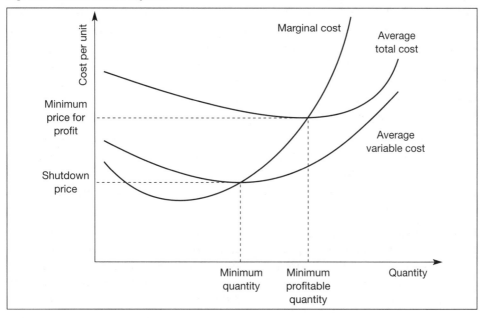

- ◆ **Shutdown price.** If your income per unit is less than minimum *average variable cost* per unit (less than the point where *marginal cost = average variable cost*) you are not covering your variable costs. In other words, if gross revenue per widget is less that $1, you might as well shut up shop and spend your days on the beach.

- ◆ **Minimum economic price.** If your income per unit is less than the lowest point in your average total cost curve (where *average total cost = marginal cost*) you are not covering fixed and variable costs. If you sell widgets for less than $3, you will make a net loss.

If you are selling between your shutdown and minimum economic prices, you are covering the variable costs of the product, but not your fixed costs. You are making a loss, but at least you are earning more than if you did nothing. For example, if you are selling widgets for between $1 and $3, you are recovering some of your fixed costs. You need to develop a sales strategy to move to full profitability

As you will already have noticed, you can apply the *normal* to marginal analysis and calculate the likelihood of various outcomes. An interesting exercise, if you feel so inclined, is to assume that costs are distributed normally around the central expectation and establish a *range* of probable outcomes.

> 'We are usually convinced more easily by reasons we have found ourselves than by those which have occurred to others.'
>
> **Blaise Pascal**

▶ Inventory costs

Too much inventory costs you money. It ties up cash in stock that can, of course, become obsolete or damaged. At the other extreme, not enough inventory tests customer loyalty and leads to lost or delayed sales. The projections discussed in Chapter 13 reveal your *required* inventory levels. However, this is not necessarily the *optimum* level, which can be identified using some simple arithmetic. The starting point is to recognize that in this respect the only costs that vary are:

◆ **Ordering costs** – the costs of processing purchase orders, taking delivery, tooling up for a production run, and so on. Ordering costs per unit decline as volumes increase due to economies of scale.

◆ **Carrying costs** – including the costs of storage, insurance and funding. These increase steadily with volume.

Figure 23.4 shows these costs separately and combined. The top curve is the sum of the figures that are used to plot the lower two curves. The point where inventory costs are lowest – the optimum inventory level where ordering and carrying costs are minimized – is where they equal each other. In other words, in any one period, the quantity of inventory that you should order is the quantity where:

Total ordering costs = Total carrying cost

or

Number of orders × cost per order = Average inventory × carry cost per unit

Fig. 23.4 Optimum inventory level

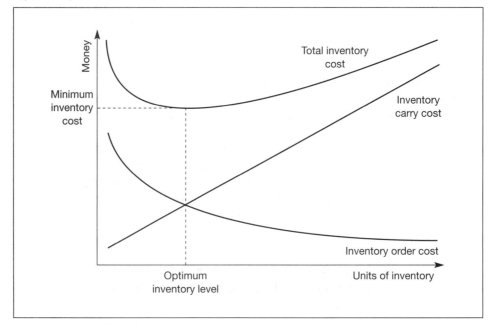

For *just-in-time* inventory management, the reorder point is triggered when inventory falls to a level equivalent to daily demand × delivery time in days. This presupposes that demand is steady and delivery is always on time. Maybe you want to carry a buffer stock?

The optimum inventory level is based on an accurate projection of sales. If demand runs higher than expected, you could run out of stock. This is another situation where the *normal* can be used:

1 Forecast sales for a given period; find the mean and standard deviation using the techniques explained on p. 361 *(Be certain about uncertainty)*.

2 Decide the acceptable risk associated with having too much or too little inventory (i.e. we will accept a 10% risk of running out of stock).

3 Find the sales volumes associated with these percentages (i.e. in the tails of the normal curve).

4 You have the required range for inventory.

Ten hard questions to ask or be asked

1 Could we improve our decision making by using quantitative techniques? Which ones?

2 Have we identified all the quantitative and qualitative factors which we should take into account before we reach a decision?

3 Is risk modelled correctly? If the normal distribution has been used, does it really apply?

4 What is the most important message from the risk assessment?

5 What is our break-even point for each product? How does it relate to our targets? Is the margin of safety adequate?

6 How much does each product contribute to the bottom line? Which is best? Worst? Why?

7 Are we operating efficiently, at a high level of capacity use? Do we have sufficient margin to meet additional demand? Do we have slack capacity that we could be using to better effect?

8 How do our prices relate to the economic minimum? Have we used common sense costing?

9 How does our inventory relate to expected demand? Do we have an acceptable buffer stock? Or too much of a safety margin?

10 Have we used the correct assumptions? What can we learn from our competitors? Clients? Independent research and commentary?

▶ Conclusion

This concludes our little foray into some of the more advanced decision-making techniques. I hope that you found it useful. It might even have encouraged you to go back through your forecasts and projections from earlier chapters. I have to say that my personal favourite is the normal distribution as applied to the future (as discussed throughout this chapter). Statisticians may not be overjoyed by the lack of rigour with which it is sometimes applied in business situations. But from a management viewpoint, any quantification of uncertainty and risk is welcome.

the finance director did it

'Then there is the man who drowned crossing a steam with an average depth of six inches.'

W.I.E. Gates

▶ Chapter survival toolkit

▶ Overview

This chapter wraps up the book by pulling together the previous chapters and summarizing some of the things that you should watch out for when forecasting, estimating, reviewing, planning, monitoring, analysing and presenting. In addition, there is a summary of what to do when things go wrong.

▶ Prerequisites

You can read this chapter at any time.

▶ Mastering managing the numbers

After reading this book, you should be able to answer the following questions:

1 How can I measure the performance of my business area? Why are trends and ratios so important?

2 What is common sense costing and why should I use it?

3 Are financial measures adequate? What other metrics should I watch?

4 How can I measure risk and use it to my advantage?

5 Why do projects, budgets and other plans go wrong, and how can I guard against it?

6 How do financial, tax and management accounts differ? Why are they each important?

7 Why should I question our bean counters? How can they help me in my job?

8 If accounting is so rigorous and pedantic, how come the same numbers can be made to tell different stories?

9 Why do I have to do the analysis myself? Why can't I trust published reports and credit rating agencies?

10 How will *managing the numbers* help me in my career?

> 'Do not put your faith in what statistics say until you have carefully considered what they do not say.'
>
> **William W. Wyatt**

> ▶ **Jargon watch**
>
> You will be happy to hear that there is almost no heavy new jargon in this chapter. Four new terms are listed at left. If you have withdrawal symptoms, you can go on to read *The finance director's language* (see p. 383) – and visit this book's website.
>
> **New beanie buzz words**
> Cookie-jar accounting
> Big bath
> Special purpose entities
> Channel stuffing

▶ Managing the numbers

Assuming that you have not skipped straight to the end to see whodunnit, I congratulate you on making it this far. We have taken a fairly hectic journey through the issues surrounding *managing the numbers* and we have covered a significant amount of ground. Thank you for staying with me. I guess that now is a good moment to pause and look back over the topics covered.

We have discussed forecasting, estimating, reviewing, analysing and interpreting numbers. Moreover, we have considered these tasks in relation to topics as diverse as evaluating production, sales and overheads; preparing budgets; appraising projects, producing financial statements and reports; measuring individual or corporate performance; raising and investing funds; and undertaking a whole range of other jobs. The close interrelationship of all numerical issues should be clear. These final few pages pull together some of the key themes in this book.

▶ Forecasting and estimating

When looking ahead, the trick is to identify what needs to be *forecast*, what can be *estimated* in relation to the forecast, and what needs to be treated as an *assumption* (a given). Examine the historical data using a spreadsheet to assist with the analysis. Find the patterns. Look for relationships with other factors, both internal (e.g. spending on advertising) and external (such as exchange rates). Apply management judgement and business knowledge, and make the forecast. Use ratios (headcount, spending, sales, etc.) to make the dependent estimations. Beg or borrow assumptions from reliable parties (government statisticians, economic institutes, etc.).

That said, query assumptions and relationships. Ask what if? For example, what if interest rates rose 5%, sales fell 5% or your competitor cut prices by 5%? Use a distribution such as the *normal* to model risk. Assess break even, capacity limits, minimum prices, etc. Do the same for each product line. Question what you are doing, and why.

▶ Planning

There is a great deal of truth in the old adage *if you can't measure it, you can't manage it.* Before you begin any analysis, or set out on a new path or project, do some planning (it seems as if I should plug my book here, *The Definitive Business Plan* 2002, 2nd edn, FT Prentice Hall). Identify what you can quantify, select performance metrics, and set milestones or targets. In other words, know in advance what you expect to see. Use the techniques in Chapters 21 to 23 estimate the risks and set margins of latitude. Then you can measure the results against these expectations to see if everything is staying on track.

Break projects into small, reversible steps. Map out your path in advance. Do not centralize budget planning; ensure that individual managers are involved and responsible. Prefer flexible, rolling budgets. Set assumptions and frameworks from the top down; set budget plans from the bottom up. Ensure that you provide an adequate contingency reserve. Do not confuse budget targets with performance measures; financial metrics should be only part of the measuring and reporting process. Continuously monitor the outturn; be prepared to restate budgets.

▶ Review

When given figures, question them ruthlessly. Do not assume that because they are in a complex spreadsheet they must be right. Check that the calculations are entered correctly – and then check the basis for the calculations. Again, check the assumptions and relationships. Beware of spurious accuracy. Create charts to see if trends look reasonable. See also the following comments.

▶ Monitoring and performance review

Anyone would be overwhelmed by too many metrics. The fewer that you can get by with, the better; 10 or 20 for any one area is probably the maximum. Remember also to look at unquantified factors, such as morale, prestige, and public relations. Guard against scope creep (where deliverable results expand over time). Be prepared to redefine targets as necessary.

Measure the trend, and the trend in the trend. For example, there are clear warning signs if sales are running below target or spending is above target. You should also be cautious if sales are dropping nearer and nearer to the target each month, or if the gap between costs and the target is narrowing over time. The same applies to non-financial indicators, such as headcount, production levels, quality control failures, bugs in software under development, and so on.

Use common-sense costing to determine the costs associated with each and every product, service and activity undertaken. Look for ratios everywhere. Always try to improve them. Be aware of the difference between profits and profitability when examining margins and your product mix.

Do not review your activities in isolation. You might be doing fine, but are your competitors doing better? Benchmark yourself against your competitors and against the *best of breed* for specific activities such as inventory control or overseas sourcing of supplies.

▶ Presentations

When called upon to present numbers, start by identifying your storyline. What is it that you want to say? There is always a message, even if it is that you are reporting or predicting 'no change'. What else do you have to tell your audience? Always assume that they are unfamiliar with the numbers, even if you told them the same story last month. Of course, be tactful. No one likes to be reminded that they were not paying attention, did not understand, or have simply forgotten. Perhaps begin with a statement such as: as *you will recall, by doing x, y, and z, we are in the situation where* ... No matter how depressing or embarrassing the subject matter, try to end on a positive note.

When you know your story, plan the steps that will take your audience through it as smoothly as possible. Try to use handouts, a whiteboard or a computer presentation. If you decide on a Microsoft PowerPoint-type presentation, keep it simple. Skip the distracting razzmatazz and fancy transitions – although judicious use of illustrations can help get the message across. Try to present data in chart format. Do not crowd charts – one message per picture is a good rule of thumb.

Round all numbers to as few effective figures as possible (e.g. two or three), and consign more detailed figures to annexes, footnotes, or at least separate tables. Do not present figures in isolation. *Sales were $x* is not very meaningful. *Sales were $x, 15% higher than in the same month last year* is more useful. Generally, prefer percentages for comparisons. Compare like with like (remember seasonality).

Rehearse your presentation. Ask yourself if it really tells the story that you want it to tell, and if the story you are telling is the right one. Then criticize it and make a list of the questions people will ask (at least some of which will be the obvious questions). Put yourself in the position of various members of your audience. Consider their personal agendas to see from which angle they will come at you. Finally, of course, prepare answers and slides or handouts for the potential questions. Always try to be one step ahead of your audience.

▶ Financial reporting

According to an old joke, every business has at least three sets of accounts: one for the tax authorities, one for the bankers, and one for the owners. Of course, the implication is that these figures are fixed or faked. You definitely do not want to be part of this. But where you are in control, you will want to restate the numbers to extract maximum value. Management, tax and financial reporting are each driven by differing objectives, and each produces a different view of the same numbers. In general, one should not influence the others directly. You want to select the most appropriate format for the task in hand – and you may well end up with three legitimately different sets of accounts.

> 'Not all dishonest accounting is legal.'
>
> **Anon.**

▶ Management accounting

For *managing the numbers* on a day-to-day basis, you need, as anyone would guess, management accounts. These will give you the most realistic view of events, since they are unencumbered by any statutory reporting requirements. Monthly figures are usually best – unless you are in retailing, in which case four-week periods offer good comparability. Use accruals accounting and common-sense costing. Bring in non financial metrics; ratios to headcount and volumes (sales, production, etc.) can be very revealing.

▶ Inspecting internal reports

Remember that your subordinates and colleagues who prepare financial reports are possibly unaware of, and probably not bound by, generally accepted accounting principles and accounting standards. These people might make mistakes of classification; and they may even indulge in deliberate window dressing, or worse. Ratios and charts can help you spot errors and oddities. Look back at Fig. 12.5 for a reminder of some areas where managers massage costs. Depending on the level of complexity of the reporting, you might need to be alert for the issues mentioned in the next paragraphs.

▶ Divisions, subsidiaries, partners and other investments

The rules for inspecting internal accounts apply when assessing any financials. In addition, there are some additional areas that deserve close attention. Crawl over the notes to the accounts; check contingent liabilities and off-balance sheet items. Recall that currency mismatches can result in unwelcome and unplanned losses (or gains). Watch for exceptional and extraordinary items which sneak in below the line in the profit and loss account.

Remember, there are numerous tricks that can be played with assets. Their sale with an agreement to repurchase at a later date can remove them from the balance sheet. They might be revalued downwards to enable the sale of assets or the whole business at below market cost. Or they might have been revalued upwards to inflate the balance sheet and the net worth of the business.

Question all transactions between related companies and business units. Market prices may go out of the window. Tax authorities and accounting regulators are strict about *transfer pricing*, but it is still common for a company to fix the rates at which it does business with related entities – and to conveniently convert profit centres into cost centres. Watch also for countertrade. Obviously, unless transactions are valued and reported honestly, this can artificially lower revenues. It can also lead to surprise hidden costs.

'There is no true number in accounting, and if there were, auditors would be the last people to find it.'

Harvey Pitt

>> **What they don't want you to know**

In addition to the tricks listed in Fig.12.5, techniques used to pad profits and smooth income include the following:

Cookie-jar accounting. Overestimating liabilities (sales returns, loan losses, etc.) in good years provides a cookie jar of hidden reserves which can be pulled out in lean years. See Chapter 15.

The big bath. Financial restructuring, with a one-off charge below the line, provides an opportunity to sweep all manner of losses under the carpet. See Chapter 19.

Merger magic. Much the same as a big bath, a merger provides an opportunity to write off operating costs, below the line of course. See Chapter 19.

Disappearing details. The details of transactions put through subsidiaries (read *special purpose entities*) can conveniently disappear from the books (Chapter 19).

Transfer tricks. Many tricks can be played with artificial prices used to record transactions between related entities (see p. 376, and Chapter 20).

(Im)materiality. It's highly convenient if bad news is below the threshold of materiality and thus does not have to be disclosed explicitly (Chapter 8).

Unrealistic revenue recognition. Force-feeding distributors ('channel stuffing'), prematurely booking shipments and recording other spook sales artificially inflate revenue (Chapter 13).

Profiting from pensions. Income from over-funded pension plans can provide windfall gains (and these may be paper profits), especially when stock markets are booming (Chapter 19).

Obscuring with options. Paying employees in stock options can keep substantial compensation packages out of the profit and loss account (Chapter 19).

Derived values. It is hard enough to assess the market value of assets and liabilities; the use of derivatives to hedge exposure can totally obscure the picture (Chapter 20).

Playing footsie. A host of other items can be relegated to the footnotes to the financial statements (i.e. hidden *off-balance sheet*), see Chapter 15.

Fraud. Finally, it has to be said, that not all dishonest accounting is legal (you did read that correctly) – as shown by numerous recent financial scandals, some mentioned in these pages.

▶ Comparing competitors

Recall that no two businesses will produce identical results even if they start with identical inputs. Important differentiating factors include relative levels of maturity, product lines, industry sectors, operating environments and operating cultures. On top of this, internal accounting policies and national accounting requirements will further influence reported results. Obviously, you need to keep this very much in mind when examining financials.

Try to restate your competitors' financials on a similar basis to yours. For every item, ask yourself why it was recorded as it was and if it could have been stated differently. Question the quality of the assets. Get hold of, or estimate, headcount, market share, and sales volumes; calculate ratios for everything and compare them to yours.

When things go wrong

No matter how thorough your planning and how diligent your stewardship, things can still go wrong. The most common problems are cost overruns or revenue undershoots. Occasionally, new targets are imposed, possibly from above because one department or division has problems, but in any event probably due to external factors such as unexpected economic developments or the withdrawal of funding. Whatever the problem, the implications are similar: the choices usually boil down to cutting costs, finding new revenue or obtaining new finance.

Why did it turn bad?

Finding out why things went wrong occasionally helps with the current situation. More often than not the information is better used for averting another crisis in the future. The discrepancy between plan and outturn will relate to value, volume, or efficiency. Invariably, you will find that the problem arose because of poor planning or ineffective monitoring. Maybe the metrics were wrong, or perhaps they were not tracked carefully enough. Did you rely only on financial yardsticks? Or did new, unmonitored, factors creep in?

Boosting revenue

By and large, boosting income is the most popular solution in a crisis, but it is usually the most difficult outcome to achieve. Start, though, by reviewing accounts receivable. If your accounting people have gone to sleep, an apparent revenue slowdown might be nothing more than inefficiencies in collecting payments due. Otherwise, lacklustre sales may be the very origin of the problem. The business is probably operating at the highest level of sales achievable without spending more on marketing and, anyway, increasing revenue usually takes time – a luxury which may be a scare resource if you are in a crisis. However, if demand for your products is elastic, you might be able to slash prices to jump-start sales. Regardless of how pessimistic you feel, you will, of course, explore other possibilities for putting more business on the books.

New funding

The financing angle may be an attractive alternative. If your crisis is very short term, you might be able to speed up collections and stretch out payables, or obtain additional credit from your suppliers. One possibility might be to dispose of assets and lease them back. You could consider trying to increase borrowing if you have the longer-term profitability, positive cash flow, and asset backing to support more debt. The final resort in debt restructuring, or refunding, is to try to raise additional equity.

Cost cutting

By far the most common reaction to the problems mentioned above is to cut costs. It's basically quick and effective – in the short-term at least. If you have arrived here via the preceding chapters, you will have realized that you should always expect the unexpected. For example, when preparing spending plans and budgets, always grade the items according to priority. You will then know exactly what to pare away to meet lower targets while limiting the other downsides. If necessary, review the plans to find ways to save or postpone costs. Remember the three places to look for savings: *value, volume, efficiency*. Some hints are included in Fig. 24.1.

Fig. 24.1 Twenty areas to scour for cost savings

1 **Revisit your customer interface**: can you cut costs by taking orders and providing routine customer assistance online or with automated telephone systems?

2 **Charge effectively**: revisit your pricing policies; charge for things which were previously free (installation, customer helpdesk); charge for catalogues and samples (perhaps refundable against orders); take deposits and stage payments.

3 **Review the design of products and services**: are they over specified? Do technological developments allow the use of new, cheaper, components or production processes?

4 **Manage inventory**: cut the cost of stock carry; order smaller amounts, more frequently (i.e. just-in-time); standardize; where practical, centralize to avoid stocking the sale items in several locations; use software for online procurement.

5 **Renegotiate contracts** for supplies, distribution, rents, etc.

6 **Look for new sources of supply**, especially in lower-cost overseas markets.

7 **Stretch cycles**: defer replacements, make things last longer.

8 **Reduce cycles**: cut production and sales cycles.

9 **Lease** instead of buying.

10 **Defer capital spending** or consider buying refurbished items.

11 **Defer research and development**.

12 **Benchmark**: cut unnecessary processes; standardize; streamline; enhance efficiency.

13 **Use technology efficiently**: do not over specify; don't jump for the most technologically advanced solution, select the most efficient; where possible use the Internet for lower cost communications; use software to enhance efficiency, know your customers better, etc.; standardize on lower-cost desktop software, share little used packages among several users.

14 **Outsource**: buy services from specialists, especially where they have economies of scale/lower costs for other reasons.

15 **Convert cost centres into profit centres**: charging each department for use of internal services will help reduce demand for formerly 'free' services; consider making internal service providers compete with external sources.

16 **Manage consumables**: control the use of consumables; standardize; where practical, centralize to avoid stocking the same items in several locations.

17 **Control the payroll**: replace at least part of pay increases with performance bonuses, stock options, etc; fully-utilize personnel via cross-training, work-sharing, flexitime; cut unnecessary overtime; consider extending overtime instead of taking on new employees; eradicate bloat.

18 **Be ruthlessly strict with spending** on telecoms, consultants, travel, entertainment, and other areas subject to abuse or sloppy controls.

19 **Involve everyone**: ask all your employees to propose cost cutting measures. They may know better than you where there is wastage and inefficiency.

20 **Form partnerships**: cooperate with suppliers, vendors, and other business partners for economies of scale and new opportunities.

The biggest opportunity for cost cutting

Simply *managing the numbers* will probably open up the greatest opportunities for cost cutting. Good planning, sensible metrics and careful measuring in themselves will lead to greater efficiency and lower costs; it will also reveal where you can effect further savings and generate more revenue.

▶ Ten hard questions to ask or be asked

1 Do you believe these numbers? (Trust your hunch if it tells you that something is not quite right.)

2 Are you comparing enough, and like with like? (One figure in isolation is pretty useless. Remember seasonality – and factors which affect seasonal factors, such as unusual weather. Adjust for differences in accounting policies, etc.)

3 Have they told you the whole truth? What figures might have been conveniently brushed aside, or concealed in an average?

4 Are these financial accounts? Management accounts? Has commonsense costing been used?

5 Are the figures based on some generally accepted accounting principles? If so, which ones? Correctly? If not, what accidental or intended trickery might have been perpetrated?

6 Is the timing correct? What if the transaction or payment happened a month earlier? Later?

7 Are the other assumptions and relationships correct? What if sales, rates, prices, etc. changed by 5%?

8 Volumes look good, what of values? Or the other way around?

9 Are you being blinkered by your own agenda? Are others pursuing their own agendas?

10 Have you asked the really hard questions – of others and of yourself?

▶ Whodunnit?

Sadly, for me anyway, we are out of space. We have reached the final paragraph or two. If this were a detective story, whom would you suspect? I suppose it depends which role you have assumed. A typical manager would point the finger at the chief financial officer, who, after all, blocks expenses claims, holds back pay increases, and pours cold water on great ideas which appear not to be viable on purely financial grounds. IT propeller heads would also tend to blame the finance top dog, because so many IT projects are good for the enterprise but hard to quantify in monetary terms. The chief executive would probably share the same view, because, after all, who wants a subordinate who can wield more power than the boss?

From an external perspective, bankers and shareholders know that the books cannot be cooked without the chief financial officer's assent. The CEO or a group of directors might be bent on paying themselves excessive bonuses, massaging the numbers, or outright theft, but the CFO will have to be in on the plot before it can hatch.

Whichever way you look at it, finance directors have a tough job. Perhaps we should offer them some sympathy. It's not easy to become a bean counter. It took hard work and dedication. However, because of this they have only themselves to blame. Accordingly, make sure that they give you the figures and support that you need to do your job. Then go out and *manage the numbers*. Its not difficult, and it will give you a significant leg up on your journey to ever greater success. I wish you luck.

the finance director's language

This glossary contains a selection of the more obscure examples of beanie-speak. There are substantially more definitions in a searchable database on this book's website.

AAA Triple-A: the **credit rating** applied to the debt of the most credit-worthy of companies and sovereign borrowers.

above the line An entry in the **profit and loss account** or **income statement** above the **net profit** row.

absorption costing A dubious accounting method of **cost accounting** where overheads are allocated to products according to how much revenue they generate. For example, a product producing 40% of sales income is assumed to be responsible for (i.e. to absorb) 40% of overheads – which could be a complete nonsense. See **activity-based costing**.

accelerated depreciation Writing off proportionately more of the value of a fixed asset in the early years of its life, usually for tax reasons. See **depreciation**.

accounting equation The mind-numbing relationship of: **assets = liabilities + owners' equity**.

accounting period principle A beanie guiding principle: reporting based on specific (short) time periods. Also known as the time period principle.

accounting principles The basic concepts applied by bean counters. See also **generally accepted accounting principles.**

accounting ratio The relationship between two amounts, expressed as a ratio to aid interpretation. Part of a beanie's **vertical analysis/cross sectional analysis**.

accounting standards National rules specifying the methodology that bean counters should use for valuation, measurement and disclosure.

Accounting Standards Board ASB UK standards setting body; established in 1990; subsidiary of Financial Reporting Council, issues **Financial Reporting Standards**, etc.

aoeounting test Examination of sample of accounting records to see if they have been kept *by the book* and no one has been dipping their fingers in the till.

accounts payable A US term; known as **creditors** or trade creditors in the UK. Payments due to be made by the company to trade creditors, such as suppliers.

accounts receivable A US term; known as **debtors** or trade debtors in the UK. Payments that are owed to the company by trade debtors, such as customers.

accruals accounting Recording payments made and received according the dates to which the transactions relate, which are not necessarily the dates when money changes hands. Contrast with **cash accounting.**

accrued expense Expense recorded as due but not paid; similar to a prepaid expense (paid but not due).

accrued revenue Revenue recorded as earned but not yet received.

accumulated depreciation The total **write down** in the **book value** of an asset since it was acquired.

acid test Accounting ratio, liquidity: current assets other than inventory, divided by current liabilities – an indicator of **working capital** which eliminates **inventory valuation** issues. Also known as the quick-ratio and liquid ratio.

acquisition cost Spending on bringing a fixed asset into use; can include delivery, installation, and other costs usually treated as current expenses.

activity-based costing A more or less common-sense approach to **cost accounting**. For example, if 20% of your overheads are attributable to production of widgets, then that is the proportion of overheads that should be charged against that activity. See **absorption costing**.

actuary A morbid beanie who calculates probabilities for an insurance company.

additional paid-in capital Funds received by a company on the sale of its **stock/shares**, in excess of their **book value**.

aging report A list of the money you are owed by customers categorized according to the length of time since the invoices were issued.

allocating costs Assigning costs to individual products, processes and departments – accountants have made this simple concept complex and error-prone. See **cost accounting**.

amortization **Depreciation** for things you can't touch (goodwill, patents, copyright, etc.): the writing off of an intangible asset over a number of months or years; repayment of a loan by instalments.

analysis of variance Accountant's puffed-up term for the examination of why things turned out differently from the plans.

annual percentage rate – APR An interest rate standardized to take account of the frequency of compounding and, fees and other sneaky charges.

annuity An annual (**interest**) payment from an investment.

APR See **annual percentage rate**.

ASB See **Accounting Standards Board**.

ask The **offer** price for a currency or other **financial instrument**.

assets An item of value owned by, or owed to, a business. Opposite: **liability**.

asset stripping Buying a company, closing it down and selling its **assets** in order to make a one-time profit.

audit A formal scrutiny of accounting methods and records.

audit qualification A black mark in an **audit report** signifying that the **auditors** found some irregularity.

audit report A formal statement indicating the basis for an **audit** and its findings: when accompanying a set of **financial statements** the audit report indicates the basis on which the accounts were drawn up (e.g. US **GAAP**), whether the figures represent a true and fair view of the business. See also **audit qualification**.

auditor A pernickety bean counter who conducts a formal scrutiny of accounting methods and records.

authorized capital Authorized share capital (UK); authorized capital stock (US): the maximum amount of **stock/shares** that a company can issue, as defined in the company articles/bylaws.

available assets Assets that can be readily turned into cash.

available balance The spending power of a bank account; the **cleared balance** plus any unused **overdraft** allowance.

average cost Total costs divided by the number of units produced. See also **marginal cost.**

averaging **Inventory valuation** method based on – guess – the average cost of the items passing through stock in a given period.

Baa Another way of saying triple-B; a **credit rating** one step above **junk.**

balance sheet A **financial statement** showing a company's standing and net wealth at a moment in time.

bank reconciliation A formal ticking back of your own records against a bank statement to confirm that both you and the bank have correctly recorded all transactions.

BBB Triple B: A medium **credit rating** – one step above **junk.**

bean counter, beanie Endearing (?) nickname for an accountant.

below the line An entry in the **profit and loss** account or income statement below the *headline* **net profit** row; often erroneously overlooked by commentators.

beta A measure of the risk associated with holding shares in a company; a distribution used in project assessment to model expected completion times.

bid The price at which you can buy a financial instrument, such as a foreign currency. The **ask** or **offer** is the price at which you can sell the same paper. The difference between the two is the dealers' **spread**, or profit. Knowing this, it is easy to work out which is the bid and which is the ask or offer price.

blue chip A **triple-A** company.

bonds Debt – usually transferable with a fixed interest rate and specified redemption date.

book rate An arbitrary rate used for bookkeeping transactions, such as a **foreign exchange book rate.**

book value A quaint accounting concept that divorces bookkeeping from reality. The book value of anything, such as a machine, is what you paid for it less some arbitrary deduction for **depreciation.**

bottom line The headline **net profit** entry in a profit and loss account.

break even The volume of sales where cumulative revenues equal cumulative costs.

budget A financial plan and, usually, an operating target covering a specific period, typically 12 months.

budget pro forma A fill-in-the-blanks framework used to prepare a budget. See also **pro forma**.

business cycle The sequence of recession-depression-recovery-boom experienced in almost every economy; also known as a **trade cycle.**

called-up capital Money received by a company when shareholders have paid for part of the total issued **share capital.**

capacity use Production as a percentage of potential total production. Spare capacity means wasted resources, but room for growth.

capex Shorthand for **capital expenditure.**

capital Money raised by a company through the issue of **equity** and **debt.**

capital allowance The tax authorities' way of handling **depreciation**; a sum allowed to cover the cost of using/replacing **fixed assets.**

capital asset pricing model An approach to determining a company's **cost of capital** which assumes that borrowing costs are based on a risk-free interest rate plus a risk premium (or **beta**).

capital assets See **fixed assets.**

capital budget A **budget**, or spending plan, for acquiring **fixed assets.**

capital expenditure Essentially spending on items which will be consumed or used over a longer period than one year.

capital intensive Requiring a large amount money/**fixed assets** per employee or per unit of output.

capital spending Spending on capital goods which are expected to add to future output.

capitalization The stock market value of a company; the amount of money required to buy all the issued **shares/stock.**

carrying cost The cost of holding or owning assets, such as – for **inventory** – interest, insurance, obsolescence, spoilage, storage and taxes.

cash accounting Accounting based on the date when money changes hands. Contrast with **accruals accounting.**

cash budget A **budget** prepared in cash terms; a projection of **cash flow.**

cash flow The net surplus or deficit of money (i.e. folding stuff) generated by an entity or an activity (as opposed to **net profits**, which may have been earned on paper only).

cash flow statement A tabular financial report showing the net surplus or deficit of money generated by an entity or an activity. One of the key **financial statements.**

certified public accountant – CPA A bean counter with a formal qualification from a professional organization.

CFO See **chief finance officer.**

chart of accounts A list of the accounts used by an enterprise to record spending by category (e.g. office rents, stationery, sales, etc.).

chartered accountant A bean counter with a formal qualification from a professional organization.

chief finance officer/chief financial officer – CFO The top bean counter, reporting directly to the chief executive. Reportees will include a **financial controller** and **treasurer**, but preferably not the **internal auditor** who should remain independent.

circulating assets Assets which will be consumed or turned into cash in the ordinary course of business – **current assets.**

cleared balance A bank balance which includes only that money you definitely own; it excludes cheques/checks from third parties that have been added to the actual balance, but have not yet been confirmed as paid.

common sense costing Throwing ridiculous beanie concepts such as **absorption costing** out of the window and calculating total costs in the way that any sane manager would approach the topic.

common size A beanie term for converting financial amounts into **index numbers** where, for example, sales are given a value of 100 and all other amounts are shown as a percentage of that base. This assists with the comparison of two sets of accounts of differing sizes (or currencies).

common stock US term for ordinary **shares.**

company/corporation UK/US terms for an entity established for conducting business; it has a legal personality which is distinct from that of its owners and managers.

compound interest **Interest** that itself earns interest.

compounding Accumulating, or rolling up, as in **compound interest.**

comprehensive income A relatively new term: the absolute **bottom line** in a **profit and loss account/income statement** after taking account of various unrealized gains and losses which often get swept under the carpet.

comptroller An antiquated term for a **financial controller.**

conservatism A beanie guiding principle: pessimism at work; applying accounting policies and methods to arrive at the lowest possible profit figure. Also known as prudence.

consistency A beanie guiding principle: using the same accounting policies (for **depreciation, inventory valuation,** etc.) from one accounting period to the next.

consolidated Aggregated; the **financial statements** of a parent company and its subsidiaries combined as if they were a single entity.

constant prices Prices with the effect of inflation removed – as opposed to **current prices.**

contingency A bookkeeping reserve set aside to cover future costs which cannot be projected accurately.

contingent asset Possible future benefits, such as a beneficial settlement in litigation, mentioned in the **footnotes** to a **balance sheet. Contingent liabilities** are more common!

contingent liabilities Possible future costs, such as an adverse settlement in litigation, which are relegated to the **footnotes** of a **balance sheet.**

continuity principle A beanie guiding principle: the assumption that a business will continue to exist as a going concern for ever more.

contra account An account with the opposite balance than that which is usually expected – such as **depreciation** which is shown with the **assets** in a **balance sheet,** but which *subtracts* from the value of the assets.

contributed capital Paid up **share** capital in shares.

contribution This indicates the contribution to **fixed costs** and the **bottom line** derived from one unit of sales: the sales price less **variable costs** directly associated with selling the item. See also **break even.**

contribution ratio An indicator of how effectively sales contribute to the **bottom line: contribution** divided by sales price per unit.

controller See **financial controller.**

controlling interest Possession of enough voting **shares** to hold sway over decisions affecting a company's future; more than 50% guarantees an absolute majority.

conversion period The length of time between interest payments – crucial for determining **effective interest rates.**

cost accounting Accounting which apportions all **direct costs** and **overheads** in order to calculate the cost of producing one unit of anything (e.g. a widget); often highly arbitrary. See also **absorption costing, activity based costing, common sense costing, process costing, standard cost accounting.**

cost centre A department (e.g. your bean counters) or other business unit without income: maybe essential, but often looked upon as a burden. Compare with **profit centre.**

cost of capital The average interest rate paid by a company on its **debt** and **equity**

cost of ownership Advanced concept in costing which takes into account all costs, including irritations such as the cost of downtime for a computer.

cost of sales Expenses which are directly associated with producing and selling goods and services – excludes **overheads.**

Cost-volume-profit – CVP A silly beanie name for **break even** analysis.

coupon An interest payment on fixed-interest securities.

CPA See **critical path analysis.**

CPA A certified public accountant.

CPM Critical path method; see **critical path analysis.**

crash time The shortest time in which a project could be completed.

credit An amount entered in an account (traditionally on the right-hand side) recording a payment received; deferred payment; financial standing. See also **debit.**

credit rating A comment on the financial standing of an organization or country. Common ratings are triple-A (first class), triple-B (medium risk) and junk (highly speculative).

creditors UK shorthand for *trade creditors;* US terms are **accounts payable** or payables. Payments due to be made by the company to trade creditors, such as suppliers.

Critical path analysis/method – CPA/CPM A project planning technique which helps identify the shortest path to completion.

cross sectional data A snapshot at one moment in time, as opposed to a **time series.**

currency conversion The actual exchange of one currency for another when a transaction is effected (e.g. dollars for euros) – as opposed to **currency translation** which is a bookkeeping entry.

currency swap An exchange between two borrowers, each with relative advantage borrowing in different currencies.

currency translation A bookkeeping fiction to show what would have happened had two currencies been exchanged (e.g. in the instance of an unrealized investment overseas) – as opposed to **currency conversion** which is the actual exchange of one currency for another when a transaction actually takes place.

current Pertaining to the current accounting year; likely to be sold, converted into cash due or paid within the next 12 months – as in **current assets** and **current liabilities.**

current assets Assets which will be consumed or turned into cash within 12 months.

current cost accounting (Hyper) **inflation accounting** which tries to keep place with changing prices, also known as replacement cost accounting.

current liabilities Liabilities which are due for payment/repayment within 12 months.

current price Observed prices, measured in money of the day – as opposed to **constant prices** which are adjusted for inflation.

current ratio **Accounting ratio**, liquidity: current assets divided by current liabilities – indicates ability to meet daily financial commitments. Also known as **working capital** ratio.

current spending Expenditure on things which will be consumed within one year – as opposed to **capital spending** on **fixed assets**.

CVP Cost-volume-profit – **break even** analysis to you and me.

DCF See **discounted cash flow.**

debenture A **bond** issued by a company and (in the UK) secured against specific assets.

debit An amount entered in an account (traditionally on the left-hand side) recording a payment made. See also **credit**.

debt **Bonds**; money owed and repayable in the normal course of business; i.e. excluding **share capital**.

debt finance Money raised by issuing **bonds** or taking loans from banks, etc.

debt instrument Transferable **debt**.

debt rating A measure of the likelihood that a borrower will repay a loan – also known as **credit rating**.

debt service (The cost of) meeting the interest payments on a loan.

debt service coverage **Accounting ratio**, investment: **operating profit** (before interest and tax) divided by annual **interest** payments – indicator of ability to meet **debt** obligations; another way of looking at **leverage/gearing**. Also called interest cover, times interest earned.

debt/equity ratio The amount of money a company has borrowed divided by shareholders' **equity**.

debtors UK shorthand for **trade debtors;** US terms are **accounts receivable** or receivables. Payments that are owed to the company by trade debtors, such as customers.

declining balance depreciation Front-loaded **depreciation** technique which writes down the **book value** of a **fixed asset** by the same percentage amount each year. Also known as reducing balance and diminishing balance depreciation.

deflate To remove the effects of inflation.

deflator An index (such as the consumer price index) used to remove the effects of inflation.

depletion The extraction of natural resources; **depreciation** applied to mother nature.

deposit To put money in a bank account; a down payment to confirm the intention to buy; a returnable surety against a lease or rental agreement.

depreciable base The expected cost of owning and using a **fixed asset: acquisition cost** plus allowable maintenance costs, etc. less **residual value.**

depreciation A reduction in value reflecting use; the writing down of the book value of fixed assets by applying the accounting fiction that the assets lose a fixed, predictable amount of their value each year (see also **straight line, sum-of-the-years, declining balance**.

depreciation schedule A written plan showing how the beanie thinks that the **book value** of **fixed assets** will decline over their life – see also **depreciation**.

derivative One financial instrument based on another, such as an **option** or **swap**.

diminishing balance depreciation See **declining balance depreciation**.

direct costs Expenditure which is identified a part of the cost of producing a specific product or service. **Indirect costs,** such as the accountant's salary, cannot be directly linked to a specific product or service.

discount A price reduction; to sell at below the marked price or face value.

discount rate A simple **interest rate** (see **discounted cash flow**); the interest rate at which the central bank buys short-term debt from commercial banks.

discounted cash flow – DCF Investment appraisal technique (also known as **internal rate of return** and **yield**) based on financial flows and interest rates. Compare with **net present value.**

dividend/s A share in **retained earnings** which is distributed to shareholders – a pseudo-interest payment.

dividend cover Accounting ratio, investment: **earnings per share** divided by net **dividend** per share – indicates how many times the dividend is covered by profits/how much profit is being reinvested.

dividend payout ratio Dividend cover, inverted.

double declining balance depreciation See **declining balance depreciation**.

double entry accounting Bookkeeping technique which posts two entries for every transaction, a debit and a credit.

earnings Money received; in the US used loosely to mean **net income/net profit.**

earnings before interest and tax – EBIT Net profit before interest and tax; the idea being to eliminate especially variable items to make figures more comparable between companies – see also **earnings before interest, tax, depreciation and amortization.**

earnings before interest, tax, depreciation and amortization – EBITDA Net profit before all the above; the idea being to remove items which as especially variable or dependent on accounting policies in order to make figures more comparable between companies – see also **earnings before interest and tax.**

earnings per share – EPS Net profit divided by the number of **shares.**

EBIT See **earnings before interest and tax.**

EBITDA See **earnings before interest, tax, depreciation and amortization.**

effective exchange rate – EER A weighted average exchange rate, usually with weights based on a country's foreign trade. Also known as a trade weighted index or, e.g., the sterling index.

effective interest rate An interest rate standardized to take account of the frequency of compounding and, perhaps, fees and other sneaky charges.

elasticity of demand The extent to which demand responds to changes in price.

elasticity of supply The extent to which supply responds to changes in price.

emphasis of matter A statement in an auditor's report drawing attention to some issue (probably buried in the **footnotes** to the **financial statements**) but not affecting the auditor's opinion.

EPS See **earnings per share.**

equity The owners' stake in a business (i.e. assets less liabilities) comprising stocks (US) or **shares** (UK) and **retained earnings.** The issuance of ordinary shares/common stock provides the basic risk capital (risk finance).

equity method of consolidation *One line consolidation* of the financial results of an associate company in those of the parent company.

escrow account A bank balance which is held by a guardian and released to a third party on presentation of specified documents proving performance of some obligation (such as the delivery of goods).

exceptional item/s Financial amounts, not part of normal trading operations, but nevertheless consequent on ordinary activities of the company (such as the effects of changes in accounting policies) – not to be confused with an **extraordinary** item

exchange-rate gains and losses Actual or paper gains and losses resulting from exchange-rate movements alone.

expected payoff An average of projected returns, weighted by the probability of each outcome.

external audit An examination of accounting policies and records by a third party.

external auditor An outside accountant hired as a consultant to review accounting records and policies. See **audit.**

extraordinary item/s One-offs, such as the effects of natural disasters. Do not confuse with **exceptional items.**

factoring Selling **receivables** at a discount to unlock cash.

fair market value The price at which an **asset** might be sold in the open market.

farm gate value The market price of agricultural products.

FASB The US **Financial Accounting Standards Board.**

FIFO Method of **inventory valuation.** See **first in first out.**

finance lease A form of finance that makes the purchase of a **fixed asset** look like a rental contract. See **operating lease.**

financial accounting The production of **financial statements;** compare with **cost accounting** and **management accounting.**

Financial Accounting Standards Board – FASB The US standard setting body; reports to the **Securities and Exchange Commission,** issues **Statements of Financial Accounting Standards;** was established in 1973. The acronym is pronounced 'fas-bee'.

financial comptroller Another way of saying **financial controller.**

financial controller The head accountant in charge of bookkeeping and **financial reporting.** Along with the **treasurer,** reports to the **chief finance officer.**

financial instrument/s Legal documents which transfer capital, ownership and/or risk; examples include **bonds** and **shares.**

Financial Reporting Standard Pronouncement of the UK **Accounting Standards Board.**

financial statement/s Collectively, the **balance sheet, profit and loss account** (or **income statement**), the **cash flow statement,** and maybe some other presentations such as a **segment report** and **value added statements.**

financial year Accounting year; it may or may not coincide with the calendar year.

first in first out – FIFO Inventory valuation method which assumes that the first items into stock are the first to be removed.

fiscal year An accounting year.

fixed asset register A written record of **fixed assets.**

fixed asset/s Plant, property and equipment (PPE) and intangible assets (goodwill, patents, etc.) owned by a business and expected to produce income beyond the current year (does not include **inventory**).

fixed capital Non-**circulating assets.**

fixed costs Costs which, within limits, do not vary regardless of the level of production (e.g. the rent of a factory).

flexible budget A **budget** that includes several expenditure and revenue plans; the one that will be used in the event will depend on the level of some other variable such as output or sales.

float Petty cash on hand; to sell company shares to the public for the first time; to let an exchange rate find its own level.

floating Exchange rates or interest rates that are free to change under the pressure of market forces; current **assets.**

flow of funds See **cash flow.**

footnote/s Small print in **financial statements**, usually containing the most important information.

foreign exchange book rate An arbitrary exchange rate used for bookkeeping transactions.

forex Shorthand for foreign exchange.

forward contract An agreement to buy or sell a given amount (e.g., of a foreign currency) at a future date.

free cash flow Cash flow from operations less investments in operating assets – i.e., cash available for spending.

FRS US **Financial Reporting Standard.**

FRSSE UK **Financial Reporting Standard for Smaller Entities.**

Full costing Absorption costing.

full disclosure principle A beanie guiding principle: an accounting rule that requires the revelation of all material facts.

fundamental analysis Examination of share prices in relation to the underlying performance of the business. See also **technical analysis.**

future value What a sum of money will be worth at a future date, taking into account interest rates and, possibly, risks.

futures Financial instruments with a future settlement date that facilitate speculation or hedging.

GAAP Generally accepted accounting principles.

Gantt chart A pictorial presentation of activities along a timeline.

gearing Called leverage in the US: indicator of how aggressively some financial item is being used; as an **accounting ratio: debt** divided by **equity** – i.e. low gearing = low reliance on debt.

generally accepted accounting principles – GAAP Standards and guidelines for financial accounting and reporting, governing the form and content of **financial statements**. See also **international accounting standards**

going concern A beanie guiding principle: an assumption that a business will continue to exist for ever.

goods on hand Total **inventory**.

goodwill The value of a business above its net asset value – supposedly reflecting reputation, branding, positioning, etc.

gross profit Sales less the **cost of sales; net profit** is gross profit less overheads.

gross sales Sales revenue. Period.

hedge To reduce risks, especially interest rate or exchange rate risks, by some technique such as a **forward contract** or future contract; one of these techniques in action.

historic cost/s The price paid less any (arbitrary) allowance for depreciation – as distinct from market values.

historical cost accounting Accounting based on **historic costs**, rather than market prices – see also **inflation accounting**.

horizontal analysis Beanie term for **time series** analysis.

hurdle rate A yardstick against which investment opportunities are assessed – see **net present value, internal rate of return** and **cost of capital.**

hyperinflation Very rapid inflation – defined as a *doubling in the general price level in a three year period* by the **International Accounting Standards Board.**

IAS See **International Accounting Standards.**

IASB See **International Accounting Standards Board.**

IFRS See **International Financial Reporting Standards.**

imprest system A system of accounting for **petty cash** which, in principle, forces all spending of petty cash to pass through a bank account.

income Money received; in the US used loosely to mean **net income/net profit.**

income statement US term, known as the profit and loss account in the UK: one of the key **financial statements**, which shows the **net profit** or loss (**net income**) during the accounting period.

indirect cost/s Overheads; costs which cannot be directly attributed to a unit of sales (such as your bean counter's salary). See also **direct costs.**

inelastic Supply or demand which is unresponsive to changes in price.

inflation accounting Current price accounting which attempts – not very well – to grapple with the way that **book values** become unacceptably unrealistic during periods of **hyperinflation**. An alternative to conventional **historical cost accounting.**

intangible asset Invisible **fixed assets**, such as goodwill, patents, copyright, etc.

intellectual property Intangible assets which can be protected (e.g. trademarks, patents, copyrights, industrial design).

interest The price paid for the use of borrowed money; a stake in a business.

interest cover See **debt service coverage.**

interest rate Interest payments expressed as a percentage of the principal sum.

internal audit Inspection of accounting records by an entity's own accountant.

internal auditor A financial policeman or woman (am I expected to say police-person?) on the payroll who tries to prevent accounting errors and fraud.

internal rate of return – IRR A pseudo-interest rate which links outlays and returns; a key indicator in investment appraisal. See also **net present value.**

International Accounting Standard/s – IAS Standard set by the **International Accounting Standards Board** (IASB).

International Accounting Standards Board – IASB European-based body which sets **international accounting standards** with the noble aim of harmonization and eventual convergence of standards; established in 2001 to replace the IAS Committee which dates from 1973; with its predecessor the IASC has set over 40 standards.

International Financial Reporting Standard – IFRS Standard set by the **International Accounting Standards Board** (IASB).

inventory A company's stock of products held in the ordinary course of business; raw materials, work in progress and finished goods.

inventory ordering cost The costs of tooling up, taking deliveries, etc.

inventory turnover The number of times that average inventory is sold during a given period.

inventory valuation An accounting minefield; the application of arbitrary policies for determining the book value of stock in trade; techniques include **last in first out** (LIFO), **first in first out** (FIFO), **averaging, specific identification**, units of output/production/sales, etc.

investment For an economist, spending on goods with a life of more than one year (see **fixed assets**); in a financial context, the purchase of stocks and **shares**; for an entrepreneur, spending money with the expectation of future profit.

IRR See **internal rate of return.**

issued share capital The amount of **shares** that a company has sold to third parties.

journal A bookkeeping record where transactions are simply listed in date order.

junk A low-quality credit rating. See also **junk bond.**

junk bond A high-yielding **bond** rated *highly speculative*.

last in first out – LIFO **Inventory valuation** method which assumes that the most recently purchased or produced goods are sold first – essentially a tax dodge.

law of diminishing returns An economic principle which predicts that eventually output will taper off no matter how much input is provided.

ledger A book of accounts.

legal person A company/corporation is a legal person, separate from its owners and managers.

leverage Called gearing in the UK: indicator of how aggressively some financial item is being used; as an **accounting ratio: debt** divided by **equity** – i.e. low leverage = low reliance on debt.

liability/liabilities An obligation to pay money in the future (to suppliers, lenders, etc); opposite of **asset.**

LIFO Inventory valuation method – see **last in first out.**

liquid assets **Assets** that can be readily turned into cash.

loan stock **Bonds** issued by a company.

long-term Due after five years or more.

MACRS Modified accelerated cost recovery system – US tax allowance for **depreciation.**

management accounting **Financial accounting** elaborated to make it more useful for managers.

management letter A letter from the **auditor** to the directors outlining deficiencies in accounting matters (oops).

margin See **profit margin, spread.**

margin of safety The extent to which a business is operating above **break even.**

marginal cost The additional cost incurred when producing one more unit of a product.

marginal revenue The additional revenue gained by increasing sales by one unit.

market risk That part of the risk of holding a company's shares associated with the market as a whole (also known as systematic risk); the other part being **specific risk** associated with the performance of the company itself.

market share Sales of one item as percentage of total sales. The item might be a product, service, range or the entire sales of an enterprise. The market for that item might be defined geographically.

matching Creating **assets** to offset **liabilities**, or the other way around, to minimize risks.

matching principle A beanie guiding principle for **accruals accounting:** revenues and associated costs should be brought together in the same accounting period.

merchandise inventory Total **inventory.**

merger accounting Tricky techniques for pooling of interests in **financial accounting** when there is no clear acquiring company – rapidly being outlawed by accounting standards bodies.

minimum economic price The lowest price at which you can sell without making a net loss.

minority interest A significant but non-controlling shareholding in a company (in a reporting context, such an interest which is **consolidated** in the shareholder's **financial statements**).

moving average An sequence of averages, where each one is based on a small chunk of a **time series** (e.g. a three-month moving average).

net assets Essentially **assets** less **liabilities**; may be expanded to subtract liabilities which are **off balance sheet.**

net book value The price paid less any (arbitrary) allowance for, e.g. **depreciation** – as distinct from the market value.

net earnings Another way of saying **net income.**

net income US term, net profit in the UK: the excess of revenues and gains over spending and losses. In **financial statements**, a headline figure which excludes other **comprehensive income.**

net present value – NPV The **present value** of a series of cash inflows *and* outflows – a key indicator in investment appraisal.

net profit/s UK term, net income in the US: the excess of revenues and gains over spending and losses. In **financial statements**, a headline figure which excludes other **comprehensive income.**

net realizable value The net amount that could be obtained by selling an asset (i.e. after deducting finance and selling costs).

netting Balancing income and outlays to minimize risks.

non-current Not relating to the current accounting year; unlikely to be sold, converted into cash, fall due or be paid within the next 12 months.

normal distribution A bell shaped pattern found frequently in nature when a large number of observations are graphed – useful for modelling risk.

NPV See **net present value.**

objectivity principle A beanie guiding principle: data should be verifiable and free from bias.

off balance sheet Transactions, such as leases and **contingent liabilities**, which are not recorded in the **financial statements** but which, when disclosed, are mentioned in the footnotes.

offer Also known as **ask**: the price which a dealer offers you for a financial instrument, such as a foreign currency. The **bid** is the price at which you can buy the same paper back from the same dealer. The difference between the two is the dealers' **spread**, or profit. Knowing this, it is easy to work out which is the bid and which is the ask or offer price.

OFR See **operating and financial review.**

one-line consolidation See **equity method of consolidation.**

operating and financial review – OFR A commentary on corporate activities during the accounting period.

operating cost/s The normal costs of doing business, including cost of sales.

operating expense Another name for an **operating cost.**

operating lease A genuine lease, as opposed to a **finance lease** which is designed to keep capital costs out of the **balance sheet.**

operating margin Operating profit (i.e. before interest and tax) divided by sales.

operating profit Net profit before **extraordinary items**, etc.

opportunity cost What you could have had you not spent the money on something else.

option/s The right but not the obligation to buy or sell a fixed quantity of a commodity, currency or security at a fixed price on or before a particular date.

ordinary shares UK name for common stock (US): fixed units of share capital with voting rights and, all being well, regular **dividend** payments.

outturn A observed event (such as actual sales in a given month) – as distinct from a forecast or plan.

overdraft A temporary loan facility, allowing a bank account to have a negative balance up to an agreed limit.

overhead **Indirect cost** of operating that cannot be directly associated with any one product (such as your bean counter's salary).

owners' drawing The **sole trader's** equivalent of the **dividends** which are paid to shareholders.

owners' equity The net worth of a business, ultimately payable to a **sole trader** or the shareholders.

P&L Shorthand for the **profit and loss account.**

paid-in surplus US term for a **share premium**.

paid-up capital **Shares** for which the holders have paid in full.

past due Debts which have not been paid on the due date; and as time passes are increasingly unlikely to be paid. See also **aging report**.

payables A US shorthand for accounts payable; known as **creditors** or trade creditors in the UK. Payments due to be made by the company to trade creditors, such as suppliers.

payback A simple concept of how much a money project will yield, and when; **net present value** and **internal rate of return** are generally better measures.

payout ratio Cash return as a proportion of cash outlay: See **dividend payout ratio**.

PE/PEM/PER See **price earnings**.

permanent assets See **fixed assets**.

petty cash Notes and coins held to meet small incidental expenses.

plant, property and equipment, PPE Tangible **fixed assets**.

plusses, minuses and interesting ideas – PMI Edward de Bono's formalization of a decision-making technique used when the factors are hard to quantify.

pooling of interests accounting See **merger accounting**.

possible contingency A **liability** (or **asset**) which is reasonably likely to materialize and which is disclosed in the **footnotes** to the **balance sheet** – not as certain as a **probable contingency**!

PPE See **plant, property and equipment**.

prepaid expense A payment made before the effective date (e.g. rent paid in advance).

present value What a sum or flow of money would be worth if it was in your hands right now – a bird in the hand, and all that.

price earnings multiple/ratio – PE/PEM/PER Three ways of saying the same thing: current market price of **shares** divided by most recently reported annual **net profit/net earnings**.

primary segment Either a geographic or a product breakdown – whichever the reporting company selects as most important. See also **segment report**.

prime cost The core costs of production: direct materials plus direct labour.

principal The lump sum lent/borrowed – excluding interest and fees; a person acting in their own right, perhaps engaging a broker or agent.

probable contingency A **liability** (or **asset**) which is certain enough to be included in the **balance sheet** – see also **possible contingency**.

process cost accounting Methodology used to cost an item in continuous production, over a given time period.

product life cycle The sequence of development, growth, maturity and decline for a product – you want to extend the second phase.

production costs Usually the major portion of **cost of sales**, the remainder being shipping, sales commissions, etc.

productivity Output per unit of input – e.g. manufacturing labour productivity can be measured by production per person-hour.

profit and loss account – P&L UK term, income statement in the US: one of the **financial statements**, which shows the **net profit** or loss (**net income**) during the accounting period.

profit centre A business unit with revenues; a **cost centre** which makes money, even if only by selling services to the rest of the organization.

profit margin Accounting ratio, efficiency: **operating profit** (before tax, interest, etc.) divided by sales. In other words, profit per dollar of sales.

profitability The extent to which an entity earns profits; a relative term (profits as a percentage of sales) whereas profit is an absolute measure.

profit-volume – PV The **contribution ratio**.

pro-forma A matter of form: **financial statements** which are adjusted or not prepared in accordance with **generally accepted accounting principals**; an advance copy of an **invoice**; a budget framework.

program evaluation and review technique – PERT A project planning technique which helps identify the likelihood of completing the project on time.

provision A bookkeeping reserve (but not necessarily real cash) set aside and charged against **net profit/net income** to cover expected losses such as bad debts.

prudence A beanie guiding principle: pessimism at work; applying accounting policies and methods to arrive at the lowest possible profit figure. Also known as conservatism.

PV Profit-volume – the **contribution ratio**.

qualification See **audit qualification**.

quick ratio See **acid test**.

rate of return The percentage yield from an investment, usually expressed as a annual pseudo-interest rate.

ratio analysis Examination of **accounting ratios**.

real terms Adjusted for inflation: in **volumes** or **constant prices**.

realization principle A beanie guiding principle: revenue should be booked at the moment when goods change hands or services are rendered. Also known as the revenue principle.

receivables US shorthand for accounts receivable; known as debtors or trade debtors in the UK. Payments that are owed to the company by trade debtors, such as customers.

reducing balance depreciation See **declining balance depreciation**.

replacement cost accounting (Hyper) **inflation accounting** which tries to keep pace with changing prices, also known as current cost accounting.

reschedule To defer repayment of a loan.

reserves A bookkeeping entry; profits set aside rather than distributed to shareholders.

residual value The market value of an **fixed asset** at the end of its useful life. Also known as salvage value.

restructure To raise new **capital**, **reschedule**, replacing **debt** with **equity**, etc., usually in times of financial crisis.

retained earnings Net **profits/net income** which has not been distributed to shareholders.

return on assets – ROA Accounting ratio, efficiency: **operating profit** (before interest and tax) divided by total **assets** – see **return on investment**.

return on capital employed – ROCE Accounting ratio, efficiency: **operating profit** (before interest and tax) divided by (total **assets** less current **liabilities**) – see **return on investment**.

return on equity – ROE Accounting ratio, investment: **net profit** (after tax) *divided by* owners' equity – the bottom line for shareholders.

return on investment – ROI The percentage return on cash invested – see, e.g. **return on assets, return on equity, return on capital employed.** Note that **net present value** and **internal rate of return** are more precise measures for investment appraisal.

return on sales The **profit margin.**

revaluation surplus A bookkeeping profit created when, for example, the **book value** of a **fixed asset** (such as land/real estate) is reappraised upwards.

revenue costs Spending set against revenue to arrive at **net profit/net income.**

revenue principle A beanie guiding principle: revenue should be booked at the moment when goods change hands or services are rendered. Also known as the realization principle.

ROA See **return on assets.**

ROCE See **return on capital employed.**

ROE See **return on equity.**

ROI See **return on investment.**

rolling budget A **budget** which is continually extended so that it always covers, say, the next 12 months.

sales turnover UK terms for sales, often shortened to *turnover.*

salvage value The market value of a **fixed asset** at the end of its useful life. Also known as residual value.

SEC See **Securities and Exchange Commission.**

secondary segment Either a geographic or a product breakdown – whichever the reporting company did not select as the **primary segment.** See also **segment report.**

Securities and Exchange Commission – SEC The US SEC supervises American stock exchanges and sets basic reporting requirements (but it allows the **FASB** to define standards.

segment report A breakdown of financial results by either geographic area or product/service/industry lines.

sensitivity analysis Review of a plan to quantify what happens if; e.g. What if interest rates rise by 1%? What if sales fall by 10%? What if prices rise by 5%? Etc.

SFAS US **Statement of Financial Accounting Standards.**

share capital Finance raised by issuing **shares.**

share option See **stock option** and **options.**

share premium UK term for paid-in surplus (US); cash received when subscribers pay more than face value when buying **shares** directly from a company.

shareholders' equity Owners' equity for a company/corporation.

share/s UK term for what is called stock in the US – units of share capital.

shutdown price If you sell your products at or below this price, you will go out of business.

simple interest Interest which is not accumulated to earn further interest – compare with **compound interest.**

sinking fund A cash reserve set aside to fund a future obligation (**bond** repayment, replacement of **fixed assets**, etc.); real money, as opposed to the bookkeeping concept of a **provision** or reserve.

sole trader A business owned by a single person, with no distinction between personal and business **assets** and **liabilities**.

SORP See Statement of Recommended Practice.

sources and application of funds Cash flow by another name.

sources and uses of funds Cash flow by another name.

specific identification Inventory valuation method based on the known cost of the items moving through stock – does not work with homogeneous products such as beer or talcum powder. Also known as **specific unit cost.**

specific risk That part of the risk of holding shares being associated with the performance of the company itself; the other part being **market risk** which affects all shares similarly.

specific unit costs Inventory valuation method based on the actual costs of identifiable items of inventory.

spot markets Markets where financial instruments, currencies and commodities are traded for (more or less) immediate settlement.

spread The difference between the buying and selling price of a currency, financial instrument or other asset; the difference between interest rates on loans and deposits; the difference between the highest and lowest values in a set (**distribution**) of numbers.

SSAP See Statement of Standard Accounting Practice.

standard cost accounting Applies a predetermined cost to all goods whether sold or unsold.

Statement of Financial Accounting Standards – SFAS US pronouncement, issued by the Financial Accounting Standards Board.

Statement of Recommended Practice – SORP UK pronouncement now reviewed by the UK Accounting Standards Board.

Statement of Standard Accounting Practice – SSAP UK forerunner of **Financial Reporting Standards.**

stock This can be confusing: US term for **shares** (UK); the UK term for a **bond**; also the UK word for what Americans call **inventory**.

stock index A share price index.

stock option A treat for employees and other potential investors, allowing them the choice of buying **equity** in the company at a future date at a pre-agreed price. See also **options.**

stock-in-trade UK alternative to the US term **Inventory.**

straight line depreciation Depreciation technique which assumes that value of a fixed asset is written down in equal instalments (i.e. annual depreciation is the **depreciable base** divided by the expected life in years).

sum-of-the-the-years'-digits depreciation Front-loaded **depreciation**; number the years in reverse order (for an asset with a three-year life, the years are numbered (3, 2, 1)), find the sum-of-the-years'-digits (3 + 2 + 1 = 6), use this to create depreciation factors (3/6, 2/6 and 1/6) – e.g. the first year's depreciation is the **depreciable base** multiplied by 3/6.

swap An exchange of financial instruments (e.g. currency liabilities or debt) for mutual benefit.

systematic risk The **market risk** associated with a company's share valuation – as opposed to **specific risk**.

tax accounting **Financial accounting** revised to comply with tax laws.

tax avoidance Legally minimizing tax liabilities, as opposed to **tax evasion**.

tax evasion Illegally minimizing tax liabilities, as opposed to **tax avoidance**.

tax loss A loss carried forward from an earlier period to minimize taxable income.

tax shelter Something, perhaps useful, that you can spend money on to reduce or defer taxation.

technical analysis Tea-leaf gazing to predict price movements (e.g. in shares) based on the recent pattern of price movements – compare with **fundamental analysis.**

temporary difference The tax eventually due (repayable) on a passing difference between reported and taxable profits – which gives rise to a deferred tax liability (or asset).

time period principle A beanie guiding principle: reporting based on specific (short) periods. Also known as the accounting period principle.

time series A single variable (e.g. sales) tracked over time – see also **cross sectional data.**

trade credit Finance for foreign trade – not necessarily borrowing in the conventional sense.

trade creditors UK term; US equivalents are accounts payable or payables. Payments due to be made by the company to trade creditors, such as suppliers.

trade cycle The **business cycle.**

trade debtors UK term; US equivalents are accounts receivable or receivables. Payments that are owed to the company by trade debtors, such as customers.

transfer pricing Often arbitrary prices set for transactions between two related entities, which (goodness me) may result in shifting taxable profits from a high-tax to a low-tax environment.

translation See **currency translation.**

treasurer A financial specialist who is responsible for managing the cash surpluses and needs of an entity; reports to the **chief financial officer**, along with the financial controller.

treasury stock US term for **shares** that a company has bought back from the public.

trend The underlying path of a variable such as sales over time.

trial balance Originally a check to ensure that credits and debits balance; a handy summary of all accounts, extracted from a computer accounting package.

triple-A A first-class **credit rating** applied to the debt credit-worthiness of companies and sovereign borrowers.

triple-B A medium **credit rating** – one step above **junk.**

trough The lowest point in the **business cycle.**

true and fair view The guiding principle for UK **financial statements.**

turnover UK term for sales revenue.

ultra vires *Beyond the powers* of a company, as defined in its bylaws/articles.

unit cost Expenditure incurred when producing one unit of a product.

unit of measure A beanie guiding principle: report all transactions in the same currency.

unqualified audit A clean bill of health from the financial police. Compare with **audit qualification**.

value A measure based on money, as opposed to a measure of **volume**.

value added An increase in **wealth**, resulting from the activities of the company (this would include a price mark-up between buying and selling).

value added statement One of the optional **financial statements**, showing **value added** by the reporting entity.

variable An identified element which varies in size, such as demand in a sales forecast.

variable costs Costs which increase directly with output – such as spending on raw materials – see also **fixed costs**.

variance Nothing more complicated than the difference between two amounts.

vertical analysis Beanie term for the analysis of cross **sectional data** (see also **ratio analysis**)

volume A measure of quantity, not **value**.

wasting assets **Fixed assets** which are gradually exhausted in production.

wealth The total value of money and possessions owned.

what if See **sensitivity analysis**.

window dressing Creative accounting to enhance perceptions of published **financial statements**.

working capital Liquidity which enables a business to continue trading – defined as **current assets** less **current liabilities**.

working capital ratio See **current ratio**.

working funds Another name for **working capital**.

write down To reduce the recorded value of an asset to reflect, say, **depreciation** or a fall in the market price.

yield The interest or return on an investment; to produce income.

zero-based budget A **budget** prepared without knowledge of the previous year's figures – on the assumption that this will lead to more-thoughtful projections.

index